Classroom Management and Discipline

MW01242207

Classroom Management and Discipline

**Methods to Facilitate
Cooperation
and Instruction**

Paul R. Burden
Kansas State University

Longman *Publishers USA*

Classroom Management and Discipline:
Methods to Facilitate Cooperation and Instruction

Copyright © 1995 by Longman Publishers USA.
All rights reserved.
No part of this publication may be reproduced,
stored in a retrieval system, or transmitted
in any form or by any means, electronic, mechanical,
photocopying, recording, or otherwise,
without the prior permission of the publisher.

Longman, 10 Bank Street, White Plains, N.Y. 10606

Associated companies:
Longman Group Ltd., London
Longman Cheshire Pty., Melbourne
Longman Paul Pty., Auckland
Copp Clark Longman Ltd., Toronto

Senior acquisitions editor: Laura McKenna
Editorial assistant: Matthew Baker
Production editor: Linda Moser/Professional Book Center
Cover design: Michelle Szabo, New Media Designs
Production supervisor: Richard Bretan

Library of Congress Cataloging-in-Publication Data
Burden, Paul R.
    Classroom management and discipline : methods to facilitate
cooperation and instruction / Paul R. Burden.
        p.   cm.
    Includes bibliographical references and index.
    ISBN 0-8013-1185-3
    1. Classroom management—United States.   2. School discipline—
United States.   I. Title.
LB3013.B873 1995
371.1'024—dc20   94-5432
                                                                 CIP

1 2 3 4 5 6 7 8 9 10-MA-98979695

Contents

Preface

*C*lassroom *Management and Discipline* is designed to provide comprehensive, research-based coverage of the issues. It is intended to be a scholarly synthesis of the research base on classroom management and discipline yet written and formatted in a way that is easy to read, understand, and apply. It carries a very practical, contemporary, realistic view of teaching with the content organized in a logical, sequential order. Factors to establish a classroom management system effectively and maintain order are presented, and specific actions are offered to restore order if misbehavior occurs. The content is applicable for teachers at all levels—elementary, middle level, junior high, and high school.

This book is especially appropriate as the primary text for an undergraduate course on classroom management and discipline or for a seminar on student teaching or professional development. It may be used as a supplementary text for educational psychology or teaching methods courses. Additionally, the book's scholarly treatment of the issues makes it ideal for use in graduate classes, seminars, and staff development programs for inservice teachers. Teachers and students save this text for future reference due to its comprehensive coverage of the issues and its use of lists, tables, and figures for recommended practice. The information provides a foundation for decision making for the reflective practitioner.

ORGANIZATION

The content of *Classroom Management and Discipline* is comprehensive, up-to-date, and authoritative. Each chapter reflects a synthesis of research and best practice. Part I, "Introduction," explains the dimensions of classroom management, misbehavior, and various models of discipline. Part II, "Getting Organized," examines ways to prepare for the school year, organize classroom and materials, and select and teach rules and procedures. Part III, "Planning for Management," considers ways to plan for instruction with order and management in mind, motivate students, address the diversity of students, and work with parents.

Ways to establish a cooperative, responsible classroom; encourage and reinforce appropriate behavior; and manage lesson delivery are highlighted in Part IV, "Conducting the Class." Finally, Part V on "Restoring Order" provides detailed guidance for ways to successively provide situational assistance and use mild, moderate, and severe responses to misbehavior. This part also examines ways to deal with difficult students.

SPECIAL FEATURES

To maintain the reader's interest and to accommodate different learning styles and instructional settings, *Classroom Management and Discipline* contains a variety of pedagogical features.

- *Objectives.* Each chapter begins with a list of objectives that identify expected reader outcomes.

- *Decision Points.* Several Decision Points are placed in each chapter to consider the application of the content. Each Decision Point includes several sentences describing a classroom situation concerning an issue in the chapter followed by a few questions asking the reader to make decisions about the application of the concepts.

- *Teachers in Action.* Teachers-in-Action features are included in each chapter to provide descriptions by actual elementary, middle school, junior high, and high school teachers about ways they deal with particular topics addressed in the chapter. These teachers come from all parts of the country and different community sizes—from small communities such as Gillette, Wyoming and Big Lakes, Minnesota to large cities such as New York, Dallas, and San Diego. There are over 70 Teachers in Action, with an even balance for the elementary, middle, and junior/senior high school levels.

- *Major concepts.* At the end of each chapter, a list of major concepts serves as a summary of the significant concepts.

- *Discussion questions.* Questions at the end of each chapter promote discussion in a seminar, classroom, or workshop where a number of people are considering the chapter's content.

- *Supplemental activities.* Supplemental activities are suggested at the end of each chapter for both clinical (classroom) settings and for field school-based) settings to enable the reader to investigate and apply issues addressed.

- *Key terms.* A list of key terms at the end of each chapter draws the reader's attention to significant terms. Each term is highlighted in the text.
- *Recommended readings.* An annotated list of recommended readings at the end of each chapter suggests readings for further enrichment.
- *References.* Each chapter ends with references that were cited in the chapter to document the research base of the content.
- *Audiovisual resource list.* A comprehensive, annotated list of audiovisual resources related to classroom management and discipline is displayed in Appendix B. This list includes resources on classroom management, discipline in general, cooperative discipline, assertive discipline, behavior modification, violence, hostile and resistant students, at-risk students, attention deficit hyperactivity disorder, conflict resolution and problem solving, self-esteem, social skills, caring classrooms, communication, motivation, learning styles, cooperative learning, effective teaching, and parent-teacher conferences. Each item includes the title, description, cost, and mailing address and telephone number for each publisher.

ACKNOWLEDGMENTS

Many people provided support and guidance as I prepared this book. A very special acknowledgment goes to my wife, Jennie, and children, Andy, Kathryn, and Alex. Their support kept my spirits up when deadlines were pressing, and their understanding during my absences while writing enabled me to complete the project.

Laura McKenna, the editor at Longman, facilitated the preparation and refinement of this book by sharing her understanding of the content and the market. Anita Portugal provided exemplary editing assistance to refine the content and organization. Linda Moser very capably arranged for the production of the book.

A number of classroom teachers offered descriptions of their professional practice, which are included in the Teachers-in-Action features. Their experiences help illustrate the issues and bring life to the content. The teachers are Michael Abbott, Gayle Bennett, Barbara Bjorklund, Tim Block, Susan Bosco, Hildie Brooks, Trezeline Brooks, Sherry Bryant, Ron Butler, Theresa Campos, Donna Carney, Raphael Castenet, Dana Clark, Jim Clowes, Paul Couture, Fred Dahm, Tracy Douglas, Donna Erpelding, John Fallis, Shaunda Fletcher, Francine Fankhauser, Suzy Fulghum, Cammie Fulk, Nancy Fusaro, Edward Gamble, Mary Garland, Tamara George, Matthew Gilbert, Beatrice Gilkes, Patti Grossman, Debbie Guedry, Lynne Hagar, Jeanen Hanlon, Jane Holzapfel, Linda Innes, Terri Jenkins, Richard Kedward, Marc Knapp, Martha Krein, Dea Kreisman, Janet Kulbiski, Barbara Lojka, Christine MacBurney, Sandra McClellan, Marge McClintock, Nancy McCullum, Martin Miller, Russell Moore, Sanford Morris, Gwendolyn Mukes, Cindy Norris, Sandy Peer, Ellen Rayner, James Roussin, Randi Sack, Beth Salk, Dave Sampson,

Kim Schaefer, Beth Schmar, Beverly Schottler, Margaret Shields, Tom Smith, Jacqueline Stanley, Carolyn Steinbrink, Eric Stiffler, Laurie Stoltenhoff, Deb Stuto, Kathy Sublett, Claudia Swisher, Kathryn Tallerico, Dwight Watson, Jan Wilson, and John Wolters.

Pam Monroe and Julie Moore provided invaluable assistance at Kansas State University in arranging for mailings to teachers for the Teachers-in-Action features and mailings related to the permissions log. They also prepared several tables and helped coordinate many activities. Their accuracy, patience, and good humor facilitated manuscript preparation.

Finally, I would like to extend my gratitude to the following reviewers who provided thoughtful, constructive suggestions during the earlier drafts of this book:

Dale Allee, Southwest Missouri State University

Kathryn Castel, Oklahoma State University

JoAnna Dickey, Eastern Kentucky University

Janet Ellis, University of North Texas

Joann Ericson, Towson State University

Jennifer Humphries, Ashland University

Sharon Lamson, Central Missouri State University

Tom Lasley, University of Dayton

Lee Manning, Old Dominion University

John Moore, University of Kentucky

Mike Morehead, New Mexico State University

Merrill Oaks, Washington State University

Bill Samuelson, Emporia State University

Mary Shake, University of Kentucky

Rita Silverman, Pace University

Kay Stickle, Ball State University

part I

Introduction

This part serves as an introduction to the many facets of classroom management and discipline. It includes three chapters: one explains the dimensions of classroom management, one examines misbehavior, and the third reviews various models of discipline.

Chapter 1, "Dimensions of Classroom Management," introduces the issue of order in the classroom, highlights ways to establish and maintain order, and considers methods to restore order. Chapter 1 also describes the plan for this book and offers ideas for determining your own management system.

Chapter 2, "Understanding Misbehavior," examines misbehavior in context, grade level differences in misbehavior, cause of misbehavior, types of misbehavior, and degrees of severity of misbehavior. This chapter also proposes interventions for restoring order and identifies some practices to avoid.

Chapter 3, "Models of Discipline," considers the degree of control that you may choose to exert in the classroom when managing student behavior, and describes strategies of representative authors for low-, medium-, and high-control approaches to managing student behavior. Chapter 3 also offers ideas for selecting your own approach to control.

chapter **1**

Dimensions of Classroom Management

Objectives

This chapter provides information that will help you:

1. Determine what constitutes order in the classroom.
2. Identify ways that order is established and maintained.
3. Identify ways that order is restored.
4. Describe how this book is organized.
5. Identify factors you might consider when determining your own classroom management system.

One of your greatest challenges as a teacher is to maintain order in the classroom in order to achieve your academic objectives. The term *classroom management* is often used to describe the way this can occur. Classroom management refers to the actions and strategies teachers use to maintain order (Doyle, 1986). Classroom management focuses on ways to establish and maintain workable systems for classroom groups rather than on ways to spot and punish misbehavior, resolve behavioral disorders, or capture the attention of individual students.

Order means that students are following within acceptable limits the actions necessary for a particular classroom event to be successful. Order does not mean rigid conformity, conformity to the rules, or passive student behavior.

Classroom management is complex, and many variables need to be considered when making decisions about specific situations. Nevertheless, several key questions come to mind about management and control. How is order established and maintained? How might order be restored if there are disruptions? How can you determine an appropriate management system? In this chapter we introduce the important issues and provide an orientation to the content and organization of this book.

ORDER IN THE CLASSROOM

Before examining several aspects of order in the classroom, we should define three additional terms. *Misbehavior* includes behaviors that interfere with teaching, interfere with the rights of others to learn, are psychologically or physically unsafe, or destroy property (Levin & Nolan, 1991). *Off-task behavior* includes student actions that are not focused on the instructional activities, yet would not be considered disruptive or defined as misbehavior. Off-task behavior includes daydreaming, writing notes or doodling, or not paying attention. *Discipline* is the act of responding to misbehaving students in an effort to restore order.

There are several important issues concerning order. First, order is achieved within the context of the classroom, and each context makes different demands on the class members. For instance, rules are often tied to the context or phases of a class session. All rules may not be in effect when students enter, settle down or prepare for class, attend to the lesson, clean up at the end of a lesson, or exit the classroom.

Decision Points

Teachers often have special procedures and behavioral guidelines for times when students work in small groups or in a lab setting. Suppose you are dividing your class into small groups to examine and test rock and mineral samples in various ways. How might your decisions about guidelines to maintain control be affected by the age level and maturity of the students? How might you need to monitor students differently to maintain control in small groups as compared to whole-class instruction?

Second, learning and order are closely related, and a minimal level of orderliness is necessary for instruction to occur. Learning is served by instructional functions such as covering the curriculum and promoting mastery of the content. You can achieve order by using managerial functions such as organizing groups, establishing rules and procedures, reacting to misbehavior, and monitoring and pacing classroom events (Doyle, 1986).

Third, order affects students' involvement in learning tasks. Student engagement is essentially a byproduct of well-conceived and well-orchestrated group activities. Thus, to be an effective classroom manager, you may place your emphasis on managing the group rather than managing individual students.

Finally, cooperation is the minimum requirement for appropriate student behavior. Order is achieved *with* students and depends upon their willingness to be part of the sequence of events. You can achieve cooperation with both active and passive involvement and also by not engaging students in instructional tasks. For instance, a whole-class discussion can operate with only a few students participating while other students may be only listening. Order in seatwork exists as long as students are not interacting or distracting each other, even though they may not be participating in working on the content.

ESTABLISHING AND MAINTAINING ORDER

Establishing and maintaining order are achieved in a variety of ways, but primarily by actions taken to get organized for the school year, to plan for management, and to conduct the class.

Getting Organized for the School Year

Establishing order begins with carefully preparing for the start of the year, organizing the classroom and materials, and selecting rules and procedures.

Preparing at the start of the year includes getting ready for management and instruction, establishing a plan for dealing with misbehavior, and planning for the first day and week of school. The way the desks, tables, and other materials are arranged also affects order.

Determining and teaching rules and procedures also establishes order. Some rules may be context specific, especially for certain phases of a lesson. While you may spend much time talking about rules and procedures, most socialization of students to the classroom system seems to be indirect. Informality appears to increase the overall effectiveness of classroom rule systems.

The more explicit the rules and the more clearly you communicate them, the more likely you will care about maintaining order and not tolerate inappropriate and disruptive behavior. Simply stating a rule is not enough. You must demonstrate a willingness and an ability to act when rules are broken. For this reason, reprimands and consequences play an important role in the rule-setting process.

Classroom order rests on a teacher's ability to communicate to students an understanding of events and processes and a willingness to cope with complex situations. You are the rule maker, but you must live up to students' expectations for competence in handling the system.

To establish order, you must teach, demonstrate, establish, and enforce procedures and routines at the start of the year. Successful managers hover over activities at the beginning of the year and usher them along until students have learned the work system.

Planning for Management

Another aspect of establishing and maintaining control is to plan carefully for ways to manage instruction, motivate students, address student diversity, and work with parents.

Teachers in Action

Establishing Rules for Controlling Conduct

Beatrice Gilkes, high school computer science teacher, Washington, D.C.:

To help maintain control, I ask my students to discuss realistic expectations for all persons in the classroom, including myself, that will help lead to the students being successful. Next, we discuss and select specific rules of behavior that affect maximum learning success. Throughout, we emphasize three key words—love, respect, and commitment. We then commit ourselves to these rules, and student recommendations for penalties are included in the agreement. Students place this list of rules in their notebooks. This approach to getting a commitment from the students about classroom conduct has been effective for me in 40 years of teaching.

Teachers in Action

Well-Planned Instruction Helps Maintain Order in the Classroom

Sherry Bryant, middle school social studies teacher, Rochester, New Hampshire:

If you want order, then be overplanned and organized. Keep students busy and involved. Have things planned for students who finish early. I find it's easiest to have things for them to work on memorizing (states, capitals, location of states, and so on). Another thing they enjoy doing when they finish their work is getting a set of numbered index cards on which I have written questions about what we have learned this year. An answer sheet is provided, and they can quiz themselves or turn it into a game with other students. They also can read the books displayed that tie into the topic we are learning about.

Be prepared so that you can stand at the door and greet them as they enter the room, letting them know that you're glad they are there and that you are ready to have a good day with them.

I find it useful to have a folder for each class containing the materials that I will need for that class. I do weekly plans and have all the materials for the next week run off and organized before I leave for the weekend.

When planning for instruction, be aware of certain factors that bear on the order and control to be established during lesson delivery. These factors include decisions about the degree of structure of the lesson, the type of instructional groups to use, and the means of holding the students academically accountable.

The willingness of students to stay on-task and maintain self-control and order is affected by their motivation to learn. As a result, give your attention to strategies that could be used throughout each lesson to motivate students.

Similarly, the degree to which students feel that their individual characteristics have been considered will affect their willingness to stay on-task and maintain self-control. It is important, therefore, to understand their characteristics and to address their diversity.

Working with parents is another means of maintaining order. When parents and teacher communicate and get along, students will more likely receive the needed guidance and support and will likely have more self-control in the classroom.

Conducting the Class

You can establish and maintain control by developing a cooperative classroom, reinforcing and encouraging appropriate behavior, and focusing on order when conducting the lesson.

You can take actions to develop a cooperative classroom by helping promote students' self-esteem, building positive teacher-student relationships, building group cohesiveness, and encouraging students to assume responsibility for their behavior. All of these factors can influence their willingness to maintain self-control and contribute to order.

There are certain actions you can take at the beginning, middle, and end of a lesson that affect order. These include taking attendance, giving directions, distributing materials, handling transitions, summarizing the lesson, and preparing to leave.

While routines guide behavior and stabilize actions, lessons still have an improvisational character (Erickson, 1982). Thus, the form of a particular lesson is jointly negotiated and constructed between you and your students, and order is thus subject to the contingencies of multiple interpretations, preferences, and errors. Delicate and complex processes of sustaining order must be balanced.

Much of your attention is taken up gathering information about student movement within the classroom and communicating this information to them. As the arrangement of students becomes more complex and the demands on you increase, it becomes more difficult to monitor and cue; thus, there is a greater probability of a breakdown of order. For example, a classroom with five small groups working on cooperative tasks as part of a social studies project will be more difficult to monitor than a classroom with a whole-class format.

Teachers in Action

Keeping the Classroom Positive

Carolyn Steinbrink, middle school American history teacher, Shenandoah, Iowa:

I think the students need to know the boundaries and at the same time see me as a person who helps them meet their own needs while staying within rules. One of the ways I do this is by saying "no," but at the same time helping the student stay within the limits of acceptable behavior.

For example, I have a rule about staying in the classroom during the class period. But a student may say, "May I go to my locker? I left my assignment and notepaper there." I would say, "Yes, when the bell rings. You may turn in your assignment between classes. I will loan you paper which you can replace when you bring in your assignment." In this way, the student knows how to handle the problem that has occurred by forgetting the assignment in the locker. And I have explained how to take care of the situation in a way that does not set up numerous other requests from other students to get things from their lockers.

METHODS OF RESTORING ORDER

In spite of actions you may take to establish and maintain control, off-task behavior and misbehavior occur. You will then need to restore order. For students who are showing signs of getting off-task or who are off-task, situational assistance can be provided to help them get back on-task. Mild, moderate, or severe responses can be used for students who are misbehaving.

Situational assistance includes actions that teachers take to help students cope with the instructional situation and to keep them on-task or get them back on-task before a problem becomes more serious. This includes providing cues, helping them through hurdles, redirecting behavior, altering the lesson, or other techniques.

Mild responses are nonpunitive responses to misbehavior that get the student back on-task. You may use nonverbal responses such as signals; or verbal responses might be necessary.

Moderate responses to misbehavior might be needed to get the student back on-task and to restore order, such as removing desirable stimuli with logical consequences, or behavior modification. You may also need to use severe responses such as reprimands to help restore order.

Decision Points

Under most circumstances, teachers use mild, moderate, and severe responses to misbehavior in sequence, but sometimes a step might be skipped. Imagine that two students in your sixth-grade class are having a loud argument. How might your response differ if you taught a first- or a tenth-grade class? How might your response differ if one student was mildly hyperactive? Or if one student had a history of disturbances and the other student did not?

THE PLAN OF THIS BOOK

This book focuses primarily on ways to establish, maintain, and restore order in the classroom. Rather than proposing one model for teachers to follow, it synthesizes information from researchers and practitioners on the issues of management and discipline, with an emphasis on order. Based on this synthesis, categories of teacher actions become apparent, and these actions serve as the organizational framework for presenting the content.

Some guiding assumptions about management and order emerge from the information available. It is important to recognize that there are some qualifications to the conclusions that you may draw from this review of available literature on management, discipline, and order.

Organization

In addition to this chapter, the introduction includes chapter 2 on characteristics of misbehavior, and chapter 3 on orientation to models of discipline offered by other authors.

Next, based on the synthesis of research, there are three parts about ways to establish and maintain control. Part II, Getting Organized (chapters 4-6), considers ways to prepare for the school year, organize the classroom and materials, and select and teach rules and procedures. Part III, Planning for Management (chapters 7-10), examines planning for instruction, motivation, the diversity of students, and working with parents. Part IV, Conducting the Class (chapters 11-13), explores ways to establish a cooperative classroom, encourage and reinforce appropriate behavior, and manage lesson delivery.

Finally, Part V, Restoring Order (chapters 14-17), examines situational assistance, mild to severe responses to misbehavior, difficult students, and legal aspects of discipline.

An outline of chapter headings and a list of objectives are included at the beginning of each chapter. A list of major concepts, discussion questions, suggested supplemental activities, key terms, recommended readings, and references are found at the end of each chapter. Supplemental activities are provided for clinical settings where individuals or groups may examine these issues in a location other than a school, and for field settings, while the investigation of the issues would be conducted in school.

Two features in each chapter enrich and extend the content. The Decision Points feature includes a description of a situation related to the chapter content, and several questions are posed asking you to consider how you might apply the chapter content to the situation described. Several Decision Points are included in each chapter. In addition, each chapter includes several Teachers-In-Action features. These are descriptions by teachers from all grade levels, from large and small schools, and from all regions of the country about how they address particular issues discussed in the chapter.

Guiding Principles

The content and organization of this book are based on the following principles about classroom management, discipline, and order that are derived from and supported by research and practice.

1. Misbehavior can be minimized by an effective management system that is designed to establish and maintain order.
2. Ways to establish and maintain order need to be infused into the way lessons are planned and delivered.
3. The *Law of Least Intervention* should be used when trying to restore order: You should first provide situational assistance and then progressively use mild, moderate, and severe responses to the misbehavior in an attempt to restore order.
4. The context of events and the teacher's thinking and experiences influence the selection of procedures to establish, maintain, and restore order.
5. Managing classrooms is a decision-making process that can be guided by relevant research and practice.

Qualifiers

While this book represents a synthesis of information about management, discipline, and order, it is important to recognize some relevant qualifications.

1. *Research-based guidance is not available on a number of issues since not every aspect of classroom management and discipline has been researched* For example, it would be useful to have information about how student or teacher ethnicity affects decision making about some aspect of management; however, only limited information is available. Or, it would be helpful to have information about how teachers at different grade levels provide situational assistance to students who show signs of getting off-task; but no studies are currently available on this issue.

2. *While research has been conducted on management and discipline, the studies have often examined classrooms with routinized, predictable academic*

tasks and activities with a fairly high degree of teacher control in a direct instruction format Information provided by these studies about handling, for example, transitions during a class session need to be kept in the context of that direct instruction format. It would be interesting to know how teachers using cooperative learning or other types of instructional formats handle transition.

3. *All studies and information on a given management issue may not lead to consistent conclusions* For example, recommendations from researchers and practitioners about praising students vary. Part of the reason is that praise and encouragement are different, but in studies, the terms are often used synonymously. Praise to one researcher might mean encouragement to another researcher. It may be difficult to draw consistent conclusions from the body of studies in this area.

The varying conditions under which an issue was researched is another reason for difficulty in drawing consistent conclusions. Studies on routines, for example, may have examined different grade levels, different instructional approaches, or many other variables that might lead to differing conclusions.

DETERMINING YOUR MANAGEMENT SYSTEM

Your goals, values, and beliefs about classroom management will undoubtedly affect your decisions about the management system that you would like to establish. The grade level at which you teach will also affect your decisions. Effective ways of establishing, maintaining, and restoring order with fourth graders may not work with tenth graders, and vice versa. In addition, the length of your teaching experience will likely have a bearing on your management system. Those who have not taught very long will likely have limited experiences to draw upon when making decisions.

You will need to take into account characteristics of your students as you decide on your management system. Their age, maturity, past disciplinary record, background and interests, and other factors need to be considered. The school may provide guidelines relating to management.

To help determine the management system that is best for your particular circumstances, you can ask yourself a series of questions to examine criteria about yourself, the students, and the school (see Table 1-1).

MAJOR CONCEPTS

1. Classroom management refers to the actions and strategies teachers use to establish order.
2. Order means that the students are following within acceptable limits the actions necessary for a particular event to be successful.
3. Misbehavior includes behaviors that interfere with teaching, interfere with the rights of others to learn, are psychologically or physically unsafe, or destroy property.

TABLE 1-1 Questions to help determine what classroom management system to adopt

1. *Teacher Criteria:* Consider your goals, values, and beliefs.
   a. What are my primary goals in classroom management?
   b. Which classroom management approaches address these goals?
   c. What are my values or beliefs concerning classroom management?
   d. Which classroom approaches recognize my values and beliefs?
   e. Which of the classroom approaches that recognize my values and beliefs are also consistent with my values and beliefs? (These would be your preferred classroom approaches.)
2. *Student Criteria:* Consider their needs and problems.
   a. What are the ages and levels of maturity of my students?
   b. Which of my preferred classroom management approaches are best suited to my students' ages and maturity?
   c. What is the past disciplinary record of my students?
   d. Which of my preferred classroom approaches are best suited to my students' past disciplinary record?
   e. What are the backgrounds, interests, and abilities of my students?
   f. Which of my preferred classroom management approaches are most suited to my students' backgrounds, interests, and abilities?
   g. How much support can I expect from my students' parents?
   h. Which of my preferred classroom management approaches are best suited to the expected level of parental support?
3. *School Criteria:* Consider its policies and procedures.
   a. What district and school guidelines relate to classroom management?
   b. What aspects of my preferred classroom management approaches might conflict with the district and school guidelines?
   c. Which of my preferred classroom management approaches coincides most and conflicts least with the district and school guidelines?

SOURCE: Duke, D. L. and A. M. Meckel, *Teacher's Guide to Classroom Management.* Copyright © 1984. Reprinted by permission of McGraw-Hill, Inc.

4. Off-task behavior includes student actions that are not focused on the instructional activities, yet are not considered disruptive or defined as misbehavior.
5. Discipline includes actions that teachers take to restore order.
6. Order is established and maintained primarily by actions taken to get organized for the school year, to plan for management, and to conduct the class.
7. Order can be restored by providing situational assistance, followed by mild, moderate, and severe responses to the misbehavior as needed.
8. Your goals, values, and beliefs about classroom management will undoubtedly affect your decisions about the management system that you would like to establish.

DISCUSSION QUESTIONS

1. What is the difference between off-task behavior and misbehavior?
2. From your own experiences, how did effective teachers you had or those you observed establish, maintain, and restore control in the classroom?

3. What is the value of considering guiding principles about classroom management, discipline, and control?
4. What are some of your personal and professional characteristics that might affect decisions you make about classroom management and control?

SUPPLEMENTAL ACTIVITIES

For Clinical Settings

1. Identify guiding principles that you would use in your classroom management.
2. Answer the questions about teacher criteria in Table 1-1 concerning your goals, values, and beliefs.

For Field Settings

1. Ask several teachers specifically how they establish, maintain, and restore order.
2. Ask several teachers what guiding principles they use when deciding how to manage their classrooms and maintain order.
3. Talk with the principal or others to find out what policies or expectations exist in the school or district for management, discipline, and control.

KEY TERMS

Classroom management	Misbehavior
Discipline	Off-task behavior
Law of Least Intervention	Order
Mild responses	Situational assistance

RECOMMENDED READINGS

Berliner, D. C., & Rosenshine, B. V., Eds., (1987). *Talks to Teachers*. New York: Random House.
Provides a research-based examination of many aspects of classroom teaching. One chapter deals specifically with managing the classroom, and several other chapters examine related issues.

Good, T. L., & Brophy, J. E. (1994). *Looking in Classrooms*, 6th ed. New York: HarperCollins.
Includes two chapters on preventing and coping with problems. Other chapters examine related aspects of instruction and the means to establish and maintain order. Looks at classroom life in a holistic, complex manner.

REFERENCES

Doyle, W. (1986). Classroom organization and management. In M. C. Wittrock, Ed., *Handbook of Research on Teaching,* 3rd ed. (pp. 392–431). New York: Macmillan.

Erickson, F. (1982). Classroom discourse as improvisation: Relationships between academic task structure and social participation structure in lessons. In L. C. Wilkinson (Ed.), *Communicating in Classrooms* (pp. 153–181). New York: Academic Press.

Levin, J., & Nolan, J. F. (1991). *Principles of Classroom Management: A Hierarchical Approach.* Englewood Cliffs, NJ: Prentice Hall.

chapter **2**

Understanding Misbehavior

Objectives

This chapter provides information that will help you:

1. Recognize that misbehavior needs to be seen in the context of the circumstances and requires considerable interpretation.
2. Identify the physiological, physical, and psychosocial factors that may contribute to student misbehavior.
3. Identify types of misbehavior by individuals and groups.
4. Recognize mild, moderate, and severe forms of misbehavior.
5. Recognize that teachers can take a series of actions to intervene to re-establish order.
6. Identify certain disciplinary practices to avoid.
7. Identify legal guidelines concerning discipline.

Misbehavior is any student behavior that is perceived by the teacher to compete with or threaten the academic actions at a particular moment. Misbehavior creates disruptions in the flow of classroom activities, but not every infraction of a rule is necessarily misbehavior. For this reason, misbehavior needs to be seen as action in context and requires considerable interpretation when decisions are made about the misbehavior.

To make appropriate decisions regarding misbehavior, you first must be familiar with its nature—misbehavior in context; causes, types, degrees of severity; and interventions that might be used. We address these issues in this chapter.

It is important first to recognize that the best way to deal with discipline problems is to avoid them. You should develop challenging, interesting, and exciting lessons and treat students with dignity and respect. You should also establish an effective management system, as we describe in later chapters. If misbehavior then occurs, you can consider the guidelines and principles presented in this chapter.

MISBEHAVIOR IN CONTEXT

Students who are off-task are not performing the planned instructional activity. They may be pausing to think about an issue, daydreaming, or doing other things that are nondisruptive but prohibit them from being engaged in the work. Students who are off-task will need to be addressed differently from those who are purposely misbehaving and interfering with academic activities.

You may need to intervene to stop the misbehavior. Recognize that your decisions about interventions are complex judgments about the act, the student, and the circumstances at a particular moment in classroom time (Doyle, 1986).

Some student actions are clearly misbehavior and require teacher intervention. In many cases, however, the situation is not quite so simple. Some student actions that appear to be quite similar are reacted to differently by teachers when the actions are performed by different students at different times or in different contexts (Doyle, 1986). In this *differential treatment*, teachers may react differently when considering the context of the student actions (Hargraves, Hester, & Mellor, 1975).

The key to understanding misbehavior is to view what students do in the context of the classroom structure. As mentioned previously, management refers to the teacher's actions and strategies for maintaining order. Not every infraction of a rule is necessarily misbehavior. For instance, inattention in the final few minutes of a session will often be tolerated because the lesson is coming to an end. You would most likely intervene when inattention is evident earlier in the period.

Misbehavior, then, needs to be seen as "action in context" (Mehan, Hertweck, Combs, & Flynn, 1982), and requires interpretation based on what the teacher knows about the likely configuration of events (Hargraves et al., 1975). You need to make reliable judgments about the probable consequences of students' actions in different situations. Consistency in your response does not mean that you need to behave in the same way every time, but rather that your judgments are reliable and consistent.

CAUSES OF MISBEHAVIOR

One way to understand classroom control is to determine *why* students misbehave. In some cases, the reasons are complex and personal and perhaps beyond your comprehension or control. Some misbehavior arises from common, general causes that can be anticipated.

Behavior is neither entirely internally nor externally caused, but is the result of the interaction between the individual and the environment. Specifically, the physiological, physical, and psychosocial environments combine to affect behavior (Evans, Evans, & Schmid, 1989).

The Physiological Environment

The *physiological environment* includes those *biophysical variables* that affect behavior, such as illness, nutritional factors, neurological functioning, temperament, genetic abnormalities, physical disabilities, and drugs or medication. These fall into three categories. First, behavior problems may be related to health factors. An allergy, lack of sleep, illness, or an inadequate diet may greatly affect ability to complete assignments or interact with others (Heron & Heward, 1982). For some children, excessive sugar has an affect on their behavior and may cause hyperactivity.

Physical impairments such as visual or hearing loss, paralysis, or a severe physiological disorder may also contribute to behavior problems. Medications or drugs, whether legal or illegal, may also be a factor. Restlessness, inattention, and mood swings are just some of the side effects that can be related to use of these substances. Some physiological factors are under the control of the teacher and parents, and some are not.

An example of a neurological condition is *attention deficit disorder*, a mental disorder in which the area of the brain that controls motor activity doesn't function as it should. This is among the most common childhood mental disorders and affects about 4 percent of school-age children, according to the National Institute of Mental Health. Such students may be inattentive (easily distracted, don't follow directions well, shift from one unfinished task to another, and seem not to be listening), hyperactive (talkative, fidget, and squirm), and impulsive (don't wait their turn, blurt out answers, and engage in dangerous activities without considering the consequences). There is some evidence that this may have a genetic cause, though environmental factors may play a part as well (Brown, 1993).

The Physical Environment

The *physical environment* includes *elements of the setting* that are used or present in everyday living. These can be considered in four categories: (1) Resources or conditions in the home and community may be related to behavior problems. Problems may be associated with a lack of adequate clothing or housing; parental supervision and types of discipline; home routines; significant events such as divorce or the death of a friend or relative; and community sources. There has been considerable concern and debate over the effects of television on the beliefs and conduct of children. Violence on television is seen by some to influence students to be more aggressive. (2) School factors can be related to behavior problems. These include the curriculum; effectiveness of teachers, administrators, and staff; school routines; adequacy of facilities; and

---

Teachers in Action

Elements of the Setting Affect Behavior

Debra Young Stuto, sixth-grade teacher, Omaha, Nebraska:

To be effective in handling students, you must spend time to understand the causes of the behaviors and the misbehaviors. For example, there was no way that Quincy would learn anything on the day that we had fishsticks for lunch. Quincy *hated* fishsticks. It took me several weeks of horrible scenes every Friday to fit fishsticks with Quincy's misbehavior.

Quincy was the oldest child of several little brothers and sisters, and his mother recently had had a new baby. There was no way that he was going to have a sack lunch from home on "fishstick days." Thursday night, I made Quincy a peanut butter and jelly sandwich as I made my own son's sandwich, and I put it on his desk in the morning so it was there when he walked in. Neither of us mentioned it, and every Thursday I do the same thing. Now Quincy can learn on fishstick days.

---

even other students in the classroom. (3) Classroom arrangements may play a role. The physical arrangement, temperature, noise, and lighting may have a significant effect on student performance (Evans, Evans, & Mercer, 1986). Student crowding may also be involved (Paine, Radicchi, Rosellini, Deutchman, & Darch, 1983; Zentall, 1983). (4) Instructional factors may be the most important of all the physical factors that directly affect student behavior. They include the learning climate, the appropriateness of the curriculum and instructional materials, and the effectiveness of the instructional delivery.

Decision Points

How you deliver instructions may contribute to student off-task behavior. This may include the way you provide for student involvement, handle questions, and use various instructional strategies. Suppose you are delivering a math lesson to your eighth-grade class. What could you do to assess your instructional delivery to be sure it does not contribute to student misbehavior?

Many elements of the physical environment such as the classroom setting and instructional program directly affect student behavior and are under the immediate control of the teacher. You should examine the variables within the classroom.

Teachers sometimes needlessly create disciplinary problems by the way they manage and conduct their classes (Emmer, Evertson, Clement, & Worsham, 1994;

Teachers in Action

First Impressions

Hildie Brooks, seventh- and eighth-grade health teacher, Manhattan, Kansas:

Freddy reminded me of a teaching concept many teachers seem to quickly forget—to accept each student without passing judgment when the student walks into your classroom. The first day of class is always an interesting experience. The students are trying to "figure out" the teacher, and vice versa.

When Freddy boldly walked into my room after the bell had rung and announced that he was going to be in my class, I thought that a real discipline problem had just arrived. Calmly, I requested that he check with the school office to make sure the change was correct. While Freddy was out of the room, I was able to prepare myself for his second entrance. When he came in, I quietly explained that his previous behavior was not acceptable and requested that he stand at the end of the line and wait quietly to receive his book and his seating assignment. Once class began, Freddy was very quiet.

The following day, I was apprehensive about how Freddy would behave in class. The physical education teacher had warned me that he particularly disliked this student. For some reason, Freddy was very quiet in my class. In fact, he continued to be surprisingly quiet throughout the first week. As time progressed, Freddy proved to be a diligent student, an active participant, and a positive influence in the classroom.

At the end of the term, I told Freddy how much I enjoyed having him in class and that I learned an important lesson from him. I had jumped to a quick conclusion that he might be a discipline problem, but he was really a delightful student. I will try not to classify students as problem students based on one incident.

What is interesting is that Freddy is a problem for a number of teachers. I can only guess why Freddy behaved so nicely in my class. There are three behaviors that I consciously did—I did not let Freddy make me angry, I stated the classroom policies in a calm voice, and I respected Freddy as a person by not intimidating him in front of his peers.

Emmer, Evertson, & Anderson, 1980; Moskowitz & Hayman, 1976). These inappropriate behaviors include being overly negative, maintaining an authoritarian climate, overreacting to situations, using mass punishment, blaming students, lacking a clear instructional goal, repeating or reviewing already learned material, pausing too long during instruction, dealing with one student at length, and failing to recognize student ability levels. While few teachers can avoid all of these behaviors all of the time, effective teachers appreciate the potentially damaging effects of classroom order and discipline. Being aware of these characteristics is the first step in avoiding them. It is useful to periodically reflect upon your own teaching behavior to determine if you are taking actions that are contributing to inattention or misbehavior.

The Psychosocial Environment

The *psychosocial environment* comprises factors such as *values, motivation, preferences, and conditioning history.* This environment can be examined in three ways. First, emotional and learning impairments may affect student behavior. These problems hinder ability to reason or interact with others in an appropriate manner. They may be the result of developmental delay, communication disorders, mental retardation, or learning disabilities. For instance, the long-term effects of alcohol and drug abuse on the fetus are only now beginning to be understood. Children with fetal alcohol syndrome may be hyperactive or impulsive. Crack babies—children born to women who were using crack during pregnancy—may exhibit similar behaviors.

Second, intrapersonal factors refer to variables such as interests, values, and motivation. These personal factors determine the sorts of activities students are interested in and thus influence their behavior. For example, you could assess your students to determine specific activities in which they are interested.

Expectations—the predicted outcomes of future events—also determine how behavior will be evaluated (Algozzine, Schmid, & Mercer, 1981). Expectations may influence the way teachers, students, and parents interact with others. For example, you might have a student who has had a history of behavior problems in earlier grades. You might then unintentionally expect this student to act inappropriately even before misbehavior occurs. You may behave antagonistically to the student, give him or her few opportunities to respond, and fail to notice appropriate behavior while often noticing inappropriate behavior. Similarly, some students may have an expectation that they are unable to achieve or that a certain teacher is unfair. This predicted outcome may cause them to give up or behave in a manner to fulfill the expectation.

Finally, the quantity and quality of interpersonal interactions of parents, teachers, and peers often affect student behavior. Much of what we do is dictated by the reaction of others, but not all reactions are equally valued. Praise from a friend or someone who is admired may be more reinforcing than praise offered by someone whose opinion the student does not highly value. It is important that you determine whose opinions are most valued by your students.

You could encourage your students to praise and reinforce one another. This might be done as part of the students' evaluation of the work of the entire class in a cooperative group activity. Or you might model thanking a student for sharing a good idea during a discussion, then ask the students to compliment each other when they see some noteworthy activity of other students in future classes.

Students often do things to gain the teacher's attention and recognition. Your behavior may dictate their behavior. A teacher who is overly stern, gives little praise, and creates an oppressive climate does little to motivate or foster appropriate student behavior. In fact, teachers often precipitate inappropriate behavior by shouting, handling students physically, and imposing arbitrary and authoritarian rules (Bullock, Reilly, & Donahue, 1983). A good learning environment results from praise, an organized implementation of the instructional program, and fair disciplinary practices (Smith, Neisworth, & Greer, 1978). Teachers who create such a climate are viewed positively by students who often welcome and seek praise from such a teacher.

TYPES OF MISBEHAVIOR

Sometimes individual students misbehave; sometimes a group of students or even the entire class misbehaves. This needs to be taken into account as you select an appropriate response.

Misbehavior by Individuals

Inappropriate behavior by individual students can be classified into four general categories:

1. *Hyperactivity*—a high level of activity and nonaggressive contact, often due to neurological dysfunctions. Behaviors include (a) unable to sit still, and fidgets; (b) talks too much; (c) cannot wait for pleasant things to happen; (d) constant demand for attention; (e) hums and makes other noises; (f) excitable; (g) overly anxious to please; and (h) awkward and poor general coordination.
2. *Inattentiveness*—the inability to complete work and activities, and has a high level of distractibility. Behaviors include (a) doesn't stay with games and activities; (b) doesn't complete projects; (c) inattentive and distractible; (d) doesn't follow directions; (e) withdraws from new people and is shy; (f) sits fiddling with small objects; and (g) unable to sit still and fidgets.
3. *Conduct disorder*—the inability to accept correction, tends to tease others, and shows a high level of defiance. Behaviors include (a) doesn't stay with games and activities; (b) cannot accept correction; (c) teases others; (d) discipline doesn't change behavior for long; (e) is defiant and "talks back"; (f) moody; (g) fights; and (h) has difficulty in handling frustration.

Decision Points

Let's assume that a student in your ninth-grade class is defiant and talks back. You would consider the student's age level and maturity when deciding how to handle the situation. What other factors might you consider when pondering a decision?

---

4. *Impulsivity*—has constant demand for attention, with an orientation to the present, and unpredictability. Behaviors include (a) reckless, and acts carelessly; (b) has numerous accidents; and (c) gets into things.

Another way to look at student behaviors is to examine the range of inappropriate to appropriate behaviors. Table 2-1 presents the behavior network proposed by Evans, Evans, and Schmid (1989) after they reviewed lists of bothersome behaviors identified by authors such as Evans, Evans, and Mercer

TABLE 2-1   Behavior network continuum

Inappropriate Behaviors	Appropriate Behaviors
Begins tasks only after reminding	Begins tasks promptly
Does not attend to task	Attends to task
Fails to complete task	Completes task
Does not follow directions	Follows directions
Does careless or sloppy work	Completes neat work
Is out of seat	Remains in seat
Interrupts others	Speaks when appropriate
Talks out of turn	Talks with permission
Does not tell the truth	Tells the truth
Uses abusive language	Speaks appropriately
Withdraws from others	Interacts with others
Requests constant reassurance	Participates without constant reassurance
Makes self-deprecating comments	Makes realistic statements about self
Cries at inappropriate times	Cries at appropriate times
Engages in inappropriate age-play	Engages in appropriate age-play
Fails to initiate contact with others	Initiates contact with others
Fails to engage in group activities	Initiates contact with group
Gives up easily	Is persistent
Refuses to share with others	Shares with others
Appearance of mood does not fit setting	Appearance of mood fits setting
Claims illness without apparent physical cause	Is ill with apparent cause
Runs away	Accepts consequences of behavior
Is uncooperative	Cooperates wtih others
Is disorderly in class and school	Follows class and school rules
Is assaultive	Resolves problems without violence
Destroys property	Respects property
Exhibits temper tantrums	Resolves problems appropriately
Steals	Takes things with permission
Cheats	Completes own work

SOURCE: Evans, W. H., S. S. Evans, and R. E. Schmidt, *Behavior and Instructional Management: An Ecological Approach.* Copyright © 1989 by Allyn & Bacon. Reprinted by permission.

(1986); Reinert (1980); and Veldman and Worsham (1983). This network presents appropriate behaviors allowing behaviors to be evaluated along a continuum. This continuum also reinforces the notion that a behavior management system should seek not only to reduce inappropriate behaviors but also to increase appropriate behaviors.

The inappropriate behaviors listed in Table 2-1 are not necessarily characteristic of all grade levels. Some of them may be more common in elementary classrooms (e.g., student tattles, cries, refuses to share with others, requests constant reassurance) while other behaviors of a more serious nature may be more common in secondary classrooms (e.g., student is assaultive, cheats, steals). Yet many of the behaviors could be expressed by students at any grade level.

Misbehavior as a Group

Management involves establishing and maintaining order with a *group* of students. Beyond individual misbehavior, the group as a whole sometimes exhibits inappropriate behavior. Seven types of group management problems include (a) a lack of unity; (b) nonadherence to behavioral standards and work procedures; (c) negative reactions to individual members; (d) class approval of misbehavior; (e) prone to distraction, work stoppage, and imitative behavior; (f) low morale and hostile, resistant, or aggressive behavior; and (g) inability to adjust to environmental change, such as a change in seating arrangement or classroom routines (Froyen, 1993).

DEGREES OF SEVERITY

Misbehavior ranges from mildly to severely disruptive. Severely disruptive behavior and crime in schools includes violence, vandalism, coercion, robbery, theft, and drug use. These behaviors typically occur outside the classroom in the lunch room, corridors, or outside the building. Moderate misbehavior involves tardiness, cutting class, talking, calling out answers, mild verbal and physical aggression, inattentiveness, and failure to bring supplies and books. Most misbehavior is comparatively mild and is related to attention, crowd control, and getting work accomplished in the classroom.

When selecting an appropriate response, you need to take into account the degree of its severity. You can evaluate severity by factors such as appropriateness, magnitude, intent, and extent to which a behavior differs from what is expected in a particular setting (Evans et al., 1989). The degree of your response should match the degree of severity of the misbehavior. Table 2-2 presents examples of mild, moderate, and severe misbehavior. Teachers often ignore certain minor misbehaviors because their intervention may be more disruptive than the misbehavior. You should consider and prepare procedures for dealing with the types of misbehaviors listed in Table 2-2, especially mild misbehavior that might be expressed more frequently.

TABLE 2-2   Examples of mild, moderate, and severe misbehavior

1. *Mild Misbehaviors*
   Minor defacing of school property or property of others
   Acting out (horseplaying or scuffling)
   Talking back
   Talking without raising hand
   Getting out of seat
   Disrupting others
   Sleeping in class
   Tardiness
   Throwing objects
   Exhibiting inappropriate familiarity (kissing, hugging)
   Gambling
   Eating in class
   Making disruptive sounds
2. *Moderate Misbehaviors*
   Unauthorized leaving of class
   Abusive conduct towards others
   Noncompliant
   Smoking or using tobacco in class
   Cutting class
   Cheating, plagiarizing, or lying
   Using profanity, vulgar language, or obscene gestures
   Fighting
3. *Severe Misbehaviors*
   Defacing or damaging school property or property of others
   Theft, possession, or sale of another's property
   Truancy
   Being under the influence of alcohol or narcotics
   Selling, giving, or delivering alcohol, narcotics, or weapons to another person
   Assault or verbal abuse of the teacher
   Assault of other students
   Incorrigible conduct, noncompliance
   Sexual misconduct
   Coercion

SOURCE: Borich, Gary D., *Effective Teaching Methods,* 2nd ed. Copyright © 1992 by Macmillan College Publishing Company, Inc. Reprinted by permission.

Decision Points

Consider the mild misbehaviors listed in Table 2-2 and add any examples that you can think of. From the list, which ones would you consider to be minor and not worthy of intervention? How might your decision to ignore certain minor behaviors be affected by the grade level at which you teach?

INTERVENTIONS FOR MISBEHAVIOR

Students and teachers interact to define and sustain order. The teacher is the primary custodian of the classroom and must decide when and how to intervene into the flow of activities to repair disorder. An ***intervention*** is an action taken

Teachers in Action

Don't Jump to Conclusions, Let the Student Talk

Dea Kreisman, elementary resource teacher, Aurora, Colorado:

As a resource teacher in charge of discipline, I have found that it is critical that all sides of a story be listened to and considered to determine who is at fault. Avoid automatically accusing a student of wrongdoing just because he or she has a history of discipline problems.

David, a fifth-grade student, had been sent to me for inappropriate behavior on a fairly regular basis during the first semester. I learned very quickly that if I gave him the opportunity to tell his side, even if he was at fault, he would be honest with me and accept the consequences accordingly. By the second semester, his behavior had improved. He would be very upset, however, if he felt he was not being dealt with fairly.

In a recent incident, a paraprofessional referred David to me, but she had jumped to conclusions and had not given David an opportunity to tell his side. She quickly judged him to be at fault. David wrote the following note to me about the incident.

The Truth

While on the timeout wall at recess, with Lauren seven meters away, I threw one single pebble that hit her hair. Then she and Jamara went to Ms. Nortin (who always listens only to the first person to tell the story), and they told her that I pulled Lauren's hair and threw large rocks at Jamara's legs. Ms. Nortin then gave me a behavior report that I didn't fill out in a nice way. I'm sorry that I didn't fill out the report appropriately, but I was angry at Ms. Nortin about the way she handled the situation. And I'm frustrated because I was found guilty without a trial. Therefore, I wish to have that trial to give more attention to my side of the story.

Thank you for your time and understanding,
David

by the teacher that is intended to stop the disruptive actions and return to the academic flow of activities.

Interventions can repair temporary disturbances in order, but they cannot establish order when order in the program does not exist. The degree of order, instead, depends upon the strength of the academic program and the timing of interventions so they occur before the disruptions have gained strength (Kounin, 1970).

Intervention decisions are typically based on the teacher's knowledge of who is misbehaving, what the misbehavior is, and when it occurs. Decisions to intervene are based on information about whether the behavior is serious and distracting, and decisions about the intensity of the intervention depend on the student's history of inappropriate behavior (Pittman, 1984). You should not automatically jump to conclusions if an incident involves a student with a history of behavior problems.

Decisions to intervene are often made under conditions of uncertainty. That is, early cues may be ambiguous, yet you may have only a limited amount of time to make a judgment and act. To reduce uncertainty, teachers sometimes categorize students in terms of their persistence and their visibility in the social structure of the group. Teachers learn the likely configuration of events associated with actions by different students and take this into account when deciding whether an intervention is necessary (Doyle, 1986). It is helpful to discuss the problem with the student to clarify it from both your perspective and the student's and to consider the possible interventions.

Recent research suggests that there is growing interest toward helping students learn to cope with classroom processes rather than having teachers implement behavior modification programs. This includes teaching social and cooperative skills, coping strategies, participation skills, and self-monitoring and self-control strategies (Doyle, 1986). Management and discipline procedures have been proposed to help students make responsible choices (Albert, 1989; Bauer & Sapona, 1991; Keating, Pickering, Slack, & White, 1990; Savage, 1991).

Based on this review, we can conclude that interventions (a) are used to repair disorder rather than create order, (b) involve complex decisions about the probable consequences of particular actions by particular students at specific moments in the activity flow of a class session, and (c) can themselves disrupt order.

The Principle of Least Intervention

The *principle of least intervention* states that when dealing with routine classroom behavior, misbehaviors should be corrected with the simplest, least intrusive intervention that will work (Slavin, 1994). If this is not effective, you move up to a more intrusive approach.

The main goal is to handle the misbehavior in an effective manner that avoids unnecessarily disrupting the lesson (Evertson & Harris, 1992). To the extent possible, the lesson should continue while the misbehavior is handled.

How do you apply this principle of least intervention? When you notice a student starting to lose interest in the lesson or beginning to get off-task, you can provide situational assistance—actions to help the student cope with the situation and keep the student on-task. If the student then is off-task, you can select mild responses to get the student back on-task. If mild responses are not effective, you can use moderate responses. If moderate responses do not work, you move to severe responses. This continuum of teacher responses is displayed in Table 2-3, and details are provided in chapters 14 and 15.

TABLE 2-3 A continuum of teacher responses to misbehavior

Teacher Response	Provide Situational Assistance	Use Mild Responses	Use Moderate Responses	Use Severe Responses
Purpose	To help the student cope with the instructional situation and keep the student on-task	To take nonpunitive actions to get the student back on-task	To remove desired stimuli to decrease unwanted behavior	To add aversive stimuli to decrease unwanted behavior
Sample Actions	Remove distracting objects Provide support with routines Reinforce appropriate behaviors Boost student interest Provide cues Help student over hurdles Redirect the behavior Alter the lesson Provide nonpunitive time-out Modify the classroom environment	Nonverbal Responses Ignore the behavior Use signal interference Use proximity control Use touch control Write notes to student Verbal Responses Reinforce peers Call on the student during the lesson Use humor Send an I-message Use positive phrasing Remind student of the rules Give student choices Ask "What are you doing?" Give a verbal reprimand Use differential reinforcement	Logical Consequences Behavior modification techniques Time-out Loss of privileges	Reprimands Overcorrection Physical consequences
Degree of Teacher Control	Low →			High ↑

27

SOME PRACTICES TO AVOID

This book focuses on effective ways to establish, maintain, and restore control in the classroom. Fortunately, a number of strategies are successful in achieving these purposes. Research and practice suggest, however, that some strategies are inappropriate or unsuccessful in restoring control.

Weber and Roff (1983) found that disadvantages outweigh advantages regarding harsh reprimands, threats, and physical punishment. Practitioners have identified additional approaches that have questionable effectiveness. The message is clear—*teachers should avoid the following practices:*

1. *Harsh and humiliating reprimands.* A harsh reprimand is very negative verbal feedback. Teachers may be carried away with this verbal thrashing and humiliate the student. Research reports suggest that the use of harsh reprimands is an ineffective, inefficient, and costly strategy. Harsh reprimands include speaking to the student in an exceptionally stern manner, yelling, and screaming. All of this may progress to the point where the student is humiliated. Teachers sometimes voice harsh reprimands when they have lost emotional control in response to the misbehavior.

2. *Threats.* A ***threat*** is a statement that expresses the intent to punish if the student does not comply with the teacher's wishes. Most practitioners and researchers believe the disadvantages of using threats outweigh any possible benefits. Teachers may warn students to alert them to potential consequences, but a threat often expresses more severe consequences than would normally be expected and may be stated when the teacher has lost emotional control.

3. *Nagging.* Continual or unnecessary scolding only upsets the student and arouses the resentment of other students. The teacher may consider these scoldings to be minilectures, but they are seen as nagging from the students' point of view.

4. *Forced apologies.* Forcing a student to express an apology that is not felt is a way of forcing him or her to lie. This approach solves nothing.

5. *Sarcastic remarks.* ***Sarcastic remarks*** are statements that the teacher uses to deride, taunt, or ridicule the student. While the teacher may consider this a means of punishment, they create resentment; they may lower the student's self-esteem, and may lower the esteem of the teacher in the eyes of the students.

6. *Group punishment.* ***Group punishment*** occurs when the entire class or group is punished because of the misbehavior of an individual. Peer pressure is intended to help modify the individual's behavior. Group punishment is difficult to use effectively, and the undesirable side effects are likely to outweigh the advantages. It forces students to choose between the teacher and a classmate. Many students will

unite in sullen defiance of the teacher and refuse to blame the classmate if group punishment is used. Even if they go along with the teacher, the punishment will engender unhealthy attitudes.

7. *Assigning extra academic work.* When assigning extra academic work as a punishment, the teacher implies that the work is unpleasant. It is often in the form of homework that is not normally required. The student then associates schoolwork with punishment. This is not the message teachers should convey.

8. *Reducing grades.* Penalizing a student academically for misbehavior again creates an undesirable association. Students who are penalized for misbehaving may develop an attitude of "What's the use?" toward academic work. Furthermore, reducing grades for misbehavior confounds the grade, which is intended to report only the student's academic progress.

9. *Writing as punishment.* After students misbehave, teachers may have them copy pages out of a dictionary, encyclopedia, or other book, or have students write a certain statement ("I will not do such and such again.") a number of times. Unfortunately, this approach leads to hostility in the students, gives the impression that writing is a bad thing (English teachers would be upset about the message being conveyed here), and is not logically linked to what the students may have done. It is not wise to use writing as a punishment.

10. *Corporal punishment.* **Corporal punishment** is a strategy in which the teacher inflicts physical pain on the student to punish the latter for misbehaving. Research findings are clear in suggesting that corporal punishment has far more disadvantages than advantages. Teachers should not use corporal punishment. Many districts have a policy either prohibiting the use of corporal punishment or establishing specific guidelines for its limited use.

11. *Physical labor or exercise.* A teacher may use push-ups or some other physical action as punishment. However, the teacher may not be familiar with the student's physical abilities, and the student could get hurt. In addition to concerns about student safety, having them do extra exercises in physical education in response to misbehavior may cause them to lose interest in the physical activities when the teacher assigns them as punishment.

12. *Suspension.* Except in extreme cases, suspension causes students to lose class time and fall behind in academic work. That in itself is bad, yet the suspended student may welcome the time off from school and thus suspension may not be seen as punishment.

In summary, practitioners and researchers have pointed out that the practices highlighted here should be avoided. Instead, you should use the effective strategies discussed in the next three chapters for dealing with misbehavior.

LEGAL ASPECTS OF DISCIPLINE

Your decisions about responding to student misbehavior should be made with an understanding of the legal aspects of discipline. The basis of teacher control of students, conduct regulations, due process considerations, legal aspects concerning various disciplinary actions, tort liability, disciplining students with disabilities, and remedies for unlawful disciplinary actions are all issues that need to be taken into account when responding to misbehavior.

You should recognize that rulings and interpretations may change as new court cases are resolved. These guidelines are subject to change, and it is useful to consult with your principal as the need arises when dealing with disciplinary issues discussed below.

While the law concerning student discipline remains in a state of flux, judicial decisions support the following generalizations (McCarthy & Cambron-McCabe, 1992).

1. School authorities must be able to substantiate that any disciplinary regulation enacted is reasonable and necessary for the management of the school or for the welfare of pupils and school employees.
2. All regulations should be stated in precise terms and disseminated to students and parents.
3. Punishment for rule infractions should be appropriate for the offense and the characteristics of the offender (e.g., age, mental condition, prior behavior).
4. Students cannot be punished for the acts of others.
5. Some type of due process should be afforded to students prior to the imposition of punishments. For minor penalties, an informal hearing suffices; for serious punishments, more formal procedures are required (e.g., notification of parents, representation by counsel, opportunity to cross-examine witnesses).
6. Students can be punished for misbehavior occurring off school grounds if the conduct directly relates to the welfare of the school.
7. Suspensions and expulsions are legitimate punishments if accompanied by appropriate procedural safeguards and not arbitrarily imposed.
8. The transfer of students to different classes, programs, or schools for disciplinary reasons must be accompanied by due process procedures.
9. If not prohibited by state law or school board policy, reasonable corporal punishment can be used as a disciplinary technique.
10. Academic sanctions for nonacademic reasons should be reasonable, related to absences from class, and serve a legitimate school purpose.
11. School personnel can search students' lockers or personal effects for educational purposes upon reasonable suspicion that the students possess contraband that will disrupt the school.

12. Strip searches should be avoided unless evidence substantiates that there is probable cause to search or an emergency exists.

13. The use of canines to sniff objects is generally not viewed as a search, but courts are not in agreement regarding whether their use with students is a search and that requires individualized suspicion.

14. Chemical screening of students comes within the purview of the fourth amendment and requires reasonable suspicion that an individual student is using drugs.

15. If students are unlawfully punished, they are entitled to be restored (without penalty) to their status prior to the imposition of the punishment and to have their records expunged of any reference to the illegal punishment.

16. School officials can be held liable for compensatory damages if unlawful punishments result in substantial injury to the students involved (e.g., unwarranted suspensions from school); however, only nominal damages, not to exceed one dollar, can be assessed against school officials for the abridgement of students' procedural rights (e.g., the denial of an adequate hearing). (pp. 229-230)

When responding to student misbehavior, your decisions should be guided with an understanding of the legal aspects of discipline. Students' rights thus are protected and you do not put yourself in jeopardy for disciplinary actions that you might take.

MAJOR CONCEPTS

1. Misbehavior is any behavior that is perceived by the teacher to compete with or threaten the academic actions at a particular moment in a classroom activity.

2. Teacher decisions about interventions are complex judgments requiring interpretation of the act, the student, and the circumstances at a particular moment.

3. Physiological, physical, and psychosocial conditions combine to affect student behavior.

4. There are several types of misbehavior which might be expressed by individuals or by a group of students.

5. Misbehavior ranges from mildly to severely disruptive behavior.

6. An intervention is an action taken by the teacher that is intended to stop the disruptive actions and return to the academic flow of activities.

7. When students show signs of losing interest in the lesson, teachers should first provide situational assistance. Then in sequence use mild, moderate, and severe responses if the misbehavior continues.

8. Avoid certain practices that have been proven to be ineffective, such as harsh reprimands, threats, physical punishment, group punishment, and reducing grades.

DISCUSSION QUESTIONS

1. Provide some examples to illustrate how the context of the misbehavior might affect the teacher response.
2. Identify ways in which the teacher might contribute to the occurrence of misbehavior.
3. How might the cause of the misbehavior affect the teacher's choice of an appropriate response?
4. Why should the degree of teacher response match the degree of severity of the misbehavior? Give examples.
5. What are the merits and disadvantages of moving from providing situational assistance to using severe responses?
6. What have been your experiences when teachers you have had used inappropriate disciplinary practices?

SUPPLEMENTAL ACTIVITIES

For Clinical Settings

1. Identify causes of misbehavior in the physical environment. What could you do in your classroom to minimize misbehavior due to aspects of the physical environment?
2. Identify ways you might respond to individual misbehavior due to hyperactivity, inattentiveness, and conduct disorder.
3. Review Table 2-3 and consider additional examples for teacher responses at each of the four steps.

For Field Settings

1. Ask several teachers to give examples of how the context of the misbehavior affects their response.
2. Talk to teachers at various grade levels to identify differences in students' developmental characteristics and the effect these have on the teacher's approach to discipline problems.
3. Talk to several teachers to learn their views on mild, moderate, and severe behavior. Ask how they respond to the misbehavior at each level.

KEY TERMS

Attention deficit disorder	Physical environment
Corporal punishment	Physiological environment
Differential treatment	Principle of least intervention
Group punishment	Psychosocial environment
Intervention	Sarcastic remarks
Misbehavior	Threats

RECOMMENDED READINGS

Albert, L. (1989). *A Teacher's Guide to Cooperative Discipline: How to Manage Your Classroom and Promote Self-Esteem.* Circle Pines, MN: American Guidance Service.
Includes a section on the theory and practice of cooperative discipline, four sections on corrective actions for four types of behaviors, a section on taking supportive actions, and a section on taking cooperative action. Well written and organized. Based largely on Dreikur's disciplinary concepts.

Biehler, R. F., & Snowman, J. (1993). *Psychology Applied to Teaching,* 7th ed. Boston: Houghton Mifflin.
Chapter 3 provides detailed descriptions of the physical, social, emotional, and cognitive characteristics for the following grade levels: preschool and kindergarten, primary grades, elementary grades, junior high, and high school.

Evans, W. H., Evans, S. S., & Schmid, R. E. (1989). *Behavior and Instructional Management: An Ecological Approach.* Boston: Allyn & Bacon.
Includes chapters on assessing and targeting behaviors, intervening, increasing appropriate behavior, decreasing unwanted behavior, and related issues. Focuses primarily on behavior, its causes, and appropriate interventions to promote or inhibit certain behaviors.

McCarthy, M. M., & Cambron-McCabe, N. H. (1992). *Public School Law: Teachers' and Students' Rights,* 3rd ed. Boston: Allyn & Bacon.
Includes 14 chapters covering all aspects of teaching and teachers and student rights. Has a separate chapter on student discipline. Comprehensive coverage.

REFERENCES

Albert, L. (1989) *A Teacher's Guide to Cooperative Discipline: How to Manage Your Classroom and Promote Self-Esteem.* Circle Pines, MN: American Guidance Service.

Algozzine, R., Schmid, R. E., & Mercer, C. D., Eds., (1981). *Childhood Behavior Disorders.* Rockville, MD: Aspen Systems

Bauer, A. M., & Sapona, R. H. (1991). *Managing Classrooms to Facilitate Learning.* Englewood Cliffs, NJ: Prentice Hall.

Brown, D. (1993, April 8). Hyperactivity disorder begins to give up secrets. *Wichita Eagle,* pp. 1, 5.

Bullock, L., Reilly, T., & Donahue, C. (1983). School violence and what teachers can do about it. *Contemporary Education, 55*(1), 40-44.

Doyle, W. (1986). Classroom organization and management. In M. C. Wittrock, Ed., *Handbook of Research on Teaching,* 3rd ed., (pp. 392-431). New York: Macmillan.

Emmer, E. T., Evertson, C. M., & Anderson, L. (1980). Effective classroom management at the beginning of the school year. *Elementary School Journal, 80,* 219-231.

Emmer, E. T., Evertson, C. M., Clements, B. S., & Worsham, M. E. (1994). *Classroom Management for Secondary Teachers,* 3rd ed. Boston: Allyn & Bacon.

Evans, W. H., Evans, S. S., & Mercer, C. D. (1986). *Assessment for Instruction.* Boston: Allyn & Bacon.

Evans, W. H., Evans, S. S., & Schmid, R. E. (1989). *Behavior and Instructional Management: An Ecological Approach.* Boston: Allyn & Bacon.

Evertson, C. M., & Harris, A. H. (1992). What we know about managing classrooms. *Educational Leadership, 49*(7), 74-78.

Froyen, L. A. (1993) *Classroom Management: The Reflective Teacher-leader,* 2nd ed. Columbus, OH: Merrill Publishing Co.

Hargraves, D. H., Hester, S. K., & Mellor, F. J. (1975). *Deviance in Classrooms.* Boston, MA: Routledge & Kegan Paul.

Heron, F. M., & Heward, W. L. (1982). Ecological assessment: Implications for teachers of learning disabled students. *Learning Disability Quarterly, 5,* 117-126.

Keating, B., Pickering, M., Slack, B., & White, J. (1990). *A guide to Positive Discipline: Helping Students Make Responsible Choices.* Boston, MA: Allyn & Bacon.

Kounin, J. S. (1970). *Discipline and Group Management in Classrooms.* New York: Holt, Rinehart & Winston.

McCarthy, M. M., & Cambron-McCabe, N. H. (1992). *Public School Law: Teachers' and Students' Rights,* 3rd ed. Boston: Allyn & Bacon.

Mehan, H., Hertweck, A., Combs, S. E., & Flynn, P. J. (1982). Teachers' interpretations of students' behavior. In L. C. Wilkinson, Ed., *Communicating in the Classroom* (pp. 297-321). New York: Academic Press.

Moskowitz, G., & Hayman, J. (1976). Success strategies of inner-city teachers: A year-long study. *Journal of Educational Research, 69,* 283-289.

Paine, S. C., Radicchi, J., Rosellini, L. C., Deutchman, L., & Darch, C. B. (1983). *Structuring your Classroom for Academic Success.* Champaign, IL: Research Press.

Pittman, S. I. (1984, April). *A cognitive ethnography and quantification of teachers' plans for managing students.* Paper presented at the annual meeting of the American Educational Research Association, New Orleans, LA.

Reinert, H. C. (1980). *Children in Conflict.* 2nd ed. St. Louis: C. V. Mosby.

Savage, T. V. (1991). *Discipline for Self-control.* Englewood Cliffs, NJ: Prentice-Hall.

Slavin, R. E. (1994). *Educational Psychology: Theory and Practice,* 4th ed. Boston: Allyn & Bacon.

Smith, R., Neisworth, J., & Greer, J. (1978). *Evaluating Educational Environments.* Columbus, OH: Charles E. Merrill.

Veldman, D. J., & Worsham, M. (1983). Types of student classroom behavior. *Journal of Educational Research, 76*(4), 204-209.

Weber, W. A., & Roff, L. A. (1983). A review of teacher education literature on classroom management. In W. A. Weber, L. A. Roff, J. Crawford, & C. Robinson, Eds., *Classroom Management: Reviews of the Teacher Education and Research Literature* (pp. 7-42). Princeton, NJ: Educational Testing Service.

Zentall, S. S. (1983). Learning environments: A review of physical and temporal factors. *Exceptional Education Quarterly, 4*(2), 90-110.

chapter 3

Models of Discipline

Objectives

This chapter provides information that will help you:

1. Identify the features of low, medium, and high control approaches to management and discipline.
2. Identify the characteristics of the discipline models proposed by educators who are representative of the low, medium, and high control approaches.
3. Identify actions to take when deciding on your approach to control.

Since management deals with maintaining order, you need to think about how you will maintain control over your students. How much freedom or control do you want to establish? What are your purposes for insisting on this degree of control? What are your responsibilities and the students' responsibilities?

As a starting point, it is useful to see how other educators have dealt with this issue of control. Some educators endorse many freedoms for students with limited controls, while others endorse stronger controls with limited student freedoms. Their various views will help you gain a philosophical perspective about the range of possibilities for decisions that you might make. As you proceed through this book, you can see how the ideas fit into the continuum of low to high control, then decide on your strategies. No single model is advocated or represented in this book.

This chapter provides a brief orientation for various models of control, ranging from low to high control. It is not intended to offer extensive information about each model to the point where you would be skilled enough to enact that model. For that purpose, more extensive summaries of these models are available from other sources (e.g., Charles, 1992; Edwards, 1993; Wolfgang & Glickman, 1995). The original sources mentioned in this chapter for the respective models provide a fuller description.

THE DEGREE OF CONTROL

When deciding how to handle management and discipline, you probably will take into account your views of child development, your educational philosophies, and other factors. These views can be categorized in various ways, but perhaps the most useful organizer is by the degree of control that you exert on the students and the classroom. A continuum showing a range of low to high teacher control illustrates the educational views, and the differing models of discipline can be placed on the continuum. This continuum is based on the organizer that Wolfgang and Glickman (1995) developed when examining models of discipline.

A *model of discipline* is a set of cohesive approaches to deal with establishing, maintaining, and restoring order which represent a certain philosophical perspective on a continuum of low to high teacher control. A number of authors have proposed particular approaches for handling misbehavior, such as using logical consequences or assertive discipline (both discussed later). It is useful to examine these discipline models by placing them on this continuum (see Table 3-1). As discussed in the following sections, each area of the continuum has unique characteristics.

Your approach to control and order may fall into one particular part of the continuum but this does not mean that you will follow this approach in every situation. You may branch out and use other strategies as the situation warrants.

It is sometimes difficult to place a particular author in a certain part of the continuum since several actions may be proposed in the author's model. Kounin (1970), for example, suggests some low, medium, and high control strategies, but overall, his strategies seem to fit best in the medium control approach on the continuum.

Now, let's look at the models at each point on the continuum.

LOW TEACHER CONTROL APPROACHES

Low control approaches are based on the philosophical belief that students have primary responsibility for controlling their own behavior and that they have the capability to make these decisions. Children are seen to have an inner potential, and opportunities to make decisions enable personal growth. The child's thoughts, feelings, ideas, and preferences are taken into account when dealing with instruction, management, and discipline.

The teacher has the responsibility for structuring the environment to facilitate students' control over their own behavior. When determining rules, for example, teachers guide the discussion and help students recognize appropriate

TABLE 3-1 A continuum of teacher control in classroom management and discipline

	Low Control Approaches	Medium Control Approaches	High Control Approaches
Degree of teacher control	Low	Medium	High
Degree of student control	High	Medium	Low
Degree of concern for students' thoughts, feelings, and preferences	High	Medium	Low
Characteristic teacher actions	Transactional analysis Congruent communication Group management	Logical consequences Encouragement Cooperative discipline Reality therapy Control theory Lesson and group management	Structuring classrooms, limit setting, cooperation, backup systems Behavior modification Assertive discipline Corporal punishment
Representative proponents	Eric Berne Thomas Harris Haim Ginott Fritz Redl William Wattenberg	Rudolph Dreikurs Linda Albert Jane Nelsen William Glasser Jacob Kounin	Fredric Jones B. F. Skinner Lee Canter Siegfried Engelmann James Dobson

behavior and select related rules and consequences. When misbehavior occurs, the teacher helps students see the problem and guides them in making an appropriate decision to resolve the problem.

With this philosophical belief, students have a high degree of autonomy while the teacher exerts a low degree of control. This does not mean that the classroom is a chaotic place for learning. There are standards that the students will help develop, and the teacher is ultimately responsible for enforcing the standards to enable learning to take place in an orderly environment. Low control educators might use transactional analysis, congruent communication, and various forms of group management to deal with misbehavior.

Several educators have described cohesive approaches that are characteristic of the low teacher control approach. Eric Berne and Thomas Harris have written about the way teachers speak to children; this is called transactional analysis. Haim Ginott has sensitively written about ways that teachers can speak to students to express helpfulness and acceptance. Fritz Redl and William Wattenberg offer insights into the psychological and social forces within students and classrooms that affect student behavior. Each of these educators offers actions that teachers can take to reflect the low teacher control position.

Transactional Analysis: Berne and Harris

When a box of supplies is knocked off a table, you may express disappointment that the incident happened, ask who did it, or ask what needs to be done to clean up the mess. These statements come from three ego states within the teacher. These ego states are a central part of *transactional analysis* (TA), which is the analysis of verbal interactions.

Transactional analysis was originated by Eric Berne in his book *Games People Play* (1964). Thomas Harris, who studied with Berne, followed with *I'm OK—You're OK* (1967). These books primarily dealt with communication between adults. These same principles and concepts were used to help teachers deal with children in books such as *TA for Kids* (1971), *TA for Tots* (1973), and *TA for Teens* (1973) by Alvyn Freed; *Born to Win* (1971) by James and Jongeward; and *Games Students Play* (1972) by Ken Ernst.

According to Berne, people's *ego states* are developed from life experiences and retained consciously and subconsciously in the brain. These experiences are stored as if on an audiotape and then played back as situations arise. There are three types of ego states: parent, child, and adult.

The *parent ego state* includes all the "tapes" stored from experiences we have had with our parents or parent substitutes when we were young. These tapes are "recorded" as truths, rules, or laws since we heard them as young children. Statements from the parent ego state may include, "Never tell lies." "Don't go out alone at night." "Finish your work before you go out and play." The parent ego state controls and directs the individual.

The *child ego state* includes responses that children make to things they see and do. It is their compulsive, expressive side. Feelings are often expressed through the child ego state, such as, "Why do I always have to clean up after you? I hate this work, and I'm not going to do it." Fortunately, positive feelings and expressions are also included, such as curiosity and creativity.

The *adult ego state* applies conscious thought and judgment to a situation. The adult tests the rules of the parent ego state and updates and changes them if necessary. When thinking of a particular parent statement, the adult might ask, "Does drinking coffee really stunt growth?" The adult ego state also determines when the child's feelings can be expressed. The adult ego state helps express rational, problem-solving statements such as, "I see that you made a mistake here. What is needed to correct it?"

As a teacher, you need to remain in the adult ego state and teach your students to do the same. If students are given opportunities to have their adult ego states develop, they will become rational people with an understanding of themselves and others. They will also be able to use their child and parent ego states in a constructive manner.

As people interact, their statements arise from parent, child, or adult ego states. Since a fundamental premise of transactional analysis is that all individuals need to feel adequate, it is important that people recognize the ego source of statements they make. To interact effectively, especially concerning a problem, it is important that they have compatible transactions. That is, each person should be speaking from the same ego state (e.g., adult-to-adult transactions). If the transactions are crossed, such as adult-to-child, then effective communication is impeded. Incompatible communications create conflict and also erode the student-teacher relationship. To use transactional analysis in the classroom, you should teach your students how to use TA in their verbal interactions.

Decision Points

After a series of events where a student in your sixth-grade classroom has poked and bothered two other students without provocation, you decide to have a private talk with the student. The student talks only about her dislike of the other two students and the mean things they say to her. Select some sample statements that you might make at this time based on your adult ego state to focus the student's attention on the problem and possible solutions.

The Ginott Model: Haim Ginott

Haim Ginott (1922–1973) was a professor of psychology at New York University and at Adelphi University. Among educators, he is most known for his books that address relationships between adults and children. *Between Parent and Child* (1965) and *Between Parent and Teenager* (1969) offered ideas for effectively communicating with children. Ginott focused on how adults can build the self-concepts of children, especially emphasizing that adults should avoid attacks on the child's character and instead focus on the situation or actions.

Later, Ginott carried these principles to educators in *Teacher and Child* (1972), proposing that teachers maintain a secure, humanitarian, and productive classroom through the use of congruent communication and appropriate use of praise.

Congruent communication is a harmonious and authentic oral approach in which teacher's messages to students match the students' feelings about the situations and about themselves. In this way, teachers can avoid insulting and intimidating their students and instead express an attitude of helpfulness and acceptance while showing increased sensitivity to student needs and desires.

There are several ways that teachers can express congruent communication, all directed at protecting or building students' self-esteem.

• *Deliver sane messages.* ***Sane messages*** address situations rather than students' characters. They accept and acknowledge student feelings. Too often, teachers may use language that blames, orders, admonishes, accuses, ridicules, belittles, or threatens children. This language does not promote children's self-esteem. Instead, Ginott proposes that teachers use language that focuses on the situation and the facts, not threatening the child's self-esteem.

• *Express anger appropriately.* Ginott points out that students can irritate, annoy, and anger teachers. Anger is a genuine feeling, and teachers should express their anger in reasonable and appropriate ways that do not jeopardize student self-esteem. An effective way is simply to say, "It makes me angry when . . ." or, "I am appalled when . . ." In this way, the students hear what is upsetting the teacher without hearing "put-down" statements such as, "You are so irresponsible when you . . ."

• *Invite cooperation.* Provide opportunities for students to experience independence, thus accepting their capabilities. Give students a choice in matters that affect classroom life, including seating arrangements and certain procedures. Avoid direct, long drawn-out directions, and instead give a brief statement and allow students to decide what their specific course of action should be. By inviting cooperation, you begin to break down students' dependency on yourself.

• *Accept and acknowledge student feelings.* Teachers sometimes tell students that they have nothing to worry about when a problem occurs. Instead, listen to students and accept the feelings they are expressing as real. Serve as a sounding board to help students clarify their feelings and let them know that such feelings are common.

• *Avoid labeling.* Ginott maintains that labeling is disabling. There is no place for statements such as, "You are so irresponsible, unreliable." "You are such a disgrace to this class, this school, your family." When students hear these statements, they begin to believe them, and then they may start to develop a negative self-image. Avoid labeling, while striving to be helpful and encouraging.

• *Use direction as a means of correction.* Ginott proposes that when a problem situation arises, teachers describe the situation and offer acceptable alternative behaviors. Instead of criticism, provide students with guidance about what they should be doing. For example, when a student spills supplies on the floor, offer suggestions about ways to clean up rather than criticize the student.

• *Avoid harmful questions.* Ginott points out that an enlightened teacher avoids asking questions and making comments that are likely to incite resentment and invite resistance. For example, don't ask "Why" questions such as, "Why can't you be good for a change?" "Why do you forget everything I tell you?" Instead, point out that there is a problem and invite the student to discuss ways to solve the problem.

• *Accept students' comments.* Students may ask questions or make statements that seem unrelated to the topic under discussion. Show respect and give the student credit for the question or comment because it may be important to the student in some way.

• *Do not use sarcasm.* While you may use sarcasm to be witty, it may sound clever only to yourself and not to the students receiving the comments. Students may feel hurt, with damaged self-esteem.

• *Avoid hurried help.* When a problem arises, listen to the problem, rephrase it, clarify it, give the student credit for formulating it, and then ask, "What options are open to you?" In this way, you provide students with an opportunity to acquire competence in problem solving and confidence in themselves. Hurried responses are less likely to achieve these purposes.

• *Be brief when dealing with minor mishaps.* Long, logical explanations are not needed when the mishap is a lost paper, a broken pencil, or a forgotten assignment. Brief statements should be solution oriented.

Decision Points

Assume that one of your students working in a small group began to talk angrily to another group member and stood up and tossed some papers aside. How would you communicate with that student using Ginott's principles of congruent communication (e.g., to express sane messages, express anger appropriately, invite cooperation)? If the student was of a different ethnic group from yours, how might that affect your actions? If the action was more disruptive, such as punching, how would that affect your actions?

Group Management: Redl and Wattenberg

Fritz Redl and William Wattenberg described techniques for maintaining control and strengthening emotional development in students. In *Mental Hygiene in Teaching* (1959), they discuss the psychological and social forces that affect student behavior and provide common sense applications of humane personal relations. Redl later summarized many of their recommendations in *When We Deal with Children* (1972).

There are several key features to the techniques that Redl and Wattenberg offer. First, one of their most important observations is that students behave differently in groups than they do individually. Redl and Wattenberg see the group as an entire organism with each student playing a role in its functioning. Groups may have leaders, clowns, "fall guys," and instigators. A student finds a place within a group and becomes a part of the organism. A role is played because it fills a personal need or because the group expects or enjoys this. Thus, group expectations influence individual behavior, and individual behavior affects the group.

Redl and Wattenberg maintain that groups create their own psychological forces that influence individual behavior and teachers need to be aware of group dynamics so they can maintain effective control. Group dynamics are involved, for example, when one or more students serve as scapegoats for a problem involving other students or when one student receives preferential treatment. These group dynamics are unwritten codes of conduct, and when the group's code of conduct runs counter to that of the teacher, conflicts can occur.

Group behavior is influenced by how students perceive the teacher and the roles that the teacher plays. The teacher, for example, might have a role as a helper in learning, judge, referee, detective, model, ego supporter, surrogate parent, friend and confidant, or other roles. Teachers assume roles due to group needs as well as their own preferences. The class functions better when teachers remain consistent in the roles they assume.

Teachers can deal with conflict through *diagnostic thinking*. This involves first making a preliminary hunch about the underlying cause of the problem. Obvious facts then need to be gathered. The teacher then adds hidden factors, such as background information about the students involved or knowledge of a similar previous situation. Teachers are then ready to draw a conclusion and act. Redl and Wattenberg point out that teachers need to be flexible in this diagnostic procedure, especially by putting themselves in place of the students, to identify student feelings in a given situation.

Finally, various influence techniques can be used to maintain control. Redl and Wattenberg urge that before teachers take action to correct a situation, they ask themselves several questions: What is the motivation behind the misbehavior? How is the class reacting? Is the misbehavior related to interaction with me? How will the student react when corrected? How will the correction affect future behavior?

MEDIUM TEACHER CONTROL APPROACHES

Medium control approaches are based on the philosophical belief that development stems from a combination of innate and outside forces. Thus, the control of student behavior is a joint responsibility of student and teacher. Medium control teachers accept the student-centered psychology that is reflected in the low control philosophy, but they also recognize that learning takes place in a group context. Therefore, the teacher promotes individual student control over behavior whenever possible, but places the needs of the group as a whole over the needs of the individual students. The child's thoughts, feelings, ideas, and preferences are taken into account when dealing with instruction, management, and discipline, but ultimately the teacher's primary focus is on behavior and meeting the academic needs of the group.

Students are given opportunities to control their behavior to help them develop the ability to make appropriate decisions, yet they may not initially recognize that some behavior might be a hindrance to personal growth and development. Students need to recognize the consequences of their behavior and make adjustments to reach more favorable results.

Rules and procedures are often developed jointly by teacher and students. Teachers may begin the discussion of rules by presenting one or two rules that must be followed; or the teacher may hold veto power over rules the students select. This represents a higher degree of control than is used by low control teachers. Medium control teachers then would be responsible for enforcing the rules and helping students recognize the consequences of their decisions and actions. Medium control educators might use logical consequences, cooperative discipline, reality therapy, control theory, or lesson and movement management to deal with misbehavior.

Several educators have described cohesive approaches for dealing with students which represent the medium teacher control approach to control and order. Rudolf Dreikurs, for example, provides insight into mistaken goals that students have when misbehaving, and offers suggestions for ways that students can receive logical consequences for their actions. Linda Albert has taken Dreikurs' concepts and organized them into a program called cooperative discipline. Dreikurs' suggestions were further adapted by Jane Nelsen. The principles of reality therapy and control theory are endorsed by William Glasser. Finally, Jacob Kounin's work on lesson and group management seems to fall into the medium teacher control category.

Logical Consequences and Cooperation: Dreikurs, Albert, and Nelsen

According to social psychologist Alfred Adler, people are motivated by the need to be accepted by others—to belong and to receive recognition. A well-behaved student has discovered that social acceptance comes from conforming to the group and making useful contributions to it. A child who lacks a sense of belonging, however, tries to gain acceptance through behaviors that are annoying, defiant, hostile, or helpless. Rudolf Dreikurs, Linda Albert, and Jane Nelsen are among the educators who have taken Adler's principles and applied them to classroom management and discipline.

Logical Consequences. Rudolf Dreikurs (Dreikurs, Grunwald, & Pepper, 1982) expanded on Adler's concepts and provided a useful means for teachers to work with students without reliance on punishment. At the heart of his suggestions is the use of ***logical consequences***, which are events arranged by the teacher that are directly and logically related to the behavior. Based on Dreikurs's ideas, you can use several techniques to help misbehaving students behave appropriately.

First, identify the goal of the misbehavior. Examine the key signs of the misbehavior and also consider your feelings and reactions as a means to tentatively identify the goal of the misbehavior. The goal may be to gain attention, to seek power, to seek revenge, or to display inadequacy. Then disclose this goal to the student in a private session for confirmation. This is a positive way to confront a misbehaving student. Its purpose is to heighten the student's awareness of the motives for the misbehavior.

Second, alter your reactions. Once the goal of misbehavior has been identified, first control your immediate reaction so that your response does not reinforce the misbehavior. For example, if the student's goal is to seek attention, never give the student immediate attention, but try to ignore the behavior whenever possible. Later, have a discussion with the student to identify alternatives for changing the behavior.

Third, provide encouragement statements to students. ***Encouragement statements*** consist of words or actions that acknowledge student work and express confidence in them. Encouragement statements help students see what they did to lead to a positive result and also help them feel confident about their own abilities. For example, you might say, "I see that your extra studying for the test paid off because you did so well." The focus is on what the student did that led to the result obtained.

Encouragement should not be confused with praise. Praise is an expression of approval after a student has attained something; the focus of praise statements is typically on your being pleased about something. A praise statement might be, "I'm so glad that you got the highest mark in the class on your project." An encouragement statement might be, "Your creativity and organization made a big difference in how well you did on your project."

Most important, use logical consequences. Instead of using punishment, Dreikurs prefers to let students experience the consequences that flow from misbehavior. A logical consequence is an event arranged by the teacher that is directly and logically related to the misbehavior. For instance, if a student leaves paper on the classroom floor, the student must pick the paper up off the floor. If a student breaks the rule of speaking out without raising his or her hand, the teacher ignores the response and calls on a student whose hand is up. If a student makes marks on the desk, the student is required to remove them.

In summary, Dreikurs views his approaches as democratic in that teachers and students together decide on the rules and consequences, and they have joint responsibility for maintaining a positive climate. This encourages students to become more responsibly self-governing. To Dreikurs, discipline is not punishment; it is teaching students to impose limits on themselves. With Dreikurs' approaches, students are responsible for their own actions, have respect for themselves and others, have the responsibility to influence others to behave appropriately, and are responsible for knowing rules and consequences.

Cooperative Discipline. Based largely on the philosophy and psychology of Alfred Adler and Rudolf Dreikurs, Linda Albert (1989) developed a management and discipline plan called cooperative discipline, mentioned earlier. Similar to

---

Teachers in Action

Cooperative Discipline

Dwight Watson, third-grade teacher, Raleigh, North Carolina:

Third-grade students are highly susceptible to peer pressure. Using a cooperative form of discipline in my classroom encourages a positive form of peer pressure. Here's how it works. Each week, the students choose circles from a bag. The circles are color-coded to indicate group placement. The students do not sit together, but they are aware of the others in their group because they too have the same circle color. The circles are taped onto the upper right hand corner of each desk.

Since I have 25 students, I place five circles of different colors in a bag (five each of yellow, blue, green, red, and purple). Larger circles of the same color are laminated and mounted on the wall. When a student misbehaves, his or her name is placed in the larger color circle that is on display. The group with the fewest names is the winner for the week. I provide a reward to the winning group at the end of the week. Rewards may include a paperback book, a box of crayons, scissors, colored pencils, rock samples, rulers, magnifying glasses, and protractors.

This strategy works because students learn to encourage their peers to behave for the benefit of the group. They are also delighted that they can choose which group they are in each week. By randomly choosing circles from the bag, every student has an opportunity to be grouped with every other student in the classroom. They appreciate the fairness of this discipline model because no group is saddled for too long with a student who might have a tendency to be a behavior problem.

Dreikurs, *cooperative discipline* is founded on three concepts of behavior: (a) students choose their behavior; (b) the ultimate goal of student behavior is to fulfill the need to belong; and (c) students misbehave to achieve one of four immediate goals (attention, power, revenge, avoidance of failure).

Albert's cooperative discipline includes five action steps: pinpoint and describe the behavior, identify the goal of the misbehavior, choose intervention techniques for the moment of misbehavior, select encouragement techniques to build self-esteem, and involve parents as partners. Her cooperative discipline program, therefore, is designed to establish positive control through appropriate interventions and to build self-esteem through encouragement.

The building blocks of self-esteem are helping students feel capable, helping students connect (become involved and engaged), and helping students contribute. To achieve the goals of cooperative discipline intervention and encouragement strategies, use democratic procedures and policies, implement cooperative learning strategies, conduct guidance activities, and choose appropriate curriculum methods and materials.

Positive Discipline. Jane Nelson has also adapted Rudolph Dreikur's concepts into a program called ***positive discipline***. In *Positive Discipline,* Nelsen (1987) identified kindness, respect, firmness, and encouragement as the main ingredients of this program for parents and teachers. There are several key elements to Nelsen's approach: (1) Use natural and logical consequences as a means to inspire a positive atmosphere for winning children over rather than winning over children. (2) Understand that children have four goals in misbehavior (attention, power, revenge, and assumed inadequacy). (3) Kindness and firmness need to be expressed at the same time when addressing misbehavior. (4) Adults and children must have mutual respect. (5) Family and class meetings can be effective. (6) Offer encouragement as a means of inspiring self-evaluation and focusing on the actions of the child.

Nelsen has described how positive discipline principles can be applied through classroom meetings. In *Positive Discipline in the Classroom,* Nelsen and colleagues (1993) provide detailed descriptions for conducting effective meetings. In addition to eliminating discipline problems, they help students develop social, academic, and life skills and help them feel that they are personally capable, significant, and can influence their own lives.

Reality Therapy/Control Theory: William Glasser

William Glasser, a psychiatrist, received national attention with the publication of *Reality Therapy* (1965), which proposed a different approach in treating behavioral problems. Instead of looking for the antecedents of the inappropriate behavior, Glasser maintained that solutions could best be found in the present. While initially working with juvenile offenders, he became interested in helping teachers deal with discipline problems.

Over the years, Glasser's ideas concerning discipline have changed. Initially he proposed the strategies of reality therapy (1965); later he extended these ideas to control theory (1984, 1986). More recently, he has described how to manage students without coercion in quality schools (1992).

Glasser took his ***reality therapy*** message to educators in *Schools without Failure* (1969). He noted that successful social relationships are basic human needs. Glasser maintained that students have a responsibility for making good choices about their behavior and that they must live with their choices. In reality therapy, teachers and students need to jointly establish classroom rules, and the teacher is to enforce the rules consistently without accepting excuses. When misbehavior occurs, the teacher should ask the student, "What are you doing? Is it helping you or the class? What could you do that would help?" The student is asked to make value judgments about the behavior, and the teacher can suggest suitable alternatives. Together, they create a plan to eliminate the problem behavior. When necessary, the teacher needs to invoke appropriate consequences.

Over time, Glasser expanded his reality therapy concepts. With the development of control theory (1986), he added the needs of belonging and love,

control, freedom, and fun. Without attention to those needs, students are bound
to fail. Glasser maintained that discipline problems should be viewed as total
behaviors, meaning that the entire context of the situation needs to be examined
in an effort to seek a solution. For example, physical inactivity may contribute
to misbehavior, whereas it might be overlooked if the situation is examined in
a more confined way.

With *control theory*, you must recognize that students want to have their
needs met. Students feel pleasure when these needs are met and frustration when
they are not. You must create the conditions in which students feel a sense of
belonging, have some power and control, have some freedom in the learning
and schooling process, and have fun. Students will then not be frustrated and
discipline problems should be limited.

Based on Glasser's principles of reality therapy and control theory, Diane
Gossen (1992) has proposed restitution as an approach based on the recognition
that all young people make mistakes. *Restitution* involves the student's remedying
the problem created by his or her actions. By focusing on how the student can
correct the mistake, this approach emphasizes positive solutions to problems.

The Quality School (1992) describes Glasser's recent effort to improve
schools. He now takes a broader, organizational perspective. Glasser asserts that
the nature of school management must be changed in order to meet students'
needs and promote effective learning. In fact, he criticizes current school
managers for accepting low-quality work. Glasser's newest book, *The Quality
School Teacher* (1993), offers specific strategies for teachers to move toward
quality schools.

The Kounin Model: Jacob Kounin

Jacob Kounin was a professor of psychology at Wayne State University. He made
hundreds of videotapes of teachers in the classroom to identify differences
between teachers who managed their classes well and those who did not.
Kounin's research, published in *Discipline and Group Management in Classrooms*
(1970), provides rich insight into the preventive facets of misbehavior but little
information about techniques of corrective discipline.

The *Kounin model* describes lesson and movement management as a means
to prevent and address student misbehavior. If misbehavior occurs, Kounin notes
that teachers can use two techniques to respond in an effort to get students
back on-task: withitness and overlapping. *Withitness* is a term Kounin coined
to describe the degree to which teachers can react to the target student in a
timely way when misbehavior occurs. A teacher who is "with-it" knows what is
going on in the classroom at all times, notices who is misbehaving, and responds
to the misbehavior in an appropriate and prompt manner. Good monitoring
and prompt handling of a situation are key aspects of a teacher being with-it.
Prompt handling will enable the behavior to be corrected before it increases in
seriousness or spreads to other students.

Overlapping refers to how teachers handle two or more simultaneous
events. For example, you may be talking with one group of students when an

incident arises in another small group. You can take an action (a look or statement) to address the misbehavior while staying with the first group. Your attention overlaps into all areas. Teachers more skilled at overlapping are more aware of all that is going on, thus they also have withitness. When students know that teachers are with-it and respond to misbehavior, they are more likely to stay on-task.

Another important finding by Kounin was that good *movement management* in a lesson is achieved by effective momentum, pacing, and transitions—all of which are controlled by the teacher. Kounin further discovered that there are two movement management mistakes that teachers may make: jerkiness and slowdowns. *Jerkiness* refers to changes in the flow of activities that create confusion, unnecessary activity, noise, delay, and misbehavior. It connotes failure to move smoothly from one activity to another. Jerkiness can be minimized by completing one task before starting another and using smooth transitions.

Slowdowns are delays that waste time between activities, and they occur due to overdwelling and fragmentation. *Overdwelling* occurs when teachers continue to focus exclusively on a single issue long after students have understood the point being made or when procedures take more time than necessary. For example, overdwelling arises when a teacher continues a discussion too long or has students do too many sample problems in class after they appear to understand the issues. *Fragmentation* occurs when teachers spend too much time on details or break an activity into parts when it could be carried out as a single unit. Interrupting seatwork several times, for example, with additional directions would fragment a lesson and interrupt student concentration.

Another important finding from Kounin's research is that having a group focus is essential to developing a productive, efficient classroom and maintaining concentration. In *group focus,* students pay attention to the same thing at the same time. To maintain group focus, you need to take into account (a) high participation group format, (b) the degree of accountability, and (c) attention.

Group format refers to grouping students in ways that maximize active participation. Higher participation formats require students to write answers, solve problems, read along, manipulate materials, or perform some other task during instruction. *Accountability* means that you let the students know that their performance will be observed and evaluated. Accountability may be maintained by techniques such as having students write their answers, perform, or display work in some way. *Attention* involves having students focus on the activity at all times. Kounin suggests that attention could be promoted by using techniques to alert the group, such as creating suspense, calling on students randomly, and varying the response format.

Decision Points

Let's assume that you are teaching a music lesson to third graders with a wide range of musical ability and that you want to maintain group focus with a high participation group format. How might you focus student attention and hold students accountable for such a lesson? How might you need to change your plans if you had a seventh-grade or a tenth-grade music class?

Another important element of lesson management is *satiation*, which means becoming filled up with something and getting enough of it. When students are satisfied with an activity, they show progressively less interest, and this may lead to boredom and off-task behavior. Progress, variety, and challenge can minimize satiation. Students need to feel that they are making progress toward a significant goal, and teachers may highlight the progress or provide some feedback on progress. Variety in a lesson also helps maintain attention and minimize satiation. Varying the type of activity, the level of difficulty, the way the content is presented, group structure, and the use of instructional materials can help add variety to a lesson. Students who are intellectually challenged also are less likely to reach satiation and become bored. A challenging activity produces a greater sense of accomplishment than a simple task.

Kounin also reported that when teachers took actions to stop misbehavior by one student, it affected the behavior of nearby students. This is called a *ripple effect*. Students who witnessed the teacher's actions had a tendency to behave appropriately rather than receive the same type of consequence the misbehaving student received.

HIGH TEACHER CONTROL APPROACHES

High control approaches are based on the philosophical belief that students' growth and development are the result of external conditions. Children are seen to be molded and shaped by influences from their environment; they are not seen to have innate potential. Therefore, teachers and adults need to select desired student behaviors, reinforce appropriate behaviors, and take actions to extinguish inappropriate behaviors. Little attention is given to the thoughts, feelings, and preferences of the students since adults are more experienced in instructional matters and have the responsibility for choosing what is best for student development and behavior control.

Teachers using high control approaches believe that student behavior must be controlled because the students themselves are not able to effectively monitor and control their own behavior. The teachers select the rules and procedures, commonly without student input. Teachers then reinforce desired behavior and take actions to have students stop inappropriate, undesired behavior. When misbehavior occurs, teachers take steps to stop the disruption quickly and redirect the student to more positive behavior. Behavior modification, behavioral contracting, and several reinforcers are characteristic of high control approaches. Compared to the previous models, there is more emphasis on managing the behavior of individuals than the group.

Several educators have described cohesive approaches that represent the high teacher control approach to control and order. Fredric Jones offers ideas for properly structuring classrooms, using limit setting techniques, building cooperation, and using backup procedures in the event of misbehavior. Behavior modification, as illustrated by B. F. Skinner, is a high control approach. The assertive discipline plan developed by Lee Canter includes high control approaches, but also incorporates important principles of management. Authors such as Siegfried Engelmann and James Dobson, representing the highest level of teacher control, endorse corporal punishment as a last resort in trying to control student behavior.

The Jones Model: Fredric Jones

Fredric Jones is a psychologist who has conducted research on classroom practices and developed training programs for improving teacher effectiveness in behavior management and instruction. In *Positive Classroom Discipline* (1987), Jones emphasized that teachers can help students support their own self-control. The *Jones model* recommends that teachers (a) properly structure their classrooms; (b) learn how to maintain control by using appropriate instructional strategies and limit-setting techniques; (c) build patterns of cooperation; and (d) develop appropriate backup methods in the event of misbehavior.

First, consider the rules, routines, and standards; seating arrangements; and student-teacher relationships when structuring your classroom. Rules, procedures, routines, and standards need to be taught to students so they understand the standards and expectations. Jones points out that the arrangement of the furniture can maximize teacher mobility and allow greater physical proximity to students on a moment-to-moment basis. While presenting several ways to arrange student desks, Jones indicates that any arrangement that provides quick and easy access to all students is likely to be successful. Jones also prefers to have assigned seats for students to disperse the better students among the chronic disrupters.

Maintain control by using appropriate instructional strategies and limit-setting techniques. Jones maintains that teachers lose control when they spend too much time with each student, such as during seatwork. Teachers commonly spend time to find out where a student is having difficulty, to further explain the part the student doesn't understand, and to supply additional explanations and examples. Instead, Jones recommends that teachers use the three-step sequence of praise, prompt, and leave. In this sequence, teachers first praise students for what they have done correctly so far. Second, prompt students by telling them exactly what to do next and encourage them to do it. The teacher then leaves, to let the student take the needed action and also to be available to help other students.

Decision Points

At the end of most class sessions, you have your tenth graders start their homework while you walk around to provide assistance and monitor them. Four students in the class regularly have difficulty understanding the

material and need a considerable amount of your time for additional explanations and assistance during this seatwork. What could you do to
minimize the amount of time that you need to spend with these four students? How might you involve other students to provide this assistance?

Another aspect of maintaining control is by setting limits. Jones proposed
a series of specific actions that can be taken when a student is getting off-task.
These techniques primarily involve body language to convince the student that
the teacher is in control. These steps involve being aware of and monitoring
the behavior of all students; terminating instruction when necessary to deal with
a student; turning, looking, and stating the student's name; moving to the edge
of the student's desk; moving away from the student's desk when the student
gets back to work; placing your palms on the desk and giving a short, direct
verbal prompt if the student does not get back to work; moving closer over the
desk; and finally moving next to the student behind the student's desk.

Build patterns of cooperation. Jones proposed an incentive system called
preferred activity time (PAT) that can be used so students can earn certain
benefits if they behave and cooperate. The PAT may be a variety of activities
and privileges which are given to the class as a whole at the start of a
predetermined time (a week's worth). When an individual student misbehaves,
the teacher uses a stopwatch or timer to record the length of time of the
infraction, and this amount of time is subtracted from the class' total time. On
the other hand, students can earn bonus time for the class by cleaning up the
classroom in a hurry, being in their seats in time, or some other desired behavior.

Last of all, develop appropriate backup in the event of misbehavior. Backups
are to be used systematically from lesser sanctions to more serious ones. Low-level
sanctions involve issuing a warning; pulling a card with the student's name, address,
and telephone number; and then sending a letter to the parents. (But the student
is first given an opportunity to correct the behavior; if this happens, the letter is
not sent.) Midlevel sanctions include time-out; detention; loss of privileges; and a
parent conference. High-level sanctions include in-school suspension; Saturday school;
delivering the student to a parent at work; asking a parent to accompany the student
to school; suspension; police intervention; and expulsion.

Behavior Modification: Skinner and Others

B. F. Skinner (1902-1990) spent most of his academic career at Harvard
University, where he conducted experimental studies in learning. In *Beyond
Freedom and Dignity* (1971), Skinner challenged traditional views of freedom
and dignity and instead claimed that our choices are determined by the
environmental conditions under which we live and what has happened to us.
He maintained that we are not free to choose. Skinner's work has been extended
and modified by many psychologists and educators. Its application to classroom
practice has been called ***behavior modification***, a technique of reinforcement
and punishment for shaping behavior.

Behavior modification, as proposed by Skinner and others, has several distinguishing features (Charles, 1992). Behavior is shaped by its consequences and by what happens to the individual immediately afterward. The systematic use of **reinforcers**, or rewards, can shape behavior in desired directions. Behavior becomes weaker if it is not followed by reinforcement. Behavior is also weakened by punishment. In the early stages of learning, constant reinforcement produces the best results.

Once learning has reached the desired level, it is best maintained through intermittent reinforcement provided only occasionally. Behavior modification incorporates several types of reinforcers. It is applied primarily in two ways: (a) when the teacher rewards the student after a desired act, the student tends to repeat the act; and (b) when the student performs an undesired act, the teacher either ignores the act or punishes the student; the misbehaving student then becomes less likely to repeat the act.

Several types of reinforcers can be used:

- Edible reinforcers may include candy, cookies, gum, drinks, nuts, or other snacks. These can be given at any grade level but are more common with elementary students and perhaps into the middle school grades.
- Social reinforcers include words, gestures, stickers, certificates, and facial and bodily expressions of approval by the teacher.
- Material or tangible reinforcers include objects that students can earn as rewards for desired behavior. These include decals, art and craft supplies, books, posters, pennants, toys and games, pens and pencils, rubber stamps, and the like.
- Token reinforcers include stars, points, buttons, or other items that can be accumulated for desired behavior and then "cashed" for other material or tangible reinforcers.
- Activity reinforcers are activities that students prefer. These may include running errands, assisting the teacher, having extra free time, going to the library, operating a projector or other equipment, or working on a special project.

Behavior modification works best when practiced in an organized, systematic, and consistent way. Behavior modification systems seem to fall into five categories (Charles, 1992). (1) The "catch them being good" approach involves making positive statements to students who are doing what is expected of them. For example, a teacher might thank a student for obtaining class materials and being ready to start the class. (2) The rules-ignore-praise approach involves establishing a set of classroom rules, ignoring inappropriate behavior, and praising appropriate behavior. This approach works best in elementary grades and is less effective in secondary grades. (3) The rules-reward-punishment approach involves establishing classroom rules, rewarding appropriate behavior, and punishing inappropriate behavior. This system is quite appropriate for older students. (4) The **contingency management** approach is a system of tangible reinforcers where students earn tokens for appropriate behavior that can be "cashed" at a later time for material rewards. This approach can be used at all grade levels, but is especially effective with students who have chronic behavior problems and those who are mentally retarded. (5) **Contracting** involves preparing a contract for an individual student who has chronic problems or is hard to manage. Contracts often include statements about the desired behaviors, deadlines for completion of certain acts, and reinforcers and punishments depending on whether the desired behaviors are or are not met.

Assertive Discipline: Lee Canter

Lee Canter is an educator who first came into prominence with the publication of *Assertive Discipline* (1976), which was a take-charge approach for teachers to control their classrooms in a firm and positive manner. Since that time, he has created an organization called Lee Canter and Associates, which prepares materials related to classroom discipline and conducts workshops and training programs for teachers, administrators, parents, and other educators.

Over the years, Canter expanded and built upon the basic behavior management principles from that book. Since today's teachers face even more complex situations, a more comprehensive model was developed. The revised edition of *Assertive Discipline* (1992) goes beyond the initial take-charge approach and includes additional management procedures. In the revised *Assertive Discipline*, Canter discusses the assertive attitude necessary to deal with management and discipline, the parts of a discipline plan, aspects of teaching responsible behavior, and ways to deal with difficult students. The goal of *assertive discipline* is to teach students to choose responsible behavior and in doing so raise their self-esteem and enhance their academic success.

Canter maintains that teachers have the right and responsibility to (a) establish rules and directions that clearly define the limits of acceptable and unacceptable student behavior; (b) teach these rules and directions; and (c) ask for assistance from parents and administrators when support is needed in handling student behavior. The manner in which teachers respond to student behavior affects students' self-esteem and their success in school. Therefore, teachers must use an assertive response style to state expectations clearly and confidently and to reinforce their words with actions.

A discipline plan has three parts: (a) rules that students must follow at all times; (b) positive recognition that students will receive for following the rules; and (c) consequences that result when students choose not to follow the rules. Sample rules may be to follow directions, keep hands and feet to oneself, or be in the classroom and seated when the bell rings. Positive recognition may include praise, positive notes sent home to parents, positive notes to students, or special activities or privileges.

Teachers in Action

Positive Recognition in Assertive Discipline

Cammie Fulk, fifth-grade teacher, Fulks Run, Virginia

To provide positive recognition in my assertive discipline plan, I post a personal calendar for each student each month. If a student has behaved well and completed all of the work for the day, a stamp is placed on that date. If not, then the reason for not receiving the stamp is written on that date. When a student receives five stamps in a row, a reward is given. For 10 stamps in a row, a free homework pass is provided. At the end of each month, the calendar is sent home to be signed by the parents and then returned to me. This personal calendar has become a strong motivator in my fifth grade classroom.

In addition to the personal calendars, I have a gem jar on my desk as a reward for the entire class. It is simply a clear coffee cup with three permanent levels marked on the side to indicate 5, 10, and 15 minutes of free time earned. As I observe the entire class on task, I place several gems in the jar. Gems may be marbles, bubble gum, candy corn, jelly beans, or other small items. Gems can be earned for a variety of behaviors such as good hallway behavior, the entire class on task, the entire class completing homework, or other valued actions. The sound of the gems hitting the glass cup brings smiles to my fifth graders.

Consequences are delivered systematically with each occurrence of misbehavior. The first time a student breaks a rule, a warning is given. The second time, the student may lose a privilege; for example, may have to be last in line for lunch or stay in class one minute after the bell rings. The third time, the student loses additional privileges. The fourth time, the teacher calls the parents. The fifth time, the student is sent to the principal. In cases of severe misbehavior, these preliminary steps may be skipped and the student sent to the principal.

Another part of Canter's assertive discipline plan is to teach responsible behavior. This includes determining and teaching specific directions (classroom procedures), using positive recognition to motivate students to behave, redirecting nondisruptive off-task behavior, and implementing consequences. Canter further emphasizes that successful teachers need to blend academic and behavior management efforts into a cohesive whole so that management actions are inapparent.

Canter gives special attention to dealing with difficult students, who represent perhaps 5 to 10 percent of students. In *Assertive Discipline* (Canter & Canter, 1992), recommendations are provided for conducting a one-to-one problem-solving conference between the teacher and the difficult student. The goal is to help the student gain insight into the problem and ultimately choose more responsible behavior. Guidelines are offered to provide support to build positive relationships with difficult students, and recommendations are made for developing an individualized behavior plan. Parents and administrators can offer additional support when dealing with difficult students. Canter has published a separate book on this subject: *Succeeding with Difficult Students* (1993).

Behaviorism and Punishment: Engelmann and Dobson

Many educators endorse behavior modification as an effective means to deal with misbehavior, but few support corporal punishment as one of the consequences to be used in behavior modification. Siegfried Engelmann and James Dobson are among those who support corporal punishment. More than 20 states, however, have banned its use in schools.

Siegfried Engelmann is known primarily through his books *Teaching Disadvantaged Children in the Preschool* (1966, with Carl Bereiter) and *Preventing Failure in the Primary Grades* (1969). He endorses the use of corporal punishment through the primary grades because of considerations about efficiency and academic attainment.

Engelmann is concerned that disadvantaged students do not have the same opportunities at home as middle-class students. When they start school, they are already behind the middle-class students. Engelmann is concerned about the efficiency of the learning environment so that disadvantaged students can take advantage of the available time. When students misbehave, instructional time is lost and they are further disadvantaged.

Engelmann believes that other disciplinary approaches take too much time to reconcile problems. Thus, he supports disciplinary approaches that are quick and to the point, including corporal punishment if necessary. The quickest way to stop severe misbehavior is to physically punish the student. Engelmann supports the planned, restrained use of corporal punishment as a means toward academic efficiency. He does not support physical violence or abuse.

Engelmann's later works emphasize the need to structure the classroom to establish a positive learning environment and make no mention of corporal punishment. He further highlights ways to reinforce good performance through verbal and tangible reinforcers.

James Dobson is a licensed psychologist who first gained national recognition with his book *Dare to Discipline* (1970). When the context of his book became out of date, Dobson wrote *The New Dare to Discipline* (1992) to provide parents and teachers with his updated views on child rearing. Simply stated, he maintains that healthy, happy children typically come from homes where parents achieve a balance between love and control.

While *The New Dare to Discipline* includes many chapter that are of interest primarily to parents, some material is directed to teachers. His fundamental convictions about raising children are expressed. He maintains that children thrive best in an atmosphere of genuine love, undergirded by reasonable, consistent discipline. Permissiveness has failed as an approach to child rearing, and children need to be taught self-discipline and responsible behavior. They need assistance in learning how to handle the challenges and obligations of living.

Children must understand that they must obey parents and teachers so they can be protected and taken care of. Parents and teachers have a responsibility to establish clear boundaries for appropriate behavior. In the absence of clear boundaries, permissiveness follows, resulting in disrespect, defiance, and the general confusion that occurs in the absence of adult leadership. The consequences for stepping out of these boundaries should be strong. In relating a classroom example, Dobson (1992) endorses giving children "the maximum reason to comply with your wishes" (p. 118).

Corporal punishment is acceptable under certain circumstances. Dobson states that children must learn that there are dangers in the social world, that defiance, sassiness, selfishness, and temper tantrums are behaviors that endanger life. He maintains that the minor pain from corporal punishment that follows deliberate misbehavior tends to inhibit it, just as discomfort shapes behavior in the physical world. Corporal punishment should be used infrequently. Other punishments may be preferable, such as time-out or loss of privileges.

Dobson believes it is acceptable to begin spanking children from the age of 18 months. He suggests that most corporal punishment should stop prior to the first grade (six years old). For older children and teenagers, Dobson suggests lost privileges, financial deprivation, related forms of nonphysical retribution, or other creative approaches. He notes that corporal punishment is not effective at the junior and senior high school levels, and he does not recommend its use there. It can be effective with elementary students, especially with amateur "clowns." Dobson cautions that corporal punishment that is not administered according to carefully thought out guidelines is dangerous.

Both Engelmann and Dobson believe that corporal punishment will inflict pain and thus teach the child a lesson about how to behave. They agree that it is effective and works well with young children. By startling the children with pain, only then will they learn the boundaries of acceptable behavior, to be remembered in adult life. Direct commands, reinforcement, and isolation are effective punishments.

DECIDING ON YOUR APPROACH TO CONTROL

To what degree do you want to exercise control in your classroom? That is the fundamental question when deciding on your approach to management and discipline. To answer that question, you will likely consider a number of factors, such as your views of educational philosophy, psychology, and child development. For example, when determining your approach to control, you will take into account your beliefs about the dominant influence on a child's development—from inner forces, outside forces, or a combination of the two.

Your examination of these issues will probably reveal whether you are inclined to use low, medium, or high control approaches. Another way to see where you might fit on the teacher behavior continuum is to complete a series of questions in the "Beliefs on Discipline Inventory" (see Appendix A).

After determining your position on the teacher control continuum, decide whether you want to use a particular discipline model, synthesize two or more models, or create your own approach. The teacher behavior continuum helps you see the range of possibilities for decisions you might make concerning order. Even if you choose one model, you may find that the classroom context and the events cause you to shift from that model and use elements of other approaches. You don't have to accept the entire set of actions proposed by a certain model.

When determining the relative merits of the discipline models, it may be useful to establish criteria by which to compare the relative characteristics, strengths, and weaknesses of each model. As a means of evaluation, Edwards (1993) proposes asking questions that focus on whether the plan helps the child become more self-disciplined and autonomous, promotes a good self-concept and good behavior, prevents discipline problems, is consistent with the instructional program, and is easy to implement.

This chapter provides a brief orientation to the various models of discipline, ranging from low to high teacher control. Rather than proposing one model of discipline from those described, a synthesis of information from researchers and practitioners is presented in the following chapters. This chapter offers a philosophical perspective concerning the degree of teacher control you would like to establish.

MAJOR CONCEPTS

1. When deciding how to handle management and discipline, teachers take into account their views of child development, educational philosophies, and other factors.

2. A continuum of low to high teacher control illustrates the views expressed by educators.

3. Low control approaches are based on the philosophical belief that students have primary responsibility for controlling their own behavior and that they have the capability to make these decisions.

4. Educators representative of the low control approach are Eric Berne and Thomas Harris (for transactional analysis), Haim Ginott, Fritz Redl, and William Wattenberg.

5. Medium control approaches are based on the belief that students develop from a combination of innate forces and environmental forces. Thus, control of student behavior is a joint responsibility of the student and the teacher.

6. Educators representative of the medium control approach are Rudolf Dreikurs, Linda Albert, Jane Nelsen, William Glasser, and Jacob Kounin.

7. High control approaches are based on the belief that students' growth and development are the result of external conditions. Children are seen to be molded and shaped by influences from their environment.

8. Educators representative of the high control approach are Fredric Jones, B. F. Skinner, Lee Canter, Siegfried Engelmann, and James Dobson.

9. When deciding on your approach to control, you will likely consider your views of educational philosophy, psychology, and child development. It may also be useful to identify whether you are inclined to use low, medium, or high control approaches on the teacher behavior continuum.

DISCUSSION QUESTIONS

1. What are the merits and problems that might be associated with each of the three levels of teacher control?

2. Recall a favorite teacher. What level of control did that teacher use? What are the indicators of that level of control?

3. How might you explain your rationale for using Haim Ginott's concepts of congruent communication to a parent?

4. What is the difference between praise and encouragement (as explained by Dreikurs)? What are the purposes of each?

5. Why is the Fredric Jones model included in the high control category?

6. What arguments can be developed for and against the use of corporal punishment?

SUPPLEMENTAL ACTIVITIES

For Clinical Settings

1. Prepare an essay that describes your view of child development, educational philosophy, and other factors that relate to the issue of control.

2. Prepare a list of items comprising the criteria to assess the relative characteristics, strengths, and weaknesses of each discipline model.

3. Using the criteria you selected to assess the various models of discipline, assess each of the plans proposed by the authors reviewed in this chapter.

For Field Settings

1. Talk with several students about their experiences with teachers who use low, medium, and high control approaches. Assess their experiences.

2. Talk with several teachers to learn about the degree of control they use in the classroom. See if they use one model, a combination of several models, or their own unique approach.

3. Talk with the school counselor or psychologist to receive an appraisal of the three levels of teacher control and the effects on student behavior.

KEY TERMS

Accountability	Kounin model
Adult ego state	Logical consequences
Assertive discipline	Low control approaches
Attention	Medium control approaches
Behavior modification	Model of discipline
Child ego state	Movement management
Congruent communication	Overdwelling
Contingency management	Overlapping
Contracting	Parent ego state
Control theory	Positive discipline
Cooperative discipline	Preferred activity time
Diagnostic thinking	Reality therapy
Ego states	Reinforcers
Encouragement statements	Restitution
Fragmentation	Ripple effect
Group focus	Sane messages
Group format	Satiation
High control approaches	Slowdowns
Jerkiness	Transactional analysis
Jones model	Withitness

RECOMMENDED READINGS

Charles, C. M. (1992). *Building Classroom Discipline,* 4th ed. New York: Longman.
   An entire chapter is devoted to each of the following: Redl and Wattenberg, Kounin, Skinner, Ginott, Dreikurs, Canter, and Glasser. Other chapters address additional classroom management issues.

Edwards, C. H. (1993). *Classroom Discipline and Management.* New York: Macmillan.
   An entire chapter is devoted to each of the following: Skinner, Canter, Dreikurs, Berne and Harris, Glasser, Ginott, Kounin, and Jones. Other chapters address creating a discipline program and classroom management procedures.

Wolfgang, C. H., & Glickman, C. D. (1995). *Solving Discipline Problems: Strategies for Classroom Teachers,* 3rd ed. Boston: Allyn & Bacon.
   An entire chapter is devoted to each of the following: Gordon, Berne and Harris, Raths and Simon, Dreikurs, Glasser, behavior modification, Canter, and Engelmann and Dobson. Other chapters address decision making and classroom management.

REFERENCES

Albert, L. (1989). *A Teacher's Guide to Cooperative Discipline: How to Manage Your Classroom and Promote Self-esteem.* Circle Pines, MN: American Guidance Service.

Bereiter, C., & Engelmann, S. (1966). *Teaching Disadvantaged Children in the Preschool.* Englewood Cliffs, NJ: Prentice Hall.

Berne, E. (1964). *Games People Play: The Psychology of Human Relations.* New York: Ballantine Books.

Canter, L. (1976). *Assertive Discipline: A Take-charge Approach for Today's Educator.* Santa Monica, CA: Lee Canter & Associates.

Canter, L., & Canter, M. (1992). *Assertive Discipline: Positive Behavior Management for Today's Schools,* rev. ed. Santa Monica, CA: Lee Canter & Associates.

Canter, L., & Canter, M. (1993). *Succeeding with Different Students: New Strategies for Reaching Your Most Challenging Students.* Santa Monica, CA: Lee Canter & Associates.

Charles, C. M. (1992). *Building Classroom Discipline,* 4th ed. New York: Longman.

Dobson, J. C. (1970). *Dare to Discipline.* Wheaton, IL: Tyndale House Publishers.

Dobson, J. C. (1992). *The New Dare to Discipline.* Wheaton, IL: Tyndale House Publishers.

Dreikurs, R., Grunwald, B. B., & Pepper, F. C. (1982). *Maintaining Sanity in the Classroom: Classroom Management Techniques,* 2nd ed. New York: Harper & Row.

Edwards, C. H. (1993). *Classroom Discipline and Management.* New York: Macmillan.

Engelmann, S. (1969). *Preventing Failure in the Primary Grades.* New York: Simon and Schuster.

Ernst, L. (1972). *Games Students Play.* Millbrae, CA: Celestial Arts.

Freed, A. M. (1971). *TA for Kids.* Sacramento, CA: Jalmar Press.

Freed, A. M. (1973). *TA for Tots.* Sacramento, CA: Jalmar Press.

Freed, A. M. (1973). *TA for Teens.* Sacramento, CA: Jalmar Press.

Ginott, H. G. (1965). *Between Parent and Child.* New York: Avon.

Ginott, H. G. (1969). *Between Parent and Teenager.* New York: Macmillan.

Ginott, H. G. (1972). *Teacher and Child.* New York: Macmillan.

Glasser, W. (1965). *Reality Therapy: A New Approach to Psychiatry.* New York: Harper and Row.

Glasser, W. (1969). *Schools without Failure.* New York: Harper and Row.

Glasser, W. (1984). *Control Theory: A New Explanation of How We Control Our Lives.* New York: Harper and Row.

Glasser, W. (1986). *Control Theory in the Classroom.* New York: Harper and Row.

Glasser, W. (1992). *The Quality School: Managing Students without Coercion,* 2nd ed. New York: HarperPerennial.

Glasser, W. (1993). *The Quality School Teacher.* New York: HarperPerennial.

Gossen, D. C. (1992). *Restitution: Restructuring School Discipline.* Chapel Hill, NC: New View Publications.

Harris, T. A. (1967). *I'm OK—You're OK.* New York: Avon Books.

James, M., & Jongeward, D. (1971). *Born to Win: Transactional Analysis with Gestalt Experiments.* Boston: Addison-Wesley.

Jones, F. H. (1987). *Positive Classroom Discipline.* New York: McGraw-Hill.

Kounin, J. S. (1970). *Discipline and Group Management in Classrooms.* New York: Holt, Rinehart and Winston.

Nelsen, J. (1987). *Positive Discipline,* 2nd ed. New York: Ballantine Books.

Nelsen, J., Lott, L., & Glenn, H. S. (1993). *Positive Discipline in the Classroom: How to Effectively Use Class Meetings and Other Positive Discipline Strategies.* Rocklin, CA: Prima Publishing.

Redl, F. (1972). *When We Deal with Children,* 2nd ed. New York: Free Press.

Redl, F., & Wattenberg, W. W. (1959). *Mental Hygiene in Teaching,* 2nd ed. New York: Harcourt, Brace and World.

Skinner, B. F. (1971). *Beyond Freedom and Dignity.* New York: Knopf.

Wolfgang, C. H., & Glickman, C. D. (1995). *Solving Discipline Problems: Strategies for Classroom Teachers,* 3rd ed. Boston: Allyn & Bacon.

part II

Getting Organized

This part includes three chapters on ways to get organized for management and discipline. The chapters examine ways to prepare for the school year, organize your classroom and materials, and select and teach rules and procedures.

Chapter 4, "Preparing for the School Year," offers guidelines for getting acquainted with the school environment, making management preparations, making instructional preparations, establishing a plan for dealing with misbehavior, planning and conducting the first day, and handling the first week.

Chapter 5, "Organizing Your Classroom and Materials," addresses the functions of the classroom setting, factors to be considered in room arrangement, and environmental conditions.

Chapter 6, "Selecting and Teaching Rules and Procedures," examines the need for rules and procedures, and highlights ways to select and teach them to the students.

chapter 4

Preparing for the School Year

Objectives

This chapter provides information that will help you:

1. Make managerial preparations before school starts.
2. Make instructional preparations before school starts.
4. Identify steps and features of a systematic, 7-step plan to deal with misbehavior.
4. Identify principles to consider when planning for the first day.
5. Identify actions to be taken on the first day.
6. Identify actions needed during the first week.

If you surveyed experienced teachers about the role of management at the beginning of the school year, you would undoubtedly hear comments about management and instructional preparations before school starts and about ways to plan for the first days of the year. Studies on management have verified that the first few days set the tone for the entire year (Emmer, Evertson, & Anderson, 1980; Emmer et al., 1994; Evertson & Emmer, 1982; Evertson et al., 1983; Evertson et al., 1994).

To prepare, you can get acquainted with the environment, make management preparations, make instructional preparations, establish a plan for misbehavior, and also prepare for the first day. When the year finally begins, there are certain actions that are appropriate during the first day and over the following few days.

A number of issues are addressed in this chapter, and additional details about other responsibilities are included in the following chapters.

Many other resources are available (Christopher, 1991; Moran et al., 1992; Sarka & Shank, 1990; Schell & Burden, 1992; Williamson, 1988; Wong & Wong, 1991).

STARTING THE SCHOOL YEAR EFFECTIVELY

Before school starts, you can get acquainted with the environment to better understand your district, school, classroom, facilities, and resources. You can then make preparations about your room arrangement, procedures, routines, and other matters.

Making Management Preparations

It is important to consider carefully management issues such as your school environment, room arrangement, materials, rules and procedures, communication with parents, and seating arrangements. Based on a study of experienced teachers (Schell & Burden, 1992), you could direct your attention to the following management issues.

The School Environment.   The first step is to become thoroughly familiar with the total environment: the room, school, other teachers, children, resources, and the community. You will then have more information upon which to make decisions, will probably feel more confident about your job, and will not need to devote time in the first weeks to gathering this information. Based on a study of experienced teachers (Schell & Burden, 1992), you could direct your attention to getting acquainted with instructional resources, facilities, personnel, services, district and school policies, your students, the district, and the community.

Room Arrangement.   Room arrangement is an issue that can be decided before school starts. Take into account the fixed features in the room, instructional materials and supplies, traffic areas, work areas, boundaries for activity areas, visibility of students, and the purposes of various seating arrangements (discussed more fully in chapter 5). Determine the arrangement of your desk, the student's desks, tables, book shelves, filing cabinets, and other furniture. Inquiries can be made if there is need for additional furniture.

Room Decoration.   It is important to make your classroom an attractive, comfortable place. Consider having some plants in the classroom, or even an aquarium. Displays of pictures, posters, charts, and maps also help cover the walls with informative and appealing materials. Attractive bulletin boards add color. You might prepare one bulletin board listing classroom information and use another one to display seasonal items. After school starts, you could have students prepare the bulletin boards.

Gather Support Materials.   After examining the curriculum guide and the textbooks, you might have ideas about activities for a certain unit or lesson. Supplemental materials may be needed when the time comes to teach that lesson. This is the time to gather additional support materials such as games and devices, pictures, cassette tapes, charts, maps, and graphs. The school may have discretionary funds for their purchase. They may be obtained from school supply catalogs, a local store, or garage sales.

Organize Materials.   It is useful to set up a filing system for storing district and school communications and other important documents. Papers kept in a filing cabinet include the district's policy handbook; correspondence from the principal, superintendent, or other supervisors; correspondence from professional organizations; lesson plans; and items on curricular content.

   Some teachers use file folders. A separate file folder may be created for each course unit to hold pertinent notes and resource materials. Textbooks, resource books, manipulative materials, and other types of supplies also need to be organized and stored.

Classroom Procedures.   You can follow various procedures to accomplish specific tasks. Procedures may be identified regarding handing in completed work, sharpening a pencil, using the restroom, or putting away supplies. Before school starts, identify actions or activities requiring procedures that would contribute to a smoothly running classroom, then decide what those procedures should be.

Classroom Helpers.   Teachers call upon students at all grade levels as helpers to perform various tasks. Make a list of tasks that need to be done and decide which ones students could perform. Give attention to how task assignment will be rotated to give every student an opportunity to help. Roles are often held for one or two weeks before the assignments are rotated. Depending on the grade level and circumstances, some tasks may include students as line leader, light switcher, pencil sharpener, paper collector, plant waterer, chalkboard eraser, window and blind opener, and playground equipment manager.

Class Lists and Rosters.   It is useful to plan a means to record whether students have returned their book orders, picture money, field trip permission forms, and so on. You can prepare a generic class roster listing the students' names in alphabetical order in the left column, with blank columns on the right to check off the action. It is helpful to input the list onto a computer disk so that an updated sheet can be easily generated when the roster changes.

Home/School Communication.   Open communication with parents is vital. Before school starts, many teachers prepare an introductory letter to parents to welcome them, and to inform them about the teacher, the curriculum, grading practices and standards, the homework policy, rules and procedures, and so on.

Teachers in Action

Classroom Helpers

Laurie Stoltenhoff, fourth-grade teacher, Greenwich, Connecticut:

Classroom jobs encourage self-sufficiency, a sense of responsibility, and respect. I assign necessary tasks on a weekly basis because this eliminates the need to solicit helpers on a daily basis. There are eight positions to be filled each week. I fill them by calling on the first eight students on my class list; the next week I call on the next eight students, and so on, each week. This rotation allows for each student to experience each job.

The more seriously I represent the job, the more seriously my class will take their work as classroom helpers. I post a "Help Wanted" sign on the bulletin board. Rather than use traditional job titles, I assign more "adult" titles. For example, the attendance and lunch count person is called a secretary, and the chalkboard washers are our maintenance crew. Our classroom staff seems satisfied, and they never ask for a raise!

Teachers in Action

Using a Class List for Various Purposes

Marge McClintock, fifth-grade science and social studies teacher, New Providence, New Jersey:

As soon as I am given my class list for the year, I assign them numbers in alphabetical order. The students are told their numbers and are required to write their numbers on all their work. This has several benefits. When homework or seatwork is handed in, I ask a student to put the papers in numerical order for me. I can see in an instant which numbers are missing and take whatever action is needed.

Another benefit relates to managing the students on class trips. Although I always carry a class list with me, it is much faster to have the students call out their numbers in order when they're back on the bus or whenever roll needs to be taken.

This letter can be sent home with the students on the first day. Teachers can also make plans for other types of parental communication such as phone calls, progress reports, or a Back-to-School Night.

To establish good relationships with students, you might send a postcard or a letter to your students before school starts. The greeting could include a personal and positive welcome, a list of some activities you plan for the year, and perhaps a request that the student bring something special to school.

Birthdays and Celebrations.   Depending on the grade level, you might want to arrange celebrations or parties for birthdays or other special events. If celebrating birthdays, consider having a poster or calendar that lists every student's birthday and bulletin board space for the student being honored. Decide how you want to celebrate birthdays.

Most schools have specific policies for celebrating major holidays, such as Halloween, Christmas, Hanukkah, Martin Luther King Jr. Day, and Easter. Inquire about these policies so you'll understand what is expected.

Room Identification.   On the first day of school, students need to locate your classroom. Especially for students new to the building, it is important to have the room clearly labeled. For elementary classrooms, a poster on the outside doorway should include the room number, the teacher's name, and the grade level (Room 24, Mrs. Soria, Third Grade). For secondary classrooms, the poster should include the room number, the teacher's name, the grade level and/or subject (Room 211, Mr. Wagner, World History).

This information should be written on the chalkboard so students see that they are in the correct classroom. Some type of welcoming statement should also be written on the chalkboard such as, "Welcome, I'm glad you're here."

For elementary classes, many teachers also place a name tag on each student's desk. Name tags may also be needed for other personal spaces such as student lockers, storage areas, or coat hangers.

Seat Selections and Arrangements.   A teacher may prefer to select each student's seat, while another lets the students select their seats. This decision should be made before school starts. In either case, be sure that there are enough seats for the number of students you expect. You might take the students' age level and maturity into account in your decision. Some primary teachers, for example, prefer to have several seats clustered to give the young students a "family" feeling. Other arrangements may be considered according to grade level.

Inspect the seats to be sure they are not damaged and they are of sizes to accommodate your students. You might change the seating arrangements during the year to accommodate work groups, to move students who need close supervision to more accessible seats, or simply to provide a change.

Teachers in Action

Seat Selections

John Fallis, high school trigonometry teacher, Greencastle, Indiana:

When the students enter my class on the first day, I tell them to sit anywhere they wish. Most other classes are structured in alphabetical order, so the students are pleased with having a choice. They will wave to friends with a call to "come over here."

When all the students have arrived, I walk down each row, asking them to state their names. I want each name pronounced and spelled, if necessary. Then I move around the room, trying to associate each name with the appropriate face. It may require several trips, but it won't be long until I know all the names. I then ask them to confuse me by changing seats to different locations. It is time to try to identify each student again. This needs to be done once or twice.

The new seats become the students' permanent seats, since they have scattered from their original seats. But the real benefit is knowing every name from the first day. When I need to call on them during class discussion, I know their names. They have a more positive feeling about school, and I have a better start on discipline and organization.

Distributing Textbooks.   Sometime during the first few days, you will need to distribute textbooks. You need to obtain the textbooks and prepare an inventory form on which to record each book number, with a space in which to write the student's name.

You need to think about when and how the textbooks will be distributed. Since the first day often necessitates many announcements and activities, you might want to wait until the second or third day before distributing textbooks, or distribute them just before they are needed for the first time. Attention might be given to the specific means of distribution. One way is to have students line up one row at a time and go to the table where the books are stacked. When handing the book to the student, record the student's name on the inventory form.

Opening Class Routine.   Students often work better when they know that a particular routine will be regularly followed. You can decide on the particular actions to be taken. You may need to take attendance, make announcements, and attend to other tasks at the start of the period. The purpose of a routine is to ensure an orderly transition as students enter the room and prepare for instruction. Some teachers have students review vocabulary words or problems while other tasks are performed.

PLANNING FOR INSTRUCTION

You can make preparations for instruction by deciding on a weekly schedule, collecting instructional materials, and the like. Establish a plan for handling misbehavior that may occur during instruction.

Making Instructional Preparations

Carefully consider instructional issues such as long-range plans, supplementary materials, student assessment, a folder for substitute teachers, a syllabus, and so on. Based on a study of experienced teachers (Schell & Burden, 1992), you could direct your attention to the following instructional issues.

Long-Range Plans. It is helpful to peruse the curriculum guides and other related materials so you can appreciate what should be covered by the end of the year. Some tentative decisions need to be made for the amount of time to be spent on each unit. Some curriculum guides include recommendations about the number of weeks to spend on each unit.

You may want to solicit advice from other teachers, particularly from those who teach your subject or grade level. To the extent possible, make these rough schedules conform to the school calendar by taking into account grading periods and holidays. Be careful not to overschedule yourself. Leave some time for review near the end of each unit or chapter for reteaching as the situation warrants and for unexpected occurrences such as school closings due to inclement weather.

Supplementary Materials. For each major topic included in your rough long-range plans, start an ongoing list of related supplementary materials or activities. It may include field trip locations, resource people, media, games, assignments, bulletin boards, and additional books. Inquire about library or media center resources, such as films or videotapes, and order and reserve them. You might prepare other supplementary materials to use during the first few weeks.

Skeleton Plans. A *skeleton plan* is a brief overview of intended accomplishments. It often includes a weekly list of expected accomplishments. Skeleton plans are more detailed than the long-range, yearly plans, but do not have the detail needed for daily lesson plans. Skeleton plans for the first three or four weeks serve as a guide for preparing the more detailed lesson plans.

Weekly Time Schedules. You should establish your weekly schedule before school starts and place a copy of it in your lesson plan book, for instance. The weekly schedule is often displayed in a chart, with the weekdays listed at the top and the hours listed in the left-hand column.

The class schedule for secondary teachers probably will be determined by the principal or other officers and it will display the grade level and subject to be taught during each class period. For elementary teachers, certain time slots will be reserved for activities or classes held outside the regular classroom, such as art, physical education, music, the library, recess and lunch. For the remaining time in the elementary schedule, the teacher has the flexibility to determine when and for how long each subject will be scheduled. The beginning elementary teacher may find it helpful to solicit recommendations for timing from other teachers.

Daily Lesson Plans.   After you have completed the skeleton plans for the first three or four weeks, it is time to prepare the daily lesson plans for the first week. Lesson plan formats vary; one that is often used includes boxes indicating days of the week and subjects taught. Notes may be included about objectives, a list of topics to be covered or activities to be conducted, materials, and means of assessment.

Beginning and probationary teachers are often required to show the principal or assistant principal their weekly lesson plans for the coming week. Many teachers prefer to begin the year with an interesting review of the subject as taught the previous year. This is a time to consolidate learning and review, reinforcing your knowledge of the subject matter, and identifying the students' level of understanding.

Tentative Student Assessment.   It is useful to make an initial assessment of the students' understanding and skills at the start year so you can better recognize abilities and differences within the class. These assessments could be conducted sometime during the first week, but you should think about how to plan for the assessment, then make necessary arrangements before school starts. Assessment procedures might include worksheets, oral activities, observation checklists, pretests, or review lessons. After conducting these early assessments, you could record the results on a roster that had been drawn up earlier.

Backup Materials.   It is useful to have some backup materials available when instruction requires less time than anticipated, when a change of plans is necessary, or when students finish their activities early. These backup materials may be related to the topics being covered at the time. Many teachers have a collection of puzzles, educational games, discussion questions, brain teasers, creative writing, word searches, and riddles. You can gather these materials before school starts.

Folder for Substitute Teachers.   A substitute teacher will take your place when you are absent. It is important to prepare materials for substitutes, to help support their efforts, maximize learning, and minimize off-task behavior. Many teachers prepare a folder for the substitute which includes important information. It can be kept on your desk with the plan book.

Additional information about substitute teaching is available from various sources (e.g., Collins, 1982; Downing, 1985; Peterson, 1985; Pronin, 1983). Much of it can be collected before school starts, with further information added as needed.

Teachers in Action

Preparing for the Substitute Teacher

Debra Guedry, elementary teacher, Baton Rouge, Louisiana:

I always worried about the days when I needed to be absent, and I believed that my students needed consistency in their daily and weekly routines. Having a substitute teacher required extra planning on my part of keep things running as normally as possible.

During my first few years of teaching, I found myself in a panic when I needed to be absent unexpectedly. After being in this situation several times, I decided to get organized! I prepared a "substitute folder" which is ready at all times. The folder includes the following items:

- *Names of Important People.* Principal, secretary, reliable students, nearby co-worker, and room numbers.
- *Classroom Procedures.* Daily schedule, morning routines (roll call, lunch count, duty), rainy day schedule, bell signals, lunch and recess schedules, and seating chart.
- *Discipline.* Rules and procedures, rewards and consequences.
- *Special Accommodations.* Students who attend special programs, students with special needs (physical, medical, others).
- *Materials (and location).* Lesson plans, textbooks, supplies, and so on.
- *Helpful Tips.* Have information on whole class photocopied and ready for use. Make a list of favorite class games and activities that can be used when needed. This will help eliminate discipline problems when students have completed the assigned work and have nothing to do.

Christine MacBurney, middle school language arts teacher, New Providence, New Jersey:

I have an accountability system for the substitute teacher. This is a reporting sheet that gives me feedback on each class's behavior and academic progress. It includes a five-point rating scale for behavior and general cooperation along with space for noting specific student concerns. At the beginning of the school year, I tell the students about this reporting system and discuss their responsibility toward a substitute teacher. I also tell them about specific consequences should they misbehave. I now find that my classes compete for the best ratings and comments, knowing that I "reward" the best class with a night free of homework.

Planning for Homework.   Give careful consideration to how you will evaluate students and determine report card grades. One element of evaluation often involves homework, and preparation for developing a homework policy can be made before school starts.

Prepare a homework policy in the form of a letter sent to parents at the start of the year. The policy should explain why homework is assigned, explain the types of homework you will assign, inform parents of the amount and frequency of homework, provide guidelines about when and how students are to complete homework, let parents know you will positively reinforce students who complete homework, explain what you will do when students do not complete homework, and clarify what is expected of the parent (Sarka & Shank, 1990).

Preparing a Syllabus.   You need to give students information about each course at the start of the year. You could plan and prepare this information as well as related materials before school starts. Elementary grade teachers often merely discuss this information with students. At the secondary level, they may hand each student a course syllabus that outlines this introductory information.

The *course syllabus* includes the course title, the title of the textbook and any other primary resource materials, a brief course description, and a list of course objectives, a content outline, course requirements (e.g., tests, home-work, projects), how grades will be calculated (e.g., points to satisfy each requirement and the point total needed), a description of the homework policy, the attendance and tardiness policy, and a listing of classroom rules and procedures. Some teachers also include a description of the instruction method and the activities students are to engage in.

Preparing Policy Sheets.   The syllabus might include all related classroom policies and procedures, though some teachers do not include these items. Depending on the grade level and circumstances, the teacher might not provide a course syllabus.

A teacher might prepare a policy sheet for the students. The sheet may state rules and procedures, the policy for attendance and tardiness, and the like. If a course syllabus is not used, this policy sheet might also state the grading policy.

Establishing a Plan to Deal with Misbehavior

With an understanding of management and discipline, you will need to develop a plan for dealing with misbehavior. The 7-step plan presented below begins with establishment of a system of rules and procedures. You need to provide a supportive environment during instruction as well as situational assistance when students get off-task. If the student does not get back on-task, you need to move through advancing levels of punishment. If none of these actions are effective, you may need to involve other personnel.

Many studies have reported that the amount of time spent disciplining students is negatively related to student achievement (Crocker & Brooker, 1986; Evertson et al., 1980; Stallings & Kaskowitz, 1974). You should deal with misbehavior effectively while avoiding unnecessary disruptions. Researchers and educators have also proposed movement from low to high intervention when developing a plan to address misbehavior (Charles, 1992; Levin & Nolan, 1991; Steere, 1988; Wolfgang & Glickman, 1995). Once the rules and procedures and a supportive classroom environment are in place, the teacher moves from low to high intervention, as described below.

1. *Establish your system of rules and procedures.* Establish an appropriate system of rules and procedures as a foundation for dealing with discipline. It is vital that you select a system of rules and procedures appropriate to the situation. This system should incorporate reward or reinforcement for desirable behavior and the consequences of misbehavior.

No single approach is best for all teachers and all situations. For instance, rules and procedures for a tenth-grade English class would not be appropriate for a third-grade class. Furthermore, the system needs to be consistent with established school and district policies and with your personal educational philosophy, personality, and preferences.

2. *Provide a supportive environment during class sessions.* Once the system has been established at the start of the year, you need to maintain a supportive environment. Actions taken in the normal course of instruction are for the purpose of guiding and reinforcing students toward positive behavior. You would follow them even in the absence of misbehavior.

Providing a supportive environment is accomplished primarily through cueing and reinforcing appropriate behavior, and gaining and holding attention. Cueing and reinforcing involve stressing positive, desirable behaviors; recognizing and reinforcing desired behaviors; and praising effectively. Gaining and holding attention necessitates focusing attention at the start of the lessons; keeping lessons moving at a good pace; monitoring attention during lessons; stimulating attention periodically; maintaining accountability; and terminating lessons that have gone on too long. Treat students with dignity and respect, and offer challenging, interesting, and exciting classes.

3. *Provide situational assistance during class sessions.* Students may get off-task during a lesson. This off-task behavior may take the form of misbehavior or may simply be a lapse in attention. Either way, you need to promptly provide situational assistance. ***Situational assistance*** denotes actions you take to get the student back on-task with the least intervention and disruption possible; it does *not* involve aversive nonpunitive or punitive consequences. You should be alert to a lack of involvement in learning activities, prolonged inattention or work avoidance, and obvious violations of rules and procedures. These behaviors can be dealt with directly and without overreaction.

Situational assistance can be provided by removing seductive objects, reinforcing appropriate behaviors, boosting student interest, providing cues, helping students through hurdles, redirecting the behavior, altering the lesson, and other approaches (discussed more fully in chapter 14).

Some inappropriate behaviors are of such short duration and are so insignificant that they can safely be ignored. Your use of situational assistance might be considered a "forgiveness step" for the student by recognizing that the off-task behavior is minor or fleeting and by allowing the student to get back on-task without penalty.

Decision Points

Before using mild responses for off-task behavior, teachers often provide situational assistance to get students back on-task. What are the
benefits of situational assistance? How might situational assistance differ between the eleventh grade and the fifth grade? How might ethnic
differences of students affect your decisions about the ways to provide
situational assistance?

4. *Use mild responses.* If a student continues to be off-task after situational
assistance is provided, you need to use mild corrective responses. These are
not intended to be punitive. Mild responses may be nonverbal or verbal (see
chapter 14).

Nonverbal responses include ignoring the behavior, using signal interference,
using proximity control or using touch control. Verbal responses involve reinforcing
peers, calling on the student during the lesson, using humor, giving a direct appeal
or command, reminding the student of the rule, and several other approaches.

5. *Use moderate responses.* If students do not respond favorably to mild
responses and continue to exhibit off-task behavior, you need to deliver moderate
responses (see chapter 15). These punitive responses deal with misbehavior by
removing the desired stimulus so as to minimize the inappropriate behavior.
Moderate responses include logical consequences and various behavior modification techniques such as time-out and loss of privileges.

6. *Use severe responses.* If moderate responses are insufficient, you need
to move to a more intrusive type of intervention (see chapter 15). Severe
responses are intended to be punitive, by adding aversive stimuli such as
reprimands, overcorrection, and physical consequences. The purpose of aversive
stimuli is to decrease unwanted behavior.

7. *Involve other persons when necessary.* If all efforts have failed to get
the student to behave properly, you need to involve other persons in the process.
This occurs most commonly with chronic or severe misbehaviors. You may
consult counselors, psychologists, principals and assistant principals, teaching
colleagues, college personnel, mental health centers, school social workers,
school nurses, supervisors and department heads, and parents (Steere, 1988).
Their assistance and involvement will vary depending on their expertise.

THE SCHOOL YEAR BEGINS

Getting acquainted with the school environment, making management and
instructional preparations, and establishing a plan for misbehavior are all vital
tasks. You also need to begin planning for the announcements and activities of
the first day, decide how to conduct the first day, and consider other instructional
and management issues during the first week.

Planning for the First Day

Starting the school year effectively is vitally important when establishing a system of management. Several principles should guide your decisions about planning the start of the year and your actions in the first few days (Evertson et al., 1983, 1994; Emmer et al., 1994; Good & Brophy, 1994).

1. *Plan to clearly state your rules, procedures, and expectations.* When students arrive for the first time, they may have uncertainties. They will want to know your expectations about behavior and academic work. They will want to know the rules for general behavior and also the consequences for adhering to or breaking them. Students also will wonder how you will monitor the rules and how consistently you will enforce them. They want to understand the procedures for going to the restroom, turning in homework, sharpening pencils, talking during seatwork, and the like. They will be interested in learning about course requirements, grading policies, standards for work, and other aspects of the academic program.

You need to think about these issues prior to the start of school, make decisions about them, and be prepared to convey this information to the students. Probably you will already have decided about your system of rules and procedures as part of the 7-step plan on misbehavior. It is especially important to take the necessary time during the first few days to thoroughly describe your expectations about behavior and work. Emphasize and be explicit about desirable behavior. Combine your directions about procedures, rules, and course requirements with your initial content activities to build a good foundation for the year.

2. *Plan uncomplicated lessons to help students be successful.* Content activities and assignments during the first week should be designed to ensure maximum student success. Select relatively simple lessons at the start so that few students will likely need individual help. This allows you to focus on monitoring behavior and to respond to students in ways that shape and reinforce appropriate behavior. It provides you with opportunities to reinforce academic achievement and to begin to develop positive relationships with students.

3. *Keep a whole-class focus.* Plan activities for the first week that have a whole-class focus, rather than several small-group activities. Whole-class activities make it easier to monitor student behavior and performance. You can focus on reinforcing appropriate behavior and preventing inappropriate behavior.

4. *Be available, visible, and in charge.* You must be in charge at all times. Move around and be physically near the students, and maintain a good field of vision so you can see all the students, wherever you stand. Move around during seatwork to check on student progress.

Decision Points

Effective teachers are available, visible, and in charge. Suppose that you are ready for your tenth-grade math class on the first day of school. How could you exhibit this take-charge behavior as students enter the room and you make your opening announcements and describe the planned activities? How might your approach differ for a sixth-grade class and for a first-grade class?

---

5. *Plan strategies to deal with potential problems.* Unexpected events can develop when you meet your students for the first time. These might include (a) interruptions by parents, office staff, custodians, or others; (b) late arrivals; (c) one or more students being assigned to your class after the first day; and (d) and insufficient number of textbooks or necessary materials. While you cannot foresee events, you can give thought to how you would deal with the unexpected, should it occur.

6. *Closely monitor student compliance with rules and procedures.* By closely monitoring students, you can provide cues and reinforcement for appropriate behavior. Better managers monitor compliance with rules consistently, intervene to correct inappropriate behavior whenever necessary, and mention rules or describe desirable behavior when giving feedback. Effective managers stress specific corrective feedback rather than criticism or threat of punishment when students fail to comply with rules and procedures.

7. *Quickly stop inappropriate behavior.* Inappropriate or disruptive behavior should be handled quickly and consistently. Minor misbehavior that is not corrected often increases in intensity or is taken up by other students. Quickly respond to inappropriate behavior to maximize on-task behavior.

8. *Organize instruction on the basis of ability levels.* The cumulative record folders will indicate ability levels in reading, math, and other subjects. Select instructional content and activities that meet the ability levels of your students.

9. *Hold students academically accountable.* Develop procedures that keep students accountable for their academic work. This may include papers to be turned in at the end of class, homework, in-class activities, and other means. Return the completed papers promptly and with feedback. Some teachers give a weekly assignment sheet to each student. This sheet is completed by the student, checked by the parent, and returned to the teacher daily.

10. *Be clear when communicating information.* Effective teachers clearly and explicitly present information, give directions, and state objectives. When discussing complex tasks, break them down into step-by-step procedures.

11. *Maintain students' attention.* Arrange seating so all students can easily face the area where their main attention needs to be held. Get everyone's focused attention before starting a lesson. Monitor for signs of confusion or inattention, and be sensitive to student concerns.

12. *Organize the flow of lesson activities.* Effective managers waste little time getting the students organized for the lesson. They maximize student attention and task engagement by maintaining momentum and providing signals and cues. They successfully deal with more than one thing at a time (e.g., talking with one student while keeping an eye on the rest of the class).

Conducting the First Day

The first day is often a time of nervousness for teachers and students. Fortunately, you can make decisions about a number of issues as you prepare for the day. Students, on the other hand, enter school with a lot of uncertainty. They have questions (Wong & Wong, 1991):

- Am I in the right room?
- Where am I supposed to sit?
- What are the rules in this classroom?
- What will I be doing this year?
- How will I be graded?
- Who is the teacher as a person?
- Will the teacher treat me as a human being?

You can do many things on the first day to address these concerns, as discussed in the following sections.

Greet the Students. Stand by the classroom door before class begins. As students are about to enter, greet them with a smile and a handshake. As you do this, state your name, your room number, the subject or period, if needed;

Teachers in Action

The First Class Session

Martin Miller, Jr., high school mathematics teacher, New Providence, New Jersey:

There is no second chance to make a first impression. Planning for the first class session takes as much time as preparing for any content lesson you will teach. The anxiety level for both teachers and students about that first day is high. Taking advantage of these feelings can make for a good beginning.

Students like to have guidelines about how the class will be run as well as what is expected of them academically. I always begin by welcoming them and immediately giving them something to do. I hand them their textbook and an index card. On the card, they write their name, address, telephone number, and book number.

While the students are filling out their cards and looking at the textbook, I set up my seating chart and verify attendance. Within 10 minutes of meeting the students, I begin my first lesson. By keeping clerical chores to a minimum, I try to have more time on-task. After a closure activity, somewhere in the middle of the class period, I take a few minutes to explain how their grade will be determined, the rules of the class, and when extra help sessions are available.

Next, we deal with some curriculum content and then I make a homework assignment. I tell the students that homework assignments will be written on the chalkboard every day in the same location.

Setting high standards on the first day makes the following days easier. We will always need to monitor and adjust, but this will be within the framework set on the first day.

---

the grade level or subject, and anything else appropriate, such as the seating assignment (Wong & Wong, 1991). As mentioned previously, your name, room number, section or period, and grade level or subject should be posted outside your door and on the chalkboard.

Tell Students about Their Seat Assignments. There are various ways to handle seat assignments. Some teachers prefer to let students select their seats while others prefer to assign seats. Either way, students should be told what to do as they enter the classroom.

If you determine the seating assignment, there are several ways to inform students of their seat assignment as they enter. For elementary classes, you may have name tags taped on the desks. For secondary classes, you might have a transparency displayed on the projector screen indicating the seating arrangement. A different transparency would be used for each of the class sections. Also have a copy of the seating chart in hand as you greet the students.

Correct Improper Room Entry. Observe students as they enter and take their seats. Some may not go directly to their seats or may behave inappropriately. It is important to ask a student who enters the room inappropriately to return to the door and enter properly.

Be calm but firm; tell the student why this is being done, give specific directions, check for understanding, and acknowledge the understanding (Wong & Wong, 1991). The communication might be along these lines:

Todd, please come back to the door.

I am sorry, but that is not the way you enter our classroom every day. You were noisy, you did not go to your seat, and you pushed Ann.

When you enter this classroom, you walk in quietly, go directly to your seat, and get to work immediately on the assignment that is posted.

Are there any questions?

Thank you, Todd. Now show me that you can go to your seat properly.

During this interaction, be sure to use the student's name and be polite with a "please" and "thank you."

Handle Administrative Tasks. Taking attendance is one of the first administrative tasks to be done at the start of the period. Have the students raise their hands when called to indicate that they are present and to give you an opportunity to see the face associated with the name. As you call each name, ask the student whether you pronounced it correctly.

After the first day, some teachers prefer not to continue taking attendance. Instead, they give an assignment that is to begin as soon as the students enter. After the work is underway, the teacher can take attendance by visually scanning the room; the names do not need to be called. This approach, or one similar to it, takes very little time and allows students to move quickly into the academic work.

Teachers in Action

Getting Acquainted with Each Other

Linda Innes, seventh-grade middle school language arts teacher, Kansas City, Missouri:

Since three elementary schools feed into our middle school, most of the students will not know one another at the start of the year. I like to start out the first day with a fun, nonthreatening activity that will help us get to know one another. One of my favorite activities is to have the students sit in a circle and introduce themselves using a silly adjective that starts with the first letter of the first name (Crazy Cory, Mushy Marcel, Maddening Mandy). After this, they repeat the names of those already introduced. Also, the students might mention some interests or recent activities.

At the end of the first session, I have the students fill out a "student inventory" index card. I ask them to state their name (including nickname), address, phone number, the name of the person they live with (perhaps a guardian or another person), the school they attended last year, their birthday, and the number of brothers and sisters with their ages. I also ask them to answer the following questions on the card: Do you write poems or stories? Have you ever written anything you really liked? If so, what is it? This student inventory card comes in handy as I get to know the students and understand their background.

Make Introductions. Students appreciate knowing something about the teacher. At the start of the period, give the students your name and some personal information, such as the number of years you have been teaching, professional development activities, family, personal interests and activities, hobbies, and other background information. This helps the students know you as a person and may be informative and comforting to them. This is also the time to let the students know that you are enthusiastic about working with them, and that you will be reasonable and fair with them.

Some teachers like to use this opening time to have the students briefly introduce themselves. Some get-acquainted activities could be included on the first day to help promote good feelings.

Discuss Classroom Rules and Procedures. All classrooms need rules and procedures if they are to run smoothly and efficiently. Rules should be taught on the first day to immediately establish the general code of conduct. Post the rules in a conspicuous place in the classroom. If a letter has been prepared for parents which describes the rules and procedures, give it to the students so they can take it home.

Some procedures may be taught on the first day, though many teachers prefer to teach procedures (e.g., distributing materials, getting ready to leave the classroom, handing in papers) over the next several days instead (Leinhardt, Weidman, & Hammond, 1987). In this way, all the procedures are not taught at the same time, and the students might feel less overwhelmed and more likely to remember them. Procedures can be taught when the need for them first occurs. For example, when it is time to collect papers at the end of an activity, you can teach the appropriate procedure.

Present Course Requirements. Before school started, you would have prepared the course requirements and syllabus. On the first day, students want to know what content will be covered and what is expected of them concerning grading. Take time to discuss the course content and some of the activities planned for the year. If you have prepared a syllabus, hand it out. Discuss the grading requirements for tests, homework, projects, and the like and indicate the levels required for the various letter grades.

Conduct an Initial Activity. Depending on the amount of time available, many teachers plan an initial activity related to the curriculum. It should provide a review of some subject matter that students had had in the preceding year, or may be a preview of topics to be covered. Either way, the activity should be designed so that the students can complete it with little assistance and with much success. This leaves you free to monitor the students during the activity, to provide assistance when necessary, and to take corrective action on off-task behavior.

End the Class Period. A routine to end the class period is needed, and this also must be taught. Procedures need to be established and time put aside for returning books and supplies, disposing of scrap paper and cleaning up the classroom, putting away books and other materials preparatory to either leaving the classroom (for the middle and secondary level) or moving into the next subject (elementary grades).

Handling the First Week

The first day may be a half day or on an abbreviated schedule. There may not be time to teach all the procedures, provide introductions, or conduct get-acquainted activities. These activities may be spread out over the first few days.

During the first several days, review major rules and procedures and enforce them consistently. Related information about the curriculum can be offered after the first day. Provide opportunities for students to ask questions about rules, procedures, course requirements, and so on.

Students may enter your classroom after the first day due to being transferred from another classroom, schedule changes, or late entry in school. They will have missed all of the opening information about rules and procedures, curriculum, and other issues, so it is necessary to provide this orientation for each student. This might be done privately during seatwork or recess. Some teachers assign a student to serve as a "buddy" to provide the orientation information and to answer the new student's questions.

MAJOR CONCEPTS

1. The first step in preparing for the school year is to become thoroughly familiar with the total teaching environment: the room, school, other teachers, children, resources, and the community.
2. Prior to the start of the year, you can make decisions about management issues such as room arrangement, materials, rules and procedures, communication with parents, seating arrangements, and other issues.
3. A 7-step plan can be followed to systematically deal with discipline by establishing rules and procedures, maintaining a supportive classroom environment, providing situational assistance, and moving from low to high intervention techniques when responding to continuing misbehavior.
4. Before school starts, you need to carefully consider instructional issues such as long-range plans, supplementary materials, student assessment, a folder for substitute teachers, a syllabus, and other issues and have these in place before the first day of school.
5. Several principles should guide your decisions about planning the start of the year and your actions on the first few days. These include clearly stating rules and expectations, planning uncomplicated beginning lessons, having a whole-class format, having a strategy to deal with misbehavior, monitoring student compliance, holding students academically accountable, and other concerns.
6. Students enter the first day with a lot of uncertainty, and you can plan specific actions to address these concerns.
7. There may not be time to teach all the procedures, provide introductions, conduct get-acquainted activities, or cover other information on the first day. These activities may be spread out over the first week.

DISCUSSION QUESTIONS

1. What can you gain by finding out about the local school district and the community resources?
2. What are the advantages and disadvantages of having preassigned seats for your students? What reasons might a teacher have for letting students select their seats?
3. What are the merits of the 7-step plan for systematically dealing with misbehavior? How might that plan be improved?
4. What are the reasons for making long-range instructional plans before school starts?
5. Why should a teacher plan uncomplicated lessons at the start of the school year?
6. What benefits might be gained by having students introduce themselves and using get-acquainted activities?

SUPPLEMENTAL ACTIVITIES

For Clinical Settings

1. Identify the tasks that you would like to have performed by classroom helpers. Establish a procedure for showing the students what to do in these roles. Establish a procedure for rotating these roles to other students every week or two.
2. Prepare a course syllabus that includes the course title, a brief course description, a list of course objectives, a content outline, course requirements (e.g., tests, homework, projects), how report card grades will be calculated (e.g., the points for each requirement and the point total needed for certain grades), a description of the homework policy, attendance and tardiness policy, and a list of classroom rules and procedures.
3. Prepare a detailed lesson plan for your first class session at the start of the year. Include actions you will take and information you will provide.

For Field Settings

1. Talk to teachers to identify what they do before school starts, what they do on the first day or first class session, and how they handle the first two weeks.
2. Talk to several teachers to see how they handle long-range planning and skeleton planning.
3. Ask several teachers to provide recommendations for preparing for and starting the school year.

KEY TERMS

Course syllabus	Skeleton plan
Situational assistance	

RECOMMENDED READINGS

Sarka, P. R., & Shank, M. (1990). *Lee Canter's Back to School with Assertive Discipline.* Santa Monica, CA: Lee Canter & Associates.
   Includes sections on preparing an assertive discipline plan, planning to teach specific directions, classroom organization, bulletin boards, communicating with parents, planning for homework, final preparations, and actions on the first few days. Has a K–6 focus but many ideas are applicable to the secondary level.

Schell, L. M., & Burden, P. R. (1992). *Countdown to the First Day of School.* Washington, DC: National Education Association.
   Includes specific suggestions for measures to take to prepare for the first day. Has sections on getting acquainted, the classroom environment, and instructional planning. Based on recommendations from over 300 experienced teachers. Presented in outline and checklist format.

Williamson, B. (1988). *A First-year Teacher's Guidebook for Success.* Sacramento, CA: Dynamic Teaching Co.

Includes chapters on organizing the classroom, preparations for the first day, policies and procedures, discipline, back-to-school night, parent conferences, and other practical concerns. Has an elementary focus but many ideas also relate to the secondary level.

Wong, H. K., & Wong, R. T. (1991). *The First Days of School: How to be an Effective Teacher.* Sunnyvale, CA: Harry K. Wong Publications.

Includes practical suggestions to prepare for the school year and to conduct the opening days. Covers characteristics of effective teachers, positive expectations, classroom management, lesson mastery, and professional development.

REFERENCES

Charles, C. M. (1992). *Building Classroom Discipline,* 4th ed. New York: Longman.

Christopher, C. J. (1991). *Nuts and Bolts: Survival Guide for Teachers.* Lancaster, PA: Technomic Publishing Co.

Collins, S. H. (1982). *Classroom Management for Substitute Teachers.* Eugene, OR: Garlic Press.

Crocker, R. K. & Brooker, G. M. (1986). Classroom control and student outcomes in grades 2 and 5. *American Educational Research Journal, 23,* 1-11.

Downing, D. O. (1985). *Sub Survival: A Handbook for the Substitute Elementary Teacher.* Holmes Beach, FL: Learning Publications.

Duke, D. L., & Meckel, A. M. (1984). *Teacher's Guide to Classroom Management.* New York: Random House.

Emmer, E. T., Evertson, C. M. & Anderson, L. (1980). Effective management at the beginning of the school year. *Elementary School Journal, 80,* 219-231.

Emmer, E. T., Evertson, C. M., Clements, B. S., & Worsham, M. E. (1994). *Classroom Management for Secondary Teachers,* 3rd ed. Boston: Allyn & Bacon.

Evertson, C. M., & Emmer, E. T. (1982). Effective management at the beginning of the school year in junior high classes. *Journal of Educational Psychology, 74(4),* 485-498.

Evertson, C. M., Emmer, E. T., & Brophy, J. E. (1980). Predictors of effective teaching in junior high mathematics classrooms. *Journal for Research in Mathematics Education, 11,* 167-178.

Evertson, C. M., Emmer, E. T., Clements, B. S., & Worsham, M. E. (1994). *Classroom Management for Elementary Teachers,* 3rd ed. Boston: Allyn & Bacon.

Evertson, C. M., Emmer, E. T., Sanford, J. P., & Clements, B. S. (1983). Improving classroom management: An experiment in elementary school classrooms. *Elementary School Journal, 84,* 173-188.

Good, T. L., & Brophy, J. E. (1994). *Looking in Classrooms,* 6th ed. New York: HarperCollins.

Leinhardt, G., Weidman, C., & Hammond, K. M. (1987). Introduction and integration of classroom routines by expert teachers. *Curriculum Inquiry, 17(2),* 135-176.

Levin, J., & Nolan, J. F. (1991). *Principles of Classroom Management: A Hierachical Approach.* Englewood Cliffs, NJ: Prentice Hall.

Moran, C., Stobbe, J., Baron, W., Miller, J., & Moir, E. (1992). *Keys to the Classroom: A Teacher's Guide to the First Month of School.* Newbury Park, CA: Corwin Press.

Peterson, S. (1985). *Help! for Substitutes.* Carthage, IL: Good Apple.

Pronin, B. (1983). *Substitute Teaching: A Handbook for Hassle-free Subbing.* New York: St. Martins Press.

Sarka, P. R., & Shank, M. (1990). *Lee Canter's Back to School with Assertive Discipline.* Santa Monica, CA: Lee Canter & Associates.

Schell, L. M., & Burden, P. R. (1992). *Countdown to the First Day of School.* Washington, DC: National Education Association.

Stallings, J. A., & Kaskowitz, D. (1974). *Follow-through Classroom Observation Evaluation 1972–74.* Menlo, CA: Stanford Research Institute.

Sterre, B. F. (1988). *Becoming an Effective Classroom Manager: A Resource for Teachers.* Albany, NY: State University of New York Press.

Williamson, B. (1988). *A First-year Teacher's Guidebook for Success.* Sacramento, CA: Dynamic Teaching Co.

Wolfgang, C. H., & Glickman, C. D. (1995). *Solving Discipline Problems: Strategies for Classroom Teachers,* 3rd ed. Boston, MA: Allyn & Bacon.

Wong, H. K. & Wong, R. T. (1991). *The First Days of School: How to be an Effective Teacher.* Sunnyvale, CA: Harry K. Wong Publications.

chapter 5

Organizing Your Classroom and Materials

Objectives

This chapter provides information that will help you:

1. Identify the functions of a classroom setting.
2. Identify factors to be considered when making decisions about the physical environment.
3. Determine how to effectively arrange the floor space for the teacher's desk, student desks, bookcases, filing cabinets, and activity areas.
4. Recognize ways to effectively use storage space.
5. Identify ways to use bulletin boards and wall space.
6. Identify ways to adjust the environmental conditions to create a positive ambience and a comfortable setting.

You will want to organize your classroom and materials to facilitate learning and minimize off-task behavior, and careful planning can help achieve these purposes. The organization influences students' perceptions of their place in the classroom, the types of activities that will be appropriate, and how they are expected to behave. As with so many other aspects of teaching, designing the physical environment is more complex than it first appears.

The environment can exert both direct and indirect effects on your students (Proshansky & Wolfe, 1974; Weinstein & David, 1987). The direct effect is the manner in which certain activities are facilitated or hindered, such as the way that a circular seating arrangement may enhance group discussion. The indirect effect is the manner in which the values and intentions of the teacher are communicated, how excitement toward learning is generated, the status assigned individuals and activities, and the sense of comfort or threat (Weinstein & David, 1987). The prominent location of a computer, for example, indirectly communicates certain values and intentions as does an attractive bulletin board display.

It is important to consider the effects of the environment on student behavior and to deliberately create environments that facilitate desirable behavior. Develop *environmental competence*, which is an awareness of the physical environment and its impact, and the ability to use the environment to meet your goals (Steele, 1973). Being environmentally competent helps you to plan spatial arrangements that support your objectives, be sensitive to messages communicated by the physical setting, and know how to evaluate the effectiveness of the environment. You can be alert to physical circumstances that might contribute to behavioral problems, and can modify the environment when the need arises (Weinstein & Mignano, 1993).

This chapter discusses the functions of the setting, factors to be considered when designing the physical environment, and specific ideas about floor space, storage space and supplies, bulletin boards and wall space, and the environment.

FUNCTIONS OF THE CLASSROOM SETTING

The classroom is viewed as the place where teaching and learning take place. But there is more to it. Teachers and students spend several hours each day together in classrooms, and additional purposes are served by the classroom and the way it is arranged. Steele (1973) indicates that physical settings serve six basic functions: security and shelter, social contact, symbolic identification, task instrumentality, pleasure, and growth. These provide a useful starting point for examining the classroom and the ways that you might effectively design the physical environment.

Security and Shelter

The *physical security* and shelter of students is a basic concern, involving the physical conditions that affect their senses. The temperature and quality of the air, noise, light, and the quality and comfort of the seats and other facilities are physical aspects of security and shelter. *Psychological security* and shelter, another element, means that the students feel secure, comfortable, safe, and protected.

Based on these physical and psychological issues, you could do the following to provide for the security and shelter of your students:

- Arrange for a comfortable temperature, and assure proper ventilation for fresh air (e.g., open the window for fresh air).
- Eliminate or minimize distracting noise (e.g., close the door when there is outside noise).

- Adjust lighting to a comfortable level; reduce glare.
- Add elements to soften the environment (e.g., warm colors, fabrics, textures, rugs, plants).
- Minimize distractions (e.g., don't crowd desks, keep desks away from heavy traffic zones).
- Arrange for a place for students to go if they need a break (e.g., a voluntary time-out area, a private work area, or a study carrel).

Decision Points

Students need to feel psychologically secure, comfortable, safe, and protected. If you are using cooperative learning groups in your eighth-grade English class, what could you do about the room arrangement to provide this psychological security? How might your decisions be affected by the ethnic diversity in your classroom?

Social Contact

The next function is to enable interaction among students and between teacher and students. Common arrangements are rows, clusters of two or more desks, and semicircles. The degree of student interaction and teacher directedness vary with each arrangement. The degree of interaction you want among your students should be the key determinant in selecting the seating arrangement.

Beginning teachers might want to use rows of desks because this format directs student attention to the teacher, reduces student interaction, and makes it easier for students to concentrate on individual assignments (Bennett & Blundell, 1983; Wheldall, Morris, Vaughan, & Ng, 1981). Later, when feeling more confident about classroom control, beginning teachers can more comfortably experiment with other seating arrangements.

Interaction between you and your students is also affected by the seating arrangement. In a classic study on teaching, Adams and Biddle (1970) reported that teachers interact more fully with students seated in the center of the room and with those in front; this area is called the **action zone**. These students participate actively, with more questions and comments. Whatever the seating arrangement, you should make efforts to give attention to all students.

Based on these issues, you could do the following to address the social interaction in the classroom:

- Select a room arrangement that facilitates the interaction you want to achieve among students. (Rows are more teacher centered, clusters or circles are more student centered.)
- Make efforts to interact with all students, regardless of where they are seated.

Teachers in Action

Personalizing the Classroom

Marc Knapp, sixth-grade teacher, San Diego, California:

The space behind my desk reflects me. Here you'll find my degrees, awards, and credentials. There are also family photos, and pictures of activities and places that I enjoy. This board gives me a momentary mental vacation when things become tense. It also lets students know that I have a life, and it gives me credibility as a professional educator.

When you enter the office of a doctor, attorney, or CPA, you always see credentials on the wall. You should never see a classroom without them, either. Therefore, when Alejandro's father came to school for a conference, I positioned him at a table where he could see the student award wall as well as my credentials and awards.

Russell Moore, first-grade teacher, Sterling Heights, Michigan:

The walls of my classroom are no longer spaces to be filled with commercially prepared decorations. Instead, they serve as a canvas where the students' original writings and artwork are displayed.

Once I get the furniture and materials in place, I tape large pieces of roll paper on the walls and pin yards of pleated and draped fabric to the bulletin boards to provide background for students' work. Completed student writings and drawings are trimmed and mounted on a sheet of construction paper which serves as a frame. The colors of the construction paper complement the background colors of the roll paper or fabric. I write the title for each display on cards, which also indicate the ages of the students in the display. These title cards are also mounted and displayed with the work.

This display builds a sense of student ownership of the space. By viewing their carefully displayed work, they become aware of the value I place on their work. Visitors also see the development and talents of the students, and the students are encouraged to continue to produce quality work that can be displayed. A standard of work is conveyed through the displays. And it also helps the classroom be a comfortable, attractive place.

Symbolic Identification

The physical setting provides a means for students to have **symbolic identification** within the classroom. This is personal identification through symbols such as work samples, posting of personal information, photographs, posters, and other objects. These objects can be displayed to show students' accomplishments, personal background, interests, and activities.

At the start of the year, you might have students prepare the bulletin boards as a means to show something personal. Throughout the year, the room could be decorated with samples of student work. You should feel comfortable about bringing some personal articles to the classroom to personalize the setting, such as photographs of friends and family, posters, paperweights, crafts, or trinkets.

In an effort to provide symbolic identification to personalize the classroom, you could do the following:

- Display objects that give information about the students (e.g., photographs, work samples, projects).
- Display objects that communicate something personally about yourself (e.g., photographs, trinkets, paperweights).

Task Instrumentality

Task instrumentality deals with the way the physical environment can help teachers and students carry out tasks and activities. Your students may work independently, in pairs, or in groups; the physical arrangements may help or hinder the work. Students may need to obtain supplies from various locations in the room; the storage area and the traffic patterns created thus affect this task. Students may need to be in certain areas, and this will affect the task. To complete the task, students will need to see the teacher and the presentation. These are examples of the effects of the physical environment.

Taking the task instrumentality into consideration, you could do the following (Weinstein & Mignano, (1993):

- Make sure frequently used materials are accessible.
- Make sure students know where things belong.
- Plan pathways to avoid congestion and distraction.
- Arrange seats for a clear view of presentations.
- Offer students a personal space in which to keep belongings.
- Situate your desk in an appropriate place (positioning it off to the side helps to ensure that you will circulate).
- Separate incompatible activities (e.g., noisy-quiet, messy-neat, and wet-dry).

Providing Pleasure

Another function of the setting is to provide pleasure, and making the classroom attractive is an important means toward this end. In reviewing studies on environmental attractiveness, Weinstein and Mignano (1993) noted that students who were in classrooms that they found attractive had a tendency to be more persistent on tasks, had better attendance and sense of group cohesiveness, and participated actively in class discussions.

People respond positively to variation in the environment (Olds, 1987). A classroom could include both warm and cool colors, open spaces and small private areas, hard and soft surfaces, and various textures. There should be moderate variation; too little may not be very stimulating, while too much may produce feelings of anxiety and disorder.

In order to implement these issues about providing pleasure, you can do the following:

- Use a moderate variety of warm and cool colors in the classroom.
- Use a moderate variety of textures, ranging from smooth to rough.
- Provide for a variety of spaces (e.g., open, private, formal, and informal).
- Provide a variety of surfaces, ranging from hard to soft.

Stimulating Growth

The classroom can be arranged to stimulate students' growth, especially in the cognitive area. Classrooms are often arranged to allow for teacher-directed instruction, seatwork, and some small group work. At the same time, the setting should invite children to explore, observe, test, and discover (Weinstein & Mignano, 1993).

An *open-closed continuum* could be used to categorize the materials you provide, with one end representing open-type materials that lead to many possible answers and the other end representing closed-type materials that lead to only one possible answer. One way to encourage growth is to make available materials that promote student exploration. The open-closed continuum can comprise both closed materials—puzzles and workbooks leading to one correct answer, and open materials—art materials or creative writing leading to many possible acceptable answers (Jones & Prescott, 1978).

Space also needs to be provided for students to work with these materials. Students may work at their desks, while tables, carpeted reading areas, or other locations could be arranged for their use.

Library books, computer programs, and other instructional materials could be displayed to invite the students to read, explore, and discover. Provisions need to be made in the schedule to allow students to observe the materials, select what they would like to use, and then use the materials at an appropriate location.

Taking these growth factors into account, you can do the following when arranging the physical setting:

- Provide materials that enable a range of closed (one answer) to open (many possible answers) responses.
- Display library books, computer programs, and other instructional materials for students to use.
- Make provisions in the schedule to allow students to look at, select, and use the invitational materials.

Decision Points

To promote growth, you should set up the physical environment to invite students to read, observe, and explore. Many materials can be made available and the schedule can be arranged for these activities. What could you do to achieve these purposes? In making your selections, how might you address the diversity of students?

FACTORS TO BE CONSIDERED IN ROOM ARRANGEMENT

Decisions about room arrangement must be made before students arrive on the first day, yet changes can be made throughout the year. A good arrangement can help you cope with the complex demands of teaching by minimizing interruptions, delays, and "dead" times while maintaining a comfortable environment. You should first consider the following factors, taking into account how the six functions of the classroom setting can be achieved.

1. *Fixed features.* Doors, windows, closets, electrical outlets, and lab tables are examples of features that are fixed and immovable. The permanency needs to be taken into account as the location of other, movable items is determined.

2. *Instructional materials and supplies.* Resource books, display models, handouts, maps, and other things you need should be readily accessible. Some supplies are stored in the classroom, including items such as manipulatives, art supplies, and resource books. Since students pick up these supplies from the storage area, they should be stored in a convenient location. Easy access and efficient storage mean that activities are more likely to begin and end promptly, and time spent on getting ready and cleaning up is minimized.

3. *Traffic areas.* Keep high traffic areas free of congestion. High traffic areas include the space around doorways, the pencil sharpener and trash can, group work areas, book shelves and supply areas, your desk, and student desks. These areas should be well separated from each other, spacious, and easily accessible. For example, try not to seat a student next to the pencil sharpener, because of the traffic and the possibility for distraction.

4. *Study areas.* A study area is sometimes available for an individual student or a small group of students to have a quiet place to study or work on a project. The area should be private and quiet and away from the traffic lanes. A corner of the classroom is a favored spot.

5. *Activity areas.* In this area students work on topics related to the academic program. Computers may be available here. Learning centers may be included in an activity area, where students may work individually or in small groups.

6. *Creating activity boundaries.* If several work areas are part of a classroom, you need to create boundaries to separate one from another. An area where a computer is located for use by an individual student, for example, could

Teachers in Action

Storing and Distributing Supplies

Eric Stiffler, seventh-grade middle school science teacher, Wichita, Kansas:

I like to organize my science classes into 10 groups, partly because I have 10 large desks in my room. One work group for each table works very well. I assign each group a number (1 to 10), and each group has a tray of materials which includes scissors, beakers, graduated cylinders, and rulers. I label each tray and each item in the tray with the number of the group.

When we get ready to do an activity, one student from each group goes to get the tray which holds their materials. No time is wasted explaining where the materials are. At the end of the class period, the students replace the items. I assign one student to check the trays and make sure that everything has been returned. This system has eliminated theft problems and has saved a great deal of time.

be separated from the students' desks by a divider, such as a filing cabinet or a bookcase. Areas for small group work or independent work should be separated from the area for large group instruction. The boundaries should not limit your ability to monitor the students in the work area.

7. *Visibility.* Two aspects of visibility should be considered as you arrange the physical environment. First, be sure that you can easily see students, to identify when a student needs assistance or to prevent task avoidance or disruption. Maintain clear lines of sight between work areas and areas that you will frequent.

Second, be certain students can easily see the presentations and displays. All students should be able to see the chalkboard or overhead projector screen without moving their chairs, turning their desks around, or twisting their necks. Locate the primary instructional area prominently to help students pay attention and to facilitate instruction.

8. *Purposes of seating arrangements.* The arrangement of student desks provides a framework for teacher-student interaction and student behavior (Rosenfield, Lambert, & Black, 1985). The arrangement will vary depending on the teaching method, the interaction pattern, the characteristics of the learners, and the teacher's ability to maintain control. Several possible seating arrangements are shown in Figure 5-1.

The three most common seating patterns are rows (A–C in Figure 5-1), clusters of desks (D–F), and circular (G) or semicircular (H) patterns. The purposes of seating arrangements must first be considered to suit lesson objectives. Since the purposes of the lesson objectives may vary, it may be necessary to adjust the seating pattern based on the objectives. For some purposes, you may want to direct the lesson, allow only limited student input or interaction, and promote independent work. In such a case, rows of desks (A–C) would be quite suitable.

For other lessons, you might want to promote discussion among all students, and a circular (G) or semicircular (H) arrangement that enables the students to see each other would promote this interaction. Rosenfield, Lambert, and Black (1985) reported that students in brainstorming activity who were seated in circles were far more involved than students seated in rows or clusters. Whole-group meetings are facilitated with circular or semicircular seating arrangements.

You might want high participation in discussion or on a project but with a limited number of students under a more ordered, less spontaneous environment. In this case, clusters of two to six student desks (D–E) would serve these purposes. Weinstein (1979) reported that organizing desks so that only two or three students could interact led to higher on-task behavior, less off-task movement, and less loud talking. Cooperative learning activities, for example, would be facilitated with clusters of desks.

Student self-control also needs to be considered. Some students have sufficient self-control to resist the temptation to socialize at inappropriate times, and can overcome distractions from those seated nearby. These students could be seated in clusters or close to other students. Some students, however, may lack this self-control and should be placed in rows so as to limit potential interactions and disruptions. Changes in the seating pattern can occur as students mature and gain the self-control necessary in clusters or circles.

Experienced teachers sometimes begin the year by having the seats arranged in rows because this makes it easier to maintain control. After control has been established and you are more confident about the students' self-control, clusters, semicircles, circles, or other nontraditional seating arrangements could be used. Based on their experience in managing students, some teachers may begin the year with an arrangement of desks in clusters to facilitate cooperative learning from the very start.

9. *Flexibility.* Instructional needs change, and teachers often need to make adjustments. Sometimes teacher-directed instruction is planned, while independent or group work is carried out at other times. You may need to change the arrangement to meet these purposes. The classroom design should be flexible enough to be easily modified for different activities and student groupings.

10. *Action zone.* As mentioned earlier, the action zone is the area where teachers interact more fully with students. In a classroom with rows, the action zone includes students in the center of the room (primarily in the middle row) and students in the front of the room (Adams & Biddle, 1970). There is likely an action zone in other seating arrangements, as well. The key issue is that interaction between you and students is affected by the seating arrangement. You need to be sensitive to the action zone that you may create with your arrangement. You should make efforts to give attention to *all* students without regard to the seating arrangement.

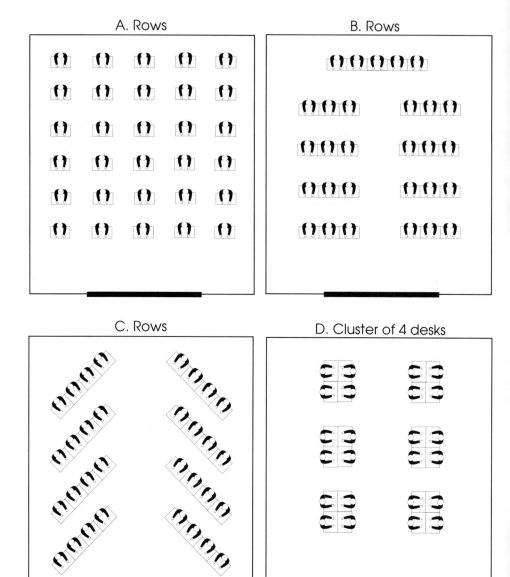

FIGURE 5-1 Possible seating arrangements

E. Clusters of 6 desks

F. Clusters of 12 desks

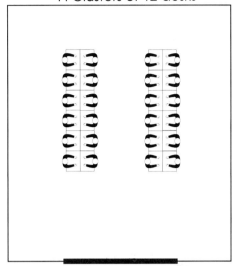

G. Circle

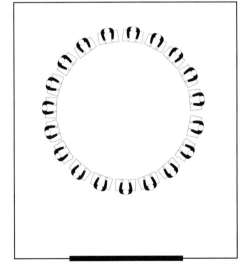

H. Semicircle

FIGURE 5-1 (*continued*)

Teachers in Action

Seating Arrangements

Sanford Morris, high school biology teacher, Buffalo, New York:

My science room has a standard 8-foot lab demonstration table at the front. I rarely use the demonstration table and find it a barrier to being with the class. I have placed another table on the other side of the demo table toward the class. The table is large enough for the overhead projector, transparency storage, and room for me to sit or stand as I use the overhead or conduct discussions.

I have arranged the students' desks in a "U" with the open part of the "U" facing the front. All seats face the center of the "U." Even with a class size of about 30, I can easily walk down the middle of the "U" and reach any student. From my position in front, I have eye contact with every student and none can hide behind another. This seating arrangement encourages active participation and diminishes behavior problems. It facilitates my style of asking questions of students and developing a dialog.

11. *Teacher proximity.* Students tend to stay on-task when the teacher is nearby, and this increases learning time. When deciding about the physical design of the classroom, you need to consider how you will be able to be close to all students during a lesson. For teacher-directed lessons, a seating arrangement that permits close contact with as many students as possible might be considered. For small group or independent work, you may choose to walk around the room, and thus the specific layout may not be of much concern as long as there is room for easy movement.

12. *Teacher's work space.* Depending on the subject area and your preferences, you may need a space to prepare materials or to conduct a presentation or demonstration. A work or display area may be needed in a lesson for art, science, home economics, and other subjects.

13. *Environmental conditions and ambience.* Lighting, noise, ventilation, and heating can affect behavior; you can adjust these to create an appropriate physical environment. For instance, light intensity can be controlled. Dim lighting during classwork, a flickering ceiling light, or inadequate darkening of the room for viewing movies or filmstrips causes unnecessary frustration, lack of interest, and off-task behavior (Levin & Nolan, 1991). There may be noise in the hallway, and you may close the door. When the room becomes stuffy, a window could be opened. When it is too hot or cold in the room, adjustments could be made.

These conditions contribute to the ambience. ***Ambience*** refers to the environment of a place, and is made up of orderliness, light, sound, texture, color, temperature, and odor (Savage, 1991). The elements can be combined in

Teachers in Action

Building Room Ownership

Nancy Fusaro, first-grade teacher, Topeka, Kansas:

At the beginning of the year, my students and I work together to organize the classroom and materials. I make sure that the space is clean and the materials are in containers that will be used for storage throughout the year. The students basically begin the year in an empty classroom. The bulletin boards and shelves are left empty so that we can fill them together. I explain the different uses of the materials and then they decide on the best place to store them. The bulletin boards are left empty until I have student work to display.

Giving the students the responsibility for organizing the classroom from the beginning has helped them develop ownership of the classroom. It also frees me at the beginning of the year to take care of planning. The class-room becomes ours from the beginning, not just mine. I am able to send my students the message that their ideas are valued and that we will be working together as a team.

Dana Clark, high school English teacher, Irving, Texas:

Wall space adds to the atmosphere of the classroom. I use all of my wall space to display my students' work. At times, we even staple poetry projects onto the ceiling. Displaying student work makes the students feel a sense of pride. They feel proud to see their work displayed, and it also adds warmth and color to the room. I also do not need to buy posters.

I have the walls sectioned based on the units of literature that are to be taught throughout the year. In the middle of the back wall is a 4-foot by 6-foot bulletin board that I cover entirely with photographs of my students participating in activities throughout the year. The students love this bulletin board because they love to see themselves and their classmates. I have had many students comment to me about how much they like my room because it is so colorful, and they feel as if it is "their" room, not simply the teacher's room.

ways that are pleasant to create feelings of warmth, comfort, and security. Room decorations can contribute to these feelings.

14. *Students with disabilities.* Students with disabilities need to be taken into account when arranging for the physical design of a classroom. A student in a wheelchair, for instance, will need sufficient aisle space to move around the classroom. A student with a hearing impairment might need to be seated

close to you with an unobstructed view, and space might need to be provided for an interpreter. A special education teacher is a good source of information for suggestions on how to arrange the physical environment to accommodate the needs of students with disabilities.

Decision Points

Students with disabilities are frequently "mainstreamed." What adjustments in the physical environment might you make for a child with a mild learning disability to enable easy access to the student when assistance is needed? How could you design the seating arrangement to promote assistance by other students?

PHYSICAL ARRANGEMENT OF THE CLASSROOM

After considering the functions of the classroom setting and the factors involved in room arrangement, you can determine the physical arrangement. Floor space, storage space, bulletin boards, wall space, and environmental conditions need to be addressed.

Floor Space

A classroom typically contains many objects such as student desks, the teacher's desk, bookcases, tables, and activity centers that take up floor space. When determining how to arrange the classroom, you need to consider the functions of the space and the factors mentioned earlier, to facilitate learning and to minimize interruptions and delays. Visiting other teachers' classrooms can suggest ideas for effective ways to arrange the floor space in your classroom.

A good starting point in planning the floor plan is to decide where you will conduct whole-group instruction. Examine the room and identify where you will stand or work when you address the entire class to conduct lessons or to give directions. This area should include a chalkboard, an overhead projector screen, a table for the overhead projector, a small table to hold items needed during instruction, and an electrical outlet. Consider the following items:

• *Student desks.* Even if other arrangements are to be used later in the year, you might start the year with student desks in rows facing the main instructional area since it is easier to manage students with this pattern. Be sure all students can see this instructional area without having their backs to it and without having to get out of their seats.

Keep student desks away from high traffic areas. Avoid placing their desks near the door, pencil sharpener, trash can, and supply areas. Leave ample aisles between the desks to enable easy movement of students and yourself when monitoring seatwork.

• *The teacher's desk.* Your desk should be situated so that you can see the students, but it is not essential that the desk be at the front of the room. Placement at the rear of the room may, in fact, help when you monitor students during independent work. Students facing away from you cannot discern when you are looking at them unless they turn around. They often assume their behavior is being closely monitored. This tends to encourage them to stay at their assigned tasks. Instead of sitting at the desk during independent work, many teachers move around the room to monitor and assist students.

If you plan to work with individual students at your desk, you need to consider traffic patterns to and from the desk. Student desks should not be so close to yours that the student will be distracted by other students approaching your desk or working with you there.

• *Bookcases and filing cabinets.* These should be placed so students' visibility of chalkboards or relevant displays is not obstructed. They should not prevent your monitoring. If a bookcase contains frequently used articles such as resource books, dictionaries, or supplies, it should be conveniently located and monitored. If it contains seldom-used items, an out-of-the-way place is best. If there is only one bookcase, it is helpful to restrict it to frequently used items.

• *Activity centers or work areas.* An **activity center** is an area where one or more students come to work on a special activity. It may be in the form of a learning center or a computer work area. One or more tables commonly serve as the work surfaces. When you select the placement of tables for this area, be sure that you can see all students in the work area, keep traffic lanes clear, and avoid congested areas. A center often will have special equipment such as tape recorders with headphones, a computer, a filmstrip projector, or other supplies. Enough table and work space must be provided for students to work efficiently. It is useful to place the work area at the side or the back of the room and to the backs of other students.

Storage Space

Teachers and students use numerous instructional materials. Not all of them are used every day and they must be stored when not in use. Storage space must be provided for textbooks and resource books, frequently used instructional materials, teacher's supplies and instructional materials, equipment, and infrequently used materials.

1. *Textbooks and resource books.* Some textbooks are not retained by students, and thus must be stored in the classroom for easy access. Resource books obtained from the school library, public library, or other sources may be available for student use. All of these books should be stored in a bookcase that enables easy access.

2. *Instructional materials.* Instructional materials will vary with the subject area that you teach. These may include rulers, scissors, special paper, pencils, staplers, tape, glue, and other supplies. Students may be expected to provide some of these supplies (and would keep them in their desks or bring them to

---

Teachers in Action

Bulletin Boards

Patti Grossman, middle school language arts and social studies teacher, Phoenix, Arizona:

For many years, I thought that the way to start the year off was to have the room totally decorated for the students; every bulletin board was perfectly done and beckoning. However, in the last few years I took a new approach.

In my classroom, there are four small bulletin boards. On one of them, I place school information such as the calendar, bell schedule, and school buttons. I dedicate each of the other three bulletin boards to the three groups of students I teach; I have each group for both language arts and social studies. On each bulletin board, I place a different color backing, a border, and a banner for that class.

On the first day of school in my language arts class, I hand out magazines, scissors, and glue. Each student is instructed to find a picture or two that represents something personal, cut it out, and glue it to the bulletin board like a collage. This gets them focusing on themselves and talking with others in the class. The nervousness of the opening day disappears, rapport develops, and the comfort level and ownership in the class begins to grow. They begin to feel that it is their room as well as mine. The collages remain all year, but papers, team charts, student work, and so on go on top of the pictures.

---

class). As with textbooks and resource books, a storage location should be selected to enable easy access to the materials. Clearly labeled containers for each of the supply items are very helpful in maintaining an orderly supply area. These materials may be stored on shelves of a bookcase or cabinet, or on a counter.

3. *Teacher supplies.* Supplies that only you will use should be kept in your desk or in storage areas used only by you. These supplies include items such as hall passes, attendance and lunch count forms, ditto masters, computer disks, computer programs, lesson plan book, tablets, file folders, and chalk. These items should be stored securely so students don't have access to them.

4. *Equipment.* Items like an overhead projector, tape recorders, computers, or other instructional media may not be used every day. These items must be stored when not in use.

5. *Infrequently used items.* Some instructional materials are used only once during the year. These include seasonal decorations (e.g., Halloween, Thanksgiving), bulletin board displays, or special project materials. Certain materials may be used for only one unit, as in the case of a model of the human eye for a science

class. Some teachers prefer to keep seasonal decorations or other infrequently used materials at their homes.

Bulletin Boards and Wall Space

Constructive use of bulletin boards and wall space can contribute to a positive environment. This can be achieved by the display of relevant material, assignments, rules, schedules, student work, and so on. Many teachers involve students in the selection of content and the preparation of bulletin boards and the use of wall space. One approach is to select a different group of students to plan and prepare a bulletin board each month.

Some teachers dedicate a certain purpose for each bulletin board. For example, one bulletin board could be used to post classroom rules, a daily or weekly schedule, classroom helpers, lunch menus, a school map, emergency information, or other information. Another bulletin board could be used to display student work. A third board could be simply for decoration, with seasonal, motivational, or artistic items. Other boards can be used to post information and news articles about school or community events. Bulletin boards might display content-related news articles, posters, or information.

Some of this material, such as a listing of classroom rules, can be displayed on wall posters if the content will not be likely to change during the year. On the other hand, designated areas of the chalkboard can display student assignments or special announcements because this information is likely to change daily.

ENVIRONMENTAL CONDITIONS

As mentioned earlier, lighting, noise, ventilation, and heating can affect behavior, and you can make adjustments to these to create an appropriate physical environment. These environmental conditions contribute to the ambience. You and your students need to feel comfortable.

One way to provide for a comfortable environment is to soften it and make it more friendly through decorations on the walls, live plants, carpeting in selected areas, and flexible lighting for certain areas. This is an opportunity to bring in items of personal interest, whether they be content-related or not. For instance, a teacher who is a hot air balloon enthusiast may display posters, pins, and models of hot air balloons.

Decision Points

Physical factors such as decorations, orderliness, lighting, noise, ventilation, and heating can contribute to the ambience of a classroom. What could you do in your classroom to make it feel like a good place to be? How could you take into account the diversity of students as you create this ambience?

By keeping the classroom clean and orderly, you also send a signal to the students that the environment is important and that it should be kept in good order. At the start of the year, you might examine how flexible lighting could be provided, if only with a table lamp in a study area. Ways to minimize disruptive sound should be considered, whether it be simply closing the classroom door or adding some carpeting or other fabric on the walls to deaden echoes.

Arrangements should be made to ensure a comfortable temperature along with good ventilation and fresh air. Sometimes, a window can be opened, and there needs to be aisle space by the window to provide access. Collectively, these environmental conditions contribute to the ambience and comfortable feelings that should be provided.

MAJOR CONCEPTS

1. The organization of the classroom influences learner perceptions of their place in the classroom, the type of activities that will be appropriate, and how they are expected to behave.
2. Physical settings serve six basic functions: security and shelter, social contact, symbolic identification, task instrumentality, pleasure, and growth.
3. When deciding how to arrange the physical environment, teachers should consider factors such as fixed features, instructional materials and supplies, traffic areas, work areas, activity boundaries, visibility, purposes of seating arrangements, flexibility, the action zone, teacher proximity, environmental conditions and ambience, and students with disabilities.
4. When deciding how to arrange the floor space, teachers need to consider the functions of the space and the various factors mentioned earlier in an effort to facilitate learning and to minimize interruptions and delays.
5. The floor space of a classroom includes student desks, the teacher's desk, bookcases, filing cabinets, tables, and activity centers.
6. Instructional materials not used every day must be stored when not in use. Storage space must be provided for textbooks and resource books, frequently used instructional materials, teacher's supplies and instructional materials, equipment, and infrequently used materials.
7. Constructive use of bulletin boards and wall space can contribute to a positive environment. This can be achieved by displaying relevant instructional material, assignments, rules, schedules, student work, and other items of interest.
8. Teachers can adjust lighting, noise, ventilation, and heating to create an appropriate physical environment. These environmental conditions contribute to the classroom ambience.

DISCUSSION QUESTIONS

1. Are some of the functions of the classroom setting more important than others? Which ones? Why?
2. What are the merits and disadvantages for placing students' seats in rows?
3. What are some factors that a teacher might take into account when deciding where to place the teacher's desk?

4. From your classroom experience, do you think there is such a thing as an action zone where the teacher gives more attention? How might the classroom environment affect this factor?
5. What are the reasons for and against having students take some responsibility for preparing certain bulletin boards?
6. In reflecting on your own schooling, what were the characteristics of classrooms that had a positive ambience?

SUPPLEMENTAL ACTIVITIES

For Clinical Settings

1. Draw a floor plan for your classroom that takes into account the issues covered in this chapter.
2. Make a list of the types of instruction or activities that you would use for each of the following types of seating arrangements: rows, paired desks, clusters of desks, a semicircle, a circle of desks, tables.
3. List the things you could do in a classroom that would contribute to positive ambience.

For Field Settings

1. Examine several classrooms and consider ways that each classroom addresses each of the functions of the classroom setting covered in this chapter.
2. Talk with several teachers about their experiences with various types of seating arrangements. Were certain types of instructional activities or instructional approaches more appropriate or effective with a certain type of seating arrangement?
3. Ask several teachers about room arrangement factors such as traffic areas, work areas, visibility, environmental conditions, and students with disabilities.

KEY TERMS

Action zone	Physical security
Activity center	Psychological security
Ambience	Symbolic identification
Environmental competence	Task instrumentality
Open-closed continuum	

RECOMMENDED READINGS

Weinstein, C. S., & Mignano, A. J. (1993). *Elementary Classroom Management: Lessons from Research and Practice.* New York: McGraw-Hill.
   Chapter 3 covers designing the physical environment. Discussion centers on six functions of the classroom setting, with specific recommendations to achieve these functions. The teacher is viewed as an environmental designer.

REFERENCES

Adams, R. S., & Biddle, B. J. (1970). *Realities of Teaching.* New York: Holt, Rinehart & Winston.

Bennett, N., & Blundell, D. (1983). Quantity and quality of work in rows and classroom groups. *Educational Psychology, 3,* 93–105.

Jones, E., & Prescott, E. (1978). *Dimensions of Teaching Learning Environments.* Pasadena, CA: Pacific Oaks College.

Levin, J., & Nolan, J. F. (1991). *Principles of Classroom Management: A Hierarchical Approach.* Englewood Cliffs, NJ: Prentice Hall.

Olds, A. R. (1987). Designing settings for infants and toddlers. In C. S. Weinstein & T. G. David, Eds., *Spaces for Children* (pp. 117–138). New York: Plenum.

Proshansky, E., & Wolfe, M. (1974). The physical setting and open education. *School Review, 82,* 557–574.

Rosenfield, P., Lambert, N., & Black, A. (1985). Desk arrangement effects on pupil classroom behavior. *Journal of Educational Research, 77*(1), 101–108.

Savage, T. V. (1991). *Discipline for Self-control.* Englewood Cliffs, NJ: Prentice Hall.

Steele, F. I. (1973). *Physical Settings and Organization Development.* Reading, MA: Addison-Wesley.

Weinstein, C. S. (1979). The physical environment of the school: A review of the research. *Review of Educational Research, 49*(4), 577–610.

Weinstein, C. S., & David, T. G. (Eds.). (1987). *Spaces for Children.* New York: Plenum.

Weinstein, C. S. & Mignano, A. J. (1993). *Elementary Classroom Management: Lessons from Research and Practice.* New York: McGraw-Hill.

Wheldall, K., Morris, M., Vaughan, P., & Ng, Y. (1981). Rows versus tables: An example of the use of behavioral ecology in two classes of eleven-year old children. *Educational Psychology, 1*(2), 171–184.

chapter 6

Selecting and Teaching
Rules and Procedures

Objectives

This chapter provides information that will help you:

1. Examine the need for classroom rules.
2. Identify guidelines for selecting rules and procedures.
3. Identify ways to teach and review the rules.
4. Examine the need for classroom procedures.
5. Identify guidelines for ways to select, teach, and review procedures.

Think about all the traffic laws that govern the use of motor vehicles. Guidelines are established for ways to signal, turn, yield the right of way, pass other vehicles, and numerous other aspects of driving. These laws have been enacted in every state to ensure the safety of drivers and others. Guidelines are also needed in the classroom to govern how the teacher and the students conduct themselves so that the learning objectives are achieved and everyone is successful.

Rules and procedures guide and govern student behavior. You need to carefully consider what rules and procedures are needed to effectively manage the class. They should then be taught to the students and reviewed regularly.

RULES IN THE CLASSROOM

Rules are general behavioral standards or expectations that are to be followed. They comprise a code of conduct intended to regulate individual behavior in an attempt to avoid disruptive behavior. Rules guide the way students interact

107

with each other, prepare for class, and conduct themselves during class. They are stated in positive terms. In addition to general rules, some rules may apply to specific situations (e.g., gum chewing is not allowed).

The effective use of rules involves several actions. You should examine the need for certain rules, select appropriate ones, select the consequences, teach the rules to the students, obtain student commitment to them, and periodically review the rules.

Examine the Need for Rules

Teaching and learning involve complex interactions under many conditions. Learning activities and student involvement vary considerably, and rules of conduct can be used to govern student actions. Rules provide guidelines for appropriate behaviors so that teaching and learning can take place. Rules should be directed at organizing the learning environment to ensure the continuity and quality of teaching and learning, and not simply be focused on exerting control over students (Brophy, 1988).

Rules need to be realistic, fair, and reasonable. They should meet the following purposes: (a) the teacher's right to teach is protected; (b) the students' rights to learning are protected; (c) the students' psychological and physical safety are protected; and (d) property is protected (Levin & Nolan, 1991).

When considering rules, you need to examine the way you teach and the environment you would like to maintain. Factors to be considered include your educational philosophy, the age and maturity of the students, school rules and expectations, the climate to be developed, and the rationale for a particular rule.

Select the Rules

After considering the need for rules, you are ready to select those that are appropriate for your classroom. Sample rules include: (a) follow the teacher's directions; (b) obey all school rules; (c) speak politely to all people; and (d) keep your hands, feet, and objects to yourself. These rules are probably appropriate for all grade levels (K-12).

Because of differences in student maturity and developmental levels, certain rules may be needed for certain grade levels. For example, students in the primary grades (K-3) often need direct guidance on many matters. Some additional rules that would be appropriate for these grades may include: (a) follow directions the first time they are given; (b) raise your hand and wait to be called on; (c) stay in your seat unless you have permission to stand; (d) do not leave the room without permission.

Some rules about materials and starting class are often instituted for departmentalized settings and grade levels. For example, rules might include: (a) bring all needed materials to class, and (b) be in your seat and ready to work when the bell rings at the start of the period.

Below are listed guidelines to consider when selecting rules.

Teachers in Action

Model What You Want from Students

Sherry Bryant, middle school social studies teacher, Rochester, New Hampshire:

It took me years to realize that I was a model for my students. You don't need rules as much as you need to be a model of what you want and expect. If you want students to be kind, then model kindness. If you want students to do their homework, expect them to do it, but also do yours. If you want them to listen, then listen to them. To show that learning is fun, share your learning with them. Decide how you want your classroom to be, and then teach and model in the same way.

Be honest, share yourself, have self-confidence, smile, make mistakes and learn from them. Know that you make a difference. Always greet your students as they enter the classroom and be at the door as they leave to say goodbye or to give an encouraging word.

1. *Make classroom rules consistent with school rules.* Before you identify classroom rules, you must become familiar with school rules and recognize your responsibilities to them (Boostrom, 1991). For instance, school rules may identify behaviors that are specifically forbidden (e.g., no running in the halls), or specifically required (e.g., a student needs a hall pass when out of the classroom during class time).

2. *Involve students in making the rules to the degree that you are comfortable and to the degree that the students' age level and sophistication permit.* Among other things, student involvement in selecting rules will be affected by your philosophical perspective. Many teachers do not provide for student choice in rule setting; they may clearly present the rules and discuss the rationale for them. Other teachers find that students feel greater commitment and are more likely to adhere to the rules if they help formulate the rules and consequences. You can be an effective manager whether or not you involve students in identifying rules.

If students are involved in identifying rules, you can exert different degrees of direction during discussion about them. You may begin with a general discussion of rules of everyday life. Rich discussions can be prompted by questions such as: What is the purpose of traffic lights? Why do people need to pass a written test about traffic laws and a driving test to obtain a driver's license? Why were rules established for sports such as basketball and football? What would a basketball game be like without rules?

This can be followed by a guided discussion about appropriate rules to guide students' actions. Since students may not identify all areas that you consider

Teachers in Action

Involving Students in Selecting Rules

Tracy Douglass, third- and fourth-grade teacher, Phillips, Maine:

At the start of the year, I allow from one to three days to pass *without* establishing rules. During this time a chart is placed on an easel where students can list problems and incidents that (a) they have been involved in, (b) they observed but weren't involved in, or (c) they think might happen. They can write these items either before or after school or during recess. I might also add an item to the list.

After one to three days, we sit in a circle and have a discussion about how these incidents affect our ability to learn. From this discussion, we develop a list of things we need to be able to learn. An example might be, "We need to be able to hear the person who is speaking." These statements can then be reduced and reframed as rules. This process leads to positively stated rules. The need mentioned here might result in a rule such as, "Look at and listen to the person who is speaking." I try to have no more than four or five rules or procedure statements.

I always include some role playing in this discussion because the students then better understand what constitutes appropriate and inappropriate behavior. Our list is then printed on chart paper and posted in a conspicuous place. During the next two weeks, we refer to the chart at the start of each day, then review it from time to time.

important, you may need to prompt the discussion. Teachers often guide students into identifying about five rules as a means to focus on important behavior. The degree of formality as to managing acceptance of the rules varies; you may want the class to vote on the list or you may prefer to handle approval by consensus.

3. *Identify appropriate behaviors and translate them into positively stated classroom rules.* Since rules are a general code of conduct, they should focus on the conduct desired. Students respond better when the rule is stated in a way that expresses the desired behavior. To the extent possible, try to state rules positively. Instead of "no fighting," state the rule as, "Keep your hands and feet to yourself." Instead of "no teasing, swearing, or yelling," state the rule as, "Speak politely to all people."

4. *Focus on important behavior.* When identifying appropriate student behavior, you could make a list of student actions for various settings. Rules should focus on important behavior that meets one of the purposes mentioned earlier. If you had a rule for every type of behavior, major and minor, you would have a very extensive list. Rules should focus only on important behavior.

5. *Keep the number of rules to a minimum (four to six).* By focusing on important behavior, the number of rules can be limited. Four to six rules is a good number for important behaviors. The rules can be written in broad enough language that they encompass related behaviors. For example, the rule, "Follow the teacher's directions" covers important behavior and is broad enough to deal with a number of circumstances. By selecting rules with that degree of generality, the number can be limited to between four and six.

6. *Keep the wording of each rule simple and short.* A rule that has several conditions and qualifiers in its wording may be confusing. It is better to keep the wording simple and short so the meaning is clear and recognizable.

7. *Have rules address behaviors that can be observed.* Sometimes rules focus on an attitude, such as, "Be kind to others." What constitutes being kind is open to many interpretations. A certain action might be viewed by one student as being unkind, whereas another student might not see it that way. To avoid problems of this nature, it is preferable that the rule address behaviors that can be observed. In this way, the behavior did or did not occur, and there is no gray area of interpretation.

8. *Identify rewards when students follow the rules and consequences when students break them.* Students need to know what will happen if they break the rules. They may then choose to follow the rule rather than incur the consequence. If a student chooses to break the rule, then that student chooses the consequence.

Students also need to know what good things will happen if they follow the rules. Rewards and incentives should be established to influence students to follow the rules (more about encouraging and reinforcing appropriate behavior in chapter 12).

Decision Points

Many teachers have about five classroom rules that apply to general behavior standards. If you were teaching in an eighth-grade social studies class, what rules would you select for your classroom that would reflect your teaching style and educational philosophy? How might you need to alter these rules if you were using cooperative learning groups?

Select Rewards and Consequences

As previously mentioned, both rewards and penalties need to be identified relative to rules. Rewards may include reinforcers of a social nature, activities and privileges, tangible reinforcers, and token reinforcers (discussed more thoroughly in chapter 12). Students need to be told that these reinforcers will be delivered if they follow the rules.

Social reinforcers may take the form of written and verbal comments from the teacher, nonverbal facial or bodily expressions, and proximity. *Activities and privileges* can include being selected to be a classroom helper or having a

***

Teachers in Action

Rules and Consequences

Margaret Shields, high school mathematics teacher, Pittsburgh, Pennsylvania:

I select four rules that are stated positively, identifying what students are expected to do rather than what they shouldn't do. These rules are: (1) do not disrupt the learning of others, (2) be prompt, (3) be ready (physically and mentally), and (4) be seated. I emphatically state that students do not have the right to interfere with anyone else's learning.

Consequences are essential to the rules. They should be hierarchical and, more importantly, be matters that are under control of the teacher. For example, do not include a one-day suspension as a consequence if you do not have the authority to suspend students. My consequences are: (1) a warning, (2) detention after school, (3) a phone call to the student's home, (4) a referral to the office.

Don't make idle threats. Students know from others whether you really call their homes. Respect from students is essential in a well-managed classroom. Respect is earned, it is not automatic. Many inexperienced teachers demand respect before they have earned it. Be patient. If you are fair and consistent, respect will follow.

***

privilege such as playing a game, reading for pleasure, or working at the computer. *Tangible reinforcers* may be such articles as bookmarkers, certificates, or posters. *Token reinforcers,* such as points, stars, or tickets, can be "cashed" at a later time for a tangible reinforcer.

Students need to be told what consequences will be delivered if they choose to break a rule. When a student gets off-task, first provide situational assistance in an effort to get the student back to work. If the student stays off-task, deliver mild responses such as nonverbal and verbal actions. If that doesn't work, you can move to moderate responses (logical consequences and behavior modification), then implement severe responses (reprimands and overcorrection) if needed.

Teach and Review the Rules

The presentation and discussion of the rules are intended to help students understand them, recognize their related responsibilities, and build a commitment to follow them. Below are listed guidelines to follow for teaching and reviewing rules.

1. *Plan to discuss and teach the rules in the first session.* When making plans for the first day of school, include time to discuss the rules in the first session in which teachers meet the students. Students need to know the rules from the start.

Teachers in Action

Teaching the Rules

Laurie Stoltenhoff, fourth-grade teacher, Greenwich, Connecticut:

When we discuss the rules on the first day, I begin by describing a lunchroom with no rules (no assigned tables, no order to buying lunch, no requirement for disposing of garbage). Fourth graders are quick to surmise that lunch period would be chaotic. It may be fun for a while, but their lunch period would soon become an unpleasant experience.

I then carry this discussion into the classroom. We brainstorm why we need rules. What problems would we face? Students often say that everyone would talk at once, there would be little or no learning, and the room would sound like a gym. We then create a rule to avoid each possible negative outcome. We first list all possible rules and then restate the rules that are selected into positive statements.

Finally, I divide the class into groups of four or five and have them illustrate a rule of their choice. While they perform this task, I neatly write the rules on a poster, which is displayed throughout the year.

You should teach the rules as if they were subject matter content; this could include a handout, a transparency, discussion, practice, and even a quiz. Include an explanation of the rules, rehearsal, feedback, and repeat teaching (Evertson, 1985; Evertson, Emmer, Sanford, & Clements, 1983). If different rules apply for various activities (e.g., large-group work, small-group work, labs, independent work), these should also be clarified at this time.

2. *Discuss the need for rules.* It is important the students recognize the rationale for the rules because this can build understanding and commitment to them. If there is a sound rationale for a rule, students are more likely to follow and not challenge it. As mentioned earlier, this can begin as a general discussion about the need for rules in all aspects of life (e.g., for driving a car, for playing in a softball game). This discussion can then lead into the need for rules in the classroom to help teaching and learning.

3. *Identify specific expectations relevant to each rule; provide examples and emphasize the positive side of the rules.* Examples of specific behaviors that meet or break a rule should be identified. This will help clarify your expectations. Since the wording of the rules is often brief and somewhat general, this discussion allows you to clarify both acceptable and unacceptable behavior for each rule.

4. *Inform students of the consequences when rules are followed and also when they are broken.* Point out that you are helping them make good decisions about their behavior. When they make good decisions, positive results will follow. When they don't make good decisions, results will be negative. Appropriate

decisions are rewarded; inappropriate decisions are not. After discussing the general reasons for providing consequences, you should discuss the specific consequences that will be used.

5. *Verify understanding.* As in any subject matter lesson, student understanding of the rules and consequences must be verified. This may take the form of questions, a game format, or even a quiz. If there is evidence that students do not fully understand the rules and consequences, repeat teaching may be needed.

6. *Send a copy of your discipline policy home to parents and to the principal.* It is helpful to send a copy of the classroom rules and consequences to the parents. Include a sheet that the parents sign indicating they have read the policy and have reviewed it with their child. This helps develop understanding and commitment to the policy. This signed form should be returned to you. It is helpful to provide the principal with a copy of your policy.

7. *Post the rules in a prominent location.* The rules should be written on a poster and displayed in a prominent place, perhaps on a side wall where students will easily see them. This display is a constant reminder that the rules exist to guide behavior.

8. *Remind the class of the rules at times other than when someone has just broken a rule.* Rather than waiting for a rule to be broken, it is better to select a time when there have been no problems to remind them about the rules. It is helpful to anticipate potential problems and remind students of the rules before the problems occur.

Teachers in Action

Reviewing Rules before an Event

Mary Garland, sixth-grade teacher, Omaha, Nebraska:

Before going on a field trip, doing a special project, visiting with a guest speaker, or undertaking any new activity, I take time to review the rules and expectations. I call this a preteaching lesson, and it is a valuable preventive disciplinary strategy. It may take just a few minutes or perhaps an entire class period. I carefully prepare the lesson to review the rules and guidelines.

I identify expected learning outcomes and establish a set of rules and consequences for appropriate and responsible behavior. This gives the students an opportunity to learn about the event, practice the academic and social skills needed for the activity, and feel confident as they enter a new situation. This preteaching lesson helps me and the students avoid embarrassment by being well prepared for the activity and helps lead to more positive outcomes.

Teachers in Action

Getting a Commitment from Students

Sandra McClellan, third-grade teacher, High Point, North Carolina:

On the first day of school, my third graders and I discuss the rules that they think we need to have for the year. We develop a list of desired behaviors and then write rules along with consequences to reinforce those behaviors. We follow these rules for a week and then we amend them as needed. The list of rules and consequences is then signed by all class members and posted as our constitution. Next, the list is sent to the parents in a newsletter to be signed and returned. A copy is also given to the principal.

Claudia Swisher, high school English teacher, Norman, Oklahoma:

The students write their own rules using Steven Glenn's model for classroom meetings. I set up the activity by saying there are district and school policies we need to follow, we will have no more than five rules, and rules need to be stated positively. I tell the students that I might list certain behaviors as rules that are not open to student discussion. For example, I tell classes that we need a rule about language. The first class to come up with such a rule stated it as, "Use appropriate language, apologize for slips." I now recommend that one every year.

After setting these parameters, the students in each of my five classes brainstorm possible rules and then carefully word them in positive terms. I compile these top five rules from each of my classes, and the next day the students in each class vote again on the top five rules from this new list. The rules receiving the most votes from all classes are the ones that we use throughout the year.

This approach to rule setting has been very positive each year. Students who write the rules have ownership in them, police each other's behavior, and remind each other of the rules. They are proud to explain the rules to new students. I feel that my students' behavior is positive most of the time because they have participated in this process.

For example, before an activity takes place which requires students to move around the classroom, it is a good idea to remind them about the rule to "keep your hands and feet to yourselves." You alert them to the rule and the appropriate behavior, and this presumably will minimize poking and shoving during the activity.

9. *Review the rules regularly.* At all grade levels, it is important to review the rules frequently for several weeks at the start of the year. Daily review during

the first week, three times a week during the second week, and once a month thereafter is a good approach. In the first few weeks, it may be useful for the students to evaluate their behavior and consider whether improvement is needed. Periodic review throughout the school year is then appropriate, especially right after a holiday or after the winter or spring break.

Review rules with each new student who might transfer into the class after the start of the year. In that case, it is often helpful to talk to the new student yourself and also assign him or her to a student who knows and follows the rules to help explain them to the new student.

Obtain Commitments

After initially teaching the rules to the students, have them express their understanding of the rules and indicate their intention to follow them. While this can be done in several ways, one of the most effective is to have students sign a copy of the paper that lists the rules and includes a statement such as, "I am aware of these rules and understand them." Each student thus affirms understanding of the rules. You can keep these signed sheets. An extra copy could be given to students for placement in their desk or in a notebook. As discussed earlier, sending a copy of the discipline policy home to the parents is another means of obtaining commitment.

PROCEDURES IN THE CLASSROOM

Procedures are approved ways to achieve specific tasks. They are intended to help students accomplish a particular task, rather than serve as a general code of conduct, and to prevent inappropriate behavior as in the case of rules. Procedures may be identified to direct activities such as handing in completed work, sharpening a pencil, using the restroom, or putting away supplies.

Sometimes, the word *routines* is used synonymously with procedures. Routines serve as a means to establish and regulate activities and thus increase the predictability of the teaching environment (Yinger, 1979). Routines reinforce the similarity between student and teacher perceptions of classroom events (Rohrkemper, 1985).

Procedures and routines have several advantages (Leinhardt, Weidman, & Hammond, 1987; Yinger, 1979): They increase your shared understanding of an activity, reduce the complexity of the classroom environment to a predictable structure, and allow for efficient use of time.

Leinhardt, Weidman, and Hammond (1987) observed the behavior of effective classroom managers and categorized the routines they used into (a) *management routines*, including housekeeping tasks, moving the class to different parts of the school, and setting basic behavioral limits; (b) *support routines*, including conducting a lesson, distributing papers, breaking into groups; and (c) *exchange routines*, which deal with discussion between the teacher and students and discussion among students. Weinstein and Mignano (1993) label these as class-running routines, lesson-running routines, and interaction routines.

Teachers in Action

Procedures for the Transition from Hallway to Classroom

Terri Jenkins, middle school language arts teacher, Hephzibah, Georgia:

The transition time when students move from the hallway into the classroom is challenging because teachers typically need to be outside their classroom door to monitor the hallways as well as their classroom. A routine that engages students immediately upon entering the classroom is helpful.

When my students enter, they quickly move to their seats, take out paper and pencil, and attempt to correct a sentence that I have already written on the chalkboard. The sentence contains an error in grammar, capitalization, punctuation, or spelling. When they finish, the students are to fold their paper and hold it up. As I glance from my spot by the door, I appoint the first student who completes the task to collect papers as the others hold them up. Grading is simple; each correct response is worth one point.

This technique can be used in any classroom by simply modifying the task. In math, the initial task might be a logic problem or a word problem. In science or social studies, there might be a question about the reading assignment or a review question from yesterday's lesson.

This technique can accomplish several goals. First, it engages students as soon as they enter the room, thus obviating unnecessary talking and moving around. Second, students are all prepared for the class when they work on this task because the same materials needed in class are needed for the task. For example, if the lesson requires the student to have the textbook or a calculator ready, this initial activity can require the use of the textbook or calculator. Finally, the task forces student attention toward the content. This simple technique makes monitoring students more manageable while achieving other purposes.

The effective use of procedures encompasses several actions. You should examine the need for certain procedures, select the appropriate ones, then teach and review the procedures with the class.

Examine the Need for Procedures

As a first step, you must examine the need for procedures. What activities or actions would benefit from a procedure that would regularize student conduct in the performance of that action? To answer this key question, you might think about all of the actions that take place in the classroom and identify those that would benefit from having an associated procedure.

You do not need to start from scratch in doing this assessment; research studies of management in elementary and secondary classrooms have generated

TABLE 6-1 Areas to consider for classroom procedures

1. *Room Use Procedures*
   a. Teacher's desk and storage areas
   b. Student desks and storage for belongings
   c. Storage for class materials used by all students
   d. Pencil sharpener, wastebasket, sink, drinking fountain
   e. Bathroom
   f. Learning stations, computer areas, equipment areas, centers, and display areas

2. *Transitions in and out of the Classroom*
   a. Beginning the school day
   b. Leaving the room
   c. Returning to the room
   d. Ending the school day

3. *Out-of-room Procedures*
   a. Bathroom, drinking fountain
   b. Library, resource room
   c. School office
   d. Playground or school grounds
   e. Cafeteria
   f. Lockers
   g. Fire or disaster drills

4. *Procedures for Whole-Class Activities and Instruction, and Seatwork*
   a. Student participation
   b. Signals for student attention
   c. Talk among students
   d. Making assignments
   e. Distributing books, supplies, and materials
   f. Obtaining help
   g. Handing back assignments
   h. Tasks after work is completed
   i. Make-up work
   j. Out-of-seat procedures

5. *Procedures during Small Group Work*
   a. Getting the class ready
   b. Taking materials to groups
   c. Student movement in and out of groups
   d. Expected behavior in groups
   e. Expected behavior out of groups

6. *Other General Procedures for Secondary Classrooms*
   a. Beginning the class period
      (1) Attendance check
      (2) Previously absent students
      (3) Late students
      (4) Expected student behavior
   b. Out-of-room policies
   c. Materials and equipment
      (1) What to bring to class
      (2) Pencil sharpener

(continued)

TABLE 6-1 (*continued*)

    (3) Other room equipment
    (4) Student contact with teacher's desk, storage, and other materials
  d. Movement of student desks
  e. Split lunch period
  f. Ending the class period

7. *Other Procedures*
  a. Classroom helpers
  b. Behavior during delays or interruptions

a framework that can be used to examine and identify typical procedures. A number of specific areas that might need procedures are displayed in Table 6-1, some of which are adapted from Emmer et al. (1994), Evertson et al. (1994), Jones and Jones (1990), and Weinstein and Mignano (1993).

For example, you may follow approaches in which the students work independently, in pairs, in small groups, or in large groups. Students may be asked to work at their desks, at a table or a work station, at a lab table, and so on. You may need a different set of procedures in these work settings as compared to a teacher-directed setting. Talking with other students, for instance, may not be permitted in a teacher-directed lesson but may be encouraged in a work station setting where a small group of students are working together.

Select the Procedures

When examining the items presented in Table 6-1, you need to consider the unique circumstances in your classroom. The grade level, maturity of the students, your preference for order and regularity, and other factors may be taken into account when deciding the need for a procedure. It may be that you will select many items listed in the table since they involve standard actions.

After selecting the items, decide what each procedure will be. You could draw upon your own experiences. In making your decisions, you might recollect your own schooling experiences, your observations of other classrooms, your conversations with other teachers, and your own teaching experience.

Teach and Review the Procedures

Students shouldn't have to guess whether they need to raise their hands during class period or interpret subtle signals from you to determine what you want them to do. From the first day, teach and review the various procedures that are needed. Leinhardt, Weidman, and Hammond (1987) found that effective teachers spend more time during the first four days of school on management tasks than on academic tasks.

Several steps serve as guides when teaching and reviewing classroom procedures.

1. *Explain the procedure immediately prior to the first time the activity will take place.* Rather than explain procedures for many activities and actions on the first day, plan to space your explanation over the first several days. It is often useful to wait for a situation to arise that provides an opportunity to explain the procedure. Some procedures will likely be taught early, such as asking to go to the restroom, while others, such as where to go during a fire drill, could be taught a few days later or just prior to the event.

Some procedures may be sufficiently complex or critical, such as safety procedures for a laboratory or for student notebook requirements, that you should provide printed copies. Many procedures, however, are not written because students learn them rapidly. As with rules, it is important to clearly state the procedures, discuss the rationale for them, and provide opportunities for practice and feedback, where appropriate.

2. *Demonstrate the procedure.* After the explanation, you might demonstrate what you want the students to do. For example, you could demonstrate how they are expected to use the pencil sharpener or how to obtain extra supplies. This will show students what actions are expected of them.

3. *Practice and validate understanding.* After your explanation and demonstration, students could then be asked to practice the procedure. They might be asked to line up in the manner explained to proceed to the next class. In this way, students practice the procedure. It is also useful to ask them about the procedures to see whether they understand when and how the procedures need to be used.

Decision Points

Assume that students regularly need to use supplies from a supply table in your tenth-grade classroom during class. What procedures would you determine for students to pick up the materials at the start of class and drop them off at the end of class? What novel ways could you use to check for their understanding of these procedures?

---

4. *Give feedback.* As the students are practicing the procedure, observe carefully to determine whether they do it properly. If so, provide reinforcement. If there are problems, constructively point this out and indicate how the procedure should be done.

5. *Reteach as needed.* If a number of students have difficulty during practice, it may be necessary to reteach the procedure and perhaps explain it differently. It would then be useful to demonstrate the procedure once again and give the students another opportunity for practice.

6. *Review the procedures with the students prior to each situation for the first few weeks.* Rather than go through an activity and notice a student not following the procedure properly, it is better to remind students of the details of needed actions just before they are asked to perform them. At the end of class, for instance, you could remind students of the procedure for turning in their completed work just before you ask them to turn it in. Students appreciate

the reminders instead of the criticism they might receive for not following the procedure. These reminders can be given for the first few weeks until the students have adopted the procedures.

7. *Review the procedures after long holidays.* After being away from school for many days, some students may forget some procedures. Therefore, reviewing the procedures after a long holiday is a useful step to reinforce them.

MAJOR CONCEPTS

1. Rules are behavioral standards or expectations that are to be followed. They constitute a general code of conduct intended to regulate individual behavior so as to avoid disruptive behavior.
2. Rules should meet the following purposes: (a) the teacher's right to teach is protected; (b) the students' rights to learning are protected; (c) the students' psychological and physical safety is protected; and (d) property is protected.
3. Teachers should follow various guidelines when selecting, teaching, and reviewing the rules.
4. Before teaching the rules, both rewards and penalties need to be identified.
5. Procedures are approved ways to achieve specific tasks.
6. Teachers first need to select the actions that need procedures and then determine the particular procedures that students will follow.
7. Teachers should follow the guidelines when teaching and reviewing classroom procedures.

DISCUSSION QUESTIONS

1. What are the advantages and disadvantages of involving students in the selection of classroom rules?
2. What consequences would be appropriate for mild, moderate, and severe misbehavior in the first, seventh, and eleventh grades?
3. What are the merits and problems related to sending a copy of your classroom discipline policy home to the parents?
4. Why are procedures needed in classrooms?
5. How might classroom procedures be different at various grade levels?

SUPPLEMENTAL ACTIVITIES

For Clinical Settings

1. For your grade level or subject area, select the classroom rules that you prefer. Next, develop a plan for teaching these rules to the students on the first day.
2. For your grade level or subject area, select the procedures you prefer to use for the areas identified in Table 6-1.
3. Prepare a letter which you might send to parents describing your discipline policy.

For Field Settings

1. Find out what policies exist in the school district and in your school for student conduct and academic expectations (e.g., homework).
2. Talk to two or more teachers to determine what rules and specific procedures they use. Obtain any printed guidelines that they provide students.
3. Talk with several students to learn their impressions for the reasons underlying the rules and procedures. Obtain their assessment of the appropriateness of the rules and procedures being used.

KEY TERMS

Activities and privileges	Rules
Exchange routines	Social reinforcers
Management routines	Support routines
Procedures	Tangible reinforcers
Routines	Token reinforcers

REFERENCES

Boostrom, R. (1991). The nature and functions of classroom rules. *Curriculum Inquiry, 21*(2), 193-216.

Brophy, J. E. (1988). Educating teachers about managing classrooms and students. *Teaching and Teacher Education, 4,* 1-18.

Emmer, E. T., Evertson, C. M., Clements, B. S., & Worsham, M. E. (1994). *Classroom Management for Secondary Teachers,* 3rd ed. Englewood Cliffs, NJ: Prentice Hall.

Evertson, C. M. (1985). Training teachers in classroom management: An experimental study in secondary education classrooms. *Journal of Educational Research, 79*(1), 51-58.

Evertson, C. M., Emmer, E. T., Clements, B. S., & Worsham, M. E. (1994). *Classroom Management for Elementary Teachers,* 3rd ed. Englewood Cliffs, NJ: Prentice Hall.

Evertson, C. M., Emmer, E. T., Sanford, J. P., & Clements, B. S. (1983). Improving classroom management: An experiment in elementary school classrooms. *Elementary School Journal, 84,* 173-188.

Jones, V. F., & Jones, L. S. (1990). *Comprehensive Classroom Management: Motivating and Managing Students,* 3rd ed. Boston: Allyn & Bacon.

Leinhardt, G., Weidman, C., & Hammond, K. M. (1987). Introduction and integration of classroom routines by expert teachers. *Curriculum Inquiry, 17*(2), 135-176.

Levin, J., & Nolan, J. F. (1991). *Principles of Classroom Management: A Hierarchical Approach.* Englewood Cliffs, NJ: Prentice Hall.

Rohrkemper, M. (1985). Individual differences in students' perceptions of routine classroom events. *Journal of Educational Psychology, 77,* 29-44.

Yinger, R. (1979). Routines in teacher planning. *Theory into Practice, 18,* 163-169.

Weinstein, C. S., & Mignano, A. J. (1993). *Elementary Classroom Management: Lessons from Research and Practice.* New York: McGraw-Hill.

part III

Planning for Management

The four chapters in Part III concern ways to plan for management, including planning for instruction, planning to motivate students, planning to address the diversity of students, and planning to work with parents.

Chapter 7, "Planning for Instruction," describes planning for an instructional program and individual lessons with attention to maintaining order. It discusses students' academic needs, as well as methods for holding students accountable, using time wisely, and maintaining effective records.

Chapter 8, "Planning for Motivation," addresses student motivation to learn. Specific strategies are presented along with approaches to motivational planning.

Chapter 9, "Planning to Address the Diversity of Students," explores how student differences are expressed. The chapter suggests ways to accommodate these differences.

Chapter 10, "Planning to Work with Parents," considers parental support or resistance to involvement, gives reasons for working with parents, and describes communicating with parents.

chapter 7

Planning for Instruction

Objectives

This chapter provides information that will help you:

1. Identify sources of information and ways to plan for instruction.
2. Determine factors that should be taken into account when planning lessons.
3. Identify students' academic needs.
4. Identify ways to hold students academically accountable.
5. Determine ways to use academic time wisely.

When planning for instruction, most teachers pay close attention to curriculum and the instructional process. They make decisions about instructional goals and objectives, content, and teaching strategies. They also plan how to use instructional media and the means of evaluating students.

When planning for instruction, several questions come to mind in relation to classroom management and discipline. How should you plan the instructional program? What factors should you take into account when planning lessons? What are the students' academic needs? How can students be held academically accountable? How can academic time be used wisely? What are the implications for these issues on management and order? Chapter 7 addresses these issues.

PLANNING AN INSTRUCTIONAL PROGRAM

When planning the program, you can refer to curriculum guides and the textbook teacher's manual for objectives, content, potential instructional activities, and other resources. This information can facilitate your decisions for preparing both long- and short-range plans.

Curriculum Guides and Teacher's Editions

Curriculum guides translate the broad aims of education into specific, subject-related goals, which usually are not written in behavioral terms; these goals are then translated into explicit unit objectives. *Curriculum guides* include subject-specific goals, a fairly detailed outline of curricular content, and recommended instructional activities and materials. They may include recommendations about the number of weeks to be devoted to various segments of the outline.

The school board adopts guides, which then become the official documents about the course; you are expected to use them in planning. A curriculum guide should be available for each subject at each grade level. Both long-range and short-range plans are based on these guides.

The *teacher's edition* of the textbook to be used is also informative. It describes recommended activities; objectives; resource books, videotapes, computer games or programs, or other supplements; definitions of key words; and other aids. Taken together, the curriculum guides and the teacher's editions are valuable resources.

Long- and Short-Range Planning

With the curriculum guide as your foundation, you can make plans for the year, the terms, the units, and the daily lessons. A *yearly plan* is a general outline of content, with specific ideas associated with course content, methods, and evaluation. The plan identifies the content and establishes a sequence for teaching. The curriculum guide is the chief reference document for yearly plans.

A *term plan* includes detailed outlines of the content to be covered in a marking period. It elaborates the yearly planning outlines. Term plans are divided into weeks, with an outline for instructional activities and materials for each week. *Unit plans* may outline activities and content in sequence, along with notes about text pages, appropriate examples, and selected materials.

Weekly plans lay out the week's activities within the framework of the daily schedule. Finally, the *daily lesson plan* is a direct continuation of the weekly plan. It may include notes about objectives, materials, activities, evaluation, and so on.

Teachers in Action

Long-Range Planning

Kim Schaefer, prealgebra middle school teacher, Rapid City, South Dakota:

When I start planning, I look at the whole picture. What does the curriculum cover for the year? Where am I going, and where do I have to be at the end of the year? I then break it down into semesters, nine-week sections, and finally units. What am I going to cover in those time frames?

Once I have it down in units, I find all the material that I can and then decide which material I will use and how I will use it. From there, I do a daily planning schedule one unit at a time.

PLANNING LESSONS

Preparing daily lesson plans is vital to effective management and discipline because engaging lessons can keep students on-task and can minimize misbehavior. You should take into account the degree of structure that will occur in each lesson. The grouping planned for the instructional activities will also affect student interaction. Consider homework when planning lessons, as well.

Degree of Structure in Lessons

Various instructional strategies factor into achieving lesson objectives. These strategies vary in the degree that they are teacher-directed. Instructional strategies fall on a continuum from teacher-directed, more explicit methods, to student-directed, less explicit methods (Burden & Byrd, 1994).

Teacher-directed instructional strategies include lectures, demonstrations, recitations, questions, and practice. Teachers try to control all aspects of the lesson: objectives, activities, materials, assignments, interaction, and evaluation. Other instructional strategies are more interactive, such as group and discussion methods. *Student-directed instructional strategies* emphasize inquiry and discovery.

When deciding on your strategy, you need to weigh its advantages and disadvantages along with the lesson objectives. Effective teachers use several strategies ranging from teacher-directed to student-directed. The lesson objectives may determine which approach is most appropriate. Some content may lend itself to inquiry and discovery, whereas other content may be better handled with direct instruction.

Over time, students should be given the opportunity to learn through several instructional strategies. Emmer, Evertson, and Anderson (1980) discovered that teachers who were flexible and utilized a variety of instructional strategies appeared to be more interesting to their students.

Selecting Grouping Practices

Group students in the way most appropriate for the instructional strategies and objectives. Focus upon the group as a collection of individuals who learn. Within groups, each student observes, listens, responds, takes turns, and so on. Groups can be large or small. Whole-group, small-group, and independent work are options; each affects student conduct and order.

Whole-Group Instruction. In ***whole-group instruction***, the entire class is taught. It allows you to (a) lecture, demonstrate, and explain a topic; (b) ask and answer a question; (c) provide the same recitation, practice, and drill exercises; (d) work on the same problems; and (e) use the same materials. You still can ask individual students to answer questions, monitor students as they work on assigned activities, and work with individual students. Even with whole-group instruction, however, you need to consider individual student differences.

Small-Group Instruction. There are times when the objectives can be better met with small groups. In ***small-group instruction***, students are more actively engaged, and teachers can better monitor student progress.

If there are more than six in the group, generally not everyone will actively participate. A midsize group is no more efficient for such purposes as lecture or demonstration than a large group. Educators recommend that groups comprise four or five students (Cohen, 1992), with an upper limit of six (Johnson, Johnson, & Holubec, 1990).

Since groupwork helps develop relationships, it is useful to vary group membership based on gender and ethnicity. Students with disabilities can be placed in groups with nondisabled students, to integrate them into the mainstream classroom (Johnson & Johnson, 1980; Madden & Slavin, 1983). While there may be good reasons for planning a homogeneous group for certain activities, educators in general recommend group heterogeneity (Cohen, 1992; Johnson, Johnson, & Holubec, 1990; Slavin, 1991).

Many teachers find that they can divide large classes into groups, committees, or teams, as needed, for their small-group and individualized techniques (Reid, Forrestal, & Cook, 1991). Small groups, usually used in elementary school reading and mathematics, can be formed in all grade levels and subjects.

Small groups can be based on issues, such as student ability, interest, skill, viewpoint, activity, or integration (Cohen, 1992). Groups could be set up arbitrarily. There are three types of groupings: ability grouping, cooperative learning groups, and peer tutoring.

1. *Ability grouping.* In ***ability grouping,*** students judged to be similar in their academic ability are clustered into classes. In ***within-class grouping*** subgroups are formed, with each subgroup being fairly homogeneous in terms

---

Teachers in Action

Creating Groups

Tamara George, sixth-grade teacher, Topeka, Kansas:

Grouping may be done for many reasons, and I follow different procedures to create them. For checking or reviewing, divide the groups into categories—the number of people in your family, or the color of your hair, for example.

For an important project, group according to students' ability to work together. I keep a list of each group, and can make changes so students are not always working with the same people. I find it very important to have one organized or motivated person in each group.

Claudia Swisher, ninth-grade English teacher, Norman, Oklahoma:

Students interact in group or cooperative activities at least once a week. I think about how to establish groups, move students into their groups, and avoid wasting time when shuffling chairs. I also want to give each student a chance to work with every other student in the class and get to know each one.

I assign groups heterogeneously with a balance of strong and weak students, boys and girls, and well behaved and poorly behaved. I set up new groups for each new unit of student, which lasts about two to three weeks.

Since I share my classroom with another teacher, we leave the desks in the traditional rows. I use this arrangement for groups, changing my seating chart for each unit and assigning the groups at the same time. Students who sit close together make up a group of four. Through the entire unit, they are seated together.

When it is time for groupwork, the students in each group simply rotate their positions. In this way, the four members face each other and communicate easily; and the noise level can be kept low. At the end of the activity, the students return their desks to row order with little trouble, and the room is ready for the next teacher. I am much more enthusiastic about cooperative work since I have control over the logistics of my situation.

---

of ability. Within-class grouping has been most widely researched in elementary math classes, and results suggest that small numbers of groups are more effective than large numbers. Group assignments can be flexible, role models for low achievers are available, teacher morale is higher, and stigmatizing is minimized (Slavin, 1994).

2. *Cooperative learning.* **Cooperative learning** is a grouping in which students work in small, mixed-ability learning teams. Such groups can be formed at various grade levels and in different subject areas.

Through cooperative learning, students understand that they are responsible not only for their own learning but also for the learning of their team members. Cooperative learning approaches are often used to supplement other practices. In spite of renewed interest in them, classes are structured for cooperative learning for only 7 to 20 percent of the time (Johnson, Johnson, & Holubec, 1990).

Cooperative learning occurs in three ways: (a) assignment of individual students to specific responsibilities within a larger group task or project; (b) assignment of students to a shared project or task; (c) assignment to groups to study and be responsible for group members' learning. Additional resources on cooperative learning include Slavin (1987, 1991, 1994), Johnson and Johnson (1994), and Sharan and Sharan (1992).

3. *Peer tutoring.* This approach involves students teaching students (Goodlad & Hirst, 1989). The two types of **peer tutoring** are (a) cross-age tutoring, in which older students work with younger ones; and (b) peer tutoring, in which students in the same class work together. There are several advantages to peer tutoring (Johnson & Johnson, 1994): (a) peer tutors are often effective in teaching students who do not respond well to adults; (b) peer tutoring can develop a bond of friendship between tutor and tutored, which is important for integrating slow learners into the group; (c) peer tutoring allows the teacher to teach a large group of students, while giving slow learners the individual attention they need; and (d) tutors benefit by learning to teach.

Peer tutoring can be practiced at all grade levels. Before having students work in pairs, you need to clarify its purposes, obtain the necessary materials, and provide an appropriate work area where the students can work without disturbing other students. You might offer guidance about working and studying together.

Decision Points

When arranging for small group instruction, you could have students involved in cooperative learning. Suppose that you had your eighth-grade students work in cooperative groups on a project about the geography of the United States. What procedures would you use to establish and maintain order when the students are working in these groups?

Independent Work.   You might give students opportunities to work on tasks of their own choosing, or assign activities that enable students to work alone. Good and Brophy (1994) found that one-third of elementary teachers attempt to individualize instruction and that one-fifth of secondary teachers attempt to do so.

When assigning independent work, you may involve students in any of a number of instructional strategies. In **inquiry and discovery approaches,** students learn about the process of discovery by collecting data and testing hypotheses. Teachers guide students as they discover new meanings, practice the skills, and undergo the experiences that will shape their learning. These approaches include computer-assisted instruction, learning centers, learning stations, laboratory, discovery techniques, and others.

Not all independent work involves inquiry approaches. *Mastery learning* is an individualized approach that follows a structured curriculum divided into small segments of information, with corresponding skills to be learned (Bloom, 1981). It is designed to ensure that all students achieve the lesson's objectives and to allow each student enough time to do so. Mastery learning is based on traditional group instruction and individual remediation and enrichment.

CONSIDERING STUDENTS' ACADEMIC NEEDS

When teaching methods respond effectively to the student academic needs outlined in this chapter, learning is significantly increased and misbehavior is dramatically decreased (Jones & Jones, 1990). By addressing their academic needs, you focus on helping them feel safe and secure, and on developing a sense of competence and success in their school environment. As they better understand your decisions about the purpose and meaning of instruction, have opportunities to make decisions and set goals, and monitor their own progress, they find the environment safe and supportive.

Jones and Jones (1990) have identified the following 13 academic needs in a review of the literature on motivation. These issues should be taken into account when you plan for instruction.

1. *Understand and value the learning goals.* Students are more likely to become involved in activities that have a clear goal. Students will derive greater satisfaction and enjoyment from an activity that has a definite aim. Roehler, Duffy, and Meloth (1987) found that when teachers learned to give detailed explanations about the purpose of instructional activities, students demonstrated significantly greater understanding of and appreciation for the purpose of the instruction.

Consider the alternative if you do not clearly communicate the learning goals so your students can understand them. They may "go through the motions" of an activity without understanding its purpose or its relationship to other content. They may be concerned with only completing the assignment, rather than attempting to understand its purposes and objectives. Some students may become passive when they see no academic purpose and consider assignments to be "busy work" with no specific learning objective.

2. *Understand the learning process.* You can do at least three things to help students understand the learning process. (a) Increase student motivation by providing information about the learning process. Students can learn how individuals differ in their preferred learning style, that different tasks lead to certain learning outcomes, and that activities can be selected to support specific learning outcomes and student learning styles. (b) Be clear about choices you

offer. By giving students explanations you allow them opportunities to think carefully and select appropriate choices. (c) Improve evaluation when teaching about the learning process. You can more carefully clarify the learning goals and their relationship to instructional methods, and then match the evaluation to these goals. This clarity of goals, teaching methods, and the evaluation process can increase students' motivation, reduce their frustration, and enhance achievement.

3. *Be actively involved in the learning process.* Students may become bored and restless during periods of passive learning. Conversely, they can be stimulated when actively and emotionally involved in learning. Misbehavior is also significantly less during lessons that require students to use higher levels of cognitive skills, incorporate their feelings, and relate material to their own lives.

Students are not involved in the learning process to the extent preferred. John Goodlad's (1984) study found that across all grade levels, teachers talked three times as much as students did. It is common to have uninvolved students who listen to a teacher or who are involved in seatwork.

Studies completed at the Center for Early Adolescence suggest that primary-age and adolescent children require particular emphasis on active participation. Guidelines provided in the *Middle Grades Assessment Program* (Dorman, 1981) include suggestions about (a) actively engaging students in manipulating materials and objects; (b) having students work in small groups; and (c) having students ask questions of each other as well as of their teacher.

4. *Relate subject matter to their lives.* Relating the information in the lesson to some meaningful event or idea in students' lives will help them remember that information. It is more difficult for them initially to learn and retain information unimportant to them than it is to learn meaningful information.

Studies on motivation substantiate this concept. For example, McClelland's theory and subsequent research on achievement motivation suggest that individuals will be more highly motivated to achieve if they can be shown how their efforts relate to their everyday lives (McClelland & Alschuler, 1971).

Decision Points

Students have the academic need for the subject matter to relate to their lives. For a seventh-grade class covering the geography of their state, how could you plan the lesson to relate to the students' lives? What might you do to also take into account the students' different learning styles as well as their cultural differences?

---

5. *Control the learning environment by setting goals or following students' interests.* An impressive body of research indicates that student learning is enhanced when students have the opportunity to be involved in selecting learning materials and establishing learning goals. They need opportunities to explore topics they find exciting and interesting. You can provide them with a sense of control through giving them a voice in (a) what material to work on; (b) when work will be accomplished; (c) how it will be completed; (d) the level

---

Teachers in Action

Helping Students See Content Relevance

Donna Erpelding, third-grade teacher, Manhattan, Kansas:

I believe that nothing should be taught in isolation. Every skill, every objective, and every fragment of information should fit into a bigger picture. My job is to paint the bigger picture of relevancy for the student. I find that is easier to do if I focus on a theme and relate content to the theme.

I *try* to express the meaningfulness of the lesson with creativity, enthusiasm, and a spirit of "Ah!" Whatever we are doing, the students need to see its relevance to the theme or to their individual worlds. I believe a lot of what is taught is lost, in the absence of the sense of connectedness or relevancy.

---

of difficulty of the assignment; (e) self-correcting and self-monitoring of work; and (f) individual goal setting.

6. *Experience success.* Successful experiences help develop feelings of self-worth and confidence toward new activities. Teacher effectiveness research suggests that learning is enhanced when students experience high rates of success in completing tasks. Following successful experiences, students tend to raise their expectations and set higher goals; failure is met with lowered aspirations (Diggory, 1966).

If students are not offered activities in which they can succeed, they can be expected to withdraw or act out. You can help them experience higher rates of success by having them set individual goals and evaluate their own learning, as well as through cooperative learning, peer tutoring, and effective teacher monitoring and repeat teaching (Jones & Jones, 1990; Kolesnik, 1978).

7. *Receive realistic and immediate feedback that enhances self-efficacy.* Effective feedback enables students to better understand where they stand in relation to achieving goals, the progress they have made toward a goal, and what they need to do to continue or to improve. Effective praise also communicates your belief that the student can reach predetermined goals, that the student's effort is a major factor influencing the outcome, and that how a student's progress compares with that of other students is not important.

8. *Receive appropriate rewards for performance gains.* Rewards are one proven way to motivate students to put forth effort, especially when the rewards are offered in advance as incentives (Good & Brophy, 1994). Extrinsic rewards are not needed for tasks that students find intrinsically satisfying, but they are sometimes needed to stimulate effort on tasks that are difficult or tedious.

Recognize that extrinsic rewards can reduce intrinsic interest in a task (Morgan, 1984). Rewards appear to be most useful when they simultaneously reinforce performance and provide feedback about mastery of the material (Bandura, 1982; Deci & Ryan, 1985; Lepper, 1981).

9. *See learning modeled by adults as an exciting and rewarding activity.* When motivating students to learn, you can model learning (Brophy, 1987) by: (a) modeling interest in learning and motivation to learn; (b) projecting intensity; (c) projecting enthusiasm; and (d) modeling task-related thinking and problem solving. Express the importance you hold for learning, for example, by responding to student questions with enthusiasm, curiosity, and interest.

10. *Experience an appropriate amount of structure.* Develop clear expectations about student behavior and academic performance. Students need to understand how the classroom will operate, how problems will be resolved, and how they will be involved in influencing curricular and instructional decisions. Be cautious about maintaining excessive dominance or control when developing the structures necessary to create a safe, clearly understood environment.

11. *Have time to integrate learning.* Since students may learn a great deal in the course of one day, they need time to integrate the new ideas they encounter. Students learn at various rates and in different ways, so it is important to slow down and provide all of them an opportunity to organize the new ideas. Plan activities that are designed to help students summarize new learning and relate this new knowledge to previous learning and to their lives.

12. *Have positive contact with peers.* Creating positive peer relationships appears to meet a basic personal need that is prerequisite to productive participation in learning. Working with peers has the potential of fulfilling this need. With cooperative learning, students' initial learning, retention, and transfer of concepts tend to be higher than when they work individually (Johnson & Johnson, 1994; Johnson, Johnson, & Holubec, 1990).

13. *Receive instruction matched to their level of cognitive and skill development and learning style.* Students differ in their levels of cognitive development and learning styles. Give each student tasks that are hard enough to require some effort and that increase competency, but are easy enough to be completed with no more than minimal assistance. Deborah Stipek (1993) stated, "The importance of tasks being matched to each child's skill level cannot be overemphasized. It is necessary for intrinsic motivation and optimal learning. As difficult a principle as this is to implement, it is the most important one for motivation and learning" (p. 90). If the same or a limited range of instructional methods is used with every student, some students may become frustrated, experience failure, and respond by misbehaving.

PLANNING TO HOLD STUDENTS ACADEMICALLY ACCOUNTABLE

Procedures to help manage student work must be selected. *Academic accountability* means that the students must complete certain activities related to the instructional objectives. Research studies of elementary and secondary classrooms

Teachers in Action

Student Accountability through an Information Sheet

Francine Fankhauser, junior high school English teacher, Federal Way, Washington:

I provide my students with an "Information Sheet" at the beginning of each major literature unit. The sheet has three parts. The first part lists *student expectations,* showing how we will cover the reading material (e.g., *Romeo and Juliet* and be read orally; *Call of the Wild* will be read independently) and explains the other tasks that students are expected to complete during the unit (library research, presenting a scene from a play, completing study questions, and so on).

The second section provides *grading information* by indicating required reading assignments, the format of quizzes and tests, participation requirements, and the respective points for all required work.

The third section is *a calendar* that notes daily activities, assignments, supplemental films, quizzes, tests, and school events. Students have told me that they value the calendar the most because it allows them the flexibility to organize their own work. They know what point they need to reach for discussion sessions and other due dates so they can arrange their study time according to their personal schedules. I have found that empowering students to do this results in higher self-esteem and greater success.

An added benefit is that students who are absent are able to keep up with their assignments and return to class prepared. Parents also appreciate the information sheet because it makes them aware of the curriculum. This is especially useful to parents who need to give their child extra assistance.

provide insight into ways that students can be held academically accountable (Emmer et al., 1994; Evertson et al., 1994). Teacher responsibilities for holding students academically accountable are displayed in Table 7-1, some of which are adapted from Emmer et al. (1994) and Jones and Jones (1990).

The following elements should be considered:

- Determine a system of grading (e.g., letter grades or numerical grades, and measures for nonachievement outcomes). This decision might have been made for you by the school district as reflected in the report card format. Use evaluation measures (e.g., tests, written or oral reports, homework, ratings, projects) throughout the marking period, and describe the grading system to the students.

TABLE 7-1 Holding students academically accountable

Take into account the grade level and subject area when decisions are made on the following issues in an effort to hold students academically accountable.

1. *The Grading System*
   a. Select a grading system
   b. Select types of evaluation measures
   c. Determine how grades will be assigned
   d. Address nonachievement outcomes
   e. Communicate the grading system to students
   f. Design a gradebook
   g. Report grades and communicate to parents
2. *Assignments*
   a. Post assignments
   b. State requirements and grading criteria for assignments
   c. Long-term assignments
3. *Work and Completion Requirements*
   a. Identify work requirements
      (1) Use of pencil or pen
      (2) Headings on papers
      (3) Writing on the back of the paper
      (4) Neatness and legibility guidelines
   b. Identify completion requirements
      (1) Due dates
      (2) Late work
      (3) Incomplete work
      (4) Missed work
   c. Make provisions for absent students and make-up work
      (1) Have an assignment list or folder
      (2) Identify a due date
      (3) Select a place to pick up and drop off absent assignments
      (4) Provide a regular time to assist students with make-up work
4. *Monitoring Progress and Completion of Assignments*
   a. Determine when and how to monitor in-class assignments
   b. Determine when and how to monitor longer assignments, projects, or works in progress
   c. Determine when and how to monitor in-class oral participation or performance
   d. Determine which activities will receive a grade and which will be used only for formative feedback for the student
   e. Select checking procedures that will be used in class
      (1) Students exchanging papers
      (2) Marking and grading papers
      (3) Turning in papers
5. *Providing Feedback*
   a. Decide what feedback will be provided to students, and when it will be provided
   b. Determine what records students will keep concerning their progress
   c. Select incentives and rewards
   d. Record scores in the gradebook
   e. Post selected student work

Teachers in Action

Accountability in Makeup Work

James Roussin, grades 7 to 12 English and literature teacher, Big Lake, Minnesota:

I use an assignment notebook to bring students up-to-date about missed assignments. First I recruit a student who likes to write (you might want to assign two students who take turns, or an alternate person if you use only one student). It is very important that you select someone who likes to write. Writing can be "a misery" for a student who hates writing, or who is not careful about details. I have a separate assignment notebook for each class, and there is a designated area for the notebooks.

The recording student dates each entry and keeps a running log of what went on during that class period. The log might look like this:

Friday, April 15, English 10, 5th period.
Learning Goal: Know the four kinds of sentences.
Today, Mr. Roussin had us practice writing different kinds of sentences. We worked out of the blue *Building English Skills* book. The assignment was on page 234. We had to do all of exercise A and 1 to 10 in exercise B. Mr. R. first explained the sentences and then we practiced in the book. I thought writing complex sentences was especially hard. You might want to ask Mr. R. to go over these later on. There was no homework! Mr. R. did say that we would have to know the four kind of sentences by next Wednesday. He is planning a quiz for next Friday.

I ask the student recorder to write what he or she feels was especially difficult with the lesson so an absent student will learn how easy or difficult the lesson was. When the student returns, I suggest a discussion with the student recorder, after which I will answer additional questions at the end of the period. The student recorders become an integral part of the classroom, and they know their work is valued. I reward these students with a can of "pop" on occasion or a candy bar. This is a small fee to pay for an important management tool.

- Make decisions about assignments. This includes deciding where and how you will post assignments, as well as the requirements and criteria for grading. Students should understand that completed assignments are part of the grading system.

- Decide on work and completion requirements. Students need to have guidelines or work requirements for the various assignments. Details about due dates, late work, and missed assignments due to absence should be explained. The relevant procedures will help students understand expectations held of them and should minimize questions on a case-by-case basis.

- Monitor student progress and completion of assignments. You may want to use some in-class activities as exercises but not count performance on these in your grading. The activities may be written, oral, or performance demonstrations. Progress should be monitored. In many cases, the entire class is at work on the designated activity; this enables you to walk around and observe each student carefully to see how the student is progressing.

- Provide students with feedback about their progress. Feedback of in-class activities may take the form of statements to individuals or to the class. Students may exchange papers to evaluate progress on formative exercises. Papers or projects that are to be part of the report card grade should be collected, graded, and returned promptly. In this way, students receive regular feedback about their progress throughout the marking period. Computer programs available for maintaining a gradebook can easily generate progress reports for both students and teacher.

Decision Points

Effective teachers hold students academically accountable in many ways. Assume that you require your tenth-grade English students to complete three tests, seven homework assignments, and two cooperative projects for the report card marking period. What provisions would you have for absent students and make-up work? How do these provisions hold students academically accountable? How might your procedures differ for second-, sixth-, and twelfth-grade classes?

USING ACADEMIC TIME WISELY

When considering how to use academic time wisely, it is useful first to examine the time available for instruction. Students are in school for several hours a day, yet much of that time is consumed in recess, lunch, time between classes, and homeroom or announcement times. Of the allocated time, some is used for announcements, collecting or distributing papers and supplies, transitions between activities, and other noninstructional events. Thus, the actual academic time is less than the allocated time.

Some students may be daydreaming or be off-task, so the time spent in learning is less than the allocated time. The time students are paying attention and are engaged in action is called *time-on-task*. *Academic learning time* refers to the amount of time a student engages in learning tasks that yield fairly high rates of success (Strother, 1984). What really counts is for students to be successful during that allocated time. As you can see, the amount of engaged time is much less than the time students are in school.

Let's consider a 45-minute class. Within this allocated time, 5 minutes may be spent on taking attendance and making announcements, 5 minutes on describing an activity and giving directions, 5 minutes for cleanup and preparation to finish the class. That leaves 30 minutes of academic time, but students may not be fully engaged even during all of that time. Furthermore, their engagement during this time may not be entirely fruitful.

The amount of time students are engaged in learning is positively related to their achievement in the content area. A student who is continually off-task will not achieve as well as one who remains on-task. Students often are off-task in obvious ways, such as getting out of their seats, reading notes, or talking to other students. Off-task behavior can often manifest itself in daydreaming or other types of mental or emotional disengagement that can be difficult to detect.

To engage students in learning, you could (a) elicit the desired behavior; (b) provide opportunities for feedback in a nonevaluative atmosphere; (c) plan group and individual activities as motivational aids; (d) give meaningful verbal praise; and (e) monitor seatwork and check it (Borich, 1992). You can begin and end lessons precisely on time, reduce transition time between tasks and activities in a lesson, and minimize waste time in an effort to maximize time-on-task and student engagement (Wyne & Stuck, 1982).

The time available for instruction increases when you (a) follow schedules; (b) begin and end activities on time; (c) facilitate transitions from activity to activity; and (d) assign scheduled activities first priority rather than engaging in spontaneous alternative activities (Rosenshine, 1980).

Effective management and scheduling can lead to increased learning and a reduction in discipline problems (Berliner, 1979). Good and Brophy (1994) indicate that time-on-task is important, but the task itself must be relevant, appropriate, lead to a reasonably successful outcome (such as designing the difficulty of the assignment to enable the student to solve at least 80 percent of the problems correctly), and be followed by timely feedback. Instructional time should be allocated in relation to the importance of the academic task.

MAJOR CONCEPTS

1. Since the curriculum guides are adopted by the school board as official documents for the goals and content of a particular course, teachers are expected to use these curriculum guides in their planning.

2. Using the curriculum guide as the foundation, teachers make plans for the year, the terms, the units, and the daily lessons.

3. Instructional strategies fall on a continuum from teacher-directed, more explicit methods all the way to student-directed, less explicit methods.

4. Teachers need to consider the type of student grouping that is most appropriate for the instructional strategies and objectives, including whole-group, small-group, and independent work.

5. Students have a number of academic needs that should be considered as lesson plans are made.

6. Academic accountability involves requiring the student to complete certain activities related to the instructional objectives being considered.

7. Effective use of academic learning time can lead to increased learning and a reduction in discipline problems.

DISCUSSION QUESTIONS

1. How might the degree of structure of an instructional activity affect student behavior? What might teachers do to minimize misbehavior?

2. What are the merits of whole-group, small-group, and independent work? What might teachers do to minimize misbehavior with each strategy?

3. Why should teachers consider students' academic needs when planning lessons? What is the connection between this and classroom management and discipline?

4. How does holding students academically accountable relate to classroom misbehavior?

5. What are some ways that teachers could maximize the amount of time-on-task?

SUPPLEMENTAL ACTIVITIES

For Clinical Settings

1. For each type of grouping (whole-group, small-group, and independent work), how might you monitor student progress and provide feedback?

2. Identify how you will establish academic accountability procedures for: assignments, work and completion requirements, monitoring progress and completion of assignments, and providing feedback (see Table 7-1).

For Field Settings

1. Ask several teachers for suggestions for effectively using whole-group, small-group, and independent work.

2. Talk to teachers about how they hold students academically accountable for each area listed in Table 7-1.

KEY TERMS

Ability grouping	Student-directed instructional strategies
Academic accountability	Teacher-directed instructional strategies
Academic learning time	Teacher's edition
Cooperative learning	Term plan
Curriculum guides	Time-on-task
Daily lesson plan	Unit plan
Inquiry and discovery approaches	Weekly plan
Mastery learning	Whole-group instruction
Peer tutoring	Within-class grouping
Small-group instruction	Yearly plan

RECOMMENDED READINGS

Burden, P. R., & Byrd, D. M. (1994). *Methods for Effective Teaching.* Boston: Allyn & Bacon.
Provides thorough coverage of all aspects of general teaching methods, including planning, instructional strategies, instructional delivery, media and resources, guiding student study, evaluation, grading, and other related topics.

Johnson, D. W., Johnson, R. T., & Holubec, E. J. (1990). *Circles of Learning: Cooperation in the Classroom,* 3rd ed. Edina, MN: Interaction Book Co.
Defines cooperative learning and provides thorough descriptions for its use in the classroom.

Jones, V. F., & Jones, L. S. (1990). *Comprehensive Classroom Management: Motivating and Managing Students,* 3rd ed. Boston: Allyn & Bacon.
Chapter 6 offers a detailed description of ways to enhance students' motivation to learn by examining their academic needs.

Slavin, R. E. (1991). *Student Team Learning: A Practical Guide for Cooperative Learning,* 3rd ed. Washington, DC: National Education Association.
Includes thorough descriptions for several types of cooperative and team learning strategies.

REFERENCES

Bandura, A. (1982). Self-efficacy mechanism in human agency. *American Psychologist, 37,* 122-147.

Berliner, D. (1979). Tempus educare. In P. Peterson & H. Walberg, Eds. *Research on Teaching: Concepts, Findings, and Implications.* Berkeley, CA: McCutchan.

Bloom, B. S. (1981). *All Our Children Learning.* New York: McGraw-Hill.

Borich, G. (1992). *Effective Teaching Methods,* 2nd ed. Columbus, OH: Merrill Publishing.

Brophy, J. (1987). On motivating students. In D. C. Berliner & B. V. Rosenshine, Eds., *Talks to Teachers* (pp. 201–245). New York: Random House.

Burden, P. R., & Byrd, D. M. (1994). *Methods for Effective Teaching.* Boston: Allyn & Bacon.

Cohen, E. G. (1992). *Designing Groupwork: Strategies for the Heterogeneous Classroom,* rev. ed. New York: Teachers College Press.

Deci, E., & Ryan, R. (1985). *Intrinsic Motivation and Self-determination in Human Behavior.* New York: Plenum.

Diggory, J. (1966). *Self-evaluation: Concepts and Studies.* New York: John Wiley.

Dorman, G. (1981). *Middle Grades Assessment Program.* Chapel Hill, NC: Center for Early Adolescence.

Emmer, E. T., Evertson, C. M., & Anderson, L. M. (1980). Effective classroom management at the beginning of the school year. *The Elementary School Journal, 80,* 219–231.

Emmer, E. T., Evertson, C. M., Clements, B. S., & Worsham, M. E. (1994). *Classroom Management for Secondary Teachers,* 3rd ed. Englewood Cliffs, NJ: Prentice Hall.

Evertson, C. M., Emmer, E. T., Clements, B. S., & Worsham, M. E. (1994). *Classroom Management for Elementary Teachers,* 3rd ed. Englewood Cliffs, NJ: Prentice Hall.

Good, T. L., & Brophy, J. E. (1994). *Looking in Classrooms,* 6th ed. New York: HarperCollins.

Goodlad, J. I. (1984). *A Place Called School: Prospects for the Future.* New York: McGraw-Hall.

Goodlad, S., & Hirst, B. (1989). *Peer Tutoring: A Guide to Learning by Teaching.* New York: Nichols.

Johnson, D. W., & Johnson, R. T. (1980). Integrating handicapped students into the mainstream. *Exceptional Children, 47*(2), 90–98.

Johnson, D. W., & Johnson, R. T. (1994). *Learning Together and Alone: Cooperative, Competitive, and Individualistic Learning,* 4th ed. Boston: Allyn & Bacon.

Johnson, D. W., & Johnson, R. T., & Holubec, E. J. (1990). *Circles of Learning: Coopera-tion in the Classroom,* 3rd ed. Edina, MN: Interaction Book Co.

Jones, V. F., & Jones, L. S. (1990). *Comprehensive Classroom Management: Motivating and Managing Students,* 3rd ed. Boston, MA: Allyn & Bacon.

Kolesnik, W. (1978). *Motivation: Understanding and Influencing Human Behavior.* Boston: Allyn & Bacon.

Lepper, M. (1981). Intrinsic and extrinsic motivation in children: Detrimental effects of superfluous social controls. In A. Collins, Ed., *Aspects of the Development of Competence: The Minnesota Symposia on Child Development, vol. 14.* Hillsdale, NJ: Erlbaum.

Madden, N. A., & Slavin, R. E. (1983). Cooperative learning and social acceptance of mainstreamed academically handicapped students. *Journal of Special Education, 17,* 171–182.

McClelland, D., & Alshuler, A. (1971). *The Achievement Motivation Development Project.* USOE Project No. 7-1231 (Final Report). Washington, DC: Office of Education, Bureau of Research.

Morgan, M. (1984). Reward-induced decrements and increments in intrinsic motivation. *Review of Educational Research, 54,* 5–30.

Reid, J., Forrestal, P., & Cook, J. (1991). *Small Group Learning in the Classroom.* Portsmouth, NH: Heinemann.

Roehler, L., Duffy, G., & Meloth, M. (1987). The effects and some distinguishing characteristics of explicit teacher explanation during reading instruction. In J. Niles, Ed., *Changing Perspectives on Research in Reading/Language Processing and Instruction.* Rochester, NY: National Reading Conference.

Rosenshine, B. V. (1980). How time is spent in elementary classrooms. In C. Denham and A. Lieberman, Eds. *Time to Learn* (pp. 107-126). Washington, DC: National Institute of Education.

Sharan, Y., & Sharan, S. (1992). *Expanding Cooperative Learning through Group Investigation.* New York: Teachers College Press.

Slavin, R. E. (1987). Ability grouping and student achievement in elementary schools: A best-evidence synthesis. *Review of Educational Research, 57,* 293-336.

Slavin, R. E. (1991). *Student Team Learning: A Practical Guide for Cooperative Learning,* 3rd ed. Washington, DC: National Education Association.

Slavin, R. E. (1994). *Educational Psychology: Theory into Practice,* 4th ed. Boston: Allyn & Bacon.

Stipek, D. J. (1993). *Motivation to Learn: From Theory to Practice,* 2nd ed. Englewood Cliffs, NJ: Prentice Hall.

Strother, D. B. (1984). Another look at time-on-task. *Phi Delta Kappan, 65*(10), 714-717.

Wyne, M. D., & Stuck, G. B. (1982). Time and learning: Implications for the classroom teacher. *The Elementary School Journal, 83*(1), 67-75.

chapter **8**

Planning for Motivation

Objectives

This chapter provides information that will help you:

1. Identify factors that contribute to motivation.
2. Select techniques that capture and maintain student interest in the subject matter and highlight its relevance.
3. Select techniques that promote success and help students maintain expectations for success.
4. Select techniques that express interest in the content, project enthusiasm, and provide feedback and rewards for performance.
5. Identify the three critical time periods of a learning activity, and the motivational factors that need to be considered for each.

Imagine that one of your students doesn't seem interested in the subject matter of your course. The student exerts minimal effort on classroom activities, seatwork, projects, homework, and tests. The student gets off-task easily, bothers other students, and disturbs classroom order. It may be that there are many such students in your class, and you are searching for ways to get these students interested and engaged.

This is where motivation ties in. If you can motivate students, they are more likely to participate in activities and less likely to get off-task and contribute to disorder. An effective manager deliberately plans for ways to motivate students.

Since motivation is a complex, multifaceted issue, it is helpful first to examine some of the reasons for its complexity in an effort to gain an understanding of its principles. Next, we will look at specific strategies that you can

145

use to motivate your students. Finally, a system for motivational planning is offered for three critical time periods in a learning event.

THE COMPLEX NATURE OF MOTIVATION

Most educators use the word ***motivation*** to describe those processes that can arouse and initiate behavior, give direction and purpose to behavior, continue to allow behavior to persist, and lead to choosing or preferring a particular behavior (Wlodkowski, 1984). Of course, teachers are interested in a particular kind of student motivation—the motivation to learn. Teachers who ask questions such as, "How can I help my students get started?" or, "What can I do to keep them going?" are dealing with issues of motivation. Slavin (1994) suggests that motivation is the influence of needs and desires on the intensity and direction of behavior.

Before considering the processes or strategies you might initiate to arouse, direct, and maintain student behavior to learn, it is useful to examine two related factors. First, recognize the merits and limitations of relying on intrinsic and extrinsic motivation. Next, recognize that there are several theoretical views of motivation, each having implications for the strategies you select.

Intrinsic and Extrinsic Motivation

There are two broad categories of motivation—intrinsic and extrinsic. ***Intrinsic motivation*** is a response to needs within the student, such as curiosity, the need to know, or feelings of competence and growth. Internal satisfaction a student feels about a particular task is another aspect of intrinsic motivation. For example, some students might find activities involving movement to be intrinsically satisfying. ***Extrinsic motivation*** is motivation from outside the learner and has to do with external rewards for completion of a task. Words of praise from the teacher, a higher grade, or a privilege are examples.

Numerous studies have been done on intrinsic and extrinsic motivation (e.g., Lepper, Greene, & Nisbett, 1973; Lepper & Greene, 1975; Morgan, 1984; Pittman, Emery, & Boggiano, 1982). The reinforcement of extrinsic motivation can be effective; but be aware that excessive use of rewards may be decreasingly successful in new situations, foster dependence on the teacher, and undermine intrinsic motivation.

Research on the effects of extrinsic rewards on intrinsic motivation suggests caution toward giving material rewards for activities that are intrinsically satisfying. Make everything you teach as intrinsically interesting as possible, and avoid offering material rewards when they are unnecessary. At the same time, do give extrinsic rewards when you feel they are needed (Lepper, 1983). For example, rewarding students for participating in an exciting activity is not necessary, whereas extrinsic rewards may be needed after an activity that students find less intrinsically interesting and satisfying.

Decision Points

Teachers plan lessons with a view toward both intrinsic and extrinsic motivation. If you were teaching an eleventh-grade course on contemporary political issues, how might you satisfy the students' intrinsic needs (the need to satisfy curiosity, the need to know, the need for feelings of competence and growth, the need to be physically active) through your selection of the content, instructional strategies, and requirements for completion? How can you simultaneously accommodate students' individual differences in interests, knowledge, skills, and learning style preferences?

Theoretical Views of Motivation

Many factors will determine whether your students will be motivated to learn. Several theoretical views of motivation attempt to explain aspects of student interest: the behavioral view, the cognitive view, the humanistic view, and achievement motivation theory.

While no single view explains student interest, those interpretations provide insight into individual differences in student desire to learn. The four views to be presented can serve as the basis for motivating your students (Biehler & Snowman, 1993). While both types of motivation—intrinsic and extrinsic—are elements of these views, extrinsic motivation is dominant in the behavioral view, whereas intrinsic motivation is dominant in the cognitive view, the humanistic view, and achievement motivation theory.

The Behavioral View.   Behavioral theorists stress that individuals are motivated when their behavior is reinforced. Research has shown that people will exert greater effort with reinforcement (Robbins, 1984). Students are motivated to complete a task because they receive extrinsic or intrinsic rewards. For example, a student may complete a task without protest because the score so gained will contribute to a good report card grade and praise from the teacher and parents.

With the *behavioral view* of motivation, a person's internal cognitive needs are not as important as the reinforcers that control the behavior. Rein-forcers are any consequences which, when delivered immediately following a response, increase the probability that the behavior will be repeated.

The Cognitive View.   The *cognitive view* of motivation suggests that we are motivated to understand the world, to have control over our lives, and to be self-directed. Cognitive theorists stress that individuals are motivated when they experience a cognitive disequilibrium in which they try to find a solution to a problem. *Cognitive disequilibrium* occurs when a student realizes that he or she needs to know more about a particular subject. For example, when using a computer to prepare a class report, the student may have to prepare a table that includes columns of information. Cognitive disequilibrium is created when the student realizes that he or she does not know how to prepare such tables. The student is motivated to find a solution to the problem—to learn how to compose such tables. People are also motivated by curiosity, an urge to explore, or simply an impulse to try something that is fun (White, 1959).

The Humanistic View.   The *humanistic view* suggests that we are motivated by a need for growth and the development of self. This view highlights intrinsic motivation. Perhaps the best-known theory of motivation in this category is Abraham Maslow's *hierarchy of needs* (1954). Maslow hypothesized a hierarchy of five needs because needs are different at different times: (a) physiological—bodily needs such as hunger, thirst, sleep, and shelter; (b) safety—safeguards from physical and emotional harm; (c) social—affection, belongingness, acceptance, and friendship; (d) esteem—self-confidence, prestige, power, autonomy, achievement, recognition, and attention; and (e) self-actualization—the drive to maximize one's potential; growth and self-fulfillment.

In this hierarchy, deficiency needs (physiological, safety, belongingness and love, and esteem) must be satisfied before growth needs (self-actualization, knowing and understanding, aesthetic) can exert influence. When individuals have satisfied their lower, or deficiency, needs, they will then feel motivated to satisfy higher growth needs. Behavior at a particular moment is usually determined by their strongest needs.

Achievement Motivation Theory.   *Achievement motivation theory* organizes the reasons people have for wanting to achieve something. By knowing why your students want to achieve, you will be better able to select instructional strategies that will promote their motivation to learn.

Maslow's distinction between safety and growth choices is similar to the concept of *level of aspiration,* which stresses that people tend to want to succeed at the highest possible level while at the same time avoiding the possibility of failure. When students are successful, they tend to set realistic goals for themselves, and successful experiences strengthen a need for achievement. Some individuals may experience a *fear of success*—they worry that being successful may interfere with positive relationships with others.

MOTIVATIONAL STRATEGIES IN THE CLASSROOM

A number of educators have proposed strategies to motivate students to learn. Keller (1983), for example, suggests that you consider four *dimensions of motivation:* (a) *interest,* the extent to which the learner's curiosity is aroused and sustained over time; (b) *relevance,* the learner's perception that instruction is related to personal needs or goals; (c) *expectancy,* the learner's perceived likelihood of success through personal control; and (d) *satisfaction,* the learner's intrinsic motivations and responses to extrinsic rewards.

Some educators have organized their recommendations around intrinsic and extrinsic motivation (e.g., Good & Brophy, 1995; Kaplan, 1990; Slavin, 1994).

Others have provided recommendations based on a synthesis of the issues (e.g., Biehler & Snowman, 1993; Gage & Berliner, 1991). Full-length books are devoted to motivating students (e.g., Spaulding, 1992; Stipek, 1993).

Guidelines discussed below represent a synthesis of recommendations from all of those sources, and are organized into six categories of actions. Specific actions may apply to more than one category; they are placed within the category that serves its dominant purpose. These strategies are summarized in Table 8-1.

1. *Capture student interest in the subject matter.* One of the first tasks in motivating students is to arouse their curiosity and sustain their interest over time (Keller, 1983). Useful techniques for capturing student interest address the inner need to know or to satisfy curiosity; thus the techniques are intrinsically satisfying. Try to incorporate the approaches described below. These approaches are especially useful with new material. Suggestions for maintaining ongoing student interest in the lesson or unit are offered in a later section.

• *Take student interests into account.* To capture student interest, it is useful first to recognize what the students' interests are. You can then adapt the content and select instructional activities that address these interests.

Various approaches will identify these interests. As you near the start of a new unit, you might briefly describe what issues and activities you are currently planning. Students might then be asked to indicate topics or activities they are especially interested in and to offer additional suggestions. This interaction could take the form of an informal discussion.

You may prefer to draw a "web" of issues on the chalkboard. To do so, write the main topic in the center of a circle; draw lines diagonally from the circle; write the related issue on each line. As additional lines are drawn to represent related topics, the diagram will resemble a spider's web. Still more connecting lines may be drawn. For example, a unit in health may have First Aid written in the center of the web. Connecting lines may describe burns, broken bones, shock, poisoning, calling for help, and so on. Each line may relate to connecting lines for greater detail.

Another way to identify interest is through a questionnaire about the unit topics and proposed activities. You may also devise your own ways to gather student input. The key is to identify student interest in the subject matter and the possible instructional strategies, and take them into account in your planning decisions. With this information, you will be able to make better decisions to capture student attention throughout all sessions.

Decision Points

To capture student interest, take student interests into account when making planning decisions about content, instructional strategies, and performance requirements. How would you gather information from fifth graders to determine their interests? How might your approaches be different for first graders or for eleventh graders? What approaches could you use that do not rely on reading and writing? What approaches involve student interaction to identify the interests?

TABLE 8-1 Strategies for motivating students to learn

1. *Capture Student Interest in the Subject Matter*
   a. Take student interest into account.
   b. Capitalize on the arousal value of suspense, discovery, curiosity, exploration, and fantasy.
   c. Try to make study of the subject matter as active, investigative, adventurous, and social as possible.
   d. Use questions and activities to capture student interest in the subject matter.
   e. Use games, simulations, or other fun features.

2. Highlight the Relevance of the Subject Matter
   a. Select meaningful learning objectives and activities.
   b. Relate the subject matter to students' everyday experiences and backgrounds.
   c. Call attention to the usefulness of the subject matter.
   d. Have students use what they previously learned.

3. Help Students Maintain Expectations for Success
   a. Have students set short-term goals.
   b. Help students assess their progress toward their goals.
   c. Allow students a degree of control over their learning.
   d. Draw attention to the successes students have achieved.

4. Design the Lesson to Maintain Interest and Promote Student Success
   a. State learning objectives and expectations, and provide advance organizers.
   b. Vary instructional approaches and present the subject matter in interesting, novel ways.
   c. Plan active student involvement.
   d. Select stimulating, appropriate tasks.
   e. Occasionally do the unexpected.
   f. Use familiar material for initial examples, but provide unique and unexpected contexts when applying concepts and principles.
   g. Design activities that lead to student success.
   h. Provide an appropriate level of challenge or support.
   i. Plan for individual, cooperative, and competitive activities.
   j. Adapt tasks to match motivational needs.
   k. Promote feelings of control by giving students a voice in decision making.
   l. Communicate desirable expectations and attributes.
   m. Minimize performance anxiety.
   n. Establish a supportive environment.

5. Express Interest in the Content and Project Enthusiasm
   a. Model interest in learning and motivation to learn.
   b. Model task-related thinking and problem solving.
   c. Project enthusiasm.

6. Provide Feedback and Rewards for Performance
   a. Provide frequent opportunities for students to respond and to receive feedback about their academic work.
   b. Offer rewards as incentives.
   c. Give some rewards early in the learning experience.
   d. Help students attribute achievement to effort.
   e. Help students recognize that knowledge and skill development are incremental.
   f. Provide remedial socialization for discouraged students.

• *Capitalize on the arousal value of suspense, discovery, curiosity, exploration, and fantasy.* Stimuli that are novel, surprising, complex, incongruous, or ambiguous help lead to cognitive arousal, called ***epistemic curiosity*** (Berlyne, 1965). This is behavior aimed at acquiring knowledge and the means to understand and master the environment. When students' epistemic curiosity is aroused, they are motivated to find ways to understand the novel stimulus. This is especially important at the start of a learning experience when you are trying to enlist attention.

Epistemic curiosity can be aroused through (a) surprise; (b) doubt, or conflict between belief and disbelief; (c) perplexity, or uncertainty; (d) bafflement, or facing conflicting demands, and (e) contradiction (Berlyne, 1965). With these strategies, a conceptual conflict is aroused. The motivation lasts until the conflict is resolved or until the students give up. If they cannot resolve the conflict, they will become bored or frustrated, so the activity should lead to conflict resolution. Learning tasks that involve fantasy are also intrinsically satisfying (Lepper & Hodell, 1989).

Let's look at some examples of these strategies. Surprise could result when an activity leads to an unexpected ending, for example, a ball passing through a metal ring when cold cannot pass through after being heated. Doubt could be created when students are asked if the interior angles of a triangle always total 180 degrees. Perplexity or uncertainty could be created when a number of possible solutions to an issue are available but none seems absolutely right. Bafflement occurs when there does not seem to be a reasonable solution to an issue. Contradiction arises when the solution is opposite to general principle or common sense. Fantasy can be created by using an imaginary situation as the content for the activity, such as turning the lights out, describing a cave that the students might be exploring, and then having them write a creative story about their imagined trip in the cave.

• *Try to make study of the subject matter as active, investigative, adventurous, and social as possible.* Students will find the subject matter more intrinsically interesting if they are actively involved in the lesson. You can arouse their interest if the activities you select have built-in appeal. The students' first learning experience with a new topic should incorporate these characteristics.

Provide opportunities for students to move and be active. They might manipulate objects at their desks, move around the room for an activity, or engage in movement. Students might be allowed to investigate topics through activities that are part of an activity center or cooperative learning tasks. Learning can be made adventurous and entertaining through the use of unusual decorations and activities. In addition to doing independent work, students need opportunities for social interaction through pairing or small groups.

• *Use questions and activities to capture student interest in the subject matter.* At the beginning of a lesson, stimulate curiosity by posing interesting questions or problems. Students will feel the need to resolve an ambiguity or obtain more information about a topic. For example, you might ask students to speculate or make predictions about what they will be learning, or raise questions that successful completion of the activity will enable them to answer.

Teachers in Action

Using Fun Activities to Motivate Students

Jim Clowes, middle school geography teacher, Beloit, Wisconsin:

Routine activities are vital to maintaining control in a middle school setting. I use several activities that are related to geography. One is "The Map Game" where students approach maps displayed around the room and identify places named in the lesson. Another approach involves a small inflatable globe. Students remain in their seats while they toss the globe to one another, identifying on the globe places that I have named. Students look forward to these activities. I never use them as a reward for good behavior since my class knows that good behavior is expected.

These activities enhance regular learning and provide an excellent change of pace, which is needed in the middle-school classroom. In a 45-minute class, it is vital to change activities two or three times. I use the approaches described here two or three times a week to contribute to the variety. When fun learning activities are used on a regular basis, discipline problems become nonexistent.

You may plan these questions and activities as a means to induce curiosity or suspense. Divergent questions that allow for several possible acceptable answers are useful (e.g., What do you think the author was trying to express in the first eight lines of this poem?). Include opportunities for students to express opinions or make other responses about the subject matter.

• *Use games, simulations, or other fun features.* Activities that students find entertaining and fun can attract their attention. Students find these intrinsically satisfying. An ***instructional game*** is an activity in which students follow prescribed rules unlike those of reality as they strive to attain a challenging goal. Games can help students learn facts and evaluate choices. Many games combine well with the drill and practice method of learning.

An ***instructional simulation*** recreates or represents an event or situation that causes the student to act, react, and make decisions. Simulations offer a framework for using the discovery method, the inquiry approach, experiential learning, and inductive approaches to instruction. Simulations help students practice decision making, make choices, receive results, and evaluate decisions.

Games, simulations, and other activities with fun features motivate students, promote interaction, present relevant aspects of real-life situations, and make possible direct involvement in learning. Games and simulations are commercially available, with many now designed for use on computers. You can also devise your own games and simulations for use in the classroom.

2. *Highlight the relevance of the subject matter.* Another important motivational task is to help the student understand that the subject matter is related to their personal needs or goals (Keller, 1983). Actions taken to achieve this purpose can arouse curiosity and sustain interest over time. You might take the following actions as a means of highlighting the relevance of the subject matter.

- *Select meaningful learning objectives and activities.* Students will be motivated to learn only if they see its relevance. Select academic objectives that include some knowledge or skill that is clearly worth learning, either in its own right or as a step to a greater objective. Avoid planning continued practice on skills that have already been mastered, memorizing lists for no good reason, looking up and copying definitions of terms that are never meaningfully used, and other activities that do not directly relate to the learning objective.

- *Relate the subject matter to the everyday experiences and backgrounds of the students.* Students may find little meaning in definitions, principles, or other general or abstract content unless the material can be made more concrete or visual. Promote personal identification with the content by relating experiences or telling anecdotes illustrating how the content applies to the lives of specific individuals. An initial lesson on fractions, for example, might include a discussion of how the students divide a pizza at home.

- *Call attention to the usefulness of the subject matter.* Students are more likely to appreciate the relevance of the subject matter if you discuss in what way it would be useful to them, both in school and outside. Discuss the reason why the learning objective is important, in its own right or as a step to additional, useful objectives. Relate the subject matter to today's situation and everyday life. Call students' attention to the usefulness of the knowledge and skills taught in schools to their outside lives.

You could have your students think about the topics or activities in relation to their own interests. This helps them understand that motivation to learn must come from within, that it is a property of the learner rather than a task to be learned. You might ask them, for example, to identify questions about the topic that they would like to have answered.

- *Have students use what they previously learned.* Another way to clearly demonstrate subject relevance is to have students use what they previously learned. This may be easy to do since one learning objective often serves as the foundation for the next. For example, when discussing the reasons for the Civil War, you could ask the students if their earlier study of the U.S. Constitution and the Bill of Rights point to the reasons.

In this way, you reinforce previous learning and highlight the importance of each learning objective. You demonstrate that each objective will have subsequent use. Whenever possible, call for previously acquired facts and concepts.

3. *Help students maintain expectations for success.* Help students see that they can be successful through personal control (Keller, 1983). Students' motivation is enhanced when they maintain expectations for success. Techniques for this purpose address the students' inner need to be competent, and thus

Teachers in Action

Students Seeing the Purpose and Importance of Their Work

Barbara Bjorklund, kindergarten teacher, Becker, Minnesota:

Students at every level need to see the purpose and importance of their work, written or otherwise. This tends to motivate students internally. I have moved away from the use of stickers, stars, and happy faces. I now use approaches that promote understanding, sense of ownership, and self-evaluation while reducing the focus on extrinsic rewards and outside approval.

I do this by discussing the word "quality" during the first weeks of school. This is discussed relative to books, toys, cleaning up after a snack, or any other matter that might be meaningful about the activity at hand. For example, one of the final activities in our study of the nursery rhyme "Humpty Dumpty" is the students' preparation of a four-picture cut-apart sequence of the rhyme. I explain the procedures that they need to follow to prepare the card sequence and then, as a group, the students suggest various characteristics they think would show quality work.

Students usually comment immediately on "good coloring," and I prompt them for specifics such as coloring in one direction and staying within the lines. We then move to other matters such as cutting with the scissors and placing the story elements in the correct order. We also discuss the importance of quality. I write their reactions down; this serves as a reference. After everyone is clear on *what* we're doing and *why*, then we begin.

As another example, I have students check their work with me before taking it home. At this point, which I view as crucial, I say, "Tell me about your work." "What do you like about your work?" "What did you do that is quality?" In the case of "Humpty Dumpty," the students might say something about the coloring, cutting, or sequencing.

If a child has not done a quality job for his or her abilities, this needs to be addressed. Because my approach doesn't involve stickers and stars, I think it is wise to inform parents about it.

the techniques are intrinsically satisfying. The following approaches present a means to help students maintain expectations for success.

- *Have students set short-term goals.* Students will work harder for goals they set themselves than for goals set by someone else. In **Individually Guided Motivation** (Klausmeier et al., 1975), students meet with their teachers on a regular basis to set specific, measurable goals for the week. For example, students might select a score they expect to obtain on an upcoming test or project. At the next goal-setting conference, the teacher would discuss each student's

Teachers in Action

Planning to Fail or Succeed

Michael Abbott, teacher in an alternative high school, Livonia, Michigan:

We prepare a newsletter that describes our activities. At the start of the year, we take time to get acquainted and to orient the students to our expectations. The following is an actual lesson that was used and reported in the newsletter to demonstrate some of the orientation activities.

TEACHER: There will be no note-taking today. Instead, you'll be brain-storming about something and I'll do all the writing on this chart. Today, I'd like you to tell me all the things that you can do to guarantee to me that you will fail a class. Absolute failure! Don't be shy, you said you were the experts.

STUDENT: Don't study.

TEACHER: That was a good one. Any others?

STUDENTS: Don't do homework. Leave books at home. Daydream in class. Fight with the teacher.

TEACHER: Wow, one at a time. I need to get these down.

STUDENTS: Have a bad attitude toward school. Procrastinate. Be disorganized. Forget books, pencils, and other stuff for class. Sleep in class. Skip class. Just don't try.

TEACHER: This is a good list. Let's stop now. You're right, you are the experts on failure. By the way you're going, I will be writing all day.

Let's look at what we have here. What can we learn from this? Because you knew how to fail so well, what else does that tell you?

STUDENT: It shows that if we know how to fail, then we also know how to be successful.

TEACHER: Good answer. You all know how to get better grades. If you want success, then you need to do what leads to success. Is there anything else that we can learn here?

STUDENT: We do things that lead to failure.

TEACHER: You bet! Failure just doesn't fall out of the sky. It doesn't just happen; we do it deliberately. Every time we do not study or skip class or leave our books at home, we make a conscious decision toward failure.

It's hard to believe that people fail on purpose, but you just proved that it happens. On reflection, most of us know what we need to do to improve any part of our lives. When it's clear, it's easier to succeed.

So what changes do you plan to make in your life to improve your grades? Go slow, I'm taking notes again. I want to read them back to you at the end of the marking period.

attainment of the goals, and set new goals for the following week. During these meetings, the teacher would praise students for setting and then achieving the goals, and would help them learn to set ambitious yet realistic goals. This goal-setting and review process can increase student achievement (Klausmeier et al., 1975). Given your grade level and time constraints, you may need to modify this program to fit your situation.

Students who set short-term goals have higher intrinsic interest, higher feelings of self-efficacy, and improved performance in the content area (Zimmerman, 1989). Attainment of short-term goals seems to enhance both learning and motivation. When students achieve their goals, they have a sense of mastery that serves to make the activities more interesting.

You should help students identify short-term goals and set appropriate standards for them to judge their progress. Goal setting is effective when goals are proximal (focusing on an immediate task) rather than distant, specific rather than global, and challenging rather than too easy or too hard. Students must take the goals seriously and be committed to them.

• *Help students assess their progress toward their goals.* Students may need help in assessing progress toward established goals by using appropriate standards for judging levels of success. Breaking a large goal down into several smaller parts is a useful way to help students assess progress. For example, instead of simply stating that a student will do better in the next report card period, identify several smaller goals aimed at improving homework, tests, and the like.

Some students will need detailed feedback about both the strengths and the weaknesses of their work. Simply reporting a grade, for example, may not be sufficient. The student would profit from additional information concerning improvements made on earlier work as well as specific ways to improve.

• *Allow students a degree of control over their learning.* Students who feel they can control the learning situation (where, when, how) and the learning outcomes (seeking the level they want to achieve) are more intrinsically motivated (Lepper & Hodell, 1989). This helps them feel that they can be successful. Depending on your situation, you may be able to give students some choices in instructional activities, when they are due, and how they should be completed. Then, students are more likely to have expectations for success.

• *Draw attention to the successes students have achieved.* You can also draw attention to the successes students have achieved. You can make statements about class progress toward achieving the goals and about their overall work. Displays and announcements about the work of individual students or groups would also draw attention to the successes that students have experienced.

4. *Design the lesson to maintain interest and promote student success.* Motivation to learn is enhanced when students are interested in the subject matter and expect to be successful (Keller, 1983). The lesson should be designed to accomplish these ends. The following techniques are intended to achieve these purposes through both intrinsic and extrinsic motivation.

• *State learning objectives and expectations, and provide advance organizers.* Students need to know exactly what they are supposed to do, how they will be evaluated, and what the consequences of success will be. Avoid confusion by clearly communicating objectives and expectations. At the start of a class, for example, you might describe that day's assignment, your expectations for how the assignment will be completed, the form of the paper to be turned in, the means of evaluation and relative point value in the grading period, and other expectations you hold.

Your description also serves as an organizer for the students so they understand what will happen in class. This introduction should also include a description of the value of the subject matter to be examined and the related tasks. Students can then better appreciate the material and have a reason to be motivated.

• *Vary instructional approaches and present the subject matter in interesting, novel ways.* After capturing student interest at the start of a lesson, maintain interest through varied approaches such as lectures, demonstrations, recitations, practice and drills, reviews, panels and debates, group projects, inquiry approaches, discovery learning and problem solving, role playing and simulation, gaming, and computer-assisted instruction (Burden & Byrd, 1994).

As effective as a strategy may be, students will lose interest if it is practiced too often or too routinely. Vary your strategies over time and try not to use the same one throughout an entire class period. Try to make sure something about each task is new to the students, or at least different from what they have been doing. Call attention to the new element, whether it be new content, media involved, or the type of responses required.

• *Plan for active student involvement.* Too often, students just sit, listen, read, and write. Some students would prefer to be more actively involved. For example, students might conduct a debate concerning a controversial issue, prepare a product as a result of a group project, or conduct a survey in the class or outside. Students become actively engaged and circulate in the classroom as they complete the various tasks.

• *Select stimulating, appropriate tasks.* The tasks themselves need to relate to the lesson's objectives and stimulate student interest. You could stimulate interest by selecting tasks that relate to one of the three types of curiosity (Kreitler et al., 1975): (a) perceptual curiosity, in which curiosity is piqued by what they observe around them; (b) manipulative curiosity, in which curiosity is awakened through active manipulation of an object; and (c) conceptual curiosity, in which curiosity involves the desire to know about or to solve a mystery.

• *Occasionally do the unexpected.* Another way to maintain student interest and to claim attention is by doing something unexpected. Note what usually goes on and do something different. Instead of preparing a worksheet, have the students prepare it. If your discussions in social studies have been about the effects of certain events on the United States, focus discussions on the effects on your community. If you normally have a reserved presentation style, occasionally include some dramatic elements. An occasional departure from what the students have come to expect adds fun and novelty to instruction and helps maintain student interest.

• *Use familiar material for initial examples, but provide unique and unexpected contexts when applying concepts and principles.* When you want to build interest, involve the familiar. For applications once learning has been achieved, however, it is the unique and unexpected that keep interest high and help students transfer what they have learned. For example, when teaching the classification system of plants and animals, you might begin by classifying different breeds of dogs to illustrate classification. You could then have them develop a classification for music sold on compact disks and cassette tapes at a local music store.

• *Design activities that lead to student success.* Students are motivated to learn when they expect to be successful. Therefore, make sure that they fairly consistently achieve success at their early level of understanding, then help them move ahead in small steps, preparing them for each new step so they can adjust without confusion or frustration. Pace students through activities as briskly as possible while thoroughly preparing them for new activities.

• *Provide an appropriate level of challenge or support.* Activities should be at an appropriate level of difficulty. Students lose interest rapidly if they are not able to succeed because the work is too hard, or if they are able to succeed too easily. Assessments conducted before instruction determine what your students already know and thus help you decide on the appropriate degree of difficulty for the work at hand. Careful observation of students at work will help inform you of the level of difficulty.

• *Plan for individual, cooperative, and competitive activities.* Interest is maintained when there is variety in the way the learning activities are structured. Some activities, such as seatwork, may be completed individually. Other projects can be completed in cooperative learning groups with four to six students in each group.

Competitive activities also provide excitement and rewards. Students can compete either as individuals or as teams, depending on the activity. Team approaches may be more desirable because they can be structured so students cooperate with members of their team. Make use of group competitive situations that stress fun rather than winning.

Decision Points

Structuring learning experiences in various ways helps maintain student interest. Assume you are teaching a ninth-grade math class: identify how you would use individual, cooperative, and competitive activities. What are the merits and disadvantages of each approach? How might the inclusion of some students with disabilities affect your handling of these activities?

• *Adapt tasks to match motivational needs.* Individual differences in ability, background, and attitudes toward school and specific subjects should be considered as you make decisions about motivational strategies. Some students need more structure than others. Other students need more reinforcement and praise. Some students are more motivated to learn than others. You will need to select motivational strategies that are most effective for your students and adjust the frequency and intensity of their use depending on individual needs.

- *Promote feelings of control by giving students a voice in decision making.* Giving students some choices within a framework allows them to follow their interests. The range of choices may be limited or broad. For example, you might identify several tasks and then let students select the order in which they will complete the tasks. You might identify several alternative tasks that address a given objective and then let students select the task they prefer. Still another approach is to solicit student input in task selection. The degree of control you permit will be affected by their age and maturity, among other factors. Students appreciate even a limited degree of choice.

- *Communicate desirable expectations and attributes.* If you treat your students as if they already are eager learners, they are more likely to become eager learners. Let them know that you expect them to be curious, to want to learn facts and understand principles, to master skills, and to recognize what they are learning as meaningful and applicable to their everyday lives. Encourage questions and inquiry. Through these means, you communicate desirable expectations and attributes.

- *Minimize performance anxiety.* To motivate students to learn, they need to believe that they will be successful in their efforts. If you create situations that cause tension, pressure, and anxiety, your students will likely choose safety and remain uninvolved for fear of failure. On the other hand, if you minimize risks and make learning seem exciting and worthwhile, most students will join in.

One way to reduce anxiety is to make clear the separation between instruction or practice activities designed to promote learning and tests designed to evaluate student performance. Most activities should be structured as learning experiences rather than tests. You might say, for example, "Let's assess our progress and learn from our mistakes."

Avoid using only one or two exams or projects as the sole means for determining the report card grade. To encourage participation, make it clear that students will not be graded on their questions or comments during recitation. Don't impose conditions or restrictions on assignments, homework, or projects that might get in the way of students' giving full effort. For example, requiring that all papers be typed perfectly, with no formatting errors, would seem to be a barrier to some students.

- *Establish a supportive environment.* Be encouraging and patient in an effort to make students comfortable about learning activities and to support their learning efforts. Establish a businesslike yet relaxed and supportive atmosphere. Reinforce students' involvement with the subject matter and eliminate any unpleasant consequences. Organize and manage your classroom to establish an effective learning environment.

5. Express interest in the content and project enthusiasm. To be motivated to learn, students need to be interested in the subject matter and see

Teachers in Action

Giving Personal Attention and Reinforcement

John Wolters, sixth-grade teacher, Manhattan, Kansas:

"Just what are you doing with my daughter?" came from the mother of one of my students as she sat down for our first parent-teacher conference. Keeping as calm and collected as I could, I tried to surmise if this was a call for panic or if I was to be commended for a job well done. Before I could respond, she went on. "Before sixth grade, Amber was a girl who just went through the motions when it came to school stuff. Her grades had been steady Cs and Ds, with an occasional B. She never talked about school at home, and doing homework was like pulling teeth."

"But this year, we have a different girl at home. She comes home and isn't seen until her homework is done. Amber hasn't missed a day yet, and even came to school sick one day when she didn't want to miss a science experiment. I had hopes that this would mean better grades, but I was floored when you sent home this sheet with all As and Bs. What are you doing with her? Do you share your secrets?"

I had no idea of Amber's previous record since she came new to our school that year. From the first day, she appeared to be a diligent worker, but it appeared that school didn't come naturally for her. I didn't think I would need to take any additional steps to motivate her.

I gave Amber personal attention in several ways. This worked for her. During recess I would talk with her and other students, trying to bring out similarities that each of them might not have found in one another as quickly if I had not intervened. Amber sincerely appreciated the notes that I wrote to her which focused on something she had done well. Sometimes the notes just affirmed a positive quality I had noticed about her. She even wrote "thank you" notes to me; some included questions she wanted me to answer in a note to her.

When I included comments on her papers about something she had done well, she continued doing well in that area. If I pointed out something that could be done better, she made noticeable improvement in the following papers. She also responded to expectations I put before the class—they became personal goals for her. If her work was late, she came to me and told me exactly why it was late and when I could expect it to be turned in. She said that she would work hard not to let it happen again.

Before Amber's mom left, I assured her that Amber had the major role in the changes that had taken place. What I had done to help Amber, I had done with the rest of the class as well; yet not all of the students made as much progress as Amber.

its relevance (Keller, 1983). By expressing interest in the content yourself and projecting enthusiasm, you address these motivational issues.

- *Model interest in learning and motivation to learn.* Let your students see that you value learning as a rewarding, self-actualizing activity that provides personal satisfaction and enriches your life. Share your thinking about learning and give examples of its application. In this way, students see how an educated person uses information in everyday life. For example, a social studies teacher might relate how her understanding of community, state, and national events helped her make informed decisions when voting on candidates during political elections.

- *Model task-related thinking and problem solving.* Think "out loud" as you demonstrate to students how they might approach an issue or problem; let them see how *your* mind approaches a problem. Modeling opportunities arise whenever an activity calls for use of a cognitive process or strategy. For example, you can model for them how to conduct an experiment, identify the main ideas in paragraphs, develop a plan for writing a composition, or deduce applications of a general principle to specific situations.

- *Project enthusiasm.* Everything you say should communicate in both tone and manner that the subject matter is important. If you model appropriate attitudes and beliefs about topics and assignments, the students will pick up on these cues. Use timing, nonverbal expressions and gestures, and cueing and other verbal techniques to project a level of intensity and enthusiasm that tells the students that the material is important and deserves close attention. (Enthusiasm is discussed more fully in chapter 12.)

Decision Points

First graders like a teacher to be animated and exciting. Yet maintaining a high degree of enthusiasm all the time may present some problems. What might these problems be? Exhibiting little enthusiasm all the time also may pose a problem. How can you determine an appropriate degree of enthusiasm? How might your approach to displaying your enthusiasm be different in fourth grade, ninth grade, or twelfth grade?

---

6. *Provide feedback and rewards for performance.* Students need to reach a point of satisfaction for what they are doing and what they are achieving (Keller, 1893). This satisfaction is the result of their intrinsic motivations about what they are doing as well as their responses to extrinsic rewards. You can help students be satisfied by providing feedback and rewards for their performance.

- *Provide frequent opportunities for students to respond and to receive feedback about their academic work.* To be satisfied about their work, students need to receive feedback. Give them opportunities to respond actively, to interact either with you or with one another, to manipulate materials, or respond in some way other than merely listening or reading. Drill, recitation, boardwork, and seatwork can be useful. In addition, active response opportunities can occur through projects, experiments, role plays, simulations, or other creative applications of what has been learned. Students also like activities that allow them to create a finished product. All of these activities offer opportunities for students to work and respond to instructional stimuli, and as well give you opportunities to offer feedback about their work.

Students need to receive immediate feedback that will guide subsequent responses. For example, you might have five students work simultaneously on math problems at the chalkboard while you and the rest of the class observe them. You then could offer the students feedback about their work and discuss how to overcome the difficulties they found in arriving at a solution. Students profit from this feedback, which guides them in solving future problems. Grading is not involved.

Feedback also takes the form of grades for course requirements including homework, projects, quizzes, and tests. Since students need frequent feedback, plan to include many avenues for them to demonstrate competence. Do not rely on just two tests and three homework assignments, for example, as the justification for a report card grade and as the means to provide students with feedback throughout the grading period. More frequent feedback is needed throughout the grading period.

Frequent, regular feedback gives students reinforcement for their successes and indicates areas that need improvement. This helps them feel satisfied about their work, and it can be a tool to fuel extra effort and commitment in the event of dissatisfaction.

• *Offer rewards as incentives.* Rewards motivate many students to put forth effort, especially if they are offered in advance as incentives for reaching a certain level of performance. To ensure that rewards act as incentives for everyone and not only those of high ability, see that all students have reasonable opportunities to receive rewards.

When students receive consequences that they value, they become satisfied with themselves. This helps motivate them to continue working in ways that lead to success. Rewards can be delivered in various ways including: (a) grades; (b) spoken and written praise; (c) activity rewards and special privileges (opportunities to play games, use special equipment, or engage in special activities); (d) symbolic rewards (honor roll, posting good papers); (e) material rewards (prizes, trinkets); and (f) teacher rewards (opportunities to do things with the teacher). As discussed previously, be cautious about relying too heavily on extrinsic rewards since this may become counterproductive.

Grades can be an important motivational tool if they are used to give information, rather than to punish; if you explain the purpose of tests, how they are prepared, and how to interpret them; and if you view tests and grades as evidence of growth and mastery.

• *Give some rewards early in the learning experience.* By receiving some type of reward early in the learning experience, students understand why they are working and will likely put forth more effort to receive additional rewards. The reward may simply be praise or an opportunity for a special activity. A reinforcer given early in the learning experience as you plan to use it later lends the reinforcer value that influences student performance. Ultimately, students will feel satisfied—a motivator to learn.

Select easy tasks in the early steps of the learning activity. This offers you opportunities to deliver praise and rewards, which in turn help influence subsequent student behavior. Every student should be able to receive some type of positive reinforcement early in the lesson. For example, you might select fairly simple sentence translations in the first part of a French class, then gradually move on to more difficult translations later. This gives you an opportunity to reward and reinforce students at an early point.

• *Help students attribute achievement to effort.* For students to feel satisfaction about their work, they must actually be successful. Success doesn't just happen, however—students must put forth effort. They need to see that their effort is related to their achievement and feelings of success.

You can help students recognize that achievement is related to effort by drawing attention to the effort they exert in certain tasks. For example, when Gina has achieved a better report card grade, you could say, "Gina, coming in for extra help and putting in extra study time really paid off during this grading period. You raised your grade by 14 points. Congratulations!"

Statements drawing attention to effort can also be made during class sessions. In an art class, you might say "Reggie, your careful application of the water colors has helped you show realistic images." The student is reinforced due to specific actions and effort, and is likely to continue those actions.

• *Help students recognize that knowledge and skill development are incremental.* Students may not see that each small step they take helps them become more knowledgeable and skilled. If they recognize the importance of each small step, they will realize that their learning is incremental, and they will have a greater sense of success and satisfaction.

To help students recognize this, show how their understanding of each part of the subject contributes to their understanding of the whole. For example, when teaching students how to do a layup in basketball, help them recognize and practice each important part of the actions—dribbling, dribbling while running, raising the correct foot and arm when releasing the ball, and so on. Students realize that their skill development is incremental, and they can feel satisfaction as they successfully perform each step of the process.

• *Provide remedial socialization for discouraged students.* Some students may become discouraged at the first sign of difficulty, especially if they've had a history of failures. You may need to provide more intensive and individualized encouragement for these students than for the rest of the class to help them achieve success. The strategies previously described can be used, with greater attention given to these students. For example, you may need to take extra steps to help discouraged students recognize the importance of their effort as a means to lead to success. Or you may need to draw extra attention to the incremental steps that result in their knowledge and skill development. Discouraged students may also need further help with their study skills so they can be successful.

MOTIVATIONAL PLANNING

There are three critical periods in a learning event during which particular motivational strategies will have a maximum impact on motivation (Wlodkowski, 1984, 1985). These are:

1. *Beginning a lesson*—when the student enters and begins the learning process.
2. *During a lesson*—when the student is involved in the body or main content of the learning process.
3. *Ending a lesson*—when the student is completing the learning process.

For each of these time periods, two general motivational factors serve as categories for specific strategies. Strategies should address attitudes and needs when beginning a lesson, stimulation and affect during a lesson, and competence and reinforcement when ending a lesson. These critical time periods and their accompanying motivational factors are examined in the following section. As you plan a lesson, also plan for motivation, and plan that each time phase of the learning sequence includes positive motivational influences.

Beginning a Lesson

At the beginning of a learning activity, you need to consider two motivational factors when selecting motivational strategies: *attitude* and *needs*. Attitude deals with the student's view of the subject matter, the general learning environment, and other factors. Needs deal with the students' basic needs at the time of learning.

As you plan for the beginning of a learning event, ask yourself two questions:

- What can I do to establish a positive learning *attitude* for this learning sequence?
- How do I best meet the *needs* of my learners through this learning sequence?

Attitude. *Attitude* is the student's stance toward the learning environment, teacher, subject matter, and self. When planning to incorporate motivational factors at the beginning of a lesson, you need to select strategies that positively affect the students' attitude about themselves, yourself as the teacher, the subject, and the learning situation while also establishing learner expectations for success.

To positively affect attitude about yourself as the teacher, you might plan to establish a relationship with the students by sharing something of value with them, listening to them with empathy, treating them with warmth and acceptance, and using class or individual meetings to establish relationships. To positively affect attitude toward the subject and learning situation, plan to make conditions surrounding the subject positive, model enthusiasm for the subject, associate the student with other students who are enthusiastic about the subject, positively confront the student about erroneous beliefs, and make the first experience with the subject matter as positive as possible.

You can positively affect the students' attitudes toward themselves by promoting success, giving encouragement, emphasizing students' personal causation in their learning, and using group process methods to enhance a positive self-concept. Finally, when trying to establish learner expectancy for success, you could interview students and help them set goals or contracts for their learning.

Needs.   A *need* is a condition experienced by the individual as a force that leads the person to move in the direction of a goal. Maslow's hierarchy of needs provides a framework to examine strategies that teachers could select in addressing students' needs at the beginning of a lesson. When planning for meeting physiological needs, you could select content, examples, and projects that relate to the students' physiological needs, and could be alert to restlessness so you can relieve the causes producing it. For example, students may not be physically comfortable after sitting for long periods of time or after being asked to do one task for a long time. Instead, have a change of activities or break the tasks up into shorter segments.

When addressing safety needs, plan to select content, examples, and projects that relate to the safety needs of students; reduce or remove elements in the learning environment that lead to failure or fear; and introduce the unfamiliar through the familiar. To reduce the fear of failure, provide opportunities for practice and tell students that the practice activities will not be graded.

When planning for belongingness and love needs, select content, examples, and projects that relate to these needs; create components of the learning environment that tell students they are wanted and cared for; and designate classroom duties and responsibilities in such a way that each student becomes a functioning member of the group. Assigning some work to be completed in groups, for example, would allow opportunities for the social interaction that is so important.

Esteem needs can be addressed by offering learning goals that affirm the student's identity or role; subject matter, assignments, and learning modes that appeal to and complement student strengths and assets; subject matter that enhances the student's independence as a learner and a person; and activities to allow students to publicly display and share their talents and works. For example, a composition or writing project could require the students to incorporate information about their ethnic heritage, and the projects could be displayed.

To address self-actualization needs, give students the opportunity to select topics, projects, and assignments that appeal to their curiosity, sense of wonder, and need to explore; encourage divergent thinking and creativity in the learning process; and provide the opportunity for self-discovery.

Decision Points

Students have safety needs that should be taken into account when planning the beginning of a lesson. One aspect of safety is not fearing to try new things and being willing to participate in class activities. Students need to feel secure that they will not be criticized for a wrong answer or for sharing information in class. What specific actions could you take to ensure student safety in these ways? How could safety be provided in practice activities or group discussions?

During a Lesson

During a learning activity, two motivational factors need to be considered— *stimulation* and *affect*. Stimulation deals with attention and involvement during the learning process. Affect deals with the affective or emotional experience of the student while learning.

As you plan for this part of the learning activity, ask yourself two questions:

- What about this learning sequence will continuously *stimulate* my learners?
- In what way is the *affective experience* and *emotional climate* for this learning sequence positive for learners?

Stimulation. **Stimulation** has to do with holding attention and building involvement. When you introduce or connect learning activities, draw attention to the new learning activity or topic. Use movement, voice, body language, and props to vitalize and accentuate classroom presentations. To promote interest and involvement, relate learning to student interest, and use humor, examples, analogies, stories, and questions. When asking questions, limit informational questions and selectively increase questions that require comprehension, application, analysis, synthesis, and evaluation. To create disequilibrium, introduce contrasting information, play the devil's advocate, and be unpredictable to the degree that students enjoy the spontaneity. To be unpredictable, for example, you could alter your conduct of each review session before a test.

Affect. **Affect** pertains to the feelings, concerns, values, and passions of the students while learning. When planning lessons, try to encourage and integrate learner emotions, and maintain an optimal emotional climate within the learning group. Feelings are the emotions that accompany the *how* and *what* a student is learning. Awareness and communication allow feelings to become a vital and influential aspect of motivation.

Integrate what is being taught with how the student feels *now* about the content and then establish a relationship between this content and the student's life. You can also take steps to establish a climate that promotes positive interrelationships among class members.

Ending a Lesson

At the end of a learning activity, two motivational factors are considered: *competence* and *reinforcement*. Competence deals with the degree of progress the students feel they have made. Reinforcement deals with feedback on their progress.

When you plan for the ending of a learning activity, ask yourself two questions:

- How does this learning sequence increase or affirm the learner's feelings of *competence?*
- What *reinforcement* does this learning sequence provide?

Competence.   *Competence* refers to the sense of growth and content mastery that a person recognizes. As you plan for the ending of the learning activity, take into account at least two aspects of competence. First, make sure students have opportunities to become aware of their progress and mastery. You can do this by providing feedback on mastery of learning, offering constructive criticism, and facilitating successful completion of the learning task. Second, students need to be aware at the end of the activity that they "personally caused" their own learning. This can be done by acknowledging and affirming the student's responsibility in completing the task, using a competence checklist for student self-rating, and acknowledging the risk taking and challenge involved in the learning accomplishment.

Reinforcement.   *Reinforcement* is an event of a state of affairs that changes subsequent behavior when it follows an instance of that behavior. For example, a student who is given praise for efforts made in studying for a test will tend to continue these efforts after the praise is given. Reinforcement can be in the form of artificial reinforcers such as tangible or concrete materials, or extrinsic symbols for learning behavior. Gold stars, prizes, trinkets, certificates, and points are examples. When natural consequences (e.g., reading can produce new insights and expanded awareness) of student learning are evident, emphasize the result of the learning behavior and highlight it as a part of the learning process.

You can take steps to enhance the intrinsic value of traditional grading and limit its negative intrinsic value. Provide alternative forms of feedback to students about their performance, clearly explaining the grading policy to students, and perhaps using student self-evaluation as part of the grading decision.

MAJOR CONCEPTS

1. Motivation is the process of arousing, directing, and maintaining behavior.
2. Intrinsic motivation is a response to needs that exist within the student, such as curiosity, the need to know, or feelings of competence or growth. It may also involve the internal satisfaction the student feels when performing the task.

3. Extrinsic motivation is motivation that comes from outside the learner and involves the delivery of external rewards when a student completes a task. The reward might be words of praise from the teacher, a higher grade, or a privilege.

4. Several theoretical views of motivation attempt to explain aspects of student interest: the behavioral view, the cognitive view, the humanistic view, and achievement motivation theory.

5. Many strategies can be used to motivate students to learn.

6. There are three critical periods of a learning event—beginning, during, and ending—during which particular motivational strategies will have maximum impact on motivation.

7. Attitudes and needs are motivational factors to be considered at the beginning of a lesson; stimulation and affect during the lesson; and competence and reinforcement at the end of a the lesson.

DISCUSSION QUESTIONS

1. In your schooling and through your experiences in classrooms, what types of intrinsic and extrinsic motivation do you feel are most effective?

2. What are the merits and problems involved in using games and simulations as a motivational strategy?

3. How can you determine an appropriate level of challenge or support for the students?

4. What are some factors to consider when deciding on the degree of control you will give your students in decision making about content, activities, and assignments?

5. Describe several ways that review can be conducted at the end of a lesson to give students a sense of competence about what they have just learned.

SUPPLEMENTAL ACTIVITIES

For Clinical Settings

1. Assume that you will be teaching a unit on the history of your state. Describe how you would teach the unit if you were to emphasize the humanistic view of motivation. Do the same for the other views—the behavioral view, the cognitive view, and achievement motivation theory.

2. Select a unit in a subject area of your choice. Describe the ways that you could highlight the relevance of that subject matter for your students.

3. Plan two consecutive lessons in a subject area of your choice. In the left column of each plan sheet list the sequence of events, and in the right column list and briefly describe how you intend to apply the motivational factors for beginning, during, and ending the lessons.

For Field Settings

1. Ask several students to describe what motivates them to learn and to stay involved in the lesson. Ask them to identify specific strategies that their teachers use to make learning interesting.

2. Ask several teachers how they introduce learning objectives to the students and provide advance organizers.
3. Observe several lessons being taught and identify factors that serve to motivate students to learn.

KEY TERMS

Achievement motivation theory	Individually Guided Motivation
Affect	Instructional game
Attitude	Instructional simulation
Behavioral view	Interest
Cognitive disequilibrium	Intrinsic motivation
Cognitive view	Level of aspiration
Competence	Maslow's hierarchy of needs
Dimensions of motivation	Motivation
Epistemic curiosity	Needs
Expectancy	Reinforcement
Extrinsic motivation	Relevance
Fear of success	Satisfaction
Humanistic view	Stimulation

RECOMMENDED READINGS

Good, T. L., & Brophy, J. E. (1994). *Looking in Classrooms,* 6th ed. New York: HarperCollins. Discusses many aspects of teaching, and includes a separate chapter on motivation. Thorough research-based coverage.

Spaulding, C. L. (1992). *Motivation in the Classroom.* New York: McGraw-Hill. Thirteen chapters in four sections cover understanding motivation, interventions for large groups, interventions for small groups and individuals, and planning for and monitoring change. Has an academic tone.

Stipek, D. J. (1993). *Motivation to Learn: From Theory to Practice,* 2nd ed. Boston: Allyn & Bacon. Twelve chapters designed to demonstrate how achievement motivation theory and research can help teachers develop autonomous, self-confident learners who enjoy learning activities. Well referenced, thorough, has an academic tone.

Wlodkowski, R. J. (1984). *Motivation and Teaching: A Practical Guide.* Washington, DC: National Education Association. Provides thorough coverage of ways to plan for motivational strategies at the beginning, middle, and end of a lesson. Has many practical examples.

REFERENCES

Berlyne, D. E. (1965). Curiosity and education. In J. D. Krumboltz, Ed., *Learning and the Educational Process* (pp. 67–89). Chicago: Rand McNally.

Biehler, R. F., & Snowman, J. (1993). *Psychology Applied to Teaching*, 7th ed. Boston: Houghton Mifflin.

Burden, P. R., & Byrd, D. M. (1994). *Methods for Effective Teaching*. Boston: Allyn & Bacon.

Gage, N. L., & Berliner, D. C. (1991). *Educational Psychology*, 5th ed. Boston: Houghton Mifflin.

Good, T. L., & Brophy, J. E. (1995). *Contemporary Educational Psychology*. New York: Longman.

Kaplan, P. S. (1990). *Educational Psychology for Tomorrow's Teacher.* St. Paul, MN: West Publishing.

Keller, J. M. (1983). Motivational design of instruction. In C. M. Reigeluth, Ed., *Instructional Design Theories and Models: An Overview of Their Current Status.* Hillsdale, NJ: Erlbaum.

Klausmeier, H. J., Jeter, J. T., Quilling, M. R., Frayer, D. A., & Allen, P. S. (1975). *Individually Guided Motivation.* Madison, WI: Research and Development Center for Cognitive Learning.

Kreitler, S., Zigler, E., & Kreitler, H. (1975). The nature of curiosity in children. *Journal of School Psychology, 13,* 185–200.

Lepper, M. R. (1983). Extrinsic reward and intrinsic motivation: Implications for the classroom. In J. M. Levine & M. C. Wang, Eds., *Teacher and Student Perceptions: Implications for Learning* (pp. 281–317). Hillsdale, NJ: Erlbaum.

Lepper, M. R., & Greene, D. (1975). Turning play into work: Effects of adult surveillance and extrinsic rewards on children's intrinsic motivation. *Journal of Personality and Social Psychology, 31,* 479–488.

Lepper, M. R., Greene, D., & Nisbett, R. E. (1973). Undermining children's intrinsic interest with extrinsic rewards: A test of the overjustification hypothesis. *Journal of Personality and Social Psychology, 28,* 129–137.

Lepper, M. R., & Hodell, M. (1989). Intrinsic motivation in the classroom. In C. Ames and R. Ames, Eds., *Research on Motivation in Education,* vol. 3. San Diego: Academic Press.

Maslow, A. (1954). *Motivation and Personality.* New York: Harper & Row.

Morgan, M. (1984). Reward-induced decrements and increments in intrinsic motivation. *Review of Educational Research, 54*(1), 5–30.

Pittman, T. S., Emery, J., & Boggiano, A. K. (1982). Intrinsic and extrinsic motivational orientations: Reward induced change in preference for complexity. *Journal of Personality and Social Psychology, 42,* 789–797.

Robbins, S. P. (1984). *Essentials of Organizational Behavior.* Englewood Cliffs, NJ: Prentice Hall.

Slavin, R. E. (1994). *Educational Psychology: Theory into Practice,* 4th ed. Boston: Allyn & Bacon.

Spaulding, C. L. (1992). *Motivation in the Classroom.* New York: McGraw-Hill.

Stipek, D. J. (1993). *Motivation to Learn: From Theory to Practice,* 2nd ed. Boston: Allyn & Bacon.

White, R. W. (1959). Motivation reconsidered: The concept of competence. *Psychological Review, 66,* 478–533.

Wlodkowski, R. J. (1984). *Motivation and Teaching: A Practical Guide.* Washington, DC: National Education Association.

Wlodkowski, R. J. (1985). *Enhancing Adult Motivation to Learn.* San Francisco, CA: Jossey-Bass.

Zimmerman, B. J. (1989). A social cognitive view of self-regulated academic learning. *Journal of Educational Psychology, 81,* 329–339.

chapter 9

Planning to Address the Diversity of Students

Objectives

This chapter provides information that will help you:

1. Describe student characteristics that demonstrate differences in the cognitive, affective, and physical areas.
2. Describe student differences in learning styles, creative potential, gender, language, and conditions of disabilities.
3. Describe student differences due to cultural diversity, conditions placing the student at risk, and socioeconomic status.
4. Identify ways that students' individual preferences can be assessed.
5. Determine ways that approaches can be matched to students' individual preferences.
6. Identify administrative arrangements that accommodate individual differences among students.
7. Identify curricular options that address individual differences.

People differ in countless ways and it is helpful to examine variables that account for human differences. Variables are human characteristics that differ from one person to the next, and environmental characteristics that change under different conditions (Woolfolk, 1993). For example, height, weight, and measured intelligence are variables. Gender, race, socioeconomic status, and age also are variables. Less observable but equally important variables include self-esteem, confidence, anxiety, and learning style. Environmental variables that affect learning include level of content, pace of instruction, class size, and geographic region of the school.

These examples are just a few of the human and environmental variables that create a wide range of individual differences and needs in classrooms. Individual differences need to be taken into account when methods and procedures are selected for management and discipline. We first examine the ways that students demonstrate differences. We then consider methods that accommodate these differences.

STUDENT CHARACTERISTICS THAT DEMONSTRATE DIFFERENCES

Individual differences abound, and adapting instruction to student differences is one of the most challenging aspects of teaching. Just think about the diversity apparent in a Chicago classroom, for example. There may be a wide range of student cognitive and physical abilities. The students may prefer to learn in different ways, such as in pairs, small groups, or independently. Some may prefer written work; others may learn best when performing an activity. Students may have different degrees of English proficiency while others may have a disabling condition such as a hearing disorder. A wide range of ethnic characteristics may be evident, and various socioeconomic levels are likely to be represented.

The first step in planning to address this diversity is to recognize those differences. This section explores differences in cognitive, affective, and physical areas; differences due to gender, ethnicity, learning style, language, or creative potential; differences due to exceptional and at-risk characteristics; and others.

In this chapter, we discuss categories of student differences; in the classroom, however, students rarely fall cleanly into one category or another, but may exhibit characteristics from several categories.

Differences in the Cognitive Area

Cognitive ability includes information processing, problem solving, using mental strategies for tasks, and continuous learning. Children differ in their cognitive abilities to perform these tasks. Academic ability may range from low to high. *Intelligence* refers to the capacity to apprehend facts and their relations and to reason about them; it is an indicator of cognitive ability. Two of the most prominent contemporary researchers in intelligence are Howard Gardner and Robert Sternberg.

Gardner (1985) believes that all people have multiple intelligences. He has identified seven independent intelligences: linguistic, musical, logical-mathematical, spatial, bodily kinesthetic, interpersonal, and intrapersonal. According to this theory, a person may be gifted in any one of the seven intelligences without being exceptional in the others. Gardner proposes adjustment of curriculum and instruction to individuals' combinations of aptitudes. His vision of appropriate education is clear: Do not expect all students to have the same interests and abilities or to learn in the same ways. Furthermore, do not expect everyone to learn everything, for there is simply too much to learn.

Sternberg (1988) calls for greater understanding of what people do when they solve problems so they can be helped to behave in more intelligent ways. He believes that intelligent people use the environment to accomplish goals by adapting to it, changing it, or selecting out of it.

The work of Gardner, Sternberg, and other cognitive psychologists provides ideas for teachers when selecting instructional techniques. When considering the cognitive differences of your students, you should: (a) expect students to be different; (b) spend the time and effort to look for potential; (c) realize that student needs are not only in deficit areas, and that development of potential is a need, too; (d) be familiar with past records of achievement; (e) be aware of previous experiences that have shaped a student's way of thinking; (f) challenge students with varied assignments, and note the results; (g) use several ways of grading and evaluating; (h) keep changing the conditions for learning to bring out hidden potential; (i) challenge students occasionally beyond what is expected; and (j) look for something unique that each student can do.

Slow Learners. A student who is considered a ***slow learner*** cannot learn at the average rate, even with the resources designated for the majority of students (Bloom, 1982). These students have a limited attention span and are deficient in basic skills such as reading, writing, and mathematics. They need frequent feedback, special instruction, pacing, variety, and perhaps modified materials. Some slow learners do learn but at a slow pace while others are capable but are not willing to try. These latter students are called ***reluctant learners,*** under-achievers, or recalcitrant.

For your slow learners, you should: (a) frequently vary your instructional technique; (b) develop lessons around their interests, needs, and experiences; (c) provide an encouraging, supportive environment; (d) use cooperative learning and peer tutors; (e) provide study aids; (f) teach content in small sequential steps, frequently checking their comprehension; (g) use individualized materials and instruction whenever possible; (h) use audio and visual materials; and (i) take steps to develop the student's self-concept (e.g., assign a task where the student can showcase a particular skill).

Gifted or Talented Learners. Gifted or talented students have above average abilities, and they too need special consideration. Unfortunately, some teachers do not challenge them and they simply "mark time" in school. Unchallenged, they may develop poor attention and study habits and negative attitudes toward school and learning, and waste learning time. This problem is illustrated in Figure 9-1, which reproduces a real note that a middle school teacher received.

For these students, you should: (a) not require that they repeat material they already have mastered; (b) present instruction at a flexible pace, allowing those

This is an actual petition. It was handed to the middle school math teacher by an identified gifted student who had become frustrated with his math class. The student attended a large middle school in a small city in the Midwest. Twenty other students also signed the petition before it was given to the teacher.

WANTED: WORK

I, as a concerned and bored student, am protesting against you underestimating our abilities. I'm sorry to say that I'm writing this in class, but what we do in here is really not worth working on. Review, review, that's all we do. This class is no challenge. If I've learned anything in this class, it would be boredom. I want work. We want work. I have no intention to do anything in this class except twiddle my thumbs. I've found no enjoyment in sitting here listening to my teacher repeat things I've learned in fifth grade. I'm sure others feel the way I do. Please, we want a challenge.

Sincerely,

Bob

FIGURE 9-1   A petition to be challenged

who are able to progress at a productive rate; (c) condense curriculum by eliminating unneeded assignments to make time for extending activities; (d) encourage students to be self-directing and self-evaluating toward their work; (e) use grading procedures that will not discourage them from intellectual risk taking or penalize them for choosing complex learning activities; (f) provide resources beyond basal textbooks; (g) provide horizontal and vertical curriculum enrichment; (h) encourage supplementary reading and writing; and (i) encourage the development of hobbies and interests.

Differences in the Affective Area

Education in the *affective area* focuses on feelings and attitudes. Emotional growth is not easily facilitated, yet the student's feelings about personal skills or the subject being studied are at least as important as the information in the lesson (Slavin, 1994). Self-esteem, time management, confidence, and self-direction are typical affective education goals. While affective goals have generally played a secondary role to cognitive goals, they should be given an important place in your planning and instruction. Love of learning, confidence in learning, and cooperative attitudes are important objectives that teachers should foster (Slavin, 1994). You may find a range of affective characteristics exhibited in the classroom—from low to high self-esteem, confidence, cooperation, self-direction, and the like.

To encourage affective development, you should: (a) identify students by name as early as possible; (b) accept the student as he or she is, for each has interesting, valuable qualities; (c) be aware of previous experiences that have helped shape the student's feelings; (d) observe students; notice moods and reactions from day to day; (e) make observations over time, noting trends; and observe changes, or stability, under different conditions.

Differences in the Physical Area

Perhaps the best place to observe the wide range of physical differences among students is the hallway of any junior high or middle school. Tall and short, skinny and heavy, muscular and frail, dark and fair, active and quiet, describe just a few of the extremes one can see there. Physical differences may be over-looked by teachers who are not involved in physical education (Woolfolk, 1993). *Psychomotor skills* refer to gross motor skills and fine motor skills, such as dribbling a basketball or drawing a fine line. These skills are integral parts of most learning activities. Indeed, psychomotor and affective objectives often overlap.

Physical demands upon learning are obvious with regard to handwriting, industrial arts, sewing, typing, art, and driver education. However, they must not be minimized in less obvious areas such as science labs, computer classes, speech and drama, and music. Visual and hearing deficiencies also contribute to differences. You should recognize the importance of physical skills in the total learning program and explore the possibilities for including psychomotor development activities in classroom objectives.

You should: (a) remember that students are of different sizes, shapes, colors, and physical states; (b) be aware of previous experiences that have shaped physical performance and self-expression; (c) know the normal physical pat-tern for each age level and note extreme variations; (d) provide materials for manipulation and observe carefully to see what skills emerge, or are lacking; (e) observe responses to different environmental factors and different physical activities; and (f) give students a chance to express themselves physically.

Differences in Learning Styles

Learning styles are an individual's preferences for the conditions of *where, when,* or *with what* in the learning process that can affect learning (Woolfolk, 1993). These styles may play an integral role in determining how the student perceives the learning environment and responds to it. Knowledge of learning styles could help you provide options in the classroom that would enhance learning.

Theories and research studies about learning styles are tentative and ongoing, though several promising areas of instructional assistance have emerged. These include cognitive style, brain hemisphericity, and sensory modalities.

Cognitive style should be considered in planning. Cognitive style refers to the way people process information and use strategies in responding to tasks (Good & Brophy, 1995). Conceptual tempo and field-dependence/field-independence are two categories of cognitive style that educators may consider when planning instruction. *Conceptual tempo* deals with students impulsivity or reflectivity when selecting from two or more alternatives.

Field-dependence/field-independence deals with the extent to which individuals can overcome effects of distracting background elements (the field) when trying to differentiate among relevant aspects of a particular situation.

Teachers in Action

Learning Styles

Donna Erpelding, third-grade teacher, Manhattan, Kansas:

Activities and assignments that take the students' learning styles into consideration make each child feel as if he or she is a capable and contributing member of the class. Each week I plan a thematically integrated unit. I prepare lessons and activities that address the four learning styles of the students in my classroom—the poets and artists, the scholars, the engineers, and the ambassadors.

The "poets and artists" are sensitive and like to be personally involved in the unit. They are eager to bring items from home, share personal experiences, create materials, and do other things that relate to the theme of the week. By my providing opportunities for them as well as others to share, these learners are personally involved.

Each week I also develop paper and pencil activities to extend the theme activities for the "scholars" in my room. They process information more readily by using accurate information and details. These activities enhance their learning as well as others' learning.

The "engineers" learn best through hands-on activities and manipulation of materials. Science and math instruction fits into this area. Hands-on and discovery lessons help the students understand and appreciate the world around them as well as make the theme real and meaningful to everyone.

"Ambassadors" are learners who need to see the real world application to the weekly theme. They like to talk about the theme and think "bigger and better." Collaborative learning activities are made for these learners.

By incorporating a variety of learning strategies, I have found that it is possible to provide opportunities for *all* students to learn from their own perspectives and learning style.

Brain hemisphericity is another aspect of student preferences toward learning environments. The two halves of the brain appear to serve different functions even though they are connected by a network that orchestrates their teamwork. Each side is dominant in certain respects. Left-brain dominant people tend to be analytical in orientation, being generally logical, concrete, and sequential. Right-brained dominant people tend to be more visually and spatially oriented and more holistic in thinking.

Sensory modality is a third factor in student preferences. A *sensory modality* is a system of interacting with the environment through one or more of the basic senses—sight, hearing, touch, smell, and taste (Dembo, 1994). For teachers, the most important sensory modalities are the visual, auditory, and kinesthetic. Information to be learned is first received through one of the senses. The information is either forgotten after a few seconds or, after initial processing, is stored in short-term or long-term memory. Learning may be enhanced when the information is received through a preferred sensory modality. Use a variety of approaches that enable the students to receive the content through one or more of the basic senses.

Decision Points

You might use instructional approaches that take into account students' learning styles and instructional preferences. How might you plan a lesson on impressionist painting for sixth graders? How could you account for the different learning styles and instructional preferences? For the instructional decisions that you make, how might they affect your behavior in maintaining order?

Differences in Creative Potential

Creativity is defined by Torrance (1962) as the process of creating ideas or hypotheses about ideas, testing them, modifying and retesting the hypotheses, and communicating the results. Highly creative individuals sometimes demonstrate characteristics that are not always liked by others, such as independence of thought and judgment, courage of convictions, skepticism toward the voice of authority, and displays of nonconformity (Torrance, 1965).

Creative students process information differently and react to the world in ways unlike their peers. Teachers and parents say they want children to be creative, but they too often set up constraints to prevent a truly creative child from "getting out of hand." Highly creative children tend to be estranged from their peers and misunderstood by their teachers, who reward students who exhibit conforming behavior. Too many teachers suppress individualism and creativity. You might show examples of work done by former students which reflect creativity. This leads to a discussion of the value of creativity and can encourage creative potential.

You can nurture creativity by learning about creative personalities and developing the ability to appreciate divergence. In this regard, you should: (a) listen for creative (unconventional) responses; (b) reward creative responses by asking students to elaborate upon those ideas; (c) provide some learning activities in which students may be creative, not conforming; (d) allow some work to be open-ended, perhaps messy, and ungraded, to encourage exploration and "guessing"; and (e) set up flexible learning environments in which students are free to make choices and pursue areas of personal interest.

Differences Produced by Gender

The difference in male and female learning is difficult for psychologists and educators to understand. Researchers acknowledge that many descriptions of *gender difference* reflect social and political influences and past experiences. At the same time, a strong case has been made for differences in neurological make-up between the sexes that lead them to think and learn differently.

Good and Brophy (1995) believe that gender roles to which children are socialized will interact with the student roles stressed in schools and thus foster gender differences. They also believe that these roles influence how teachers respond to boys and to girls. Research suggests that boys are more active and assertive in class, so you should avoid self-defeating patterns of interaction with low-achieving, disruptive boys. You should guard against reinforcing obedience and conformity in girls, and work toward developing their intellectual assertiveness and efforts to achieve.

Current data on scholastic achievement of males and females fail to confirm some of the traditional assumptions about gender differences. The data provide more questions than answers (Dembo, 1994), and strategies can be followed that address gender issues and reduce gender bias (Grossman & Grossman, 1994).

You should: (a) remember that differences between boys and girls are not absolute, but a matter of degree; (b) take care to provide equal opportunities for each sex (for example, encourage girls to explore math and science areas, and promote artistic sensitivity in boys); (c) recognize that knowing a student's gender is merely one piece of information about that student; (d) encourage all students to test the limits of learning and achievement; (e) find ways to position the students so as to encourage greater interaction and less gender-based distinction during learning activities; and (f) monitor your own teaching behaviors and ask others to observe your sensitivity about sex bias in responding to students, giving instructions and assistance, leading discussions, encouraging students, and dealing with misbehaviors.

Differences in Language

Some students come from homes where English is not the primary language or is not spoken at all. They may have limited proficiency in English. In descending order, Spanish, French, German, Italian, and Chinese are the top five languages other than English spoken at home. This fact has a bearing on teachers' decisions about management and work.

To address language differences, you should: (a) learn about the student's previous educational experiences, language ability, and achievement levels; (b) use alternative means of presenting material (e.g., tactile, visual, kinesthetic); (c) learn about the student's culture and be alert to cultural differences; (d) have the student work with someone who is bilingual in the same language; (e) use instructional materials that are at the proper reading level and include photos, illustrations, and content of interest to the student; and (f) share information from the student's culture and other cultures represented by your students.

Decision Points

Your students may represent several languages. Suppose that you were teaching a math lesson to your fourth-grade class. Three students spoke Spanish and limited English, two students spoke Chinese and limited English, and one student spoke Vietnamese and limited English. How might you need to vary your instruction to deal with language barriers? How might you have other students assist? What are the implications for your actions on maintaining order?

Differences Produced by Cultural Diversity

Several approaches examine individual differences created by cultural diversity. The emerging concepts of cultural pluralism and respect for cultural identity in the United States are replacing "melting pot" connotations based on a "salad bowl" concept. *Cultural diversity* is reflected in the wide variety of values, beliefs, attitudes, and rules that define regional, ethnic, religious, and other cultures. Minority populations wish their cultures to be recognized as unique and preserved for their children. The message from all cultural groups to schools is clear: make sure that every student from every cultural group succeeds.

Each cultural group teaches its members certain lessons (Kagan, 1983; Woolfolk, 1993). Differences exist in the conduct of interpersonal relationships, use of body language, cooperation with other group members, and acceptance of authority figures. You need to treat each student as an individual first, because that student is the product of many influences. Many resources are available devoted to cultural diversity (e.g., Banks, 1994; Gollnick & Chinn, 1994).

As you consider individual differences due to cultural diversity, you should:

1. Examine your own values and beliefs for evidence of bias and stereotyping.
2. Read materials written by and about members of many cultural groups.
3. Invite members of various cultural groups to discuss their values and important beliefs, keeping in mind that perceptions should not be based on the responses of only one member, and that wide variations exist.
4. Regard students as individuals first, with membership in a cultural group as only one factor in understanding that individual.
5. Learn something about students' family and community relationships.
6. Consider nonstandard English and native languages as basic for minority students, in order to promote gradual but necessary instruction in the majority language.
7. Allow students to work in cross-cultural teams and facilitate cooperation, noting emergent qualities and talents.

8. Use sociograms and other devices that indicate cross-cultural awareness and acceptance. A *sociogram* is a diagram that reflects student interactions.
9. Introduce global educational content and materials.
10. Infuse the curriculum with consistent emphasis on other cultures throughout the year.
11. Take care not to assume that culturally diverse populations are deprived.
12. Select routines that do not conflict with cultural values.

Differences Resulting from Disabilities

Exceptional students include those with conditions considered disabilities. In the United States above 10 percent of students are identified as having disabling conditions that justify their placement in a special educational program (Bullock, 1992). If gifted children are considered special education students, the figure is 15 percent.

Categories for special education services include learning disabilities; speech or language impairment; mental retardation; emotional disturbances; other impairments of health; multiple disabilities; impairment in hearing, orthopedics, or sight; and deafness/blindness.

Teachers in Action

Cultural Diversity

Suzy Fulghum, second-grade teacher, Northglen, Colorado:

During the first few weeks of school in my second-grade classroom, Red Wing was extremely shy, quiet, and nervous. Since she was not my only minority student, I decided to foster a sense of community through an activity involving a "cultural quilt."

Students made a square of different pieces of construction paper to represent their culture: family traditions, special places, religion, friends, relatives, and interests. As they worked together in cooperative groups, they talked about the composition of their squares, and shared materials. Red Wing talked about her square and answered many questions about Native Americans. She showed us her dancing costume and beadwork, and told us about their meaning.

The change in Red Wing's behavior was amazing. She talked willingly and actively participated in learning. The class became very interested in her customs and those of other minority students. We all realized that we are both alike and different from each other.

Teachers in Action

Students with Learning Disabilities in the Regular Classroom

Linda Innes, seventh-grade language arts teacher, Kansas City, Missouri:

I teach one class that is a class-within-a-class, which means students identified as learning disabled (LD) are placed in the same class with regular middle school students. To help meet state standards required for LD students, the learning disability teacher co-teaches the class with me. To meet these students' needs, I am very clear and specific when teaching or giving directions.

First, I give directions in various ways. I have two or three other students repeat the directions I just gave. Also, it is helpful to have the students write down the directions, especially if they deal with homework.

Second, I give instruction thoroughly and slowly. When the students are taking notes, I speak more slowly, write out the notes word-for-word to be viewed on the projector screen, repeat what I have written and spoken several times, and monitor the students' notes to make sure that they are copying them correctly. There are times when I or the LD teacher write the notes for some of the students or provide a photocopy because of a severe writing handicap or slow processing skills.

Third, I place each LD student next to an academically strong student who can provide help whenever necessary. I have found that the stronger students benefit as well as the LD students. LD students get the personalized attention they require, and the regular student has the opportunity to explain the information and in the process learn it more thoroughly.

Public Law 94–142 committed the nation to a policy of mainstreaming students who have disabilities by placing them in the least restrictive environment in which they can function successfully while having their special needs met (Good & Brophy, 1995). The degree to which they are treated differently is to be minimized. The **least restrictive environment** means that students with special needs are placed in special settings only if necessary and only for as long as necessary; the regular classroom is the preferred, least restrictive placement.

When considering the needs of these students, you should: (a) concentrate on student strengths, capitalizing on them to overcome or compensate for deficits (e.g., consider allowing some work to be done orally if the student has limited writing skills); (b) read about successful children and adults who have surmounted disabilities; (c) communicate often with special education teachers and collaborate with them in providing appropriate programs; (d) hold appropriate expectations for exceptional students (teachers sometimes expect too much; and it is more debilitating to some exceptional students to expect too little); and (e) model appropriate attitudes and behaviors for other students toward those with disabilities.

Teachers in Action

Getting Organized for At-Risk Students

Michael Abbott, teacher in an alternative high school, Livonia, Michigan:

This alternative high school just celebrated its twentieth birthday, and we realized that we have never had violence or vandalism in all that time. That may come as a surprise to some people since we have a large population of at-risk students. Being proactive is part of the reason for the lack of problems. The staff meets each week to discuss how things are going and where we are headed. And we address problems in a thorough way.

When attendance became a problem, for example, we brainstormed for ideas. It is now routine to talk to each person who was absent without a parent excuse the next day. This is not a scolding; rather, "We need you here." I believe the students feel we care. We call each night if the absentee did not call in. Again, it's "How are you? I was concerned." The students receive no credit on the days they don't attend. Students with unexcused absences and no good reason for being out will have to meet with their parents and one of the teachers to discuss their future in the program. The students love it here and will usually shape up before too long.

We believe the absence of violence in this school reflects the time we spend inculcating the school's values. We help students understand their role in the program, how we do things, and how we don't do certain things. Early on we deal with active listening, I-messages, a ban on violence, a ban on put-downs, and so on. We expect the students to help the class run smoothly. We tell them that they don't have to like everyone, but we do have to live together and we will use the active listening and I-messages in an effort to get along with each other.

Beyond this, we get active support of the parents and students on a leadership team that plans many of our activities. We work on developing good relationships with the students by greeting them each day, congratulating them on successes, phoning them to thank them for their help the following day, having conferences with them regularly, and so on.

Differences of Students at Risk

Other environmental and personal influences may converge to place a student at risk. ***Students at risk*** are children and adolescents who are not able to acquire and/or use the skills necessary to develop their potential and become productive members of society (Dunn & Dunn, 1992b). Conditions at home, support from the community, and personal and cultural background all affect student attitudes, behaviors, and propensity to profit from school experiences.

Students potentially at risk include those who face adverse conditions beyond their control: those who do not speak English as a first language; talented but unchallenged students; those with special problems; and many others. At-risk students often have academic difficulties and thus may be low achievers.

Students classified as at risk may include those living in poverty, in stress, or homeless. They may be abused and neglected, academically disadvantaged, overemployed, delinquent, lonely and disengaged, suicidal, chemically abusive, sexually active, homosexual, pregnant, or young parents. They may have sexually transmitted diseases, eating disorders, mental illness, or disabilities. They may be children of dysfunctional families or may be members of Satanic cults or gangs (Redick & Vail, 1991).

These disadvantaged students share some common characteristics. Not every trait discussed below need be present to qualify a student as at risk. Based on a review of research and experience (Bhaerman & Kopp, 1988; Lehr & Harris, 1988), they tend to exhibit the following characteristics: academic difficulties; lack of structure (disorganized); inattentiveness; distractibility; short attention span; low self-esteem; health problems; excessive absenteeism and truancy; dependence; narrow range of interest; lack of social skills; inability to face pressure; fear of failure (feel threatened by learning); and lack of motivation.

A study of successful teachers of low-achieving students reveal skills/competencies that can help these students (Lehr, 1987; Lehr & Harris, 1988). The skills/competencies fell into five major areas: personal skills/competencies, professional skills/competencies, materials, methods, and learning environment. Over half the teachers listed the following skills/competencies needed to teach low-achieving, at-risk students: (a) using a variety of techniques and methods; (b) reteaching and giving students time to practice the skill; (c) being positive; (d) being patient; (e) being caring, concerned, empathic, loving, respecting, and humanistic; (f) setting realistic goals and objectives (high expectations); (g) being an effective communicator with students and parents; (h) being a firm, consistent, and fair manager; and (i) using many different materials.

Differences in Socioeconomic Status

Socioeconomic status (SES) is a measure of a family's relative position in the community, determined by a combination of adult income, occupation, and level of education. SES is linked to intelligence, achievement test scores, grades, truancy, and dropout and suspension rates (Alwin & Thornton, 1984; Ballantine, 1989). The dropout rate for children from poor families is twice that of the general population, and for the poorest children, the rate exceeds 50 percent (Catterall & Cota-Robles, 1988).

Taking these factors into account, you should: (a) capitalize on students' interests; (b) make course content meaningful to the students and discuss the practical value of the material; (c) make directions clear and specific; (d) arrange to have each student experience some success; (e) be sure that expectations for work are realistic; and (f) include a variety of instructional approaches, such as provisions for movement and group work.

METHODS FOR ACCOMMODATING STUDENT DIFFERENCES

As stated earlier, students are unique but also very much alike. To address student diversity, learn student preferences and match some instruction to these preferences, provide administrative arrangements, and offer curricular options. Table 9–1 lists some questions for you to consider.

Determining Student Instructional Preferences

Students have preferences for instructional methods, and inventories can be used to determine these preferences. An *inventory* is a survey or questionnaire about interests and preferences that students complete. It helps you to make better use of the array of techniques available. You can use commercially prepared inventories or develop these inventories yourself.

One widely used *commercially prepared inventory* is the Renzulli and Smith (1978) *Learning Styles Inventory.* Students' responses range from very unpleasant to very pleasant toward projects, drill and recitation, peer teaching, discussion, teaching games, independent study, programmed instruction, lecture, and simulation.

Another inventory is proposed by Dunn and Dunn (1992a, 1992b). Their model includes 21 environmental, emotional, sociological, and physical stimuli as well as psychological preferences. In Dunn and Dunn's survey, student responses reveal preferences about the 21 stimuli. Dunn and Dunn conclude that learning style preferences are strengths, and teaching through learning styles can increase academic achievement (Dunn & Dunn, 1992a).

TABLE 9-1 Checklist for serving individual student needs

Does the learning activity:
1. Have educational merit?
2. Avoid labeling or stigmatizing the student?
3. Develop the student's strengths and talents?
4. Structure learning at the appropriate level and pace?
5. Minimize redundancy and repetition of concepts?
6. Encourage in-depth study in areas of student interest?
7. Allow frequent performance in preferred learning styles, with occasional performance in less-preferred styles?
8. Allow variety in assessment and grading procedures?
9. Encourage student participation in planning and evaluation?
10. Have potential for positive "ripple" effects to other students?

Other commercially prepared inventories are available which may demand much time and energy from both you and your students. They may be expensive; some require computer scoring which increases the cost.

Teacher-developed inventories can be used. The most efficient way to learn about individual differences may be simply to ask students. For example, they might be asked whether they prefer to draw or to write. An additional benefit of this informal self-report is the opportunity it gives you to interact with the student. Younger students particularly enjoy having the teacher play the secretarial role and write the responses. This procedure usually produces more data as well.

Matching Instructional Methods to Student Preferences

Many avenues should be taken to address the individual differences discussed in this chapter: ability, cognitive style, achievement motivation, anxiety, gender, and culture. One single approach is not justified. To use a popular phrase, "Different strokes for different folks" (Sprinthall et al., 1994).

Should you *always* try to match student preferences and instructional methods? For several reasons, the answer must be no. As Sprinthall and colleagues (1994) point out, preferences must be interpreted as current, not permanent preferences. Learners will not always be allowed to or want to function in their preferred modes after their school days are over.

Start where the learner is, i.e., in concert with the pupil's level of development (Sprinthall et al., 1994); then begin to mismatch (i.e., use a different approach from what the student prefers) by shifting to a slightly more complex level of teaching to help the student develop in many areas; have faith that students have an intrinsic drive to learn. These practices complement the recommendations of Vygotsky, Kohlberg, and others to nudge students beyond comfort zones of learning into just enough cognitive dissonance to facilitate growth. An athlete might explain it as "no pain, no gain."

Administrative Arrangements

Through administrative arrangements such as grouping, flexible pacing, and alternative assignments, instruction can be tailored to individual needs. These help students achieve the instructional objectives while providing choices about completing the tasks.

Grouping.   Grouping makes instruction differentiation more efficient and practical. When each group is challenged and stimulated, all are motivated to work harder. Differentiated materials can be used more easily. On the other hand, labeling can be stigmatizing if grouping is based on variables such as ability or achievement. Grouping too often and changing groups too infrequently can obstruct integration and cooperation.

With the proper planning, structure, and supervision, grouping is a useful way to provide for individual differences. When using grouping arrangements, you should:

1. Reform groups often on the basis of students' current performance.
2. Make liberal use of activities that mix group members frequently.
3. Adjust the pace and level of work for each group to maximize achievement. Avoid having expectations that are too low for low groups. Students tend to live up or down to teachers' expectations.
4. Provide opportunities for gifted students to work with their peers by arranging cross-age, between-school, or community-based experiences.
5. Groups are composed of individuals, so remember that all members do not have to do the same things at the same time in the same way. Retain individuality within the group.
6. Form groups with care, giving attention to culture and gender.
7. Structure the experience and supervise the students' actions.
8. Prepare students with necessary skills for being effective group members, such as listening, helping, cooperating, and seeking assistance.
9. Adjust methods when necessary. For example, expect to cover less content with cooperative learning techniques, and supplement with reading assignments, handouts, or homework.

Flexible Pacing. *Flexible pacing* arrangements include acceleration, continuous progress plans, programmed instruction, compacting of course content, and self-directed learning contracts. It is especially appropriate for highly able students to test out and take college courses while in high school. Flexible pacing does not always require accelerated content. Gifted students may want to progress more slowly through the curriculum as by studying a particular topic in greater detail or doing original work on a subject.

Continuous progress allows students to complete work and move on without having to wait for other students. Flexible pacing allows student placement in a grade or class that corresponds more closely with need. Students must be screened and monitored carefully to derive maximum benefit from the arrangement. Grading practices must be adapted to the flexible arrangements. Modifying the pace may forestall needed changes in the curriculum; rather than accommodating individual differences, it may simply result in students doing the same things at somewhat different rates.

Flexible pacing requires careful planning and monitoring by all teachers in the system. Good record keeping and an abundance of materials at all levels will help ensure success. When dealing with flexible pacing, you should: (a) develop efficient systems for recording student progress; (b) assist students to develop their own monitoring of work completed and achievement gained; (c) communicate with teachers at grade levels above your own to plan ongoing progress for accelerated students; and (d) cooperate with teachers who have students working under flexible pacing, in support of the method.

Alternative Assignments.   Alternative or differentiated assignments can be provided by altering the length, difficulty, or timespan of the assignment. These generally require alternative evaluation procedures.

Enrichment activities qualify as alternative assignments when directed toward individual student needs. There are four types of ***enrichment activities:*** (1) *Relevant enrichment* provides experiences that address the student's strengths, interests, or deficit areas. (2) *Cultural enrichment* might be pleasurable and productive for the student even if not particularly relevant to current needs. An example would be an interdisciplinary study or a global awareness topic. (3) *Irrelevant enrichment* might provide extra activity in a content area without addressing student needs. (4) The last level of enrichment, *busywork,* should be avoided.

Curricular Options

Curricular options allow students to practice self-direction and make choices. A class will represent variation in readiness for independent learning and differentiated materials. You can begin slowly with simple, short-term alternatives, and gradually allow students to become more self-directed and self-evaluative. Appropriate options include individualized study, differentiated materials, and alternative methods of assessment. Aides and parent and community volunteers also may be available to work with students on an individual basis under your direction. Computers can be used to address individual differences and preferences.

Individualized Study. Individualized study can be implemented through learning contracts or independent work. Such plans are most effective when developed by the student with your assistance. Individualized study facilitates mastery of both content and process. Not only can the student master a subject; he or she can also master goal setting, time management, use of resources, self-direction, and self-assessment of achievement. Independent study is ideal for accommodating learning styles. Individual ability is nurtured, and students often learn more than is required.

Independent study encourages creativity and develops problem-solving skills. It can be applied in any school setting and in all curricular areas. Most importantly, this method of learning accords with the goal of continuing education.

When considering individualized study, you should: (a) include the student in all phases of planning, studying, and evaluating; (b) encourage the student to ask high-order (analysis, synthesis, evaluation) questions as study goals; (c) encourage the student to develop a product as outcome; (d) provide the student with an opportunity to share the product with an interested audience; and (e) emphasize learner responsibility and accountability.

Differentiated Materials. Learning activity packets, task cards, and learning contracts are examples of ***differentiated materials*** that address individual differences through curriculum options. Learning centers, for example, include

Teachers in Action

Individualized Study

John Wolters, sixth-grade teacher, Manhattan, Kansas:

On my desk after recess was a note from Steve. It read something like this: "Your realy an awsome teacher? Your nice because you dont make us do any work, especialy in socal studes. Thanks Mr. W!" The reason Steve was probably so excited about social studies was that we had not been using the textbook for several weeks. Getting away from dependence on the textbook is one way I've learned to provide for individual differences within the classroom.

Steve had just finished a study of Mexico with the rest of the class, and he had done more work in three weeks than he had in the previous 12. I had decided to approach the study of Mexico from an independent study format, allowing each student to choose the focus of study. We began as a class by listing as many topics as we could. We then listed resources that were available. Each student was then free to choose his or her own topic(s) to study, learn the information, and present the content to the class.

What had Steve accomplished in three weeks of study about the Aztecs? He read between 75 and 100 pages of information, made a time-line, drew three maps and a sketchbook of Aztec people, and participated in a three-person panel discussion comparing the Aztecs, Incas, and Mayas. Not bad, I thought, for a student who had finished only one book so far that school year, who struggled to keep on-task during social studies discussions and work-time, and who had a track record of turning in about 50 percent of his work.

What was the difference this time? Steve felt that he was in charge, and he thrived on this feeling. No one was telling him to answer the questions on page 232, to outline pages 56 to 60, or to be ready for the test on Thursday. Steve tasted success once he got into this project. Meanwhile, some of the more academically capable students in the class struggled with this wide-open approach until it fit their strengths.

This format for covering material does not work in all subject areas all the time. It does, however, allow the students to choose topics of personal interest and create finished products that reflect their abilities. All of this results in increased motivation, creativity, and pride in the job they completed.

differentiated materials with several kinds and levels of goals and activities. Centers, packets, and cards can be made to meet a student's needs and then stored until another student needs them. When prepared properly, the materials accommodate different rates of learning and different cognitive styles.

The differentiated materials approach can be used at the secondary level as well as in the elementary classroom. At both levels, the materials should be explained and their use monitored and evaluated periodically. Ample time must be allowed for follow-up of the activity and evaluation of the learning.

When using differentiated materials, you should: (a) identify the objectives to be accomplished; (b) plan and construct (or purchase) the materials with care; (c) structure a record-keeping system to monitor student progress; (d) orient students to the materials; and (e) schedule ample time for follow-up and evaluation.

Decision Points

Differentiated materials can be used to meet the instructional objectives. If you had a ninth-grade lesson to teach on soil erosion, how could you vary your instructional materials to accommodate individual differences? How could you relate this topic to students' lives and make it interesting? How might students' individual differences affect your planning decisions?

Alternative Assessment Methods. In many cases, individualized instruction calls for alternative assessment and grading procedures. Allow students to write sample test questions, give pretests often, vary test format and type, and give detailed evaluation feedback.

MAJOR CONCEPTS

1. Teachers need to take individual differences into account as they select instructional methods and approach instruction and management.
2. People are alike in many ways, yet are different in ways that affect learning. Cognitive, affective, and physical differences are only part of the array of variables that account for student diversity.
3. Diversity can be due to influences of learning style, creative potential, gender, language, and disabling conditions.
4. Diversity can be affected by cultural diversity, conditions placing the student at risk, and socioeconomic factors.
5. Students have preferences for instructional methods, and commercially prepared or teacher-developed inventories can be used to determine them.
6. Several instructional approaches should be tried in an effort to address individual differences, but some cognitive dissonance should be maintained to facilitate growth.
7. Administrative arrangements appropriate for serving individual differences include grouping, flexible pacing, and alternative assignments.

8. Curricular options allow students to practice self-direction and make choices. These options include but are not limited to independent study, use of differentiated materials, and alternative assessment methods.

DISCUSSION QUESTIONS

1. Discuss ways in which all students are similar and the impact this has upon teaching and learning.
2. How might you present your philosophy of providing for individual differences to parents at a parent conference?
3. Are you enthusiastic or skeptical about the relevance of learning style theory and brain hemisphere research in classroom instruction? Why?
4. When handling misbehavior, should a teacher make allowances if the student has limited proficiency in English, is considered to be at risk, is gifted, or has a condition of disabilities?
5. What are the arguments for and against matching the instructional approaches to the students' preferences?
6. What are the merits and disadvantages of having alternative or differentiated assignments to address the diversity of students?

SUPPLEMENTAL ACTIVITIES

For Clinical Settings

1. Describe conditions that you have observed, thought about, or read about that contribute to the difficulty of providing for individual differences.
2. Make a list of ten or more questions that you would like to ask an effective teacher about addressing the diversity of students.
3. Analyze textbooks for your major teaching area(s) and level for ways in which they address individual differences and provide for individual needs.

For Field Settings

1. Observe a classroom for a period of time, preferably a day. Make a two-column list of examples where students were asked to conform (e.g., "Put your name in the upper right-hand corner," and "Line up at the door to go to the auditorium"), or were encouraged to express individuality (e.g., "Select a topic that interests you," and "Decide what grade you earned for this lesson.").
2. Using the categories of differences considered in this chapter as a guide, ask several teachers to describe individual differences they notice in their students. How do the teachers take these differences into account?
3. Investigate the policies of the school or district for dealing with the misbehavior of students who have disabilities.

KEY TERMS

Affective area

Alternative or differentiated assignments

Brain hemisphericity

Cognitive ability

Cognitive style

Conceptual tempo

Continuous progress

Creativity

Cultural diversity

Curricular options

Differentiated materials

Enrichment activities

Field dependence/
   field independence

Flexible pacing

Gender differences

Gifted or talented learners

Individualized study

Intelligence

Inventories

Psychomotor skills

Learning styles

Least restrictive environment

Reluctant learner

Sensory modality

Slow learner

Socioeconomic status

Sociograms

Students at risk

RECOMMENDED READINGS

Biehler, R. F., & Snowman, J. (1993). *Psychology Applied to Teaching,* 7th ed. Boston: Houghton Mifflin.
Includes four chapters on student characteristics. Particularly useful are chapters on theories of development, age-level characteristics, and dealing with pupil variability.

Gage, N. L., & Berliner, D. C. (1991). *Educational Psychology,* 5th ed. Boston: Houghton Mifflin.
Includes useful chapters on intelligence, human diversity (culture, gender, and exceptionality), and individual instruction.

Slavin, R. E. (1994). *Educational Psychology: Theory into Practice,* 4th ed. Boston: Allyn & Bacon.
Includes useful chapters on accommodating student differences; exceptional students; and social class, ethnicity, and gender.

REFERENCES

Alwin, C., & Thornton, A. (1984). Family origins and school processes: Early versus late influence of parental characteristics. *American Sociological Review, 49,* 784–802.
Ballantine, J. (1989). *The Sociology of Education.* Englewood Cliffs, NJ: Prentice Hall.
Banks, J. A. (1994). *An Introduction to Multicultural Education.* Boston: Allyn & Bacon.

Bhaerman, R. D., & Kopp, K. A. (1988). *The School's Choice: Guidelines for Dropout Prevention at the Middle and Junior High School.* Columbus: National Center for Research in Vocational Education, The Ohio State University.

Bloom, B. S. (1982). *Human Interactions and School Learning.* New York: McGraw-Hill.

Bullock, L. M. (1992). *Exceptionalities in Children and Youth.* Boston: Allyn & Bacon.

Catterall, J., & Cota-Robles, E. (1988). *The Educationally At-risk: What the Numbers Mean.* Palo Alto, CA: Stanford University Press.

Dembo, M. H. (1994). *Applying Educational Psychology in the Classroom,* 5th ed. New York: Longman.

Dunn, R., & Dunn, K. (1992a). *Teaching Elementary Students through Their Individual Learning Styles: Practical Approaches for Grades 3–6.* Boston: Allyn & Bacon.

Dunn, R., & Dunn, K. (1992b). *Teaching Secondary Students through Their Individual Learning Styles: Practical Approaches for Grades 7–12.* Boston: Allyn & Bacon.

Gardner, H. (1985). *Frames of Mind: The Theory of Multiple Intelligences.* New York: Basic Books.

Gollnick, D. M., & Chinn, P. C. (1994). *Multicultural Education in a Pluralistic Society,* 4th ed. New York: Macmillan.

Good, T. L., & Brophy, J. E. (1995). *Contemporary Educational Psychology.* New York: Longman.

Grossman, H., & Grossman, S. H. (1994). *Gender Issues in Education.* Boston: Allyn & Bacon.

Jones, V. R., & Jones, L. S. (1990). *Comprehensive Classroom Management: Motivating and Managing Students,* 3rd ed. Boston: Allyn & Bacon.

Kagan, S. (1983). Social orientation among Mexican-American children: A challenge to traditional classroom structures. In E. Garcia, Ed., *The Mexican-American Child: Language, Cognition, and Social Development.* Tempe, AZ: Center for Bilingual Education.

Lehr, J. B. (1987). *A Final Report of the Furman University Center of Excellence.* Greenville, SC: Furman Press.

Lehr, J. B., & Harris, H. W. (1988). *At-risk, Low-achieving Students in the Classroom.* Washington, DC: National Education Association.

Redick, S. S., & Vail, A. (1991). *Motivating Youth at Risk.* Gainesville, VA: Home Economics Education Association.

Renzulli, J. S., & Smith, L. (1978). *The Learning Styles Inventory: A Measure of Student Preferences for Instructional Techniques.* Mansfield Center, CT: Creative Learning Press.

Slavin, R. E. (1994). *Educational Psychology: Theory into Practice,* 4th ed. Boston: Allyn & Bacon.

Sprinthall, N. A., Sprinthall, R. C., & Oja, S. N. (1994). *Educational Psychology: A Developmental Approach,* 6th ed. New York: McGraw-Hill.

Sternberg, R. J. (1988). *The Triarchic Mind.* New York: Viking.

Torrance, E. P. (1962). *Guiding Creative Talent.* Englewood Cliffs, NJ: Prentice Hall.

Torrance, E. P. (1965). *Rewarding Creative Behavior.* Englewood Cliffs, NJ: Prentice Hall.

Woolfolk, A. (1993). *Educational Psychology,* 5th ed. Englewood Cliffs, NJ: Prentice Hall.

chapter **10**

Planning to Work with Parents

Objectives

This chapter provides information that will help you:

1. Identify the reasons for contacting and interacting with parents.
2. Describe reasons why some parents resist involvement.
3. Determine ways to develop a parental support system.
4. Identify when to contact parents.
5. Determine ways to communicate with parents.

A teacher's responsibility is to work with students, but it is important to communicate and interact with parents throughout the year. The reason for the communication will often determine the timing of the contact and how the contact will be made.

At the start, we must recognize that children come from various family settings. The majority come from two-parent families; however, 25 percent come from one-parent families. One-third of marriages are remarriages, and one of four children has one or more stepparents (Swap, 1993). Some children are cared for by a combination of community caregivers, not the traditional home. We use the term *parent* in a broad sense, to represent the primary adult or adults who have parental responsibility. This definition could include the biological parents, foster or step-parents, a grandparent, an aunt or uncle, an older sibling, or a guardian.

What are the reasons for working with parents? Why is it important to understand the parents and their point of view? When should parents be contacted? What are the ways that teachers might communicate with parents? We will examine these questions in this chapter.

REASONS FOR WORKING WITH PARENTS

Students ultimately benefit from good communication and effective working relationships between school and home. Parental involvement is associated with better attendance, more positive student attitudes and behavior, greater willingness to do homework, and higher academic achievement (Becher, 1984; Epstein, 1984; Haynes, Comer, & Hamilton-Lee, 1989; Henderson, 1987; Rich, 1988).

There are several reasons why you would want to communicate with parents:

1. *To create open, two-way communication and to establish friendly relations.* Positive contacts early in the year help establish positive, friendly relations. Parents and teachers do not see each other as adversaries but as allies in helping the student be successful. Two-way communication can be fostered, and this will result in appropriate school-community relations that will benefit everyone involved.

2. *To understand the student's home circumstances.* This information can help you decide on an appropriate course of action with the student. You may learn whether the parents are having marital problems, have limited ability to read or speak English, exert excessive pressure on the child to excel academically, or tend to be abusive to the student when there are problems at school. Such factors can be important as you decide how best to help each student academically and behaviorally.

3. *To inform parents of academic expectations and events as well as student performance.* Parents appreciate understanding your policy about homework, late papers, and grading guidelines. They also like to know what content will be covered, when quizzes or tests are scheduled, and what special events are scheduled. Introductory letters or a Back-to-School Night are helpful, as are newsletters devoted to special events, units to be covered, or the academic schedule. Finally, parents want to know how their children are doing. Report cards and conferences give information periodically, but parents appreciate learning about early indications of academic difficulties.

4. *To enlist parents' help with academic issues.* Teachers often seek help from parents at the start of the year. They may send a list of needed supplies home to supplement purchases made by the school district. You may want to identify parents who might be available to serve as aides or chaperones for regular or special events. This assistance may include preparing materials for bulletin boards, assisting during a field trip, and the like.

5. *To inform parents of disciplinary expectations and actions.* At the start of the year, teachers often inform parents of their disciplinary policy and their expectations for student conduct. As with the academic information at the start of the year, this communication is often accomplished through an introductory letter or a newsletter, or at the Back-to-School Night. When a student misbehaves, you may need to inform the parents without having to seek additional support and assistance from them.

6. *To enlist the parents' help in dealing with their children.* When students have academic difficulties, the parents should be contacted to identify ways they

might help. When students misbehave, the parents should be contacted so that you can work together to help the student stay on-task and be successful. Parents exert great influence over their children, and they can cooperate and support your actions.

You and the parents may agree on strategies to help the child, to build the child's cooperation and commitment to solving problems. A behavior modification program may be agreed on; as part of the plan, parents may withhold privileges or offer rewards. Parents have access to more attractive rewards than does the school, such as a videotape rental, a trip to the pool, or a special toy or item of clothing. Examples of reinforcers that parents could use are listed in Table 10-1.

TABLE 10-1 Possible reinforcers to be used at home

1. *Reinforcing Activities*
   Using the home computer
   Watching television
   Getting additional playtime
   Attending a recreational activity or sporting event
   Having a friend spend the night
   Driving the family car
   Taking lessons (music, dance, swimming)
   Shopping with a parent
   Going to the movies
   Using the stereo or CD player
   Getting telephone privileges
   Going out for a meal

2. *Social Reinforcers*
   Smiles
   Hugs
   Kisses
   Attention from parents
   Compliments about activities, efforts, appearance

3. *Game Activity Reinforcers*
   Playing outdoors alone, with a friend, or with a parent
   Participating in organized sports
   Playing Sega or Nintendo
   Playing computer games
   Participating in table games (cards, checkers, etc.)

4. *Consumable Food Reinforcers*
   Candy
   Fruit
   Snack food
   Gum
   Ice cream
   Cookies
   Cake
   Soda
   Juice

(*continued*)

TABLE 10-1   (*continued*)

5. *Tangible Reinforcers*
   Money to purchase desired items
   Pencils or pens
   Cassettes or compact disks
   Toys
   Games
   Pads of paper
   Books
   Jewelry
   Clothing

6. *Token Reinforcers*
   Points
   Stars
   Chips
   Play money
   Check marks

SOURCE: Walker, James E. and Thomas N. Shea, *Behavior Management: A Practical Approach for Educators,* 6th ed. Copyright © 1995 by MacMillan Publishing Company, Inc. Reprinted by permission.

UNDERSTANDING PARENTS

Parents want their children to succeed in school and generally appreciate teachers' efforts to keep them informed and involved (Berger, 1991). Parental reactions to problems vary widely. Reactions are largely determined by individual experiences, life experiences, education and training, expectations, socio-economic circumstances, and others. The reactions of the child, the teacher, and others also have a bearing on how the problem will be handled (Walker & Shae, 1995).

Why Some Parents Resist Involvement

As much as you would like the cooperation and support of parents in dealing with academic or behavioral difficulties, you may find parents apathetic or resistant to involvement. Walde and Baker (1990) maintain that some parents "simply don't give a damn" and are not concerned with their child's education, do not want to be involved, or lack the supportive skills needed.

There are several possible reasons for parental resistance.

- As students, they may have had unhappy experiences. They may view schools as being oppressive and not a place of hope for their children (Menacker, Hurwitz, & Weldon, 1988). These parents may consider it unlikely that school personnel can solve the problems.

- Parents of children who have a history of misbehavior may adopt coping mechanisms in an effort to deal emotionally with the problems (Walker & Shae, 1995). Their responses may point to self-doubt, denial, withdrawal, hostility, and frustration. (See Table 10-2 for a thorough list and description of parental coping mechanisms.) These parents may resist involvement with anyone and everyone at school.

TABLE 10-2 Parental coping mechanisms when their child has a problem

1. *Self-doubt.* The parents may doubt their worth as human beings and as parents. Their self-worth may be in doubt because of a perceived inability to give birth to or raise a child according to their expectations and the expectations of society.

2. *Unhappiness and mourning.* The child's problem is perceived as so severe that the parents' joy of life is gone. It is impossible for them to smile, laugh, converse, or take an active part in any of life's common pleasures. This parental reaction has been compared to the mourning that occurs after the death of a loved one.

3. *Guilt.* Because of the uncertain cause of their child's problem, many parents feel guilty. They believe that the child's problem is their fault. At times parents will go to extreme lengths to find a reason for the child's difficulty and may discover some insignificant personal behavior or incident in the past on which to place blame.

4. *Denial.* The parents may react to the child's problem by denying its existence. They reason that if the existence of the problem is denied, they do not have to concern themselves with it.

5. *Projection.* Many parents who recognize the existence of a problem may blame it on another person. They may blame the child's difficulty on a physician, nurse, caseworker, counselor, babysitter, or teacher. Occasionally they will project blame onto their spouse or other children.

6. *Withdrawal.* The parents may react to the child's problem by withdrawal, believing that they can find a solution if they give the problem sufficient time and personal consideration. In some cases, withdrawal leads to depression requiring professional attention.

7. *Avoidance and rejection.* To some parents, the birth or diagnosis of an exceptional child is so traumatic that they avoid contact with the child; they are unable to feed, clothe, or play with the child.

8. *Embarrassment and social isolation.* Many parents of handicapped children are embarrassed by them. In some cases this embarrassment leads to social isolation. Neither parent nor child leaves the home for shopping, walks, visits, or entertainment.

9. *Hostility.* Some parents report feelings of hostility and, on occasion, overt anger toward others who stare or ask questions about the child. The object of this hostility and anger may be anyone: a passenger on a bus, a person in the street, a friend, a neighbor, a relative, or a child.

10. *Overdependency and helplessness.* The parents may react with overdependency on their spouse, a child, a relative, or a professional.

11. *Confusion.* Most parents are confused by the child's problem. They are confused about the cause of the problem, its normal course, and its treatment. Such confusion is largely a result of a lack of factual information and guidance from professionals.

12. *Frustration.* Many parents who have decided on a course of action that is appropriate for their child become frustrated in their efforts to obtain services. They are confronted with insensitive and inadequately trained professionals. They are frustrated by the lack of appropriate services in the community.

SOURCE: Walker, James E. and Thomas N. Shea, *Behavior Management: A Practical Approach for Educators,* 6th ed. Copyright © 1995 by MacMillan Publishing Company, Inc. Reprinted by permission.

- Some parents view teachers, principals, counselors, and other school personnel as the experts in addressing misbehavior (Greenwood & Hickman, 1991; Turnbull & Turnbull, 1990). They may resist involvement because they do not want to interfere with the actions taken by the teacher or other officials.

- Some parents are threatened by the school itself and its bureaucracy. They may be intimidated by the size of the school, the need to report to the school office when visiting the school, the "busyness" of school, the lack of private areas for discussion, and so on (Lightfoot, 1978). These parents have a sense of discomfort toward the school.

- Diversity among the parent population and the sense that they are different from school personnel may make parents uncomfortable (Swap, 1993). For example, Asian immigrant parents may think that communication with teachers is considered to be "checking up on them" and an expression of disrespect (Yao, 1988). Members of other ethnic groups, likewise, may feel out of place.

- Some parents don't know what is expected of them or how they might contribute to their child's education. They may withdraw or become angry or frustrated when the school seems to be failing to meet their child's needs. They do not realize that the school would value their involvement.

- Some parents' don't become involved for practical reasons. They may not speak English or have limited competency in English. They may not drive a car, or have limited access to transportation. They may not have access to a babysitter or cannot afford one. Or they may simply be too tired after long days at work themselves.

Decision Points

Let's assume that you teach in a school that has much ethnic diversity, and that some parents do not attend the Back-To-School Night or the parent-teacher conferences at the end of the report card periods because of their cultural perceptions. How could you communicate to them that it is acceptable to attend such sessions and that their child would ultimately benefit from their attendance? What support might you seek from the principal in communicating with them?

Building a Parental Support System

It is helpful to identify ways you can build a support system so that you can communicate effectively with them and enlist their help. Joyce Epstein, a leading advocate of comprehensive parental involvement (Epstein, 1984; Epstein & Becker, 1982; Epstein & Dauber, 1991), identified five types of ***parental involvement*** (Brandt, 1989a): (a) *Type 1: parenting*—helping all families establish home environments to support learning; (b) *Type 2: communicating*—designing more effective forms of communication to reach parents; (c) *Type 3: volunteering*—recruiting and organizing parent help and support; (d) *Type 4: learning at home*—providing ideas to parents on how to help the child; and (e) *Type 5: representing other parents*—recruiting and training parent leaders.

It is important to counteract parental resistance (Moore, 1991). Recognizing that there are varying degrees of parental support and involvement, you will most likely focus on Epstein's Types 2 and 3—communicating and seeking volunteers. Other aspects of parental involvement are considered in other sources (cf., Brandt, 1989b; Epstein, 1991; Swap, 1993; Wikelund, 1990).

CONTACTING AND COMMUNICATING WITH PARENTS

As discussed, there are several reasons for working with parents. The timing of the contact will depend on the reason for it. There are three points to consider when contacting parents.

1. *Initial contact with all parents* would occur at the start of the year. These contacts would be designed to inform parents about the program, grading guidelines, the homework policy, rules and procedures, and other academic and behavioral expectations. Requests for additional classroom supplies and for parent volunteers for activities are generally made at this time. You could make these contacts through an introductory letter, a newsletter, Back-to-School Night, or other means.

2. *Ongoing contact with parents* occurs throughout the year to provide information about content being covered, the schedule for tests or other evaluation requirements, field trips, student progress, and so on. You may need parent volunteers throughout the year and may contact them as the need arises. These contacts could be made through a newsletter or information sheet, an open house, report cards, or other means.

3. *Contact with selected parents* needs to occur to inform them about unique concerns related to their child's progress. These contacts may occur when there is both positive and negative news to report. You will often contact parents when there is a problem; yet it is easy to overlook this when there is good news. Parents especially appreciate reports of good news. If a problem arises later, parents are often more willing to support and cooperate with the teacher.

Ways to Communicate with Parents

There are many ways to communicate with parents, and the method may be affected by its purpose. To discuss a serious act of misbehavior, for example, you would probably not wait for a parent-teacher conference scheduled at the end of a report card period but would likely call the parents immediately.

Much communication occurs at the start of the year in the form of an introductory letter, a letter about classroom management and discipline, a Back-to-School Night, and information sheets. Ongoing communication may be through an open house, newsletters, notes and letters, phone calls, special events and informal contacts, sending student work home, report cards, home visits, and parent-teacher conferences. To contact parents about their child's academic work or behavior, you could call them or arrange for a special conference.

Introductory Letter. Teachers sometimes send an *introductory letter* home with the students to give to their parents during the first week of school prior to the Back-to-School Night. This letter is intended to serve as a brief welcome to the new year, include some basic information about the class, and invite the parents to the Back-to-School Night that will soon follow.

The letter may include some information about the schedule, homework, absences, and the curriculum. You may mention in the letter that more will be said about these and other issues at the Back-to-School Night. A sample introductory letter to parents is displayed in Figure 10–1. You can adapt this letter to suit your particular situation.

FIGURE 10-1 Sample introductory letter to parents

September 4

Dear Parents:

Now that the school year has begun, I'd like to introduce myself. I am Melissa Riley, and I am your child's sixth grade teacher this year. I have taught in this school district for 14 years in both the fifth and sixth grades. I completed my undergraduate work at the University of Illinois and my master's degree at Kansas State University.

I want this to be a successful school year for you and your child. To ensure this success, it is important that we maintain open communication. Please do not hesitate to contact me if you have any questions or concerns. You could call me at school after dismissal between 3:30 and 4:30 p.m. at 555-7308. Or you could call anytime during the day and leave a message for me to call you back.

At various times throughout the school year, I will be sending a newsletter home with your child to provide information about classroom activities and special events. On a regular basis, your child will bring home graded assignments for you to look at. I also look forward to seeing you at the parent-teacher conferences which we schedule at the end of each report card period.

The annual Back-to-School Night for this school is scheduled for next Thursday, September 12, from 7:30 to 8:00 p.m. On that evening, I will be welcoming the parents of the students in my class. My presentation will include information about the daily and weekly schedule, the curriculum, my approach to instruction, my academic expectations and procedures, my policy on discipline, and other issues. The books and materials that we will be using this year will also be on display. I encourage you to attend the Back-to-School Night because it will give you an opportunity to understand the sixth grade program and become better acquainted with the room, the program, and myself.

Working together and keeping in good contact, I'm confident that this will be an exciting and successful school year. I look forward to meeting you at the Back-to-School Night.

Sincerely,

Melissa Riley

Letter about Classroom Management and Discipline. You need to share your plan for management and discipline with the parents and the principal. If you expect them to be involved when you need them, they need to know that you have a plan, and be aware of your rationale for rules, positive recognition, and consequences.

At the start of the year, you need to discuss rules, consequences, and other aspects of management with the students. A copy of this information sheet should be given to the students to take home. The letter should provide details of the management and discipline plan and explain why it is important. Ask the parents to discuss the plan with their children, sign the plan, and return the signature portion to you. A sample letter to parents is displayed in Figure 10-2. You may plan to adapt that letter for your particular situation.

If the Back-to-School Night is scheduled early in the year, you may ask the parents to return the signature portion at that time. Or you may prefer to wait and present the letter to the parents at the Back-to-School Night. Letters can then be sent home to parents who did not attend that evening.

Back-to-School Night. Many schools schedule a ***Back-to-School Night*** or Family Night during the first or second week so parents can receive information about the academic program, grading guidelines, the homework policy, rules and procedures, and other expectations. Requests for additional classroom supplies and for parent volunteers for activities are generally made at this time.

Some schools do not schedule a Back-to-School Night or, if they do, it comes later than the first or second week. You may find other ways to communicate with parents since it is important to establish contact as early as possible. For example, the letter about management and discipline might be expanded to include information commonly covered at a Back-to-School Night.

The scheduling of the Back-to-School Night is handled in different ways. In elementary schools, there is often a preset period of about 30 minutes when parents come to your classroom. You may be speaking to all the parents at one time; or a second 30-minute session may be held to accommodate parents who have more than one child attending the school. The schedule may be staggered. The parents may be given handouts.

Often, in middle, junior high, and senior high school, parents are given their child's schedule and they follow it just as the student would, in shortened sessions of 10 to 15 minutes. In this way, the parents see every teacher just as their child would. Teachers use this time to inform the parents about policies and expectations.

Preparing for Back-to-School Night. Back-to-School Night is often your first contact with the parents, so thorough preparation is necessary. There are many ways to prepare for this evening.

- *Prepare your own introductory letter to parents about the Back-to-School Night in your classroom* (see the sample introductory letter in Figure 10-1.). Don't rely only on notices the school sends home. Some

Dear Parents:

Now that the school year has begun, I'd like to introduce myself and give you some information about how I conduct my classes. My name is Keith McKinsey, and I am your child's eighth grade social studies teacher. I have taught in this school district for eight years. I completed my undergraduate work at the Florida State University and my master's degree at Kansas State University.

To maintain an appropriate learning environment, I have established the following classroom rules which all students are expected to follow:

1. Follow the teacher's directions.
2. Keep your hands, feet, and objects to yourself.
3. Do not swear or tease.

To encourage students to follow the rules, I will recognize appropriate behavior with praise, various types of reinforcement, and notes or calls home to you. If students choose to break the rules, I have established an escalating series of responses ranging from gentle prompts and reminders, to the use of logical consequences, and to detention. In class, we have discussed these rules, the reinforcement for following the rules, and the consequences if the students choose to break the rules. My goal is to ensure success for your child. Working together, I'm confident that it will be an enjoyable and productive school year.

Please indicate that you understand this discipline plan by signing your name below and indicate the phone numbers where you can be reached during the day and evening. You might also discuss the rules to make sure your child understands them.

Please do not hesitate to contact me if you have any questions or concerns. You could call me at school after dismissal between 3:30 and 4:30 p.m. at 555-6188. Or you could call anytime during the day and leave a message for me to call you back.

Sincerely,

Keith McKinsey

(Tear off and return the part below to Mr. McKinsey)

I have read and understand Mr. McKinsey's classroom management plan, and I have discussed it with my child.

Parent/Guardian Signature ——————————————————— Date ————

Comments:

FIGURE 10-2 Sample letter to parents about classroom management and discipline

teachers like to have their students prepare special invitations for their own families.

- *Make sure the classroom looks attractive and neat.* Post your name and room number prominently on the door and the front chalkboard. Display samples of work by all students. Display copies of the textbooks and other instructional materials.

- *Prepare a list of supplies or materials that parents might be able to provide.* This list will vary depending on the subject and grade level. It may include such items as rulers, buttons, a box of facial tissue, or other supplies. Have enough copies of the list to give to all parents.

- *Prepare separate sign-up sheets for parents.* These may concern the need for a private, follow-up conference about their child; volunteers to help at special events such as field trips; volunteers such as guest speakers in class; or volunteers to provide supplies requested by the teacher.

- *Prepare name tags for the students' desks.* You may want parents to sit in their child's seats to hear your presentation.

- *Plan a well-organized, succinct presentation.* Parents want to hear about your background and experience, behavioral and academic expectations, procedures for homework and absences, and other policies. Be sure to plan for time at the end of the presentation for questions.

- *Prepare handouts for your presentation.* Parents will receive these handouts at the Back-to-School Night. Have enough copies for all parents. A sample content outline of the presentation is shown in Table 10-3. Your handout should include details about issues such as those listed in Table 10-3. On the front page of the handout, include your name, the school phone number, and the times that you can be reached at the school at that phone number. Attach other related materials to this handout; these materials may include a sheet showing the daily or weekly class schedule, a sheet of needed materials and supplies, and a sheet dealing with the management and discipline policy. Staple all the handouts together as one set of materials in the sequence you will follow.

Conducting the Back-to-School Night.   Several guidelines should be taken into account regarding Back-to-School Night. Since your presentation is usually limited, possibly to 30 minutes, it is important to plan how to conduct yourself.

Greet parents at the door, introduce yourself, and point out the location of their child's seat. Begin your presentation using the handout you previously prepared concerning your background, the daily and weekly schedule, the curriculum, academic goals and activities, academic expectations and procedures, discipline, and so on. Hand a copy to each parent.

Have parents sign up for individual follow-up conferences if they want to talk with you at length about their child. Back-to-School Night is not intended

TABLE 10-3 Sample content outline for the Back-to-School Night

1. *Background about Yourself*
   a. College training and degrees earned
   b. Professional experience, including length of teaching service, grade levels taught, where taught
2. *The Daily and Weekly Class Schedule*
   For self-contained elementary classrooms; provide a photocopy for each parent showing times for classes and other scheduled events such as lunch, recess, and dismissal.
3. *The Curriculum, Academic Goals, and Activities*
   a. Overview of the curriculum and the topics to be covered (refer to the textbooks and related instructional materials on display)
   b. Your approach to instruction
   c. Instructional activities and special events such as field trips or unique programs
4. *Academic Expectations and Procedures*
   a. Grading guidelines and procedures (how grades are determined)
   b. Grading requirements (e.g., tests, quizzes, homework, projects)
   c. Homework (purposes, how often, make-up policy, absences)
   d. When report cards are delivered
   e. Parent-teacher conferences
5. *Discipline*
   a. Classroom rules
   b. Positive rewards
   c. Consequences for breaking the rules
   d. Incremental steps taken when misbehavior continues
   e. When parents will be contacted
   f. Parents need to sign the sheet about management and discipline policy.
6. *Ask Parents to Sign up for Selected Issues*
   a. For a private, follow-up conference about their child
   b. For parent volunteers for providing instructional materials and supplies
   c. For parent volunteers to help at special events such as field trips
   d. For parent volunteers such as guest speakers in class
7. *Express Interest in Hearing about Ideas and Concerns from Parents at Any Time*
8. *Time for Questions at the End of the Session (save several minutes if possible)*

to deal with concerns about individual students. Allow time for parents to ask questions. This will be an opportunity for you to provide clarification about issues and to hear the concerns of parents.

Information Sheets.   Not all schools schedule a Back-to-School Night, and not all parents attend a scheduled Night. You can prepare a packet to send home that provides information about the curriculum, grading expectations and requirements, rules and procedures, the discipline plan, and other matters. The sheets may be the same as those given to parents who attend the Night, or a shortened version.

Open House.   Once or twice a year, most schools schedule an open house when parents visit the classrooms to meet their child's teacher, observe the classroom and samples of student work, and learn about books and materials

Teachers in Action

Assignment Sheets

Kathy Sublett, eighth-grade history and language arts teacher, Anderson, California:

Students need to know on a weekly basis where they stand in their grades. I provide students and their parents with an assignment sheet listing the assignments, those the student has turned in, and those due next. I inform parents about this at the Back-to-School Night and also in a memo that I send home.

There are two purposes of the assignment sheet. First, it helps remind students that they are responsible for their assignments. They have only to look at the sheet to see which assignments they are missing. Second, it is self-protection against irate parents who are amazed when they receive a deficiency notice. I simply ask the parents to look at their child's assignment sheet to see what has not been turned in. The assignment sheets have helped defuse many tense situations. I can then ask the parents for their support in getting students to focus on their work.

being used. Some districts do not have a Back-to-School Night and schedule the first open house in mid-to-late September.

At the open house, teachers may give a formal presentation about the program. Some schools allow parents to drop in at any time during school hours to informally discuss issues.

Open houses are conducted well into the year, providing opportunities to display student projects. Science fairs may be scheduled at the same time to provide such an opportunity. Some parents attending the open house may not have attended the Back-to-School Night, and it is useful to have extra copies of the handout available at the Back-to-School Night to describe your policies.

Newsletters.   A newsletter periodically sent to all parents contains information about special events, content to be covered in the curriculum, tests or quizzes, student projects, or other points. Newsletters may be only one page, or may be longer according to need. You can report accomplishments of the class and of individual students.

Computers can be used to prepare the newsletters. Students could prepare the newsletter as a group or class project, under suitable circumstances.

Assignment Sheets.   Another way to communicate with parents is through an assignment sheet, which describes the assignments for the next week or two. The student is asked to show it to the parents. Some teachers may prefer that the parents sign the sheet and have it returned to school. This makes the students fully aware of what needs to be turned in for evaluation and can arrange their schedules appropriately; and the parents also are aware of what is happening.

Individual Notes and Letters.   Notes and letters are written to parents to discuss a particular issue about their child. You can use them to request that a conference be arranged with you, to invite parents to class functions, to inform parents about their child's work, or to offer suggestions.

Notes should be carefully written. They should be free of errors in spelling, grammar, and sentence structure. They should be brief, clear, honest, and factual. Educational jargon should not be used. Notes and letters are especially useful for contacting parents who are hard to reach by telephone.

Make sure that you address the letter correctly, since parent and child may not have the same last name. If the parents do not read English, try to take needed steps to write the letter or note in their native language. Avoid writing a letter when you are upset about a classroom event; calm down first. Try to end with a positive statement about working together for the benefit of the child.

Be cautious about sending notes home only when there is bad news to deliver. Certainly there are times when such notes need to be sent. You should also send notes with good news about the child's academic work or behavior. Brief, positive notes take only a few minutes to write to express your pleasure. By systematically writing one or two notes to different parents each day, you will provide good news and help build positive relationships with the parents. Parents will usually talk with their child about the note, and the child may come to school the next day with a more positive attitude.

Decision Points

Sending notes or letters home to parents is one way to communicate with them. What types of information might you convey in the notes or letters? What guidelines will you establish for yourself about the content, the writing form, the frequency, and other factors? How might you need to vary these guidelines if you were teaching respectively at the second-, sixth-, and tenth-grade levels?

Phone Calls.   Like notes and letters, telephone calls are made to parents to discuss a particular issue. The phone calls could request that a conference with you be arranged, to invite parents to class functions, to inform them about their child's work, or to offer suggestions. As with notes and letters, be cautious about calling parents only when you have bad news. Also call parents when there is good news to report.

Phone calls can be quite brief because you need have only two or three positive statements to share. They are not intended to be a lengthy discussion about the student. The parents should be asked to tell the child about the phone call.

Teachers in Action

Constructive Phone Calls to Parents

Kathryn Tallerico, high school English teacher, Brighton, Colorado:

As a tenth grader, Rudy was a bright student who had a history of being hostile, pouty, and downright rude. My two interdisciplinary team-mates and I had a series of problems with her last year, and we eventually had a conference with her father.

This year, Rudy showed up in my creative writing class. I had to work hard to face her without prejudice and to assume that she would cooperate and succeed. Well, she did. Whether it was the class, the maturation process, or both, I'm not sure, but she became a delight to teach.

After three months of bliss, I called her father and was able to sincerely praise her turnaround. I told her father how difficult it had been to like her the previous year. He simply said, "I know, I know. That's what she was like at home, too." Then he shared a bit about his personal hurt, and thanked me profusely for taking the time to bring my observations to his attention. I could hear the pride in his voice. I hung up glowing with the rare satisfaction of having witnessed major growth within the short time I got to spend with an adolescent.

The next day at school, Rudy thanked me too. She said her dad let her know how much it meant to him. She added that it was very important to her that he know how much she had truly changed. Then I thanked her, and we hugged.

In retrospect, I sincerely believe that careful, honest discussion at all stages had laid the groundwork for Rudy's dramatic growth. I use four guidelines when communicating with parents: (1) keep accurate records of the facts and rely on these when speaking to parents, (2) always have at least one truly kind or complimentary remark to make about the student, (3) record notes about the conversation and place a memo in a planner for a week or two ahead to provide the parent with follow-up information, and (4) ask the parent for information, help, and advice—communication must be two-way to be effective.

There are times when you need to contact parents about the child's misbehavior. You need to plan ahead before making the call (Canter & Canter, 1991, 1992). The call should begin with a statement of concern such as, "Mrs. Erickson, I care about Kendra and I feel that her behavior in the classroom is not in her best interest." You then describe the problem and present pertinent documentation. You go on to describe what you are doing and have done to deal with the misbehavior. At this point, it is helpful to invite parental input by asking questions such as, "Has Kendra had similar problems in the past? Why do you feel she is having these problems at school? Is there something going on at home that could be affecting her behavior?"

It is useful to obtain parental input about the problem. State what you will do to help solve the problem and explain what you want the parent to do. Before ending the telephone conversation, let the parent know that you are confident the problems can be worked out and that there will be follow-up contact from you. Then recap the conversation.

Special Events and Informal Contacts.   Throughout the year, teachers and parents may attend many special events. These may include sporting events, concerts, plays, carnivals, craft displays, and others. Contacts with parents at these events may provide brief opportunities to share a few words about their child's work. These contacts are especially useful as progress reports and as a means of discussing a particular issue.

Sending Student Work Home.   You can inform parents about their child's progress by sending home completed and graded student work. Parents can see what you have covered, the child's work, and any notes or remarks you have made.

Sending home only completed worksheets may not be very enlightening. It is useful to send tests, quizzes, homework, projects, lab reports, writing samples, and artwork, as well. Be sensitive about notes you write on the papers. These notes are evaluative statements; they should include comments about good points and improvement as well as about areas still needing attention.

Papers meant to be sent home may not be shown to the parents or not taken home. You might devise ways to have parents sign a sheet to indicate that they have seen the material. For example, a parent response sheet might list what has been sent home, with a blank space for the parents to sign and date. The student then returns the response sheet to you.

Decision Points

Sending graded student papers home is an important means of communication. What guidelines will you establish concerning comments you write on the papers, the type of papers sent home, and the means to confirm that parents did receive the papers? How might you modify your procedures if a number of parents have limited English proficiency or if several ethnic groups are represented?

Report Cards.   Parents are informed of their child's progress when report cards are distributed. Most report cards contain space in which you write a statement or indicate a code about effort and citizenship. As with notes, letters, and phone calls, you should be cautious about making only negative notes on report cards. Deserving students should receive positive notes.

When warranted, include notes on the report card to indicate a need to improve. Parents may call teachers shortly after report cards have been delivered if they have any question about them. Have documentation ready to justify what you have noted.

Home Visits. Another means for personal contact with parents is through home visits, especially for parents who are reluctant to visit the school. This type of communication is not as popular as it once was due to changing social conditions and concerns about safety of the visiting teachers. Nevertheless, home visits allow you to inform the parents about the program and the child's progress. You may choose to make home visits to those parents who did not attend the Back-to-School Night or the parent-teacher conferences. The handout prepared for the Back-to-School Night could then be given to the parents. Visiting the student's home gives you insight into the family environment.

Some school districts employ a home visitation coordinator or a parent educator who is responsible for regularly visiting students' homes to discuss the child's progress, important events in the family's life, and ways parents can support their child's learning (Olmsted, 1991). Teachers in some school districts are encouraged to visit the homes of all students before school begins (Love, 1989).

It is important to know the community before making home visits because of concerns about safety. Two teachers may visit together or a teacher and a security guard may make the visit.

Parent-Teacher Conferences

Another important way of communicating with parents is through ***parent-teacher conferences.*** Many school districts schedule a day or two at the end of each report card period for parent-teacher conferences so parents can meet individually with the teacher. Conference days are typically scheduled only for elementary grades; many middle school, junior high, and high schools do not schedule specific conferences. All parents are invited to attend these individually scheduled conferences.

In addition to the regular conferences, parent-teacher conferences are held with particular parents as the need warrants. When a student persistently misbehaves, you may ask the parents to come to the school for a conference. Prior to having such a conference, you may want to meet with the student to work out a plan to address the behavior (discussed in chapter 16). If this meeting does not lead to resolution, a meeting with the parents is warranted, and the student may be asked to attend.

Recommendations for conducting parent-teacher conferences come from many sources (cf., Jones & Jones, 1990; Rotter, Robinson, & Frey, 1987; Wolf & Stephens, 1989). Turnbull and Turnbull (1990) identified useful questions for teachers to ask themselves regarding parent-teacher conferences (see Table 10-4). To have effective parent-teacher conferences, teachers should thoroughly

TABLE 10-4 Questions for teachers to ask themselves regarding parent-teacher conferences

1. *Preconference Preparation*
   a. Notifying Families
      Did I, or the school, provide parents with written notification of the conference?
      Did I provide a means of determining that the parents know the date and time?
   b. Preparing for the Conference
      Did I review the student's cumulative records?
      Did I assess the student's behavior and pinpoint areas of concern?
      Did I make notes of the student's misbehavior to show to parents?
      Did I consult with other relevant professionals about the student's behavior?
      Did I mentally rehearse and review what I was going to say at the conference?
   c. Preparing the Physical Environment
      Did the setting provide enough privacy?
      Did the setting provide enough comfort?
2. *Conference Activities*
   a. Developing Rapport
      Did I allow time to talk informally before the start of the meeting?
      Did I express appreciation for the parents' coming to the meeting?
   b. Obtaining Information from Parents
      Did I ask enough open-ended questions?
      Did my body language indicate interest in what parents were saying? (Did I maintain eye contact and look attentive?)
      Did I ask for clarification on points I didn't understand?
   c. Providing Information to Parents
      Did I speak as positively as possible about the student?
      Did I use jargon-free language?
      Did I use specific examples to clarify my points?
   d. Summarizing and Follow-Up
      Did I review the main points to determine next steps?
      Did I restate who was responsible for completing the next steps and by when?
      Did I end the meeting on a positive note?
      Did I thank the parents for their interest in attending?
3. *Postconference Follow-Up*
   Did I consider reviewing the meeting with the student?
   Did I share the results with the appropriate other professionals who work with the student?
   Did I make a record of the conference proceedings?

SOURCE: Turnbull, Ann P. and H. Rutherford Turnbull III, *Families, Professionals, and Exceptionality: A Special Partnership,* 2nd ed. Copyright © 1990 by Macmillan College Publishing Company, Inc. Reprinted by permission.

prepare for the conference, take certain actions when conducting the conference, and plan appropriate follow-up.

Guidelines discussed in the following sections center primarily on parent-teacher conferences to address academic issues. These guidelines would need to be adapted somewhat to address individually scheduled parent-teacher conferences concerning academic or disciplinary issues.

Preparing for the Conference.   Parents need to be notified of the day and time of the conference. A letter could be sent home to both inform parents and provide information about what will occur. A sample letter to parents is shown in Figure 10-3.

Dear Parents:

Parent-Teacher Conferences at the end of the first report card period are scheduled for Thursday and Friday, October 23–24. Your scheduled appointment with me is on Friday, October 23, from 3:30 to 4:00 p.m. to discuss your child's progress. If you cannot come at that time, please let me know your best day and time, and I will try to adjust the schedule. We will be meeting in my classroom, Room 17.

During the conference, we will have time to review your child's report card, recent tests and projects, work samples, behavior and peer relationships, and other issues. You might want to jot down any questions that you would like to ask me.

I look forward to meeting you. By working together, I feel confident that this will be an enjoyable and productive school year.

Sincerely,

Sylvia Wu

FIGURE 10-3 Sample letter to parents concerning the parent-teacher conference

Preparing for the conference also involves collecting grades, documentation, and other materials. These materials may include the following:

1. A schedule showing the time for the conference with each parent.
2. A folder for each student which includes sample work, tests, and projects. This folder will be given to the parents at the conference.
3. The gradebook to show the student's grade or to refer to other details. The parents will have received the report card prior to the conference.
4. A copy of each textbook and other significant resource materials.
5. An agenda for conducting each conference. Have the student's strengths and weaknesses clearly in mind, and consider what you will say to each parent.

Finally, the physical environment needs to be prepared beforehand. You can arrange for these materials: (1) a table for the conference; (2) three or four adult-sized chairs for the table; (3) two or three chairs to be placed in the hallway for parents who arrive early for their conference; (4) a clean, tidy room. Have the students clean their desks. Place decorations on a wall. You might have flowers on the table and perhaps serve cookies.

Conducting the Conference. Discussion and questions in the conference should be planned in sequence to develop rapport, obtain information, present information, and summarize and follow-up. There are several guidelines to consider.

The following guidelines indicate a method to "sandwich" your main messages in between good news or positive statements at the start and at the end of the conference. The parents who hear favorable comments at the start are then in a comfortable frame of mind. As the conference comes to a close, it is useful to summarize your main points, then conclude with additional positive statements.

1. *Begin the conference in a positive manner.* Walk up to the parents, introduce yourself, and welcome them. Start with a positive statement about the student, such as, "Emily really enjoys providing leadership for students in her small group when working on projects."
2. *Present the student's strong points before describing the matters needing improvement.* Highlight the student's strengths as you move into a discussion about his or her performance. Show samples of the student's work to the parents. Later, identify matters that need further improvement.
3. *Encourage parents to participate and share information.* Allow opportunities to ask questions and share information about the student. Pose questions at various points to encourage their input.
4. *Plan a course of action cooperatively.* If the student needs to work on a particular issue, discuss the possible actions that you and the parents could take. Come to agreement about the course of action that each of you will take.
5. *End the conference with a positive comment.* Thank the parents for coming and say something positive about the student at the end of the conference.
6. *Use good human relations skills during the conference.* To be effective, you should be friendly and informal, positive in your approach, willing to explain in understandable terms, willing to listen, willing to accept parents' feelings, and careful about giving advice. You should avoid arguing and getting angry; asking embarrassing questions; talking about other students, teachers, or parents; bluffing if you do not know an answer; rejecting parents' suggestions; and being a "know it all" with pat answers (Linn & Gronlund, 1990).

Handling Conference Follow-up.   During the conferences, it is useful to make a list of follow-up actions. These may include providing more thorough feedback to the student during the next marking period, recommending additional readings, giving parents periodic updates, and a host of other actions. It is important to follow up along the lines identified during the parent-teacher conference.

MAJOR CONCEPTS

1. Teachers work with parents to (a) understand the home environment; (b) inform parents of academic expectations and events as well as student performance; (c) enlist parents' help with academic issues; (d) inform parents of disciplinary expectations and actions; and (e) enlist parents' help in dealing with their children.
2. Some parents may be apathetic or even resist involvement.

3. Parental resistance may be due to (a) the parents' unhappy experiences when they were students; (b) parental coping mechanisms in dealing with ongoing problems with their children; (c) the parents' view that educators are the experts; or (d) the parents' intimidation by the school and the bureaucracy.

4. The individual classroom teacher will most likely try to build a parental support system primarily by communicating to reach parents and by seeking parent volunteers to help with school-related issues.

5. The timing of the contact with parents will be based on the reason for the contact. The three main points of parental contact are (a) initial contacts with all parents at the start of the school year; (b) ongoing contacts with all parents throughout the school year; and (c) contact with selected parents concerning their child's academic or behavioral progress.

6. Initial communication with parents occurs at the start of the year in the form of an introductory letter, a letter about classroom management and discipline, a Back-to-School Night, and information sheets.

7. Ongoing communication throughout the year may occur with an open house, news-letters, notes and letters, phone calls, special events, informal contacts, sending student work home, report cards, home visits, and parent-teacher conferences.

8. To contact individual parents about their child's academic work or behavior, teachers often call the parents and sometimes arrange for a special parent-teacher conference to address the issues.

DISCUSSION QUESTIONS

1. How might information about a student's home help you as a teacher decide on an appropriate course of action? How might this information create problems for you?

2. Based on your experiences and observations, why might some parents resist involvement with their child's teacher(s)?

3. What is the appropriate point at which to contact parents if a student is exhibiting mild misbehavior? Moderate misbehavior?

4. In what ways did your teachers in the elementary and secondary grades contact and interact with your parents?

5. What are some ways that teachers can communicate with parents about academic expectations and events?

6. How can you communicate with parents who do not show up for Back-to-School Night or parent-teacher conferences?

SUPPLEMENTAL ACTIVITIES

For Clinical Settings

1. Prepare an introductory letter which you might send to parents at the start of the school year.

2. Assume that you will send four newsletters to parents during the school year. For each newsletter, select the month it will be sent and list the type of content that

you might report in each newsletter. (Would you have regular features in each newsletter? What content might be unique to each issue?)

3. Prepare a letter that you might send to parents prior to a parent-teacher conference.

For Field Settings

1. Talk with several teachers about experiences they have had with parents who resist involvement. How did these teachers still communicate with these parents? What suggestions do they offer?

2. Ask several teachers to describe the ways that they prepare for and conduct the Back-to-School Night. What recommendations do they have to aid your preparation?

3. Talk with several teachers about their experiences preparing for and conducting parent-teacher conferences. What suggestions do they offer for your handling of the conferences?

KEY TERMS

Back-to-School Night   Parent
Parent-teacher conferences   Parental involvement

RECOMMENDED READINGS

Brandt, R., Editor. (1989b). Strengthening partnerships with parents and community [special issue]. *Educational Leadership, 47*(2).
    Includes articles about successful parent involvement programs, partnerships in education, parent advisory committees, parent-teacher conferences, and related issues.

Epstein, J. L., guest editor. (1991). Parental involvement [special issue]. *Phi Delta Kappan, 72*(5).
    Includes articles on school, district, state, and federal leadership for parental involvement.

Rotter, J. C., Robinson, E. H., & Frey, M. A. (1987). *Parent-teacher Conferencing,* 2nd ed. Washington, DC: National Education Association.
    Includes information on the need for effective parent-teacher conferences, roadblocks and greenlights, interpersonal communication skills, and ideas for conducting the conference. A 32–page booklet.

Swap, S. M. (1987). *Enhancing Parent Involvement: A Manual for Parents and Teachers.* New York: Teachers College Press.
    Includes information about barriers to parental involvement, initiating positive contacts, making conferences productive, finding out what parents want, and involving parents in solving problems.

Swap, S. M. (1993). *Developing Home-school Partnerships: From Concepts to Practice.* New York: Teachers College Press.
    Provides a comprehensive overview and numerous practical suggestions for educators to strengthen school-parent relationships. Discusses benefits and barriers to parental involvement. Presents several models for this involvement. Excellent resource.

REFERENCES

Becher, R. M. (1984). *Parent Involvement: A Review of Research and Principles of Successful Practice.* Washington, DC: National Institute of Education.

Berger, E. G. (1991). Parental involvement: Yesterday and today. *The Elementary School Journal, 91*(3), 209-218.

Brandt, R. (1989a). On parents and schools: A conversation with Joyce Epstein. *Educational Leadership, 47*(2), 24-27.

Brandt, R. (1989b). Strengthening partnerships with parents and community [special issue]. *Educational Leadership, 47*(2).

Canter, L., & Canter, M. (1991). *Parents on Your Side.* Santa Monica, CA: Lee Canter & Associates.

Canter, L., & Canter, M. (1992). *Assertive Discipline: Positive Behavior Management for Today's Classroom.* Santa Monica, CA: Lee Canter & Associates.

Epstein, J. L. (1984). *Effects on Parents of Teacher Practices in Parent Involvement.* Baltimore, MD: Johns Hopkins University, Center for Social Organization of Schools.

Epstein, J. L., guest editor. (1991). Parental involvement [special issue]. *Phi Delta Kappan, 72*(5).

Epstein, J. L., & Becker, H. J. (1982). Teachers' reported practices of parental involvement: Problems and possibilities. *The Elementary School Journal, 83*(2), 103-113.

Epstein, J. L., & Dauber, S. L. (1991). School programs and teacher practices of parent involvement in inner-city elementary and middle schools. *The Elementary School Journal, 91*(3), 289-305.

Greenwood, G. E., & Hickman, C. W. (1991). Research and practice in parent involvement: Implications for teacher education. *The Elementary School Journal, 91*(3), 279-288.

Haynes, N. M., Comer, J. P., & Hamilton-Lee, M. (1989). School climate enhancement through parent involvement. *Journal of School Psychology, 27,* 87-90.

Henderson, A. T. (1987). *The Evidence Continues to Grow: Parent Involvement Improves Student Achievement.* Columbia, MD: National Committee for Citizens in Education.

Jones, V. F., & Jones, L. S. (1990). *Comprehensive Classroom Management: Motivating and Managing Students,* 3rd ed. Boston: Allyn & Bacon.

Lightfoot, S. L. (1978). *Worlds Apart: Relationships between Families and Schools.* New York: Basic Books.

Linn, R. L., & Gronlund, N. E. (1995). *Measurement and Assessment in Teaching,* 7th ed. New York: Macmillan.

Love, M. J. (1989). The home visit: An irreplaceable tool. *Educational Leadership, 47*(2), 29.

Menacker, J., Hurwitz, E., & Weldon, W. (1988). Parent-teacher cooperation in schools serving the urban poor. *Clearing House, 62,* 108-112.

Moore, E. K. (1991). Improving schools through parental involvement. *Principal, 71*(1), 17, 19-20.

Olmsted, P. P. (1991). Parent involvement in elementary education: Findings and suggestions from the Follow Through Program. *The Elementary School Journal, 91*(3), 221-231.

Rich, D. (1988). Bridging the parent gap in education reform. *Educational Horizons, 66,* 90-92.

Rotter, J. C., Robinson, E. H., & Frey, M. A. (1987). *Parent-teacher Conferencing,* 2nd ed. Washington, DC: National Education Association.

Swap, S. M. (1993). *Developing Home-school Partnerships: From Concepts to Practice.* New York: Teachers College Press.

Turnbull, A. P., & Turnbull, H. R. (1990). *Families, Professionals, and Exceptionalities: A Special Partnership,* 2nd ed. Columbus, OH: Merrill.

Walde, A. C., & Baker, K. (1990). How teachers view the parents' role in education. *Phi Delta Kappan, 72*(4), 319-320, 322.

Walker, J. E., & Shae, T. M. (1995). *Behavior Management: A Practical Approach for Educators,* 6th ed. Columbus, OH: Merrill.

Wikelund, K. R. (1990). *Schools and Communities Together: A Guide to Parent Involvement.* Portland, OR: Northwest Regional Educational Laboratory.

Wolf, J. S., & Stephens, T. M. (1989). Parent/teacher conferences: Finding common ground. *Educational Leadership, 47*(2), 28-31.

Yao, E. (1988). Working effectively with Asian immigrant parents. *Phi Delta Kappan, 70*(3), 223-225.

part IV

Conducting the Class

$\mathbf{P}$art IV includes three chapters about conducting a class that have a bearing on managing student behavior and maintaining order. These chapters address ways to establish a cooperative, responsible classroom; encourage and reinforce appropriate behavior; and manage lesson delivery.

Chapter 11, "Establishing a Cooperative, Responsible Classroom," discusses the importance of promoting cooperation as a means to establish and maintain order. Techniques are described for promoting students' self-esteem, building positive teacher-student relationships, building group cohesiveness, helping students assume responsibility for their behavior, and teaching cooperative skills.

Chapter 12, "Encouraging and Reinforcing Appropriate Behavior," explains techniques for maintaining student attention and involvement. Reinforcers are described, and strategies are proposed for using them effectively.

Chapter 13, "Managing Lesson Delivery," examines actions that can be taken at various points in a lesson that can affect order and on-task behavior.

chapter 11

Establishing a Cooperative, Responsible Classroom

Objectives

This chapter provides information that will help you:

1. Identify characteristics of positive classroom climate.
2. Determine ways that students' self-esteem can be promoted by helping them feel capable, become involved and interact with others, and contribute.
3. Identify actions teachers can take to build positive teacher-student relationships.
4. Select ways that group cohesiveness can be promoted.
5. Identify actions teachers can take to help students assume responsibility for their behavior.
6. Select programs that are available to teach cooperative skills to students.

Management deals with maintaining order, and you need to establish a cooperative, responsible classroom so that students choose to be orderly. Students need to feel that they are expected to be orderly, cooperative, and responsible. Developing a positive climate is one of the most important ways to establish and maintain student cooperation and responsibility.

Classroom climate is the atmosphere or mood in which you and the students interact. This feeling is a composite of attitudes, emotions, values, and relationships. Climate probably has as much to do with learning, productive work, and self-concept as does anything else in the program.

Teachers in Action

Classroom Climate

Theresa Campos, middle school science teacher, Houston, Texas:

I think developing a positive classroom climate is the foundation of successful teaching. I asked my sixth-grade students to identify things that help provide a good feeling for being in the classroom. These are the things that they mentioned.

- You would look forward to coming to this class if you were a sixth grader. You know you will be treated fairly and with understanding. You will be invited to feel at home.
- You know that Mrs. Campos really cares about you just as though you were one of her own children. You know this because she has told you so. She believes that a teacher is like a loving, nurturing parent away from home.
- These are some things that make us feel special:
  She keeps paper cups in her drawer and we can get one when we're thirsty or hot.
  She knows that sometimes kids feel "antsy" in the afternoon and can't sit too well. She lets us sit on our feet, kneel in our chair, or just stand for a while.
  She begins each class by looking at us and greeting us. She always says "Goodbye" when the bell rings and pats us on the back or says something nice when we leave.
  She asks us for our opinion and often talks things out when a decision needs to be made.
  She always feels our heads when we don't feel well and says we can put our heads down when we have a headache.
  She expects us to do our very best on the work we do. Sometimes she says, "Your scrap copy is fine, now make me a pretty one." We think she really knows that was the one we were going to turn in!
  She does not allow us to say "Shut up." There is a sign in her room that says, "Only friendly words are spoken here." She expects us to have good manners and follow the golden rule.
  When we misbehave, she explains that she does not approve of what we did, but that she still likes us.
  You can never "predict" what science class will be like because each day brings new excitement.
  She knows that we need something to do with our hands during morning announcements. There are wooden mind mazes, puzzles, books of word search puzzles, and other things to do.

A poor climate may be either chaotic and disorganized, or cold, unfriendly, and threatening. A general lack of humor prevails, and there may be sarcasm and animosity. A threatening environment may cause students to work under duress, making them dislike both teacher and school. If coldly and rigidly controlled, students may fear to make errors. They obey the rules for fear of reprisals.

In contrast, a good climate is warm, supportive, and pleasant. It has an air of friendliness, good nature, and acceptance. It is encouraging and helpful, with a low level of threats. Such a climate encourages work and promotes a sense of enjoyment and accomplishment for everyone (Charles, 1992).

Classroom climate is also related to student achievement (Murphy, Weil, & McGreal, 1986). Organizational patterns that result in students feeling more capable, included, and secure seem to result in higher achievement. To develop a cooperative, responsible classroom, you can take actions that (a) promote students' self-esteem; (b) promote student involvement and interaction; (c) promote success; (d) promote positive interactions; and (e) develop a nonthreatening, comfortable environment.

It is useful to examine several critical elements of climate. This chapter considers ways that you can promote student self-esteem, build positive teacher-student relationships, build group cohesiveness, help students assume responsibility for their behavior, and teach cooperative skills. With a positive climate and an emphasis on cooperation, order is promoted and maintained.

PROMOTING STUDENTS' SELF-ESTEEM

Self-esteem is the opinion that each person holds about himself or herself. The term *self-concept* is often used in its place. A strong self-concept may emerge as one experiences frequent success, or is weakened by repeated failures. You can enhance student self-concept while simultaneously increasing learning and reducing misbehavior. One of your main responsibilities is to create an atmosphere where self-esteem can grow.

What students feel about themselves will affect their efforts and actions in all aspects of school. You can help promote students' self-esteem by helping them feel capable, become involved and interact with others, and contribute to the class. This section draws from the very useful suggestions of Linda Albert (1989). A summary of suggestions for promoting students' self-esteem is included in Table 11-1.

There are also a number of useful, noneducational resources available on this topic including *Building Self-Esteem in Children* (Berne & Savary, 1992), and *Raising Self-reliant Children in a Self-indulgent World* (Glenn & Nelsen, 1989).

Help Students Feel Capable

Students who feel that they can master the required learning tasks and succeed often stay on-task and succeed. This boosts their self-esteem and helps reinforce the successful behavior and order. Students who feel capable are less likely to get off-task and misbehave.

TABLE 11-1 Ways to promote students' self-esteem

Helping Students Feel Capable	Helping Students to Interact and Become Involved with Others	Helping Students Contribute
Make mistakes okay	*Give students the five As:*	*Encourage students' contributions to the class*
Talk about mistakes	*Acceptance*	Invite students' help with daily tasks
Equate mistakes with effort	Accept sincerely and unconditionally	Request students' curriculum choices
Minimize the effects of making mistakes	Accept students' personal style	Ask for students' input for rules
Build confidence	*Attention*	*Encourage students to help with other students*
Focus on improvement	Greet students	
Notice contributions	Listen to students	Peer tutoring
Build on strengths	Teach students to ask for attention	Peer counseling
Show faith in students	Spend time chatting	Peer recognition:
Acknowledge the difficulty of a task	Ask students about their life outside school	Applause
Set time limits on tasks	Mention what you've talked about before	Appreciation and affirmation statements
Focus on past success	Eat with students	Happygrams
Analyze past successes	Invite students to eat in your room	Appreciation password
Repeat past successes	Attend school events	
Make learning tangible	Get involved in a project with students	
"I-Can" cans	Schedule individual conferences	
Accomplishment albums	Join students on the playground	
Checklist of skills	Chaperone school events	
Flowchart of concepts	Recognize birthdays	
Talks about yesterday, today, and tomorrow	Make baby-picture bulletin boards	
Recognize achievement	Send cards, messages, homework to absent students	
Applause	Show interest in students' work or hobbies	
Clapping and standing ovations	*Appreciation*	
Stars and stickers	Describe the behavior accurately	
Awards and assemblies	Use three-part appreciation statements	
Exhibits	Focus only on the present	
Positive time-out	Give written words of appreciation	
Self-approval	Teach students to ask for appreciation	

(*continued*)

TABLE 11-1 (*continued*)

Helping Students Feel Capable	Helping Students to Interact and Become Involved with Others	Helping Students Contribute

	Affirmation
	Be specific
	Be enthusiastic
	Acknowledge positive traits
	  verbally or in writing
	
	Affection
	Show affection when things
	  go badly
	Show kindness, and it will
	  multiply and be returned
	Show friendship
	Use affectionate touch
	  when appropriate	

SOURCE: Adapted from Albert, Linda, *Cooperative Discipline: A Teacher's Guide to Cooperative Discipline.* Copyright © 1989 by American Guidance Service, Inc., 4201 Woodland Road, Circle Pines, MN 55014-1796. All rights reserved. Reprinted by permission.

You can help in many ways to encourage students to feel that they are capable (Albert, 1989). First, make it acceptable to make mistakes. The fear of making mistakes undermines the sense of being capable. You can help remove that barrier by talking about mistakes, equating mistakes to effort, and minimizing the outcome of mistakes.

Build confidence that success is possible. Focus on improvement, noticing contributions, building on strengths, showing faith in students, acknowledging the difficulty of a task, and setting time limits on tasks. Focus on past successes to point out things that students do correctly. You thus encourage the good work through analyzing past successes and duplicating them.

Make learning tangible to allow students to see their progress. This can be done through the use of *I-Can cans* (cans in which the student drops sheets of paper listing the skills mastered), accomplishment albums, checklists of skills, flowcharts of concepts, and talks about yesterday, today, and tomorrow. Arrange for the students to receive recognition from others for the progress they have already made (Albert, 1989; Charles, 1992). Applause, stars and stickers, awards and assemblies, exhibits, positive time-out, and self-approval give the needed recognition.

Help Students Become Involved and Interact with Others

Students are likely to have high self-esteem when they are willing to become involved and interact with their peers, the teacher, and others. You can take the following actions to help students become willing to initiate and maintain these positive relationships (Albert, 1989):

- Accept the students sincerely and unconditionally. This includes accepting the students' personal style, as well.
- Give your attention by making yourself available to students and sharing your time and energy in various meaningful ways (see Table 11-1 for examples) (Niebrand, Horn, & Holmes, 1992).

Teachers in Action

Helping Students Feel Capable

Terry Jenkins, eighth-grade middle school language arts teacher, Hephzibah, Georgia:

Four years ago, I was teaching in an inner city school with 99 percent minority enrollment. From the beginning, I was convinced that all of these children could learn. My goal each day was to provide material and present it in such a way that ensured every student would experience some degree of success. I will never forget one series of lessons.

We began reading "The Graduation" by Maya Angelou, which recounts her own graduation and valedictory address. We then learned the Negro spiritual, "We Shall Overcome." The story and song were inspirational, but they weren't enough. I wanted to make the entire experience personal. I told the class that one day someone sitting in that very classroom would be responsible for giving a valedictory address at graduation, and that their next assignment was to prepare a speech and present it in class. The speeches were wonderful as I introduced each and every one of them as the valedictorian of that year. As they spoke, I could hear a new determination in their voices; I could see a new pride in their posture.

Three weeks ago, there was a soft tap on my classroom door and a welcome face appeared. Immediately I recognized Carol, one of those students who had given her valedictory address in my eighth-grade classroom almost five years ago. After a big smile and a warm hug, she quietly spoke "I just had to come by and personally invite you to my graduation on June 5. I'll be giving the valedictory address, and I want you to be there." With that, an irrepressible smile burst across her face. After much earned congratulations, she looked at the tears in my eyes and said, "I did it just for you." Carol had become a believer in her dreams, a believer in herself.

Self-esteem and belief in oneself are essential. I firmly believe that self-esteem must be built through real achievement. I still strive to provide lessons designed to maximize student success and ensure achievement, and I continually verbalize my own convictions that they all can be winners. I make every effort to personalize success. I realize that I cannot assure success for every student, but I now know that I truly can make a difference.

- Express appreciation and encouragement to students for what they have accomplished. In doing so, it is important to describe the behavior accurately. You could use a ***three-part appreciation statement*** which includes the students' action, how you feel about the action, and the positive effect of the action. For example, you might tell a student, "I am so proud of you because your extra studying paid off with such a good grade on your test." Written words of appreciation could also be given, and your statements should focus only on the present. In addition, teach students to ask for appreciation. For example, you could invite students to fill out a happygram for themselves and show it to you for your signature, if you approve. A ***happygram*** is a brief note to parents with good news about the student's behavior or academic work. The student can then take it home.

- Make verbal or written statements of affirmation about students' positive personality traits. When their traits are recognized, students feel good about themselves and about the fact that you noticed and commented. These ***affirmation statements*** will have more impact if they are specific, noting characteristics such as creativity, curiosity, dedication, dependability, effort, enthusiasm, fairness, helpfulness, humility, kindness, neatness, patience, strength, thoughtfulness, truthfulness, and wit.

- Say you like the student and express affection to the student. To do this, show affection when things are not going so well for the student, show kindness, show friendship, and even use an affectionate touch when appropriate.

Help Students Contribute

When the classroom is structured so that each student is asked to contribute to the welfare of the entire class, students who like to be needed in at least one aspect of their lives will be satisfied. When students contribute, they feel needed. When they feel needed, they feel they belong, and this helps develop self-esteem.

Take steps to help students contribute (Albert, 1989). Encourage contributions in various ways such as inviting help with daily tasks, requesting curriculum choices, and asking their input for rules. Encourage students to help other students by peer tutoring, peer counseling, and peer recognition (see Table 11-1 for examples).

Decision Points

When students contribute to the welfare of the class, they feel needed. When they feel needed, they feel they belong, and this helps develop self-esteem. If you had a unit on reading and using maps, what approaches could you use to help each student feel that he or she is contributing and is needed? How could you accommodate different learning styles through these approaches? What unique problems for maintaining order might be created by using a variety of approaches?

BUILDING POSITIVE TEACHER-STUDENT RELATIONSHIPS

A significant body of research indicates that academic achievement and student behavior are influenced by the quality of the teacher-student relationship (Jones & Jones, 1990). Students prefer teachers who are warm and friendly. Students who feel liked by their teachers are reported to have higher academic achievement and more productive behavior than students who feel their teachers hold them in low regard.

This research suggests that you need to learn and conscientiously apply skills in relating more positively to students. The guidelines listed below will help you build positive relationships (c.f., Charles, 1992; Good & Brophy, 1994; Jones & Jones, 1990).

1. *Use human relations skills.* When learning to manage the climate, you need **human relations skills.** Four general skills apply to almost everyone in all situations: friendliness, positive attitude, the ability to listen, and the ability to compliment genuinely (Charles, 1992). Give attention, use reinforcement, show continual willingness to help, and model courtesy and good manners.

2. *Enable success.* Students need to experience success. Successful experiences are instrumental in developing feelings of self-worth and confidence toward new activities. Students need to be provided with opportunities to accomplish and to realize significant improvements (Charles, 1992). Student learning is increased when they experience high rates of success in completing tasks (Jones & Jones, 1990). Students then tend to raise their expectations and set higher goals, whereas failure is met with lowered aspirations (Diggory, 1966).

To establish moderate-to-high rates of success: (a) establish unit and lesson content that reflects prior learning; (b) correct partially correct, correct but hesitant, and incorrect answers; (c) divide instructional stimuli into small segments at the learners' current level of functioning; (d) change instructional stimuli gradually; and (e) vary the pace or tempo to create momentum (Borich, 1992).

3. *Be invitational.* In their book *Inviting School Success,* Purkey and Novak (1984) maintain that teachers should develop attitudes and behaviors that invite students to learn. **Invitational learning** is centered on four principles: (a) people are able, valuable, and responsible and should be treated accordingly; (b) teaching should be a cooperative activity; (c) people possess relatively untapped potential in all areas of development; and (d) this potential can best be realized by places, policies, and programs that are designed to invite development and by people who are personally and professionally inviting to themselves and others.

Teachers in Action

Giving Attention to a Problem Student

Lynne Hagar, high school history and English teacher, Mesquite, Texas:

John walked into my classroom at the start of the year ready to fight me all the way. This pugnacious redhead walked, talked, and acted tough as nails, but when I spoke to him sharply, he blushed. John "knew" that he was going to fail from the beginning, he spoke terrible, redneck grammar, and pushed and shoved his way through the first few weeks.

How should I handle this firecracker of a student? Experience had taught me that a lot of love and consistency would solve many of his problems. I tried to react calmly to John's insulting comments, trusting that once he began to respond to my teaching, he would show more respect. When he became disruptive, I asked him privately to tell me if I had done something to offend him or to lose his respect. I apologized in advance for having done so. John was surprised that a teacher would be concerned about the reasons for his behavior and astonished that I had admitted I was capable of doing something wrong.

Once we had a basis for our relationship, I found something to say to John every day—not necessarily a compliment, just an acknowledgment that I recognized he was there. I tried my best to listen—really listen—when John talked to me, making eye contact and coming close to his desk. Sometimes I touched his arm in a friendly way when he entered the room, or laid my hand on his shoulder as I passed his seat. I wrote lengthy comments on his papers and added stickers when his work began to show improvement.

I soon realized that John attended school every day without fail; it was the best place in his life—the only place where he felt safe enough to express his feelings. I gave John opportunities to let his anger out on paper and to write about his feelings. I found out about things he was proud of and then built writing lessons around subjects such as rodeo riding and fast cars. Talking to the shop teacher gave me insight into the difficult time John had at home. An abusive father and economic hardships that forced him to work long hours at night contributed to John's angry manner. Being rejected by people he loved and trusted had caused him to anticipate failure in his personal relationships as well as in his academic work. I wanted him to learn from me that he was both lovable and capable.

I wish I could say that John became a model student, but he became only an average one, trying hard to please me in all that he did. He still lost his temper at times, blushed when teased, and often spoke without

(continued)

asking. But John began to reveal the intelligent side of his nature, dropped his aggressive pose, and expressed his affection for me and even, once in a great while, his gratitude for my teaching efforts. I began to love John very much and to care deeply about his success. There's something about struggling with a difficult student and succeeding in gaining his trust that gives a teacher a special warmth for that student. It's very rewarding in a unique way.

Teachers who adopt an invitational approach develop an environment anchored in attitudes of respect, care, and civility, and promote positive relationships and encourage human potential. You can be invitational in countless ways, such as through verbal comments, nonverbal behaviors, instructional approaches, and physical aspects.

Purkey and Novak identify four types of teacher behaviors toward students: intentionally disinviting ("You never do your homework."); unintentionally disinviting ("I teach only students who want to learn."); unintentionally inviting ("You did a nice job on your test."); and intentionally inviting ("Let me show you how to improve."). Additional resources on invitational learning include Purkey and Novak (1984), Purkey and Schmidt (1987), and Purkey and Strahan (1986).

4. *Use effective communication skills.* Positive teacher-student relationships are affected by communication that takes place. Effective communication allows for caring interpersonal interactions as well as for achieving personal and academic goals. There are two aspects to communication: ***sending skills*** and ***receiving skills.***

Sending skills take many forms. You send messages to deliver instruction, provide feedback about academic performance, confront students about behavior that needs to be changed, present positive expectations, and for other purposes. Use descriptive rather than judgmental language (Cangelosi, 1993).

Receiving skills are equally important. By effectively listening to students, you can help them feel significant, accepted, respected, and able to take responsibility for their own behavior (Jones & Jones, 1990; Martin, 1980). You can help students clarify their own feelings and resolve their own conflicts. Teachers, however, too often do not listen fully, and give quick answers rather than fully listening and helping the student.

Allow the student to talk without interruption while using acknowledging expressions such as "I see," "Uh-uh," or "Go on." Nonverbal expressions, such as eye contact and leaning toward the student, also let the student know that you're interested in what is being said.

You could also use a ***paraphrasing technique.*** This means that you restate the student's ideas in your own words as a means to clarify the statements and to encourage the student to say more. You can also reflect on and summarize what is being said. A useful, noneducational resource is titled *How to Talk So Kids Will Listen and Listen So Kids Will Talk* by Faber and Mazlish (1980).

5. *Establish a safe, nonthreatening environment.* Students need to feel safe and secure to be successful. They should know that you will not allow physical or verbal abuse by anyone. Without that protection, students will continually be concerned about their safety and thus will give less attention to academic responsibilities. A safe, nonthreatening environment is appropriate for learning and helps establish a good relationship with the students.

6. *Be fair and consistent.* Students want to be treated fairly, not preferentially. Your credibility is established largely by making sure that words and actions coincide and by pointing this out to the class when necessary. If students can depend on what you say, they will be less likely to test you constantly. Consistency does not mean that you need to behave in the same way at all times, but rather that your judgments be reliable and consistent (Doyle, 1986).

7. *Show respect and affection.* You must like your students and respect them as individuals. Your enjoyment of students and concern for their welfare will come through in tone of voice, facial expressions, and other routine behavior. In the early grades, physical gestures and contact are useful ways for teachers to express this warmth and affection. Secondary teachers should make efforts to get to know students personally. Students who like and respect their teachers will want to please them and will be more likely to imitate their behavior and attitudes.

8. *Communicate basic attitudes and expectations to students and model them in your behavior.* Students tend to conform not so much to what teachers say as to what they expect. You must think through what you expect from your students and then see that your own behavior is consistent with those expectations. If you expect students to be polite to each other, for example, you should treat your students in the same manner.

9. *Create open dialogue with students.* It is useful to create an open dialogue with students, but you need to decide how open and involved you wish to be with them. The degree of open dialogue may be determined by the students' age and your own personality, among other factors.

Decision Points

Teachers vary in the degree that they share personal information and opinions with students. Suppose that you have traveled extensively in the United States and that you are responsible for teaching social studies in your sixth-grade curriculum. In your everyday interactions with your students, how personal will you be and what factors will you take into account when deciding on this? To what extent will you relate personal experiences to the curriculum? How might the grade level and ethnic diversity of your students affect your decisions?

---

10. *Systematically build better relationships.* You can express interest in and concern for students by (a) monitoring the quality of your relationships with them, with a focus on maintaining a high rate of positive comments; (b) creating opportunities for personal discussions with them; and (c) showing your interest

in activities that are important to them (Jones & Jones, 1990). For example, you could deliberately plan to talk with some students in each cooperative learning group as you walk around to be available for help and to monitor their behavior.

11. *Communicate high expectations.* Teacher behaviors that create positive expectations almost always enhance the teacher-student relationship, and behaviors that create negative expectations result in poor relationships and poor student self-concepts, and thus reduce learning. For example, students often put forth a solid effort when you say that work may be hard but also express confidence that the students will be able to do it.

12. *Create opportunities for personal discussions.* Other than through day-to-day activities, teachers often find it helpful to set time aside to get to know their students. Some possible activities include: (a) demonstrate your interest in students' activities; (b) arrange for interviews with students; (c) send letters and notes to students; (d) use a suggestion box; (e) join in school and community events; and (f) introduce new students to adults in the school (Jones & Jones, 1990). Some teachers also make "good news" phone calls to parents of students who do all that is requested of them.

BUILDING GROUP COHESIVENESS

People in groups behave differently than they do individually. Groups seem to take on an identity and personality of their own, and group personalities are quite prone to change in response to group dynamics. When thinking of class-room management and establishing order, it is important to build and maintain group cohesiveness.

Group cohesiveness refers to the extent to which the group has a sense of identity and oneness. You can take the following actions to develop and maintain a positive sense of group purpose and enjoyment and to promote group cohesiveness (Charles, 1992; Jones & Jones, 1990; Wallen & Wallen, 1978).

1. *Encourage a sense of togetherness.* At the beginning of the year, try to develop the sense that the class is a unit that lives and works together, that all members are striving toward a common goal, that all face a common set of obstacles, that all benefit from helping each other, that all lose something when any member is unsuccessful, and that all can take justifiable pride in the class accomplishments.

2. *Identify the purpose of class activities.* Students resent busy work and spot it easily. It is important to convey a sense of purpose for activities by identifying specific short-range goals (e.g., having a project done by Friday; having every student give at least 90 percent correct answers on next week's exam). It is useful to tell students why they have a given assignment because they usually accept it more readily.

3. *Highlight group achievement.* Learning activities can be organized so that they lead to group rather than individual achievement. For example, the work of the math class could be evaluated in terms of what the class as a whole has

been able to achieve, or the progress of a cooperative learning group could be highlighted.

4. *Provide public recognition.* The sense of purposeful group behavior is greatly increased through **public recognition.** When students work on projects and receive public recognition for what they have done, their sense of purposeful and responsible behavior improves dramatically, with a corresponding reduction in apathetic and disruptive behavior. This recognition can be fostered in many ways, such as charting group gains, charting personal gains, informing parents, sharing in the classroom, and producing a class newsletter.

Decision Points

Group cohesiveness can be promoted by public recognition of individual and group work. If your geometry class just successfully finished a unit containing group projects and individual papers, how might you communicate your students' success to parents? How might you provide both public and private recognition to accommodate students' preferences for attention? How might you let people outside your class know of these successes in a public way?

---

5. *Stress the satisfaction the group offers.* Dramatize the many new and interesting things students can do in the group. When they complete a group activity, discuss how interesting it was and that more like it are to come. Instead of asking what was wrong with an activity, ask what they liked best. For example, after an activity or discussion, you could mention how successful it was, and ask the students why they think it was so successful. Then highlight how good it feels for the group to work so well and be successful.

6. *Increase the person's prestige within the group.* The prestige of group membership can be emphasized by reminding students that they are now third graders, seventh graders, or juniors. Favorable evaluations of the group can be given by others such as the principal, a visiting speaker, or another teacher.

7. *Engage students in cooperative activities.* Having students participate in cooperative activities helps make the group more cohesive. Competitive activities may make the group less cohesive. Many resources are available devoted to cooperative activities (c.f., Johnson, Johnson, & Holubec, 1990; Lyman & Foyle, 1990; Sharan & Sharan, 1992; Slavin, 1991).

8. *Increase the frequency of interaction.* Increasing the frequency of interaction within the group makes it more attractive to individual members. Interaction is enhanced by having students work together on planning and carrying out cooperative projects.

9. *Provide activities that help create cohesive groups.* Groups do not become cohesive simply by members spending time together. You can plan special activities, especially at the start of the year, to develop positive feelings about the group and the individual members. At the elementary level, these activities may include get-acquainted exercises, special event days, birthday

Teachers in Action

Classroom Meetings Help Group Cohesiveness

Laurie Stoltenhoff, fourth-grade teacher, Greenwich, Connecticut:

I am extremely proud of the positive rapport that I have with my students. One way that I instill mutual respect is through classroom meetings. Every Friday, I set aside at least 15 minutes for a class meeting. We all sit together on the floor to show that no one's ideas are more important than another's.

Classroom meetings provide a time for students to share their feelings openly about their school experience, and comments may be positive or negative. An important rule is that if someone wants to say something negative about a particular student, the class is not allowed to talk about that conversation outside the confines of our meeting. This is to prevent a student from being badgered.

One example is Alex, a nine-year old who desperately wants peer attention but resorts to behaving like a clown. In a recent meeting, students told him they were not comfortable with his clowning and wished that he would stop. I asked the class to share times when they enjoyed being with Alex, and they encouraged him to practice those behaviors more frequently. At the end of the meeting, Alex asked his peers, "Could you help me be better and tell me when I'm bugging you?" We talked about how to tell Alex. The class concluded that a person is more likely to respond if you ask nicely ("Alex, this is an example of something that bugs me. Please stop.") Improvement has been apparent since that meeting.

Since we regularly have class meetings, the students will give me updates on past issues, such as, "Lunch is better now. Adam doesn't show us the food in his mouth anymore!"

Class meetings show the class that I care about them outside of the traditional academic areas. It also encourages them to listen to one another. And it allows me to use peer influence to encourage behavioral changes. We all win!

bulletin boards, photo albums, and so on. At the secondary level, you can also plan get-acquainted activities and cooperative group work.

HELPING STUDENTS ASSUME RESPONSIBILITY FOR THEIR BEHAVIOR

You should not have to be a watchdog, keeping track of students' every move and pouncing on them when their behavior is inappropriate. Students need to recognize the rules and procedures and choose to follow them. Student self-control is vital to a successfully managed and orderly classroom. You can take the following actions to help students recognize their responsibilities and assume responsibility for their behavior.

1. *Teach rules, procedures, and expectations.* As mentioned in chapter 6, select rules and procedures and then teach them thoroughly. Students need to know what these expectations are. Especially for classroom procedures, self-management skills should be taught by following these steps in skill learning (Cartledge & Milburn, 1978): describe, model or demonstrate, perform, practice, and review.

For example, you might want students to pass papers to the front of the row at the end of class. To teach this procedure, first describe the way the papers are to be passed. Then physically demonstrate how the paper would be passed from one student to the next to the front of the row. Students then would be asked to perform and practice this procedure. At various times, as needed, review this procedure. This series of actions would be appropriate in teaching other procedures.

2. *Teach students how to make decisions.* Students should recognize that they continually make decisions about their academic work and their behavior. They have many choices to make but often do not recognize how they make decisions. By knowing how they can make decisions, students presumably will be better equipped to make decisions and assume the consequences for their decisions, whether good or bad. Students need to consider five factors when making decisions (Jones & Jones, 1990): knowledge, limits, options, choices, and consequences.

Decision Points

Teaching students how they can make decisions will help them assume responsibility for their behavior. Imagine that you have a first-grade class representing wide ethnic diversity and that you like to use cooperative learning groups whenever possible. When and how would you teach these decision-making skills? How might your actions be affected by the grade level of your students?

---

3. *Teach students to monitor their own behavior.* Especially for students who have difficulty controlling themselves, it is often helpful to have them monitor their own behavior to help them maintain self-control (McLaughlin, 1976). Self-management techniques have been used successfully with misbehaving students to increase their appropriate behaviors, such as improving academic skills and performance of on-task behaviors. These have also been effective in reducing inappropriate behaviors (Rhode et al., 1992).

Several approaches help students monitor and control their own behavior (Savage, 1991). One approach is to have students ask themselves questions when they are tempted to violate the rules or feel they are about to lose control. Students might ask themselves, "Is it worth the trouble it will cause me?" "Is this what I want to happen?" By pausing to question themselves, students will

Teachers in Action

Using a Peace Table to Help Students Be Responsible

Nancy McCullum, third- and fourth-grade teacher, Eugene, Oregon:

I think educators should teach students conflict resolution strategies so that the students can grow in their ability to solve problems without constantly relying on adult intervention. The Peace Table serves this purpose in my classroom and frees me from settling a multitude of minor disputes that occur in the classroom and on the playground.

The process is simple yet effective. The Peace Table is a designated area (an empty student desk works well). Students having minor conflicts may invite any other student to the Peace Table. Only one person may talk at any time. The person who asked another to the table speaks first. The speaker touches the top of the table with his or her hand until finished speaking. The first speaker describes the problem and uses I-messages to describe his or her feelings and needs. When the speaker removes the hand from the table, the second person touches the table and responds to the problems with an explanation, clarification, or whatever it takes. Removing one's hand from the table is the signal that you are finished speaking and are ready to listen.

This process goes back and forth until the pair has resolved the conflict or determined that they need a third party for assistance. If the problem has been resolved, those involved shake hands and complete a "Peacemaker Certificate," which is left at a designated place for my signature. If they need assistance, they sign up for teacher help. I use designated times for the Peace Table, such as during recess breaks or independent work, to minimize interruption of instructional time.

Students learn the process through group role playing and teacher or older student modeling. At first, some students overuse the table, but this decreases as the novelty wears off. I usually allow only two students at one time, since the process can lose its effectiveness in larger groups. Sometimes I allow three or even four students at the table, depending on their demonstrated problem-solving skills and the nature of the problem.

have an opportunity to assess the situation as well as calm down. Another approach is to suggest that students manipulate their mood when they are becoming angry or upset. They could think of some favorite activities or happy thoughts as a means to shift their focus.

Students who are becoming frustrated, angry, or upset can voluntarily go to a time-out area of the room to give them time to regain composure. Students might keep a record of such incidents and decide on their own reinforcements.

You could arrange a form for record keeping for both positive and negative incidents. Students can understand their behavior more objectively, set improvement goals, and select appropriate reinforcers.

Whatever method is used, you should discuss implementation of the approach and possibly model the actions needed. Self-monitoring helps students regain control of themselves and demonstrates your confidence in them that they can behave and exercise self-control.

TEACHING COOPERATIVE SKILLS

Another approach to establishing a cooperative, responsible classroom is to teach relevant skills. It is useful to briefly identify some social skills programs designed to contribute to order. *Cooperative skills* are those that help students get along socially. These skills include communication, cooperation, problem solving, conflict resolution, and team building.

Teaching students how to use cooperative learning as an instructional tool, as proposed by Johnson, Johnson, and Holubec (1990) or Slavin (1991), is not the same as teaching students about cooperative skills to get along socially. Some skills used in cooperative learning, however, may translate into skills for classroom cooperation. Special training programs described here can help students develop cooperative and responsible skills that will contribute to classroom order.

Burke (1992) offers comprehensive descriptions and specific activities to teach cooperative social skills to K–12 students. Her program addresses basic interactions, communication skills, team-building skills, and conflict resolution. Separate sections of Burke's book discuss students who have trouble accepting responsibility, students who need help with their interpersonal skills, students with behavior problems, and students with special needs. Activity descriptions, checklists, forms, and transparency masters are included.

Using a similar approach, Bellanca (1991) offers a series of lessons in his social skills primer which includes detailed lesson plans, overhead masters, and worksheets. The lessons address getting acquainted, friendship, responsibility, working together, problem solving, and conflict resolution.

A guide to *positive discipline* is offered by Keating and colleagues (1990). A step-by-step plan is described that includes assessment, involving others, determining expectations, teaching expectations and wise decision making, establishing esprit de corps, providing guided practice, arranging for independent practice, and then conducting a diagnostic progress check. This plan could be conducted in a single classroom or throughout the school.

Some programs describe individual or interactive activities to help students develop self-management and conflict-resolution skills (e.g., Cowan et al., 1992; Johnson & Johnson, 1991; Young et al., 1991). Other programs are directed specifically to behaviorally or academically at-risk children (e.g., Akin et al., 1990).

Cooperative skills are also taught through activities or lessons that develop student self-esteem and responsibility. Canfield and Siccone (1993) suggest

101 ways to achieve that purpose. Their book addresses commitment, role models, empowerment, teaching as a loving and a transforming activity, social responsibility in the classroom, and the classroom as a community.

Other books are also available (e.g., Beane & Lipka, 1987; Jackson, Jackson, & Monroe, 1983; Waksman, Messmer, & Waksman, 1988). These programs develop students' cooperative skills. They will help establish a cooperative, responsible classroom and thus contribute to order.

MAJOR CONCEPTS

1. Classroom climate is the atmosphere or mood in which interactions between teacher and students take place. This feeling is a composite of attitudes, emotions, values, and relationships.
2. To develop a cooperative, responsible classroom, teachers can take actions that have the intention of (a) promoting students' self-esteem; (b) promoting student involvement and interaction; (c) promoting success; (d) promoting positive interactions; and (e) developing a nonthreatening, comfortable environment.
3. Self-esteem is the opinion that each person holds about himself or herself.
4. Teachers can help promote students' self-esteem by helping students feel capable, become involved and interact with others, and contribute to the class.
5. Positive teacher-student relationships are associated with more positive student responses to school and with increased academic achievement.
6. Teachers need to learn and conscientiously apply skills in relating more positively to students.
7. Group cohesiveness refers to the extent to which the group has a sense of identity and oneness. Teachers can take actions to develop and maintain a positive sense of group purpose and enjoyment and to promote group cohesiveness.
8. Student self-control is vital to success. Teachers can take actions to help students recognize their responsibilities and assume responsibility for their behavior.
9. Programs are available to teach students about cooperation, communication, problem solving, team building, and related skills.

DISCUSSION QUESTIONS

1. From your experiences and observations, how would you describe a positive classroom climate?
2. What might be some characteristic behaviors of students who do not have very high self-esteem?
3. What are some actions that teachers might take to provide an inviting atmosphere for learning?

4. What might a teacher do to establish a safe, nonthreatening environment?
5. What are the characteristics of a cohesive classroom group? What might a teacher do to establish and maintain that cohesion?
6. What is the rationale for teaching students about decision making?
7. What are the advantages to teaching students about cooperative social skills such as cooperation, communication, problem solving, and team building? Might there be some disadvantages?

SUPPLEMENTAL ACTIVITIES

For Clinical Settings

1. Think of a lesson that you might teach and list ways that you will enable students to experience success.
2. List specific actions that you could take to help students become more willing to become involved and interact with others in your classroom.
3. List specific actions that you could take to help build cohesiveness.

For Field Settings

1. Talk with several teachers to see how they help students contribute to the welfare of the class and their classmates.
2. Talk with special education teachers to learn what forms could be used by students to monitor their own behavior. Find out if regular classroom teachers use such forms. What are the advantages of having students monitor their behavior?
3. Find out if teachers use specially designed programs to teach students about cooperation, communication, problem solving, team building, and related skills. If so, examine these programs and assess their strengths and weaknesses.

KEY TERMS

Affirmation statement	Paraphrasing technique
Classroom climate	Positive discipline
Cooperative skills	Public recognition
Group cohesiveness	Receiving skills
Happygram	Self-concept
Human relations skills	Self-esteem
I-can cans	Sending skills
Invitational learning	Three-part appreciation statement

RECOMMENDED READING

Albert, L. (1989). *A Teacher's Guide to Cooperative Discipline: How to Manage Your Classroom and Promote Self-esteem.* Circle Pines, MN: American Guidance Service. Includes seven sections covering the theory and practice of cooperative discipline, strategies for taking corrective actions for students seeking goals of misbehavior, ways to build student self-esteem, and ways to involve others. Has a K–12 focus, and is largely based on Rudolf Dreikurs' principles.

Jones, V. F., & Jones, L. S. (1990). *Comprehensive Classroom Management: Motivating and Managing Students,* 3rd ed. Boston: Allyn & Bacon. Includes 12 chapters with a K–12 focus on classroom management. Chapter 3 discusses positive teacher-student relationships and chapter 4 discusses positive peer relationships. Very thorough, and well referenced.

Purkey, W. W., & Novak, J. M. (1984). *Inviting School Success: A Self-concept Approach to Teaching and Learning,* 2nd ed. Belmont, CA: Wadsworth. Discusses invitational education, characteristics of inviting teachers, inviting skills, and related issues.

Purkey, W. W., & Strahan, D. B. (1986). *Positive Discipline: A Pocketful of Ideas.* Columbus, OH: National Middle School Association. Provides a practical description of invitational education and its application to discipline. Has many useful examples.

Slavin, R. E. (1991). *Student Team Learning: A Practical Guide to Cooperative Learning,* 3rd ed. Washington, DC: National Educational Association. Provides thorough descriptions of various approaches to cooperative learning. Descriptions, advantages, rules, and related information provided for each approach.

REFERENCES

Akin, T., Cowan, D., Dunne, G., Palomares, S., Schilling, D., & Schuster, S. (1990). *Creating Success! A Program for Behaviorally and Academically At Risk Children.* Spring Valley, CA: Innerchoice Publishing.

Albert, L. (1989). *A Teacher's Guide to Cooperative Discipline: How to Manage Your Classroom and Promote Self-esteem.* Circle Pines, MN: American Guidance Service.

Beane, J. A., & Lipka, R. P. (1987). *When the Kids Come First: Enhancing Self-esteem.* Columbus, OH: National Middle School Association.

Bellanca, J. (1991). *Building a Caring, Cooperative Classroom: A Social Skills Primer.* Palatine, IL: Skylight Publishing.

Berne, P. H., & Savary, L. M. (1992). *Building Self-esteem in Children.* New York: Continuum Publishing.

Borich, G. (1992). *Effective Teaching Methods,* 2nd ed. Columbus, OH: Merrill Publishing.

Burke, K. (1992). *What to Do with the Kid Who . . . : Developing Cooperation, Self-Discipline, and Responsibility in the Classroom.* Palatine, IL: Skylight Publishing.

Canfield, J., & Siccone, F. (1993). *101 Ways to Develop Student Self-esteem and Responsibility, vol 1: The Teacher as Coach.* Boston: Allyn & Bacon.

Cangelosi, J. S. (1993). *Classroom Management Strategies: Gaining and Maintaining Students' Cooperation,* 2nd ed. New York: Longman.

Cartledge, G., & Milburn, J. (1978). The case for teaching social skills in the classroom: A review. *Review of Educational Research, 48,* 133-156.

Charles, C. M. (1992). *Building Classroom Discipline,* 4th ed. New York: Longman.

Cowan, D., Palomares, S., & Schilling, D. (1992). *Teaching the Skills of Conflict Resolution: Activities and Strategies for Counselors and Teachers.* Spring Valley, CA: Innerchoice Publishing.

Diggory, J. (1966). *Self-evaluation: Concepts and Studies.* New York: John Wiley.

Doyle, W. (1986). Classroom organization and management. In M. C. Wittrock, Ed., *Handbook of Research on Teaching,* 3rd ed. (pp. 392-431). New York: Macmillan.

Faber, A., & Mazlish, E. (1980). *How to Talk so Kids Will Listen & Listen so Kids Will Talk.* New York: Avon.

Glenn, H. S., & Nelsen, J. (1989). *Raising Self-reliant Children in a Self-indulgent World.* Rocklin, CA: Prima Publishing & Communications.

Good, T. L., & Brophy, J. E. (1994). *Looking in Classrooms,* 6th ed. New York: HarperCollins.

Jackson, N., Jackson, D., & Monroe, C. (1983). *Getting Along with Others: Teaching Social Effectiveness in Children.* Champaign, IL: Research Press.

Johnson, D. W., & Johnson, R. T. (1991). *Teaching Students to Be Peacemakers.* Edina, MN: Interaction Book Co.

Johnson, D. W., Johnson, R. T., & Holubec, E. J. (1990). *Circles of Learning: Cooperation in the Classroom,* 3rd ed. Edina, MN: Interaction Book Co.

Jones, V. F., & Jones, L. S. (1990). *Comprehensive Classroom Management: Motivating and Managing Students,* 3rd ed. Boston: Allyn & Bacon.

Keating, B., Pickering, M., Slack, B., & White, J. (1990). *A Guide to Positive Discipline: Helping Students Make Responsible Choices.* Boston: Allyn & Bacon.

Lyman, L., & Foyle, H. C. (1990). *Cooperative Grouping for Interactive Learning.* Washington, DC: National Educational Association.

Martin, R. J. (1980). *Teaching through Encouragement: Techniques to Help Students Learn.* Englewood Cliffs, NJ: Prentice Hall.

McLaughlin, T. (1976). Self-control in the classroom. *Review of Educational Research,* 46(4), 631-663.

Murphy, J., Weil, M., & McGreal, T. (1986). The basic practice model of instruction. *The Elementary School Journal, 87,* 83-95.

Niebrand, C., Horn, E., & Holmes, R. (1992). *The Pocket Mentor: A Handbook for Teachers.* Portland, ME: J. Weston Walch, Publisher.

Purkey, W. W., & Novak, J. M. (1984). *Inviting School Success: A Self-concept Approach to Teaching and Learning,* 2nd ed. Belmont, CA: Wadsworth.

Purkey, W. W., & Schmidt, J. J. (1987). *The Inviting Relationship: An Expanded Perspective for Professional Counseling.* Englewood Cliffs, NJ: Prentice Hall.

Purkey, W. W., & Strahan, D. B. (1986). *Positive Discipline: A Pocketful of Ideas.* Columbus, OH: National Middle School Association.

Rhode, G., Jenson, W. R., & Reavis, H. K. (1992). *The Tough Kid Book: Practical Classroom Management Strategies.* Longmont, CO: Sopris West.

Savage, T. V. (1991). *Discipline for Self-control.* Englewood Cliffs, NJ: Prentice Hall.

Sharan, Y., & Sharan, S. (1992). *Expanding Cooperative Learning through Group Investigation.* New York: Teachers College Press.

Slavin, R. E. (1991). *Student Team Learning: A Practical Guide to Cooperative Learning,* 3rd ed. Washington, DC: National Educational Association.

Waksman, S., Messmer, C., & Waksman, D. (1988). *The Waksman Social Skills Curriculum: An Assertive Behavior Program for Adolescents.* Portland, OR: Applied Systems, Instructional Evaluation Publishing.

Wallen, C. J., & Wallen, L. L. (1978). *Effective Classroom Management.* Boston: Allyn & Bacon.

Young, K. R., West, R. P., Smith, D. J., & Morgan, D. P. (1991). *Teaching Self-management Strategies to Adolescents.* Longmont, CO: Sopris West.

chapter 12

Enouraging and Reinforcing Appropriate Behavior

Objectives

This chapter provides information that will help you:

1. Identify techniques to maintain student attention throughout a lesson.
2. Identify ways to focus the attention of the entire class on the academic work.
3. Identify a variety of techniques to reinforce students.
4. Determine ways to effectively use reinforcers.

You can take a number of actions to encourage and reinforce appropriate behavior, with the explicit purpose of trying to establish and maintain order. Without this encouragement and reinforcement, students may lose interest in the activities and may get off-task and misbehave.

Before the lesson begins, you will already have determined ways to get organized and to plan for management, as discussed in earlier chapters. One vital planning decision, for example, is to arrange for ways to have your students engage in meaningful lessons. Rules and procedures will have been established. You will have given consideration to motivating students and addressing their diversity. You will have made arrangements for these issues before the lesson begins, and they will affect the lesson and student order.

Once the class session begins, though, you may use many strategies to encourage and reinforce appropriate behavior. One part of this involves maintaining attention to the lesson and promoting involvement in activities. Another important part is to reinforce the desired behaviors. These issues are considered in this chapter.

Much of what is known about encouraging and reinforcing appropriate behavior comes from studies using direct instruction. Less is known about how behavior can be encouraged and reinforced through other approaches. Thus this chapter relates primarily to direct instruction. It is possible that somewhat different approaches would be successful with other approaches.

MAINTAINING STUDENT ATTENTION AND INVOLVEMENT

To effectively manage, you need to capture and hold student attention and encourage their involvement. *Attention* means focusing certain stimuli while screening out others (Slavin, 1994). General guidelines and specific techniques for maintaining attention and involvement are offered below along with recommendations for maintaining a group focus.

Techniques for Maintaining Attention and Involvement

Securing and maintaining attention is an important responsibility. If students are not engaged in learning, it is unlikely that they will learn the material and it is possible that they will get off-task and disrupt order. Preventive steps therefore need to be taken.

Minor inattention and disruptions can occur in any classroom. One of the most successful ways to handle these situations is to prevent them, or, if they do occur, to abort them quickly (Kounin, 1970). In addition to techniques that promote student attention to class activities, you may consider motivational strategies (discussed more thoroughly in chapter 8).

Recommendations to accomplish this end come from a number of sources (e.g., Eggen & Kauchak, 1994; Good & Brophy, 1994; Jones & Jones, 1990; Slavin, 1994; Wlodkowski, 1984); some of the following guidelines come from these sources.

• *Use attention-getting approaches.* You can use certain strategies to capture students' attention at the start of a lesson. These ***attention-getting strategies,*** which can be followed throughout the lesson, fall into four categories (Eggen & Kauchak, 1994): physical, provocative, emotional, and emphatic. Overuse of any one approach, however, reduces its ability to arouse and maintain attention.

(1) Physical attention-getters deal with any stimulus that attracts one or more of the senses (sight, sound, touch, taste, hearing). Pictures, maps, chalkboard, music, and manipulative objects are examples. Even your movements and vocal expression can be considered to be physical stimuli. (2) Provocative attention-getters center on unique or discrepant events. To create them, you could introduce contrasting information, play the devil's advocate, and be unpredictable to the degree that the students enjoy the spontaneity. (3) Emotional attention-getters are approaches aimed at involving students emotionally. This may be

something as simple as calling the students by name. (4) Emphatic attention-getters place emphasis on a particular issue or event. For example, you might cue students to an issue such as, "Pay careful attention now. The next two items are very important."

Decision Points

To maintain student attention, you may deliberately create dis-equilibrium by introducing contrasting information, playing the devil's advocate, or being unpredictable. If you were teaching a high school world history class, how might you create disequilibrium when discuss-ing the role of the Supreme Court throughout the history of the United States? As a means to be provocative, how might you approach a dis-cussion about the consequences to the country if there were no Supreme Court? How might student differences in learning styles affect the way you approach this topic while simultaneously giving consider-ation to maintaining order?

• *Arrange the classroom so that students do not have their backs to the speaker.* When presenting material during a lesson, students should be seated so that everyone is facing the presenter (you, a student, or a guest). This may seem like a simple task, but too often classrooms are arranged so that students do not have a full view of the presenter and the instructional medium. Not only is the presenter unable to see all the students; the students are not able to observe all of the presenter's nonverbal behaviors.

You may prefer to have all the student seats face the area where you spend most of your time in direct instruction, such as by the chalkboard or by the overhead projector. Or you may prefer to have them work in cooperative groups much of the time and thus arrange the desks in clusters. In that case, students can be asked to turn or move their chairs when you want their undivided attention.

• *Select a seating arrangement that does not discriminate against some students.* Teachers spend approximately 70 percent of their time in front of the classroom (Adams & Biddle, 1970). Students at the rear contribute less to discussions and are less attentive and on-task than those near the front. Involve-ment is more evenly distributed when high- and low-achieving students are commingled. You can enhance on-task behavior by carefully arranging the seats and moving around the room. You should experiment with seating arrangements.

• *Monitor attention during lessons and provide situational assistance as necessary.* Students are much more likely to pay attention if they know you regularly watch them, both to see if they are paying attention and to note signs of confusion or difficulty. Regularly scan the class or group throughout the lesson.

When students show signs of losing interest or becoming frustrated, you should provide ***situational assistance***—teacher actions designed to help students cope with the situation and to keep them on-task, or to get them back on-task before problems become more serious. Situational assistance may include such actions as removing seductive objects, providing support with routines, boosting interest, helping students through hurdles, altering the lesson, or even modifying the environment.

• *Keep lessons moving at a good pace.* Delays may arise when you spend too much time on minor points, so everyone waits while each student responds; passing out equipment individually, and so forth. Attention will wander while students are waiting or when a point they clearly understand is discussed needlessly (as in lengthy review lessons). You need to recognize what causes delays and minimize them in an effort to keep the lesson moving at a good pace.

• *Vary instructional media and methods.* Monotony breeds inattentiveness, and the repeated and perhaps exclusive use of one approach will soon result in a classroom of bored students. Moreover, student achievement is increased when a variety of materials and techniques are used (Brophy & Good, 1986). The overhead projector, chalkboard, videotapes, and slides will vary your approach.

You should use various methods to solicit attention, through demonstrations, small and large groups, lectures, discussions, field trips, and the like. For example, lectures can be mixed with demonstrations, group responses with individual responses, and short factual questions with thought-provoking questions. You should periodically review your methods to avoid falling into a dull routine. Not only does this decrease boredom, but it also appeals to the different student learning styles. On the other hand, you need to be cautious about introducing too much variety, because this may distract students and may decrease achievement. (Wyckoff, 1973). A happy balance must be struck.

Decision Points

Active involvement is an effective means to maintain attention and encourage interest, thus contributing to order. How might you arrange for active student involvement if you were teaching a fifth-grade unit on South America? How might you use different student groupings to achieve this involvement? How would you use instructional media and other resources to promote both involvement and content coverage? How might you hold the students accountable for their involvement? How would all of these actions contribute to order?

• *Stimulate attention periodically.* Attention wanders when instruction becomes predictable and repetitive. You can promote continual attention as a lesson or an activity progresses. You can stimulate attention by cueing students through transitional signals that a new section of the lesson is coming up. For example, you might say, "We have just spent the last fifteen minutes considering what running water erosion is. Now let's look at the ways that farmers and other people try to stop this erosion." You can use challenging statements such as, "Now, here's a really difficult (or tricky or interesting) question—let's see if you can figure it out."

• *Show enthusiasm.* Your own enthusiasm is another factor in maintaining attention. Enthusiasm can be expressed through vocal delivery, eyes, gestures, body movement, facial expressions, word selection, and acceptance of ideas and feelings (Collins, 1978; Gephart, 1981). Teacher enthusiasm has been related to higher student achievement (Good & Brophy, 1994; Rosenshine & Furst, 1971). Several studies have established that students learn more from lessons that are presented with enthusiasm and expressiveness than from dry lectures (e.g., Abrami et al., 1982; Crocker & Brooker, 1986).

You do not need to express a high degree of enthusiasm all of the time. Depending on the circumstances, you may vary the degree of enthusiasm being expressed. For example, there may be times during a lesson when you might be very animated and vocally expressive. Other times, you may choose to be mild mannered.

• *Use humor.* Students appreciate a certain amount of humor, which increases student achievement (Kaplan & Pascoe, 1977; Ziv, 1988). Occasional humor also helps maintain attention. You may enjoy making silly statements or sharing funny experiences with your students. Be cautious that jokes are not used to tease or demean a student, even if expressed humorously, because the student may interpret these statements as being serious.

• *Use questions effectively to maintain attention.* You can ask questions to achieve academic objectives. There are several guidelines for you to consider about questions.

1. Use random selection when calling on students.
2. Use variety and unpredictability in asking questions (Kounin, 1970).
3. Ask the question before calling on a particular student.
4. Wait at least five seconds after asking the question before calling on a student.
5. Have students respond to classmates' answers.
6. Do not consistently repeat answers.
7. Ask questions that relate to students' own lives or similar situations.
8. Vary the type of questions being asked.

• *Maintain individual accountability.* Students should be accountable for doing lessons and learning all of the content. It is helpful to ask a question or require the student to periodically respond (Good & Brophy, 1994). An unpredictable pattern in the way you handle questions or responses helps maintain individual accountability and causes students to be mentally engaged and to be more attentive.

Decision Points

To maintain students' attention throughout a lesson, they need to be held individually accountable. If you were teaching a third-grade lesson on fractions, what approaches could you use to hold the students individually accountable? How might your accountability procedures differ if you had students working independently, in pairs, or in small groups? How would these procedures contribute to maintaining order?

• *Pay close attention when students answer questions.* Use active listening skills. This often entails using nonverbal skills that indicate your interest in what students are saying. If you do not give attention and show interest, you communicate that what they have to say is not very important which, in turn, will discourage involvement.

Nonverbal expressions of your interest might include nodding, moving toward the student, leaning forward, maintaining eye contact with the student, and showing interest by your facial expression. Verbal expressions may include statements such as, "Uh huh," "I see," "That's a thoughtful answer," or "I appreciate your thorough, insightful answer."

• *Reinforce students' efforts and maintain a high ratio of positive to negative verbal statements.* Students attend more fully if a positive learning environment has been created. One of the best means for accomplishing this is to respond positively to their efforts. Positive and encouraging statements are very important, and students can be motivated by positive reinforcement. On the other hand, a teacher who consistently belittles students' efforts will create a negative environment that will likely lead to inattention and off-task behavior. Make many more positive and encouraging statements than negative statements. Think about it from the students' point of view; would you like to be in a classroom where you hear mostly negative statements or positive statements?

• *Vary the reinforcers.* You can reinforce students in many ways, including social reinforcers, activities and privileges, tangible reinforcers, and token reinforcers. These are described later in this chapter. Verbal praise is one of the most common approaches used as lessons are being delivered. Vary the way you give verbal statements of praise. Instead of repeatedly saying, "Nice job" or "Good answer," you should use many different statements, including those that mention more specifically what the student did that was praiseworthy ("I really like the details in your answer.").

• *Terminate lessons that have gone on too long.* When the group is having difficulty maintaining attention, it is better to end the lesson than to struggle through it. This is especially important for younger students whose attention spans are limited. Nevertheless, some teachers continue lessons in order to maintain a certain schedule. This can be counterproductive, since students may not learn under such conditions and in any case will have to be taught again.

Teachers sometimes prolong a lesson to give each student an opportunity to participate. Instead, you should tell the class that those who do not participate on a given day will have an opportunity to participate on another day.

Maintaining a Group Focus

In addition to encouraging individual attentiveness, give attention to how the entire class is focused on the work. If the class as a whole is focused and attentive, it is more likely that individual students will be attentive and involved. According to Kounin (1970), there are three aspects of maintaining a group focus.

First, maintain a group format. You must have good organizational skills, the ability to develop a cohesive environment among a group of individuals, and an inclination to cooperate. These skills are central to managing a group format; students cannot maintain focus if they are waiting for directions and materials. You should attempt to develop group cohesiveness by including low achievers in classroom flow.

You must have high but realistic expectations for your students. If you do not believe in them, they will not believe in themselves. It is difficult to develop a sense of community if you have low expectations.

Second, have a sense of group accountability. To develop a sense of accountability, you might create the feeling that everyone is responsible for what happens in the group and for learning the material that is the subject of the group's focus (Froyen, 1993). You must make all students feel they are a part of the class and can contribute to its success. You accomplish this by offering positive feedback, by calling on students of all achievement levels, and by communicating a feeling of high expectations for all.

Through feedback you can reward correct responses, help students untangle confusing ideas, and set them straight when they don't understand. They then experience a sense of fulfillment and a sense of accountability.

Decision Points

Let's assume that you are teaching a seventh-grade math lesson and that you are having five students complete sample problems at the chalkboard. How might you hold those who are still in their seats academically accountable? How could you provide feedback to the students at the board as well as to those still in their seats? How might the lack of a procedure for accountability in this setting contribute to a loss of order?

Gain the attention of the group. In direct instruction, you must have everyone's attention. Establish clear signals to gain attention and let them know that class is about to begin (e.g., "All right, let's begin."). Once you have everyone's attention, give an overview of that day's class. Some teachers write this overview on the chalkboard as a brief list of topics to be covered. The class should then move at a brisk pace without unnecessary delays. Students are more likely to be attentive if they believe they will derive some benefits.

Of course, you may use other approaches such as cooperative learning. Regardless of your approach, there will be times when you need everyone's attention. For example, part way through the class period, you may need the attention of all students who are already working in groups. In that case, you may use a chime as a signal for students to stop their work, to be silent, and to pay attention to you.

REINFORCING DESIRED BEHAVIORS

A *reinforcer* is an event or consequence that increases the strength or future probability of the behavior it follows. Reinforcement strengthens behaviors that are valued and motivates students to do things that will benefit them (Evans, Evans, & Schmid, 1989). This section reviews various reinforcers and presents guidelines for their effective use.

TABLE 12-1   Examples of social reinforcers

Verbal and Written Expressions
   Excellent
   Awesome
   Marvelous
   Good work
   Good thinking
   Very creative
   Thoughtful answer
   Much better
   Or longer phrases or sentences that specify what the student did that was praiseworthy

Nonverbal Facial or Bodily Expressions
   Looking
   Grinning
   Smiling
   Whistling
   Laughing
   Winking
   Nodding
   Raising eyebrows
   Clapping
   Raising arms
   Using a hand gesture (thumbs up)
   Doing a "high five"

Nonverbal Proximity
   Sitting, standing, or walking near the person
   Placing the student's desk next to the teacher
   Seating the student next to friends
   Joining the student for an activity
   Eating with the student

Nonverbal Physical Contact
   Hugging
   Shaking or holding hands
   Touching an arm, back, or shoulder
   Patting the back or shoulder

Teachers in Action

Giving Students Attention

Rafael Castanet, middle school art teacher, Houston, Texas:

I give students attention by showing genuine interest in their artwork, which they do in my class. I am both complimentary and critical for the students to maintain attention and focus on the lesson objectives.

For example, I try to have the lesson's objective recur in my conversations with students, such as, "Jose, what are the characteristics of Medieval and Classical art so that you can make a good comparison for your presentation?" In this way, I give students attention and also check for understanding.

I repeat new vocabulary words with the students as they work on their projects. A few well chosen words such as, "Hey, that's a good solution for your mask design, Chris. It shows you really understand symmetry and pattern." This communicates support and acknowledges the student's learning process.

It is important to recognize that the awarding of reinforcers must be contingent on the student's behavior. If a student does what is expected, an appropriate reinforcer can be awarded. Students are thus reinforced for appropriate actions and that behavior is strengthened. In the absence of the needed behavior, students do not receive reinforcers.

Types of Reinforcers

Several techniques of reinforcement are available, including social reinforcers, activities and privileges, tangible reinforcers, and token reinforcers. Many are appropriate for both individual students and the entire class. Resources are available that give more details about reinforcers (e.g., Doukoullos, 1987a, 1987b).

Social Reinforcers. **Social reinforcers** are positive consequences such as verbal or written expressions, nonverbal facial or bodily expressions, nonverbal proximity, and nonverbal physical contact. Table 12-1 lists sample social reinforcers, with examples from Evans et al. (1989), Froyen (1993), and Walker and Shae (1995). Social reinforcers are especially valued by students when given by people important to them (Evans et al., 1989). Social forms of approval are especially useful when reinforcing student behavior if you and they have a good relationship. *Praise* is an expression of approval by the teacher after the student has attained something, and social reinforcers are often used to express this praise.

Most social reinforcement should be done privately with the student, but some may be done publicly. You need to carefully consider student characteristics when deciding how to deliver praise. A second grader may think being praised in class is wonderful, whereas a seventh grader might be somewhat embarrassed by being praised in front of the class.

Social reinforcement should always be contingent on performance of appropriate behavior. You should be specific about the behavior that resulted in the praise and the reasons for giving it. With verbal expressions, the terms used, the inflection, and degree of enthusiasm should vary, as should the type of praise (private, indirect, or public). Social reinforcers should always be paired with other reinforcers.

Systematic and appropriate reinforcement improves student behavior. It helps students know that their efforts and progress are recognized and appreciated. It is important to know both when and how to praise. Guidelines for effective praise are displayed in Table 12-2.

TABLE 12-2   Guidelines for effective praise

1. Praise is most likely to be effective when delivered as spontaneous, genuine reaction to student accomplishment rather than as part of a calculated attempt to manipulate the student.
2. Praise should be simple and direct, delivered in a natural voice, without gushing or dramatization.
3. Praise in straightforward, declarative sentences ("That's interesting. I never thought of that before.") instead of gushy exclamations ("Wow!") or rhetorical questions ("Isn't that wonderful?").
4. Specify the particular accomplishment being praised and recognize any noteworthy effort, care, or perseverance ("Good! You figured it out all by yourself. I like the way you stuck with it without giving up."). Call attention to new skills or evidence of progress ("I notice you've learned to use different kinds of sentences in your compositions. They're more interesting to read now. Keep up the good work.").
5. Use a variety of phrases for praising students. Avoid overusing standard phrases.
6. Verbal praise should be backed up with nonverbal communication of approval. Praise is more effective when delivered with a smile, a tone communicating appreciation or warmth, or gestures such as a pat on the back.
7. Avoid ambiguous statements like "You were really good today." Instead, praise in a way that specifically rewards learning efforts ("I'm very pleased with your reading this morning, especially the way you read with so much expression. You made the conversation between Billy and Mr. Taylor sound very real. Keep up the good work.").
8. Ordinarily, individual students should be praised privately. Public praise will embarrass some students and may even cause problems with the peer group. It is difficult to praise students without sounding as though you are holding them up as examples to the rest of the class. Delivering praise during private interactions avoids this problem and also helps show the student that the praise is genuine.

SOURCE: Excerpted from Good, Thomas and Jere L. Brophy, *Looking in Classrooms*, 5th ed. Copyright © 1991 by HarperCollins Publishers, Inc. Reprinted by permission.

Activities and Privileges. Activity reinforcers are privileges and preferred activities. After students complete desired activities or behave in appropriate ways, you can then reinforce them with various activities and privileges. Some reinforcers could be jobs, such as classroom helper. Activity reinforcers are often very effective for reinforcing the entire class. A list of sample activities and privileges is provided in Table 12-3.

Premack (1959) observed that high probability behavior reinforces low probability behavior. The **Premack principle** is based on the rule, "If you do X, then you can do Y." For example, if Tina answers 20 questions from her language arts work, she can have five extra minutes of recess (or some other desirable bonus). The Premack principle involves the systematic use of activity reinforcers and works well when the students can select their own consequences from a limited list of activities.

To apply this principle effectively, it is important to verify that certain behaviors are desirable. When you and the student are on good terms, a student merely performing certain tasks such as straightening the room or cleaning the chalkboards with you can be rewarding. Many other activities and privileges have an intrinsic value that doesn't depend on the student's relationship with you. Running errands, studying with a friend, going to the library, being first in line, or choosing an activity are each likely to be a positive incentive that gives satisfaction in its own right. You may have students fill out a sheet at the beginning of the year to identify activities and reinforcers that they would appreciate.

TABLE 12-3 Examples of activity and privilege reinforcers

Privileges
  Playing a game
  Helping the teacher
  Going to the library
  Decorating a bulletin board
  Working or studying with a friend
  Reading for pleasure
  Using the computer
  Writing on the chalkboard
  Earning extra recess time

Classroom Jobs
  Distributing or collecting papers and materials
  Taking attendance
  Adjusting the window shades
  Taking a note to the office
  Watering the plants
  Stapling papers together
  Erasing the chalkboard
  Operating a filmstrip or overhead projector
  Cleaning the erasers

Teachers in Action

Individual and Group Reinforcement

Cammie Fulk, fifth-grade teacher, Fulks Run, Virginia:

    Within my assertive discipline program, I use reinforcers for both individuals and the entire class. For individual students, I use a personal calendar. Each month I post a new calendar for each student. If a student has behaved well and completed all of the work for the day, I place a stamp on that date. If no stamp is warranted, then I note the reason for not giving the stamp on that date. When a student receives five stamps in a row, a reward is given. For 10 stamps in a row, a free homework pass is given. At the end of the month, the calendar is sent home to be signed by the parents and then returned to me. This has become a strong motivator for my fifth graders.

    I also keep a gem jar on my desk as a reward for the entire class. It is simply a clear coffee mug with three permanent levels marked on the side. The gems may be marbles, bubble gum, candy corn, jelly beans, or other small items. As I observe the entire class on-task, I place several gems in the jar. Gems can be earned for a variety of good behaviors, good hall behavior, the entire class being on-task, the entire class completing homework, and other desired actions. The three levels in the gem jar indicate five, 10, or 15 minutes of free time they have earned. The sound of the gems being placed in the jar brings smiles to the faces of my fifth graders.

Tangible Reinforcers. Tangible or material reinforcers are objects valued in and of themselves: certificates, awards, stars, buttons, bookmarks, book covers, posters, ribbons, plaques, and report cards. Food also may serve as a tangible reinforcer: cookies, sugarless gum, popcorn, jelly beans, peanuts, candy, or raisins.

    If you are interested in reinforcing with food (M & M's, cookies, for example), recognize some cautions. Some parents may object to certain foods (such as those high in sugar), and there may be cultural differences related to food. Students may be allergic to certain foods, and there may be health and state regulations governing dispensing of food in schools.

    Since tangible reinforcers serve as external or extrinsic reinforcement, their use should be limited. Other types of reinforcers are generally more available and more reinforcing in natural settings than tangible reinforcers. When you give awards, it is a good idea to distribute them so as to include a good number of students. Don't give awards for outstanding achievement only; award for improvement, excellent effort, good conduct, creativity, and so on.

Teachers in Action

Token Reinforcement

Linda Innes, middle school language arts teacher, Kansas City, Missouri:

One year I had a second-hour class that was out of control. No work was done, everyone shouted across the room to friends, paper balls were thrown, students were verbally assaulted, and only five of 19 students were passing. To take control once again and to restore order and sanity, the students and I wrote a new set of rules that we agreed to, and I put up a chart (complete with stickers) as a visual reinforcer for their daily progress about adhering to the rules.

We wrote the rules, complete with consequences, on a large sheet of paper and posted them. The rules included raising your hand to be called on, bringing your class materials, having an attitude to learn, and staying in your seat unless given permission to leave. The chart was a grid to display the dates and the names of each student. For every day that a student abided by the new rules, the student was awarded a sticker. Three stickers were traded in as a free assignment pass. For the students who did not abide by the rules, a one- to three-word explanation was written in their calendar square noting why they did not receive a star.

By the end of their first week, control revived and we all were proud of what we had achieved. I told the students that I was bragging about them to the principal and the other teachers. The students began to study the chart and beamed with joy when the day came to trade their stickers for a free assignment pass.

An additional, unplanned motivation came from my other four classes who suddenly became quite interested in the chart. They thought it was unfair that they didn't have a chart, too. It pleased my second-hour class to know that they were envied by my other classes. An awful situation turned into a good one with the use of this token reinforcement system.

For example, you may select one or more students each week to receive awards for something of value that they have done. Awards may be in the form of a certificate and accompanied by a pencil, poster, trading card, book, or other item. You may have students select their prize from a reward box that includes jewelry, magazines, cups, and other items students would value. This can also be done by teachers who are departmentalized and who work as a team with a larger group of students.

Some schools have a student-of-the-month program, the selection criteria being the most improved grade point average or other valued behavior. Members of the student council could select the winner, who might receive a T-shirt, a pin, a poster, or some other valued prize.

Token Reinforcers. A ***token reinforcer*** is a tangible item that can be exchanged for a desired object, activity, or social reinforcer at a later time. Tokens may be chips, points, stars, tickets, buttons, play money, metal washers, happy faces, or stickers. The back-up reinforcer is the reward for which tokens can be exchanged. Token reinforcement is useful when praise and attention have not worked. Tokens are accumulated and cashed in for the reinforcer.

Using Reinforcers Effectively

It is important to recognize the general principle of reinforcement: *behaviors that are reinforced will be retained, behaviors that are not reinforced will be extinguished.* You need to carefully consider whom to reinforce, under what conditions, and with what types of reinforcement. Reinforcement is likely to be effective only to the extent that (a) the consequences of reinforcers are experienced as reinforcers by the student; (b) they are contingent on the student achieving specific performance objectives; and (c) they are awarded in a way that complements rather than undermines the development of intrinsic motivation and other natural outcomes of behavior (Good & Brophy, 1994).

When developing a system of reinforcing desired behaviors, you should keep in mind the following guidelines (Froyen, 1993):

1. Exercise care to separate the behavior you want from the attitude you desire. Focus on the behavior.
2. Be explicit about the behavior to be rewarded. The more clearly it is stated, the better students are able to produce that behavior.
3. Remember that positive reinforcement can be used to decrease the incidence of unacceptable behavior.
4. Present the reward immediately after the desired behavior has been achieved. It is important that students know why they are being commended.
5. The power of a reinforcer is partially determined by the person who delivers it, the prior history of the recipient, and the extent to which it has been used before.
6. Select powerful reinforcers by observing what children ordinarily like to do when they are able to do as they please.
7. Frequently a big incentive is necessary to get some forms of desired behavior going.
8. Rewards accompanied by social recognition can serve to unify a group and amplify the significance of the reward.
9. Do not wait for behavior to be perfect before using reinforcement. At the onset, small improvements in route to the desired behavior may be the best some students can produce.

10. A corollary to the preceding guideline: Arrange conditions so that students feel they have a high probability of obtaining the reward with a reasonable effort.
11. A cautionary addendum to the two preceding guidelines: Do not present the reinforcer before an improvement in behavior occurs.
12. Ultimately, a teacher should work toward weaning students from dependence on reinforcers so that each student reinforces him or herself. (pp. 266-269)

Reinforcers can have a positive effect on order. By reinforcing appropriate behaviors, students will be encouraged to stay on-task. You would not reinforce behaviors that do not contribute to order.

MAJOR CONCEPTS

1. Attention is the process of focusing certain stimuli while screening out others.
2. A variety of approaches can be used that cause students to pay attention to the class activities at all times.
3. A group focus can be maintained by effectively maintaining a group format, having a degree of group accountability, and obtaining the attention of the group.
4. A reinforcer is an event or consequence that increases the strength or future probability of the behavior it follows. Reinforcement strengthens behaviors that are valued and motivates students to do things that will benefit them.
5. Social reinforcers, activities and privileges, tangible reinforcers, and token reinforcers serve to reinforce desired student behavior.
6. Behaviors that are reinforced will be retained; behaviors that are not reinforced will be extinguished.
7. Certain reinforcement guidelines can be followed concerning whom to reinforce, under what conditions, and with what types of reinforcers.

DISCUSSION QUESTIONS

1. How have teachers you have had expressed enthusiasm? What conclusions can you draw about the optimal level of enthusiasm to express in your teaching?
2. What are several ways that can be used to maintain student accountability throughout a lesson?
3. If you notice some students losing interest during a lesson, what behavioral and academic issues might you consider when deciding whether to terminate the lesson?
4. When using verbal expressions of reinforcement, what are the advantages for a variety of statements and statements that are fairly specific?
5. Some teachers use food as one type of tangible reinforcer. Would you use food as a reinforcer? Why? Why not?
6. How might your selection and use of reinforcers be affected by grade level or subject area?

SUPPLEMENTAL ACTIVITIES

For Clinical Settings

1. Prepare a lesson plan for a class you might teach. Next to the appropriate part of the lesson plan, make notations for actions that you could take to maintain student attention.
2. Establish a plan for yourself to deliver a high ratio of positive to negative verbal statements in your instruction. Include when, how, and under what circumstances you will deliver the positive and negative statements.
3. Make a detailed list of social reinforcers, activities and privileges, tangible reinforcers, and token reinforcers that you will use.

For Field Settings

1. Observe and talk with two or more teachers to determine the ways that they maintain attention and also establish a group focus.
2. Talk to several teachers to find out how they question students and to hear their recommendations for asking questions to hold student interest.
3. Talk with several teachers to see how they reinforce desired behaviors.

KEY TERMS

Activity reinforcers

Attention

Attention-getting strategies

Praise

Premack principle

Reinforcers

Situational assistance

Social reinforcers

Tangible or material reinforcers

Token reinforcers

RECOMMENDED READINGS

Doukoullos, E. S. (1987a). *Positive Reinforcement Activities: Grade K-6.* Santa Monica, CA: Lee Canter & Associates.
  Presents a number of specific strategies for grades K–6 to provide positive reinforcement for individual students, for the entire class, and for the entire school.
Doukoullos, E. S. (1987b). *Positive Reinforcement Activities: Grade 7-12.* Santa Monica, CA: Lee Canter & Associates.
  Presents a number of specific strategies for grades 7–12 to provide positive reinforcement for individual students, for the entire class, and for the entire school.
Evans, W. H., Evans, S. S., & Schmid, R. E. (1989). *Behavioral and Instructional Management: An Ecological Approach.* Boston: Allyn & Bacon.
  Covers many aspects of behavior modification and behavior management. Chapter 7 covers increasing appropriate behaviors and teaching new behaviors.

Walker, J. E., & Shae, T. M. (1995). *Behavior Management: A Practical Approach for Educators,* 6th ed. Columbus, OH: Merrill.
Includes nine chapters on all aspects of behavior modification. Chapter two covers basic principles of behavior modification and chapter three covers reinforcers.

REFERENCES

Abrami, P. C., Leventhal, L., & Perry, R. P. (1982). Educational seduction. *Review of Educational Research, 52,* 446-462.
Adams, R., & Biddle, B. (1970). *Realities of Teaching: Exploration with Video Tape.* New York: Holt.
Brophy, J., & Good, T. (1986). Teacher behavior and student achievement. In M. Wittrock, Ed., *Handbook of Research on Teaching,* 3rd ed. (pp. 328-375). New York: Macmillan Publishing.
Collins, M. L. (1978). Effects of enthusiasm training on preservice elementary teachers. *Journal of Teacher Education, 29*(1), 53-57.
Crocker, R. K., & Brooker, G. M. (1986). Classroom control and student outcomes in grades 2 and 5. *American Educational Research Journal, 23,* 1-11.
Doukoullos, E. S. (1987a). *Positive Reinforcement Activities: Grades K-6.* Santa Monica, CA: Lee Canter & Associates.
Doukoullos, E. S. (1987b). *Positive Reinforcement Activities: Grade 7-12.* Santa Monica, CA: Lee Canter & Associates.
Eggen, P. D., & Kauchak, D. (1994). *Educational Psychology: Classroom Connections,* 2nd ed. Columbus, OH: Merrill.
Evans, W. H., Evans, S. S., & Schmid, R. E. (1989). *Behavioral and Instructional Management: An Ecological Approach.* Boston: Allyn & Bacon.
Froyen, L. A. (1993). *Classroom Management: The Reflective Teacher-leader,* 2nd ed. Columbus, OH: Merrill.
Gephart, W. J. (Ed.). (1981). Teacher enthusiasm. *Practical Applications of Research, 3*(4), 1-4.
Good, T., & Brophy, J. (1994). *Looking into Classrooms,* 6th ed. New York: HarperCollins.
Jones, V. F., & Jones, L. S. (1990). *Comprehensive Classroom Management: Motivating and Managing Students,* 3rd ed. Boston: Allyn & Bacon.
Kaplan, R. M., & Pascoe, G. C. (1977). Humorous lectures and humorous examples: Some effects upon comprehension and retention. *Journal of Educational Psychology, 69,* 61-65.
Kounin, J. S. (1970). *Discipline and Group Management in Classrooms.* New York: Holt, Rinehart & Winston.
Premack, D. (1959). Toward empirical behavior laws: I. Positive reinforcement. *Psychological Review, 66,* 219-233.
Rosenshine, B., & Furst, N. (1971). Current and future research on teacher performance criteria. In B. Smith, Ed., *Research on Teacher Education: A Symposium.* Englewood Cliffs, NJ: Prentice Hall.
Slavin, R. E. (1994). *Educational Psychology: Theory into Practice,* 4th ed. Boston: Allyn & Bacon.
Walker, J. E., & Shae, T. M. (1995). *Behavior Management: A Practical Approach for Educators,* 6th ed. Columbus, OH: Merrill.

Wlodkowski, R. J. (1984). *Motivation and Teaching: A Practical Guide.* Washington, DC: National Education Association.

Wyckoff, W. L. (1973). The effects of stimulus variation on learning from lecture. *Journal of Experimental Education, 41,* 85-90.

Ziv, A. (1988). Teaching and learning with humor: Experiment and replication. *Journal of Experimental Education, 57,* 5-18.

chapter 13

Managing Lesson Delivery

Objectives

This chapter provides information that will help you:

1. Identify administrative actions taken at the start of a lesson.
2. Identify actions that can be used at the start of a lesson to capture student interest and focus attention on the learning objectives.
3. Identify teacher actions that contribute to effective group management during the middle part of a lesson.
4. Identify actions teachers take at the end of a lesson to provide for lesson summary and to enable students to prepare to leave.

Teachers can take a number of actions at certain points to manage the group, maintain order and control, and fulfill administrative and academic objectives. From one perspective, these actions may be considered teaching methods; they are discussed in this chapter because they affect order. If these actions are not handled appropriately, it is likely that students will be more inclined to be off-task and possibly misbehave. It is important to examine these tasks from the perspective of management and order.

Many strategies can be used ranging from teacher-centered, explicit approaches to student-centered, less explicit approaches. ***Teacher-centered approaches*** include lectures, demonstrations, questions, recitations, practice and drills, and reviews. ***Student-centered approaches*** center on inquiry approaches, discovery learning and problem solving, role playing and simulation, gaming, laboratory activities, computer-assisted instruction, and learning or activity centers. Grouping and discussion methods may be student or teacher directed, depending on how they are used.

Actions that you take to manage lesson delivery will vary depending on the strategy selected. Since more information about managing lesson delivery is available from research and practice about teacher-centered lessons than the other instructional approaches, discussion in this chapter is organized with that perspective. Even with less teacher-centered approaches, there are times when teachers need to be directive. Information discussed in this chapter may also be applicable to various parts of lesson delivery with more student-centered approaches.

To examine teacher behaviors in managing lesson delivery, a lesson can be seen to have three parts: a beginning, a middle, and an end. Particular teacher behaviors occur during each part of the lesson, and actions in each part affect order.

THE BEGINNING OF A LESSON

A successful lesson beginning can greatly contribute to a meaningful learning experience. The beginning should be designed to handle various administrative tasks, capture the students' interest, and focus their attention on the learning objectives to be addressed. An effective beginning can increase a student's ability to focus on the objectives.

Actions you take at the start help establish an atmosphere in which students have the motivation to learn (Brophy, 1987). ***Motivation to learn*** draws on the meaningfulness, value, and benefits of the academic task to the learner. For example, math problems may be developed relating to student interests, such as selling Girl Scout cookies. Thus, the focus is on learning rather than on merely performing. Often students can be motivated at the beginning of a lesson by emphasizing the purpose of the task or the fact that students will be interested in the task.

Before you begin the substance of a lesson, take attendance and solicit attention. At the beginning, your actions include providing daily review, providing a set induction, introducing lesson objectives, distributing materials, and giving clear, focused directions. These issues will be explored in the following sections.

Taking Attendance

Elementary teachers in self-contained classrooms take attendance first thing in the morning, whereas secondary teachers take attendance at the start of each class. Whether at the start of the day or the start of a class period, a record needs to be kept for those present, absent, and tardy. This is a special concern for secondary teachers who have a new group of students coming into the room each class period. School policies should be followed when recording and responding to tardy students.

Teachers in Action

Taking Attendance and Opening Activities

Carolyn Steinbrink, eighth-grade middle school American history teacher, Shenandoah, Iowa:

    I like the class to begin the second the bell rings. This is difficult because there are a dozen little chores that need to be done before teaching begins. Attendance must be taken and recorded, make-up work needs to be assigned, and other forms may need to be filled out. While all of this is being done, the classroom may become chaotic.
    To avoid confusion while I take care of the attendance and other items, I have the students review yesterday's learning. The best approach I have found involves the overhead projector to display directions for a three-minute task using the objectives from yesterday's lesson. Students may be asked to do a quick bit of writing, discuss a question with a partner and be ready to report, take a short 3 to 5 point quiz, or any of several review techniques.

Teachers in Action

Dealing with Tardy Students

Richard Kedward, junior high school social studies teacher, Kent, Washington:

    I have noticed that most tardiness is due to the same students. I don't view tardiness as a disciplinary issue, and I think that escalating disciplinary techniques undermines the tone, atmosphere, and relationships in the classroom.
    I use the following procedures. First, I start the lesson as soon as the bell rings—no fillers, attendance, or busywork. I do not acknowledge tardy students as they enter; instead, I continue the lesson without fussing or commenting to the student. Tardy students sign in, giving a reason for their tardiness on a clipboard at the rear. I can review these reasons. If tardiness is due to habit, or no reason is given, I talk with the student privately to help the student resolve the situation.

    It is helpful not to hold up the beginning of class to take attendance. You could plan an opening activity for students to do while you take attendance. Some teachers have the first activity posted on the board for the students. Have a seating chart for each class; a substitute teacher would find this especially useful.

Soliciting Attention

Students should understand that they are expected to give full attention to lessons at all times. A lesson should not begin until you gain their full attention. There should be a predictable, standard signal that tells the class, "We are now ready to begin the lesson." The signal will vary with teacher preferences. For example, you could raise your hand, ring chimes or a bell, stand in a certain location, or make a statement. After giving the signal, pause briefly to allow it to take effect. When you have attention, move quickly into the lesson.

There are ways to solicit attention at the beginning of a lesson. They are designed both to secure the students' attention and reduce distractions that might occur (Jones & Jones, 1990).

First, select a cue for gaining attention—students often need a consistent cue. The cues may be a special phrase that the class has chosen to indicate that you want immediate attention, or it may be a nonverbal cue such as closing the door.

Decision Points

Various approaches can be used to gain attention at the start of class. Identify several cues that rely on light, sound, or movement to give the signal. How might your cues differ for kindergarten, seventh grade, and eleventh grade?

Next, it is important that no lesson begin until all students are paying attention. If lessons are begun without this, you may spend much time repeating directions. A teacher who begins a lesson in such a fashion is a poor role model, since this indicates that it is all right to talk while others are talking. You may choose to just stand silent, waiting—students soon get the message.

Finally, remove distractions. Some students cannot screen out distracting stimuli. You can help eliminate distractions by closing the door, having the students remove unnecessary materials from the tops of their desks, adjusting the blinds, or taking other appropriate actions.

Daily Review

A lesson can start with a brief review of previously covered material, correction of homework, and review of prior knowledge that is relevant to the day's lesson. The purpose of daily review is to determine whether the students have accomplished the necessary requisite knowledge or skills for the present lesson.

This review may last from three to eight minutes, the length varying according to the students' attention span and the nature of the content. Unfortunately, daily review does not occur as often as recommended (Good & Grouws, 1979). Review is especially helpful for teaching content that will be used in subsequent learning such as math facts, math computation and factoring, grammar, chemical equations, and sight-reading words.

Teachers in Action

Reviewing

Fred Dahm, eleventh-grade social studies teacher, Wisconsin Rapids, Wisconsin:

Too often students see reviewing as a dull but necessary chore. Yet it can be much more. At the end of each lesson, I assign a different student the responsibility of preparing a 5- to 10-minute review of that content for class the next day. The review can take several forms—a discussion of major points, a listing of the material covered, a game, a crossword puzzle. The possibilities are endless.

At the beginning of the semester, I also assign pairs of students to a particular unit that we will cover to write a two- or three-page newspaper that would serve as part of the review for that unit. Students can select a title and logo. The articles might include a list of materials covered, related materials available in the library, important points of each lesson, political cartoons, an editorial, a crossword puzzle, and jokes. Each item in the newspaper must be related to the unit content. The student editors then distribute the paper to classmates to begin the review session.

You can conduct daily review at the beginning of a lesson (a) to provide additional practice and reinforcement of already learned material, and (b) to allow you to correct and reteach difficult topics (Rosenshine & Stevens, 1986).

Vary the methods for reviewing material. Checking homework at the start of class is one form of review. A game format, such as a trivia game, can be used. You can review through discussion, demonstration, questioning, written summaries, short quizzes, individualized approaches, and others (Levine, 1989; Rosenshine & Stevens, 1986). As part of the review, students might answer questions at the chalkboard, in small groups, or as a class.

The following approaches are helpful (Rosenshine & Stevens, 1986):

- Ask questions about concepts or skills taught in the previous lesson.
- Give a short quiz at the beginning of class on material from previous lessons or the homework assignment.
- Students can correct each others' homework papers or quizzes.
- Students meet in small groups (two to four students per group) to review homework.
- Students can prepare questions about previous lessons or homework and ask them of each other, or the teacher can ask them of the class.
- Students can prepare a written summary of the previous lesson.
- Have students ask the teacher about problems in homework, and the teacher reviews, reteaches, or provides additional practice.

In addition, the learning of new material is enhanced by weekly and monthly reviews. For example, weekly reviews may occur each Monday, and monthly reviews every fourth Monday. They provide further opportunities for you to ensure student understanding, insure that the necessary prior skills are adequately learned, and also check on your pace of instruction (Rosenshine & Stevens, 1986).

Establishing Set

Set induction is the initial activity by which students are induced to want to learn. This helps establish the context for the learning that is to follow and helps students engage in the learning. Set induction helps students learn what the topic is in a way that is related to their own interests and their own lives.

For example, a health lesson on first aid might begin with reading a newspaper report about a recent fire or accident. After reading the article, you could ask the students what they would do if they were the first ones to arrive after the accident. Many ideas are likely to be generated. You could then bring that opening discussion to a close by saying that today's lesson will be about that very topic—what type of first aid to administer in various circumstances. You would then move into the first part of the lesson.

Effective set induction should meet several criteria (c.f., Dubelle, 1986):

1. Get the students interested in what is to be taught. This is referred to as an *initiating activity.* For example, you might begin a lesson on creative writing by turning off the lights and explaining that you will share an adventure to a distant planet. As the room remains dark, they are to imagine their trip into outer space.
2. The set induction must be connected to the lesson content that is to follow. An activity designed to gain the students' attention but not connected to the lesson does not meet this criterion.
3. Students must understand the material and/or activity. The information of the initiating activity must be stated in a clear manner so that they will not only understand the activity but also perceive its connection to the content. Later, the set induction can be referred to while you teach the lesson.
4. The set induction and the lesson content should be related to the students' lives or to a previous lesson. Students will then be more interested. For example, a lesson in measurement at the secondary level might include measuring ingredients needed to bake a cake or some other practical application. At the elementary level, a lesson in division can be related to finding softball batting averages. You can reduce anxiety by relating the lesson to material already learned.

All four criteria must be present in order for the set induction to be effective. It would be unwise to begin a lesson without giving some thought

Teachers in Action

Set Induction

Matthew Gilbert, eighth- and ninth-grade math teacher, Greenwood, South Carolina:

"How would you like to win a million dollars right now? Did I get your attention? I hope so." This is the first thing I ask my students when I introduce place value to them. This is an example of set induction. If you can get a student's attention from the beginning of class, you can focus that student on the learning. The key to learning is involvement. The more you involve the student in learning, the more likely it is that the student will learn.

Martha Palmer Krein, kindergarten and second-grade teacher, Gillette, Wyoming:

To solicit the students' attention quickly, I use the "Give Me Five" signal. At the beginning of the year, I explain that I will often hold up my hand and say, "Give me five." I tell them that I do this because my hand will help them remember to do five things.

The thumb helps them to remember that their mouths should be quiet. The pointer reminds them that their eyes should be on me. The middle finger reminds them to raise their hands and give me five back. The ring finger helps them remember that their ears should be listening to me. And their little finger reminds them to think about what I am saying. The signal is a very effective and easy way to get their attention.

and planning to effective set induction. A good beginning sets the tone for the remainder of the lesson.

Introducing Lesson Objectives

At the start of a lesson, you should clearly describe its purpose. It is helpful to discuss the activities and evaluation process, these procedures help reduce anxiety about the lesson. At the beginning, some teachers clearly explain the objectives, the activities, and evaluation procedures to be used; others write these elements on the chalkboard, or they wait for an appropriate point in the lesson, such as after set induction.

Students learn more, in less time, when they are informed of the lesson objectives (Dubelle, 1986). Furthermore, students are more likely to become involved and derive more satisfaction and enjoyment from an activity that has a definite aim. Roehler, Duffy, and Meloth (1987) reported that teachers learned to give students specific explanations concerning the purpose of activities. Results indicated that these students demonstrated significantly greater understanding of and appreciation for the purpose of the instruction. For example, when teaching students how to use the *Reader's Guide,* you might explain that the guide could be used to locate information for a research paper assigned by another teacher.

Consider the alternative if you do not clearly communicate the learning goals. Students may go through the motions of an activity without understanding its purpose or its relationship to other content. They may be concerned only with completing the assignment, rather than attempting to understand its purposes and objectives. Some students may in fact become passive when they see no academic purpose and consider assignments to be busy work with no specific learning objective.

Distributing and Collecting Materials

You often need to distribute materials to students. Their maturity should be considered as you decide the most appropriate time and way to distribute materials. Handouts, maps, or student guides can be given out at the beginning of class to focus attention on important material and to avoid later disruptions. Materials could be handed out as they enter, to save time during the lesson. You may prefer to hand out materials at the point in the lesson where they are needed.

Materials should be strategically located for ease of distribution and minimal disruption. For example, resource books that are often used should be placed where there is sufficient space when they are needed. Procedures should be established for their distribution. You may have one row at a time get the books, have one student in each row get enough copies for that row, have students pick up a copy as soon as they enter the room, or give each student a copy on entering.

Some materials that have been distributed need to be collected later in the lesson, and appropriate ways to collect them should be selected. Collection may be the same as or different from the distribution.

Giving Clear, Focused Directions

To give clear and focused directions, you must first carefully plan them. Directions are often given at the beginning of a lesson; of course, directions might also be given for activities throughout a lesson.

When *planning for directions,* you should (a) have no more than three student actions that are required for the activity to be described; (b) describe the directions in the order that students will be required to complete the tasks; (c) clarify what type and quality of product is expected; (d) make the description of each step specific and fairly brief; (e) provide written (on the chalkboard, a transparency, or a handout) and oral directions; (f) state the directions just before the activity; and (g) make provisions for assisting students who have difficulty.

Teachers in Action

Giving Directions

Ron Butler, high school social studies teacher, Gillette, Wyoming:

There are several parts in giving directions for class activities. First, I give detailed, step-by-step descriptions for what I want the students to do. This may include mentioning the pages in the textbook and the specific actions that I want the students to take. Second, I seek feedback from them to see if they understand the directions. Especially when there are several steps in the directions, I ask a randomly selected student to repeat the directions to ensure that everyone hears them again. At that time, I can correct any misunderstandings they may have. Third, I screen the steps on the overhead projector so the students can refer to them as they move along.

When *giving directions,* you need to (a) gain student attention; (b) present the directions; (c) check to see if students understand the directions ("Do you have any questions about what you need to do?"); (d) have the students begin; and (e) remediate if necessary, should one or more students not follow directions. Clearly state what books and materials are needed.

It is often helpful to demonstrate the actions expected of the students by doing one problem or activity together. Students then see what is expected before they begin to work independently. Once they begin work, you should walk around to observe them to see whether they are following directions, and to be available to answer questions. If many questions arise, it may be useful to gain everyone's attention for further explanation.

Decision Points

Before starting a review session, students need directions. What directions would you give students in a ninth-grade language arts class when having some students complete sample problems at the chalkboard? What would you have the seated students do while others are at the board? How would you check for student understanding of the directions? How might you reinforce students who follow the directions?

THE MIDDLE OF A LESSON

A number of teacher behaviors during lesson delivery contribute to effective group management. These include pacing the lesson, providing smooth transitions, avoiding satiation, managing seatwork effectively, having a task orientation, and being clear.

Pacing

Pacing is the speed at which the lesson proceeds. It is the rhythm, the ebb and flow, of a lesson. Effective pacing is neither too slow nor too fast. Adjustments in pace are made as the need warrants. To pace effectively, you should not dwell too long on directions; distribute papers in a timely and efficient manner, and move from one activity to another smoothly and without interruption. Classes that lack effective pacing may drag or may move at a pace where the students are unable to grasp the material.

Guidelines can be followed to effectively pace a lesson (Good & Brophy, 1994; Jones & Jones, 1990; Kounin, 1970). First, develop awareness of your own teaching tempo. As you gain experience, you will become more aware of your personal pace. A good means of determining your pace is to audio- or videotape your performance. You are then able to learn how fast you talk, how you move around the classroom, or how much wait time you provide your students.

Watch for nonverbal cues indicating that students are becoming puzzled or bored. Monitor attentiveness and modify your pacing as needed. If high-achieving students are looking puzzled, they and perhaps most of the class may be lost. The content may be too complex or is being covered too quickly. A good indication that your pacing is too slow is that students are becoming restless and inattentive—looking out the window or fiddling with materials on their desks.

Next, break activities up into short segments. Many teachers complete an entire activity before beginning discussion or review. It is more effective to break them up into shorter segments, and to ask questions or review these segments, than to complete the activity. For example, if a lesson includes material or activities that fall into three sections, it is useful to provide a review after each section before moving to the next one.

Provide short breaks for lessons that last longer than 30 minutes. Long lessons can lead to inattentiveness and disruptive behavior. A three- to five-minute break allows the students to return fresh to the activity. Breaks can be in the form of short games related to the activity or a stand-up-and-stretch interlude. If students can get up to mingle or just stand up and stretch, they have had enough of a break.

Vary the instructional approach as well as the content. Students become restless with only a single approach. A lesson plan that incorporates several strategies will result in better attentiveness.

Avoid interrupting the flow of the lesson with numerous stops and starts. *Jerkiness* refers to behaviors that interfere with smooth flow. This occurs when the teacher (a) interrupts an ongoing activity without warning and directs the students to begin another activity; (b) leaves one activity dangling in midair, begins another, only to return to the first; or (c) leaves one activity for another and never returns to the first one. Students never see closure to the activities they had been engaged in. Such reversals tend to leave students flustered; they have not completed the previous activity and are unprepared to begin the new one.

Avoid slowdowns that interfere with pace. *Slowdowns*—delays in momentum or pace—can occur due to overdwelling or fragmentation. *Overdwelling* develops when too much time is spent giving directions or explanations. Overdwelling is seen also when the teacher becomes so enthralled with the details of the lesson or a prop for a demonstration that the students lose sight of the main idea. For example, an English teacher may get so carried away describing the details of an author's life that the students barely have time to read the author's works. Another example is a science teacher who gets carried away describing the laboratory equipment so that the students have little time to conduct any experiments.

Fragmentation is another type of slowdown in which the lesson is divided into such minute fragments that some students are left waiting and become bored. For example, the directions for an experiment may be broken down into such small, simple parts that the students feel belittled, or an activity is done by one row of students at a time, leaving the rest waiting.

Provide a summary at the end of a lesson segment. Levine (1989) suggests that rather than plan for a single summary at the end of a lesson, it might be preferable to summarize after each main point. For example, students might be asked to write a one-sentence summary of each scene as a play is read aloud.

Smooth Transitions

Transitions are movements from one activity to another. A smooth transition allows one activity to flow into another without any breaks in delivery (Arlin, 1979; Doyle, 1984; Smith, 1984). Transitions that are not smooth create gaps in delivery. Approximately 15 percent of classroom time is devoted to transitions (Rosenshine, 1980).

Transition time can occur when (a) students remain at their seats and progress from one subject to another; (b) students move from their seats to an activity in another part of the classroom; (c) they move back to their seats; (d) they leave the classroom to go outside or to another part of the building; or (e) students return to the classroom from outside or another part of the building (Paine et al., 1983).

Disorder and misbehavior can arise during transition times. Arlin (1979) reported that there was almost twice as much disruption during transition (including hitting, yelling, and other inappropriate actions) as during non-transition time. There are several reasons why transitions can be problematic (Gump, 1987). First, you may have difficulty getting the students to finish an activity, especially if they are deeply engaged in it. Second, transitions are more loosely structured than instructional activities, and there typically is more freedom to socialize and move around the room. Third, students may "save up" problems or tensions and deal with them during transition time. For example, a student may ask to use the restroom, complain to you about another student, or ask permission to get something from a locker. Finally, there may be delays in getting students started in the new activity.

To reduce the potential for disorder during transitions, you should prepare students for upcoming transitions, establish efficient transition routines, and clearly define the lesson boundaries (Ross, 1985). Jones and Jones (1990) offer several suggestions for effective transitions:

- Arrange the classroom for efficient movement, so that you and the students can move freely without disturbing those who are working.
- Create and post a daily schedule and discuss changes each morning. Posting a daily schedule will help eliminate student confusion.
- Have material ready for the next lesson. Prepare and gather materials to ensure that class time is not taken and that activities flow smoothly.
- Do not relinquish students' attention until you have given clear instructions for the following activity. All too often, teachers allow the class to become disruptive while they pause between activities or lessons to prepare for the next lesson. It requires considerable time and energy to regain attention.
- Move around the room and attend to individual needs. This enables you to notice any minor disturbances that might become major problems.
- Remind students of key procedures associated with the upcoming lesson. Reviewing standard procedures and discussing unique procedures help promote smooth transitions because students know what is expected of them.
- Develop transition activities. After lunch, physical education, or recess, students are excited and may not be ready for quieter work. You could choose structured transition activities to prepare them for the next class session. These might include reading to students, discussing the daily schedule, having students write in a journal, or another activity that may not necessarily deal with the content of the next session. After this transition time, they will likely be more ready to begin the next session.

Decision Points

Assume that you have planned a lesson for a third-grade class in which the students will hear a five-minute tape recording of a story, draw a picture about some aspect of the story, and then write two paragraphs about the story. What arrangements would you need to make to ensure smooth transitions throughout the lesson? How might the directions for the lesson take into account the need for smooth transitions?

Avoiding Satiation

Satiation means that students have had enough of something, and this may lead to boredom, restlessness, and off-task behavior. For example, students may enjoy seeing a videotape, writing a creative story, or working in pairs on a project. When these activities are used too often or for too long a time, however, students will start to lose interest, become bored, and will likely get off-task. You need to guard against planning activities that will lead to satiation.

There are three ways to avoid satiation (Kounin, 1970). First, have students experience progress, which is the sense they have of steadily moving toward a significant objective. Pacing and group focus help achieve this sense. To promote feelings of progress you need to avoid dwelling on one topic too long. Second, provide variety as an effective way to avoid satiation. At the same time, routines are necessary to preserve order and organization. You need to sense when enough is enough. Instructional variety helps invite inquisitiveness, excitement, and interest.

Third, select an appropriate degree of challenge in the academic work. Students do not tire of success if the success genuinely tests their abilities and culminates in personally relevant accomplishments. When the challenge is sufficient to court and fortify students' best efforts, satiation is seldom a problem.

Managing Seatwork Effectively

Seatwork involves students working on assignments during class which provide practice or review of previously presented material. Students spend hundreds of hours during a school year doing seatwork privately at their desks (Good & Beckerman, 1978; McDonald, 1976). It is imperative that you structure seatwork so that it is done effectively while enabling students to experience a high rate of success.

Guidelines for successfully implementing seatwork come from many sources (Anderson, 1985; Emmer et al., 1994; Jones & Jones, 1990; Rosenshine & Stevens, 1986; Weinstein & Mignano, 1993). The following recommendations represent a synthesis from these sources:

1. Recognize that seatwork is intended to practice or review previously presented material. It is not suited to learning new material.
2. Devote no more time to seatwork than is allocated to content development activities.
3. Give clear instruction—explanations, questions, and feedback—and sufficient practice before the students begin their seatwork. Having to provide lengthy explanations during seatwork is troublesome for both you and the student. Explain why the activities are being done and how to do the seatwork.
4. Work through the first few problems together before having the students continue independently. This offers a model for completing the work and gives the students an opportunity to ask questions.
5. Decide if you will allow talking during seatwork. It is often desirable to start with no talking during seatwork and have students work alone. After a month or two, teachers sometimes allow students to talk quietly with others to seek or provide help. Clarify when quiet talking is allowed.
6. Circulate from student to student during seatwork, actively explaining, observing, asking questions, and giving feedback. Monitoring

students to provide this positive and corrective feedback is very important.

7. Determine how students will seek help from you. Ask them to raise their hands when they need help. You can then go to them or signal them to come to you.

8. Determine when students can leave their seats. To eliminate unnecessary wandering around the room, decide when and for what purpose students can get out of their seats. For example, students may get supplies, sharpen pencils, or turn in papers only when necessary.

9. Have short contacts with individual students (i.e., 30 seconds or less).

10. Break seatwork into short segments rather than plan one long time slot. Rather than have one lengthy presentation followed by extended seatwork, break up instruction into segments with brief seatwork after each segment.

11. Arrange seats to facilitate monitoring (e.g., face both small groups and independently working students).

12. Establish a routine for seatwork activity which prescribes what students will do when they have completed the exercises. Students may complete an additional enrichment assignment for extra credit, or may use the time for free reading or to work on assignments from other classes.

Task Orientation

Task orientation has to do with your concern that all relevant material be covered and learned as opposed to having students mired in procedural matters or extraneous material. Task-oriented teachers plan an appropriate amount of time lecturing, asking questions, and engaging the students in activities directly related to the material that is to be learned. Achievement is reported to be higher in classrooms of task-oriented teachers than in classrooms where teachers tend to be off-task (Rosenshine, 1983).

Task-oriented teachers are goal oriented, and they plan instructional strategies and activities that support these goals. They also have a high, but realistic, set of expectations for their students. To be task oriented in the classroom, you should (a) develop unit and lesson plans that reflect the curriculum; (b) handle administrative and clerical interruptions efficiently; (c) stop or prevent misbehavior with a minimum of class disruption; (d) select the most appropriate instructional model for objectives being taught; and (e) establish cycles of review, feedback, and testing (Borich, 1992).

Clarity

Clarity refers to the precision of your communication about the desired behavior. Clarity in teaching helps students understand better, work more accurately, and be more successful (Gephart, Strother, & Duckett, 1981). Effective teachers exhibit a high degree of clarity by giving clear and explicit directions, instructions, questions, and expectations. If you are constantly asked to repeat questions, directions, and explanations, or if your students do not understand your expectations, you are not manifesting clarity.

Clear directions, instructions, and expectations need to be given. Students then know what is expected of them and can act accordingly on activities, assignments, and other tasks. If you are not clear when giving directions, for example, the student may not complete the assignment in the way you intended, may become confused, and may need additional time and attention to complete the assignment later in the manner intended.

To be clear in the classroom, (a) inform the learners of the objective; (b) provide learners with advance organizers; (c) check for task-relevant prior learning, and reteach, if necessary; (d) give directions slowly and distinctly; (e) recognize the ability levels of students and teach to those levels; (f) use examples, illustrations, and demonstrations to explain and clarify; and (g) provide a review or summary at the end of each lesson (Borich, 1992).

THE END OF A LESSON

As stated earlier, an effective lesson has three important sections: a beginning, a middle, and an end. All three sections must be planned and implemented effectively if a lesson is to be successful. Simply ending a lesson when the bell rings or when you have covered the planned material is not appropriate. In such cases, students are not given the opportunity to place the lesson in context with other related lessons or are not permitted to ask questions that might clarify a misunderstood point. Providing a summary is imperative for a successful lesson. Furthermore, students need time at the end of the lesson to get ready to leave the classroom or prepare for the next lesson.

Closure to Part of a Lesson

Closure refers to actions or statements that are designed to bring a lesson presentation to an appropriate conclusion (Shostak, 1986). Closure has three purposes:

1. *Draw attention.* Closure should draw attention to the end of a lesson segment or the lesson itself. Often students need to be cued that they have completed an important segment of the lesson or that it is time to wrap things up. They might be cued with a statement that it is time to summarize key concepts.

2. *Help organize.* Closure should help organize learning. The many pieces of the lesson should be related to the whole. Some students are able to see this by themselves while others need assistance. To this end, you might provide a diagram, illustration, outline, or other type of summary indicating how all of the lesson content is related.

3. *Consolidate.* Closure should consolidate or reinforce the major points. You might emphasize or highlight certain concepts at this point. The main objective is to help the student retain the information for future use.

The second and third purposes involve summarizing, which is addressed later. The time at the end of a lesson segment or the lesson itself can be used for homework assignments. Between lesson segments, students may have five to ten minutes to start the assignment while you move around the room to answer questions.

Decision Points

Let's assume that you are teaching a high school history lesson in which a series of significant dates and related events have been discussed. How might you bring closure to this part of the lesson in a way that helps students see how all the dates and events are related? How might you involve students in this closure? How might you take into account students' varied learning styles?

Summarizing the Lesson

Summarizing the main points can help students gain a better idea of the content or clarify misunderstandings. You should plan to stop the lesson several minutes before the bell rings to begin the summation. Make sure that you have everyone's attention beforehand. You should avoid merely reiterating the content during the lesson (Levine, 1989). Ask questions that encourage the students to relate key aspects of the lesson or to evaluate key points. Also ask their opinions about what they believe are the key points.

To add interest, vary the way the lesson summary is conducted. On some days you may simply ask a series of questions. On other days, you may ask several students to go to the chalkboard to solve a problem and discuss the thought process involved. A game format could be used as a means of summary, such as questions out of a hat or a "Trivial Pursuit" approach. Several creative approaches will offer the desired variety to summaries.

The *summary* determines whether the students have grasped the main ideas (Rosenshine & Stevens, 1986). For example, your summary might reveal that several students do not understand the key concepts of a math lesson. It would be foolish to teach the next math lesson as though all students understand the concepts. You can use the information gathered during the summary to adjust the next day's lesson plan.

Getting Ready to Leave

Students may need to leave the classroom at the end of the lesson. For students in middle, junior high, or senior high schools, the bell will ring at the end of the period and the students will have just a few minutes to get to their next class in another room. For elementary students, the end of a lesson may signify a brief break before the next subject in their classroom, or it could mean that it is time to go to another classroom for another subject such as art, music, or physical education.

You should plan to complete instruction and the lesson summary by the end of the class period so that students are not delayed in moving to the next class. You should not teach right up to the bell because time needs to be allowed for several other events. First, you must allow time for students to return books and supplies to the designated locations.

Students need time to dispose of scrap paper and to straighten the classroom. They need time to put away their books, papers, pencils, and the like before leaving. You may plan to reserve from one to four minutes at the end of a lesson to allow sufficient time for these actions to be completed before the bell rings. Students then should be dismissed on time. You need to schedule this time when planning lessons.

MAJOR CONCEPTS

1. When beginning a lesson, teachers need to take attendance, solicit attention, provide daily review, provide a set induction, introduce lesson objectives, distribute materials, and give clear, focused directions.
2. When conducting a lesson, effective teachers pace the lesson appropriately, provide smooth transitions, avoid satiation, manage seatwork effectively, have a task orientation, and are clear in their presentation.
3. An effective teacher ends a lesson with a summary of the important concepts covered and allows students time to get ready to leave the room after the lesson or prepare for the next lesson.

DISCUSSION QUESTIONS

1. From your own school experiences, what approaches to review did you find the most successful? What are the merits of using different approaches for review?
2. What are some factors that teachers might take into account when deciding on a particular approach to distribute materials to students?
3. What consequences might occur if a teacher has poor pacing? How can a teacher overcome these problems?
4. Identify situations during a lesson where transitions are needed. How can a teacher ensure smooth transitions at these points?

5. Recall several examples when your teachers were not clear in providing directions, instructions, or expectations. What effect did this lack of clarity have on you as a student?

6. What are some ways that a summary of a lesson could be provided by either the teacher or the student?

SUPPLEMENTAL ACTIVITIES

For Clinical Settings

1. List a number of ways that you could conduct daily and weekly review.
2. Prepare guidelines for the selection of seatwork tasks and the assigning and monitoring of seatwork.
3. List a number of approaches that you could use to summarize a lesson. Some of the techniques could be directed by you and some could involve students in an active way.

For Field Settings

1. Find out how teachers record daily attendance and how that information is conveyed to the school's office. How do they record tardiness?
2. Talk with two or more teachers to determine the ways that they begin and end a lesson.
3. Talk with several teachers to obtain recommendations for ways to effectively use seatwork.

KEY TERMS

Clarity	Seatwork
Closure	Set induction
Fragmentation	Slowdowns
Initiating activity	Student-centered approaches
Jerkiness	Summary
Motivation to learn	Task orientation
Overdwelling	Teacher-centered approaches
Pacing	Transactions
Satiation	

RECOMMENDED READINGS

Burden, P. R., & Byrd, D. M. (1994). *Methods for Effective Teaching.* Boston: Allyn & Bacon. Includes materials for the beginning, middle, and end of a lesson. Has a K–12 focus on general teaching methods including planning for instruction, presenting instruction, organizing and managing instruction, considering learners' instructional needs, evaluating student performance, and improving teaching.

REFERENCES

Anderson, L. (1985). What are students doing when they do all that seatwork? In C. W. Fischer & D. C. Berliner, Eds. *Perspectives on Instructional Time* (pp. 189-202). New York: Longman.

Arlin, M. (1979). Teacher transitions can disrupt time flow in classroom. *American Educational Research Journal, 16,* 42-56.

Borich, G. (1992). *Effective Teaching Methods,* 2nd ed. Columbus, OH: Merrill Publishing.

Brophy, J. (1987). On motivating students. In D. C. Berliner & B. V. Rosenshine, Eds., *Talks to Teachers* (pp. 201-245). New York: Random House.

Doyle, W. (1984). How order is achieved in classrooms: An interim report. *Journal of Curriculum Studies, 16*(3), 259-277.

Dubelle, S. (1986). *Effective Teaching: Critical Skills.* Lancaster, PA: Technomic Publishing Co.

Emmer, E. T., Evertson, C. M., Clements, B. S., & Worsham, M. E. (1994). *Classroom Management for Secondary Teachers* 3rd ed. Boston: Allyn & Bacon.

Gephart, W. J., Strother, D. B., & Duckett, W. E. (1981). *Practical Applications of Research, Newsletter* (Phi Delta Kappa Center on Evaluation, Development, and Research), *3*(3).

Good, T., & Beckerman, T. (1978). Time on task: A naturalistic study in sixth grade classrooms. *Elementary School Journal, 78,* 193-201.

Good, T., & Brophy, J. (1994). *Looking into Classrooms,* 6th ed. New York: HarperCollins.

Good, T., & Grouws, D. (1979). The Missouri mathematics effectiveness project. *Journal of Educational Psychology, 71,* 143-155.

Gump, P. V. (1987). School and classroom environments. In D. Stokols & I. Altman, Eds., *Handbook of Environmental Psychology* (pp. 691-732). New York: Wiley.

Jones, V., & Jones, L. (1990). *Comprehensive Classroom Management: Motivating and Managing Students,* 3rd ed. Boston, MA: Allyn & Bacon.

Kounin, J. S. (1970). *Discipline and Group Management in Classrooms.* New York: Holt, Rinehart & Winston.

Levine, J. M. (1989). *Secondary Instruction: A Manual for Classroom Teaching.* Boston: Allyn & Bacon.

McDonald, F. (1976). Report on phase II of the beginning teacher evaluation study. *Journal of Teacher Education, 27,* 39-42.

Paine, S. C., Radicchi, J., Rosellini, L. C., Deutchman, L., & Darch, C. B. (1983). *Structuring Your Classroom for Academic Success.* Champaign, IL: Research Press Company.

Roehler, L., Duffy, G., & Meloth, M. (1987). The effects and some distinguishing characteristics of explicit teacher explanation during reading instruction. In J. Niles, Ed., *Changing Perspectives on Research in Reading/Language Processing and Instruction.* Rochester, NY: National Reading Conference.

Rosenshine, B. (1980). How time is spent in elementary classrooms. In C. Denham & A. Lieberman, Eds., *Time to Learn.* Washington, DC: National Institute of Education.

Rosenshine, B. (1983). Teaching functions in instructional programs. *Elementary School Journal, 83,* 335-351.

Rosenshine, B., & Stevens, R. (1986). Teacher functions. In M. C. Wittrock, Eds., *Handbook of Research on Teaching,* 3rd ed. (pp. 376–391). New York: Macmillan.

Ross, R. P. (1985). *Elementary School Activity Segments and the Transitions between Them: Responsibilities of Teachers and Student Teachers.* Unpublished doctoral dissertation, University of Kansas.

Shostak, R. (1986). Lesson presentation skills. In J. Cooper, Ed., *Classroom Teaching Skills* (pp. 111–136). Lexington, MA: Heath.

Smith, H. A. (1984). The marking of transitions by more- and less-effective teachers. *Review of Educational Research, 49*(4), 557–610.

Weinstein, C. S., & Mignano, A. J. (1993). *Elementary Classroom Management: Lessons from Research and Practice.* New York: McGraw-Hill.

part V

Restoring Order

Part V comprises four chapters about restoring order when students misbehave. These chapters include detailed guidance for successively providing situational assistance, then using mild, moderate, and severe responses to the misbehavior. This part also considers dealing with difficult students and examines legal aspects of discipline.

Chapter 14, "Providing Situational Assistance and Using Mild Responses," describes strategies of situational assistance to help students stay on-task when there are indications that the students may get off-task. If students do not respond to situational assistance, various nonverbal and verbal responses can be used.

Chapter 15, "Using Moderate and Severe Responses," begins with cautions and guidelines about punishment. After that orientation, strategies are described for moderate and severe responses to misbehavior.

Chapter 16, "Dealing with Difficult Students," describes characteristics of difficult students, the teacher's responsibility toward them, and specific approaches to use in the classroom. Outside resources are identified.

chapter 14

Providing Situational Assistance and Using Mild Responses

Objectives

This chapter provides information that will help you:

1. Describe the reasons for providing situational assistance.
2. Identify ways that situational assistance can be provided.
3. Determine the reasons for using mild responses to misbehavior.
4. Identify nonverbal mild responses.
5. Identify verbal mild responses.

Even with an effective management system in place, students may lose interest in the lesson and get off-task. Before this happens, you can give situational assistance to help the students cope with the instructional situation by removing seductive objects, boosting student interest, providing cues, and redirecting behavior. These approaches are designed to recapture student attention and motivate the students to stay involved in the lesson. The students are guided back into the lesson and order is maintained.

Nevertheless, students may get off-task and misbehave. Mild responses to the misbehavior should be used to get the student back on-task. Mild responses involve low teacher control and are nonpunitive. Both nonverbal and verbal mild responses can be a means of maintaining order.

The approaches described in this chapter are not highly intrusive; their aim is to keep students on-task. There is evidence that teachers who are most effective in resolving behavioral problems use minimally intrusive yet prescriptive methods such as gaining attention by touching or moving close to misbehaving students, then cueing appropriate behavior (Brophy & McCaslin, 1992).

SITUATIONAL ASSISTANCE

There are many disruptive behaviors in the classroom, including verbal inter-ruptions (whispering, talking, calling out, laughing), off-task behaviors (drawing, looking out the window, daydreaming, writing a note to a friend), and disrespect toward teachers and students (talking back, teasing, arguing). These behaviors are often called *surface behaviors* because they are typical and do not express any deep-seated problems. Nevertheless, surface behaviors can be disruptive, and it is important to have a systematic intervention plan that clearly communicates disapproval to the student who passes notes, calls out, walks around, or inter-feres with instruction in any way (Canter & Canter, 1992; Lasley, 1989).

Before surface behaviors escalate, you need first to be aware that they exist. Jacob Kounin's (1970) classic study of orderly and disorderly classrooms sup-ported the belief that effective managers know what is going on in the class-room. Kounin called this ability *withitness,* or the ability to observe what is going on at all times and to communicate this awareness to the students.

To communicate that you have noticed the off-task behavior, you should first provide *situational assistance*—actions designed to help the students cope with the instructional situation and to keep them on-task or to get them back on-task before problems worsen. Problem behaviors thus can be stopped early before they escalate or involve other students.

If students remain off-task after situational assistance is provided, move on to *mild responses.* These nonverbal and verbal, nonpunitive responses are designed to get the student back on-task. The continuum of responses to misbehavior illustrates that situational assistance is the starting point when dealing with off-task behavior.

In an early work on behavior management intervention, Redl and Wineman (1957) identified 12 behavior influence techniques for managing surface behaviors. Their work has been expanded and reorganized by others, including Levin and Nolan (1991) and Weinstein and Mignano (1993). The organization of this section represents a synthesis of their suggested techniques.

Before looking at specific strategies, you should recognize the link between motivation, order, and the need to provide situational assistance. When you plan a lesson, incorporate ways to motivate students, as discussed in chapter 8. They are more likely to stay on-task when their needs for interest, relevance, expectancy, and satisfaction are addressed. Otherwise, the students are more likely to lose interest and exhibit off-task behaviors such as looking out the window, passing a note, doodling, and talking to other students. These off-task behaviors contribute to disorder.

Strategies for Providing Situational Assistance

Situational assistance is the initial response needed for off-task behavior. These actions should help students get back on-task by considering their motivational needs. You may need to boost student interest, explain the relevance

---

Teachers in Action

Providing Situational Assistance

Mary Garland, sixth-grade teacher, Omaha, Nebraska:

We have a "Responsible Behavior" chart that lists the sequence of opportunities available to students to help them make responsible decisions. When a student first displays an inappropriate behavior, I use a nonverbal cue (proximity, eye contact, a signal) to help redirect the student and offer an opportunity to choose responsible behavior. No other action is needed if the student gets back on-task.

If the student continues the inappropriate behavior, I use a verbal cue (calling out the student's name, giving a reminder of the importance of the lesson) to help redirect the student to responsible behavior and provide another opportunity to choose responsible behavior. If this measure fails, the student has chosen to receive a predetermined consequence.

All my interventions are made calmly and quickly while maintaining my dignity and that of the student. The "Responsible Behavior" chart gives misbehaving students an opportunity to correct their behavior. Of course, if the misbehavior is serious, the nonverbal and verbal cues are omitted and other consequences are delivered.

---

of an issue, or do something else to help the student see the intrinsic or extrinsic satisfaction that the lesson provides. By guiding back into the lesson, you help maintain order.

Remove Distracting Objects.   Students sometimes bring objects to school which may be distracting. Young children may bring games or toys. Older students may be distracted by combs, key, or magazines. When you see that these objects are keeping the students from the assigned tasks, simply walk over to the target student and collect the object. Quietly tell the student that the object can be picked up after class. Be kind and firm; no discussion is necessary. Inform students that they should store such objects in an appropriate place before school.

Provide Support with Routines.   Students appreciate and often find comfort in knowing what is going to happen during the class period or during the day. They like to know where, when, why, and with whom they will be at various times. It is helpful to announce and post the daily schedule. Changes in the schedule should be announced in advance, if possible. Even for a single lesson, students often appreciate knowing at the start what activities are planned for the lesson. Knowing the schedule lends a sense of security and direction.

Routines for entering and leaving the classroom, distributing papers and materials, and participating in group work contribute to this sense of security.

Reinforce Appropriate Behaviors. Students who have followed the directions can be praised. This communicates to the student who is off-task what is expected. A statement such as, "I'm pleased to see that Juan has his notebook ready for today's lesson," communicates what is expected. Appropriate behavior is reinforced while simultaneously giving a signal to students who are off-task. This approach is more common in elementary classrooms; students at the secondary level may consider it to be somewhat juvenile.

Boost Student Interest. Student interest may wane as the lesson proceeds. You should express interest in the student's work when the student shows signs of losing interest or being bored. Offer to help, noting how much work has been completed, noting how well done the completed part of the task is, or discussing the task. These actions can help bring the student back on-task. Interest boosting is often needed when students do individual or small group classwork.

For example, when a student appears to be off-task while working in a small group, you could walk over and ask how the group is doing. You might ask the student a question about the group's progress. Take a matter-of-fact, supportive attitude when trying to boost student interest.

Provide Cues. Sometimes all the students are asked to do one thing, e.g., prepare their materials or clean up at the end of class, and cues can be given. ***Cues*** are signals that it is time for a selected behavior. For example, you may close the door at the start of class as a cue that instruction is about to begin and that everyone is expected to have all materials ready. Or the lights could be flipped or a bell sounded to signal time to begin cleanup or to finish small group work.

For these situations, you can select an appropriate cue and explain its use. Using the same cues consistently usually results in quick responses. You are conveying behavioral expectations and encouraging constructive, on-task behavior.

Decision Points

Assume that your ninth-grade English class is working in cooperative groups on a seven-day project. The students enter and go immediately to their groups and start work. On some days and during some sessions, however, you need to give some information to all the students. How can you cue, as a signal for students to stop and pay attention to you? How can you cue that it is time to prepare to leave the class at the end of the period?

Help Students over Hurdles. A student who is experiencing difficulty with a specific task can be aided by ***hurdle helping*** (Redl & Wattenberg, 1959). This teacher action is designed to help students overcome a problem and thus keep them on-task. Hurdle helping may consist of encouraging words from you, an offer to assist with a specific task, or making available additional materials or equipment. For example, in a seatwork activity in which students need to draw several elements, including straight lines, you might notice that one student is becoming upset because her lines are not straight. You could help her by handing her a ruler. You help before the student gives up on the assignment or become disruptive.

Redirect the Behavior.   When students show signs of losing interest, you can ask them to answer a question, to do a problem, or to read as a means of drawing them back into the lesson. Students should be treated as if they were paying attention and should be reinforced if they respond appropriately. It is important not to embarrass or ridicule them by saying that they would have been able to answer the question if they had been paying attention. Simply by asking a content-related question, students will recognize that you are trying to draw them back into the lesson. Redirecting student behavior discourages off-task behavior.

Alter the Lesson.   Lessons sometimes do not go as well as you would like, and students may lose interest in the lesson for a variety of reasons. The lesson needs to be altered in some way when students daydream, write notes to friends, yawn, stretch, or move around in their seats. This allows for a change of activities such as small group discussions or games that students like and require their active participation. Select a different type of activity from the one that has proven to be unsuccessful. When you alter the lesson early, you are able to keep student attention focused on the lesson and maintain order. For example, if a whole-class discussion proves to be unsuccessful, you might have students work in pairs on a related issue that deals with the lesson's objectives.

In your initial planning, take student interests and abilities into account and plan for several activities in each lesson. The need to alter the lesson once underway is thereby minimized. Some of these activities should require active student participation. Consider the length of time allocated to each activity by taking into account the students' age and maturity.

Provide Nonpunitive Time-out.   Students who become frustrated, agitated, or fatigued may get off-task and disruptive. When you notice this happening, you could provide a nonpunitive time-out. A *time-out* is a period of time when the student is away from the instructional situation to calm down and reorganize his or her thoughts. The student then returns to the task with a fresh perspective. This time-out is not intended to be a *punitive response,* or a punishment for the off-task behavior.

When a time-out is needed, ask the student to run an errand, help you, get a drink, or do something else not related to the class activity. Be alert to signs of frustration and agitation and be ready to respond quickly.

Teachers in Action

Altering the Setting

Tim Block, tenth-grade biology teacher, Clay Center, Kansas:

Joe was a very good biology student, and everything seemed to be easy for him. He finished seatwork or lab work well before the other students. Then he wanted to entertain the class or flirt with the girls. This, of course, distracted the other students.

I sat down with Joe and reviewed our classroom rules, which are: (1) No student will be allowed to keep another student from learning; and (2) No student will be allowed to keep me from teaching. Joe understood how his behavior could have an effect on the performance of other students. He agreed that it would be a good idea for him to sit alone at his desk at the front of the room.

Knowing his need for social contact and his ability in biology, I gave him a lab coat and designated him "student lab assistant." He did a fine job moving from one lab station to another, giving direction, not answers. Joe was not threatened by authority, his self-image was bolstered, and his status in his sophomore social hierarchy was not damaged by my obvious disciplinary action. When I altered Joe's role in the classroom, his behavior improved.

Sometimes it is useful to designate a small area of the room specifically for time-out. This could be a desk placed in a corner, partially hidden by a filing cabinet. The student could go to this semiprivate area to calm down and prepare to continue with the lesson. You could also suggest that the students be allowed to go to this area when they think they need it. Students who use the corner for nonpunitive time-out should be allowed to decide themselves when they are ready to return.

Modify the Classroom Environment. The classroom environment may itself contribute to off-task behavior (Long, Frye, & Long, 1989). The arrangement of the desks, tables, instructional materials, and other items may give rise to inefficient traffic patterns or limited views of the instructional areas. Other factors include the boundaries between areas for quiet student and group projects and access to supplies. In addition, both your actions and those of the students may affect their behavior.

Once misbehavior develops, you may need to separate the students or change the setting in some way. Examine the disturbance and identify the element that contributes to it. Modification in arrangement may include moving tables, student desks, or the storage area.

MILD RESPONSES

Students may misbehave even after you have developed a system of rules and procedures, provided a supportive instructional environment, and given situational assistance to get misbehaving students back on-task. In that case, mild responses should be used. *Mild responses* are nonpunitive, at the same time providing guidance to appropriate behavior. Nonverbal and verbal mild responses are meant to stop the off-task behavior and restore order. The continuum of teacher responses (see Table 2-3) to misbehavior illustrates the movement to more directive responses if situational assistance is not successful.

Nonverbal Responses

Even with situational assistance, students may get off-task. Nonverbal responses are taken as a nonpunitive means to get the student back on-task. *Nonverbal responses* may include deliberate ignoring, signal interference, proximity control, and touch control. These are taken in increasing order of teacher involvement and control.

Shrigley (1985) studied 523 off-task behaviors, and found that 40 percent could be corrected by the nonverbal responses discussed here. Five percent were corrected by ignoring the behavior, 14 percent by signal interference, 12 percent by proximity, and 9 percent by touch control. Nonverbal approaches successfully extinguish many off-task behaviors. If these approaches are not effective, higher control approaches such as verbal interventions need to be used.

Ignore the Behavior.   Intentionally ignoring minor misbehavior is sometimes the best course of action as a means to weaken the behavior. This is based on the reinforcement principle of *extinction;* that is, if you ignore a behavior and withhold reinforcement, the behavior will lessen and ultimately disappear. Minor misbehaviors that might be ignored are pencil tapping, body movements, hand waving, book dropping, calling out an answer instead of raising a hand, interrupting, whispering, and so on. Behaviors designed to get your attention or that of their classmates are candidates for extinction, or ignoring the behavior.

Ignoring the behavior is best used to control only the behaviors that cause little interference to teaching/learning (Brophy, 1988). It should be combined with praise for appropriate behavior (Kindall, Workman, & Williams, 1980). Extinction is inappropriate for behaviors (e.g., talking out, aggression) reinforced by consequences that you do not control, or for behaviors (violence) that cannot be tolerated for any length of time (Kerr & Nelson, 1989). If the behavior continues after a reasonable period of deliberate ignoring, you should be more directive.

There are limitations to ignoring the behavior (Morris, 185). One risk is that students may conclude that you are not aware of what is happening and may continue the behavior. While you may ignore the behavior and not give the student the desired attention, other students may give such attention. Furthermore, the student may continue the behavior for a while after you ignore it;

Teachers in Action

Using Body Language and the Teacher Look

Lynne Hagar, high school history and English teacher, Mesquite, Texas:

Nonverbal responses are one of the keys to behavior control. Did you ever watch a traffic cop and wonder how he or she makes those big, powerful automobiles do his or her bidding? The answer lies in body language. The traffic cop stands confidently and assertively, makes gestures, uses eye contact, and has forceful hand and arm signals that are clearly recognizable.

A traffic cop doesn't have to be a large or powerful person to be effective; neither does a high school teacher. I am a small woman, but I can effectively control 30 senior students just by using my voice and my body language. When I want a certain behavior to stop, the first thing I do is to look at the student. Even if that student is not looking at me, he or she eventually becomes aware that I am staring. Then I point at the student and nonverbally indicate that the behavior is to stop. For example, a finger placed on my lips indicates that talking needs to stop.

Often, a questioning or disapproving look or gesture can stop undesirable behaviors right there. I may have to move into a student's personal space or comfort zone to stop a behavior, but a combination of a look and physical proximity are effective about 90 percent of the time. I might even casually rest my hand on the student's desk, never stopping teaching, and stay put for a minute or so until I'm sure the student is back on-task.

My advice is to practice "the look" in the mirror until you get it right. It shouldn't be a friendly look, but it doesn't have to be angry either. Think of a movie star who has a power look, and imitate that. The same is true of assertive body language. Learn to say in your manner, "I am in charge here."

Move around the classroom. Getting close to your students is essential, not only when you are correcting them but also when you want to reassure them or reinforce their positive feelings about you and your classroom. A friendly touch on the shoulder as you are helping a student with a problem or a hug when a student has a big success can go miles toward cementing your positive relationship with that student.

---

however, if deliberate ignoring is effective, the student will eventually stop the behavior. For some behaviors, extinction is too slow to be of practical value. Aggressive or hostile behaviors may be too dangerous to ignore.

Use Signal Interference. **Signal interference** is a nonverbal signal to communicate to the disrupting student that the behavior is not appropriate. Signals must be directed at the target student. They let the student know that the behavior is inappropriate and that it is time to get back to work.

Nonverbal signal interference may include making eye contact with the student who is writing a note, shaking a hand or finger to indicate disapproval of inappropriate behavior, or holding a hand up to stop a student's calling out. These actions should be done in a businesslike manner. You need to move to the next level of intervention if these disruptive behaviors persist.

Use Proximity Control. Proximity control is your physical presence near the disruptive student to help the student get back on-task. This is warranted sometimes when you can't get the student's attention to a signal because the student is engrossed in an inappropriate action. For example, a student may be reading something other than class-related material or may be writing a note. While doing this, the student may not even look up at you. Signals then will not work. While conducting the lesson, you walk around the room and approach the student's desk. It is then likely that the student will notice your presence and put the material away without a word being spoken.

Some proximity control techniques may be subtle, such as walking toward the student, while others such as standing near the student's desk are more direct. If students do not respond to proximity control, you need to move to a more directive level of intervention.

Use Touch Control. Without a verbal exchange, you may place a hand on the student's shoulder in an effort to achieve calm, or take the student's hand and escort the student back to the seat. These are examples of *touch control*—mild, nonaggressive physical contact to get the student on-task. It communicates that you disapprove of the action. Touch control may redirect the student into the appropriate behavior, such as repositioning the student's hand where it belongs—on the desk.

You may take into account the circumstances of the behavior and the characteristics of the student when deciding whether and how to use touch control. Students who are angry or visibly upset sometimes do not want to be touched, and some do not want to be touched at any time. How well touch will be received depends on where it occurs and how long it lasts. A touch on the back, hand, arm, or shoulder is acceptable to many students, whereas touch to the face, neck, leg, chest, or other more personal areas are often not acceptable. Brief touch is considered acceptable; the longer it continues, the less acceptable it becomes, and it may even be considered a threat.

Decision Points

Let's assume that you are monitoring your second-grade students while they work independently at their seats. Though you want all students in their seats at this time, one student walks over to a shelf to look at something. You walk over to her. Would you use touch control? Why or why not? If so, how might you touch the student and for how long? Would you make different decision if the student was a sixth grader or a ninth grader? How might your understanding of students' individual differences affect your decisions?

Teachers in Action

Personal Notes to Students

Jacqueline Miles Stanley, middle school health teacher, Little River, South Carolina:

I have always enjoyed writing notes to students and found that they respond positively. Sometimes, students do not respond to my usual low-level assistance to correct problem behavior. Ted is one such student. No matter what the situation, he always had to have a word with me, and I felt the need to have a word with him, too. Maybe personal notes would work with him.

On one of the larger Post-It note sheets that I use, I wrote a note to Ted explaining how I felt about his behavior and what I expected from him. When he took his seat on the following day, I posted the note where only he could read it. He had a great day, and much to my delight at the end of the class, I found a little note stuck to my book. It said, "Thank you. Ted."

Now I use notes all the time to engage students in the lesson, to caution them about behavior, or to praise them. Since the other students don't know what the note says, it is a good way to help students save face, and this saves me time during class.

Write Notes to Students.   Another private way to help get a misbehaving student back on-task is through personal notes. Events during the lesson and before or after class sometimes do not allow you the opportunity to talk with a student about a problem behavior. You could write a brief personal note that could be given to the student at the start of class the next day. This would give you an opportunity to describe the problem, your concerns about it, the potential consequences to the student and others in the class, and recommendations you have for correcting the behavior. You could also give a note to the student to provide reinforcement and encouragement once the problems have been overcome.

Verbal Responses

While nonverbal mild responses may be effective, verbal responses present nonpunitive, mild responses to misbehavior. Their purpose is to get the student back on-task with limited disruption and intervention. Various verbal responses are described below.

Reinforce Peers.   When students are reinforced for appropriate behavior, others are likely to imitate that behavior (Bandura, 1986). When a student misbehaves in a minor way, you could reinforce peers seated near that student.

In *peer reinforcement,* you praise a student who is on-task but seated near a misbehaving student, to focus class attention on appropriate behavior rather than inappropriate behavior. This subtle method allows the misbehaving student to get back on-task. Furthermore, you give no particular attention to the misbehaving student with the use of peer reinforcement. This seems to be more effective at the elementary level because younger students are more interested in pleasing the teacher.

Peer reinforcement is a subtle way of redirecting students into appropriate behavior. For example, two students may be talking when they shouldn't be as they work on an assignment. Instead of drawing attention to the disruptive behavior, you might say to another nearby student, "I'm glad to see you working so quietly on your assignment. Keep up the good work." This strategy does not rely on waiting for the misbehaving student to exhibit appropriate behavior before making statements of praise. Of course, you should reinforce the disruptive students once they exhibit the desired behavior.

Call on the Student during the Lesson. You can recapture a misbehaving student's attention by using his or her name in the lesson, such as, "Now, in this next example, suppose that John had three polygons that he. . ." You could ask a question of the student to recapture the student's attention. Calling on the student in these ways allows you to communicate that you know what is going on and to capture the student's attention without citing the misbehavior.

Be cautious—students' dignity should be preserved. If you call on students in these ways only when they misbehave, they will sense that you are just waiting to catch them misbehaving, and this strategy will backfire by creating resentment (Good & Brophy, 1994).

Use Humor. Humor is a gentle reminder to students to correct their behavior. Humor directed at the situation or even at yourself can defuse tension due to the misbehavior. It can depersonalize the situation and thus help resolve the problem.

You must be careful that the humor is not sarcastic. Sarcasm refers to statements that are directed at or make fun of the student; they are intended to "put down" or cause pain. Instead, humor is directed at or makes fun of the situation or the teacher. The student then may reconsider his or her actions and get back on-task.

Send an I-Message. An I-message verbally prompts appropriate behavior without a direct command. Gordon (1974, 1991) developed this technique for verbally dealing with misbehavior. An I-message is a statement you make to a misbehaving student.

An *I-message* has three parts: (a) a brief description of the misbehavior; (b) a description of its effects on you or the other students; and (c) a description of your feelings about the effects. For example, you might say, "When you tap your pen on the desk during the test, it makes a lot of noise and I am concerned that it might distract other students."

Teachers in Action

Giving Students Choices

Terri Jenkins, middle school English teacher, Hephzibah, Georgia:

Avoiding conflict is important for classroom survival. This is especially true if one student is trying to seek power or attention. Giving the student a choice in resolving a problem defuses the situation and avoids a conflict.

A student may be playing with a toy or object brought from home, and you simply want the object to be put away so there is no distraction. You might say, "Joy, that noise is bothering me. Please put the toy back in your book bag, or you may put it on my desk for now. Thank you." You should then walk away.

The students have the power to make a choice. They do not feel challenged, and usually respond appropriately. The behavior stops, and little instructional time is lost. Choices should not be either punitive or rewarding. They should be designed to stop the misbehavior.

When giving choices, you should be polite and courteous, being careful that your tone is emotionless. After stating the choices, you should say "Thank you" then walk away from the student. It becomes obvious that you expect the student to comply.

In another example, a student may be talking with a neighbor while you are giving instructions. You might say, "Brian, I really need quiet while I am giving directions so that everyone can hear. You have a choice. You may remain where you are and stop talking to Mary, or you may choose to reseat yourself somewhere else in the classroom. Thanks." You should realize that giving good choices takes practice.

I-messages are intended to help students recognize that their behavior has consequences to other students and that you have genuine feelings about the actions. Since I-messages leave the decision about changing one's behavior up to the student, they are likely to promote a sense of responsibility.

Use Positive Phrasing. ***Positive phrasing*** is used when inappropriate off-task behavior allows you to highlight positive outcomes for appropriate behavior (Shrigley, 1985). This usually takes the form of "When you do X (behave in a particular appropriate way), then you can do Y (a positive outcome)." For example, when a student is out of her seat, you might say, "Renee, it will be your turn to pick up supplies when you return to your seat."

Through positive phrasing, you redirect students from disruptive to appropriate behavior by simply stating the positive outcomes. In the long run, students begin to believe that proper behavior does lead to positive outcomes.

Remind Students of the Rules.   Every classroom needs to have a set of rules that govern student behavior, along with consequences for breaking them. When students see that consequences of misbehavior are in fact delivered, reminders of the rules can help them get back on-task because they do not want the consequences. When one student is poking another student, for example, you might say, "Delores, the classroom rules state that students must keep their hands and feet to themselves."

A reminder often ends the misbehavior because the student does not want the consequence. If the inappropriate behavior continues, you must deliver the consequence, otherwise the reminder will be of little value because students will recognize that there is no follow-through.

Give Students Choices.   Some students feel defensive when confronted about their misbehavior. You can give them choices about resolving the problem. This allows the student to feel that he or she settled the problem without appearing to back down. All the choices you give should lead to resolution of the problem.

Decision Points

In your eleventh-grade American history class, your students are working in small groups on a project lasting three days. In one group, one student has been saying nasty things to others in the group and is trying to undermine the group's efforts. If you were to give the misbehaving student a choice at this point, what would it be? How might your choice be different if the student was misbehaving during independent work? How might your choice be different if this were a fifth-grade class? How might you determine if the student's learning style had something to do with his or her action?

Ask "What Are You Doing?"   Glasser (1969) proposes that teachers ask disruptive students three questions, to direct them back to appropriate behavior: (a) What are you doing? (b) Is it against the rules? (c) What should you be doing? These three questions can have a positive effect because the student has to state what he or she did, acknowledge that it was against the rules, and then state what should be done.

Of course, some students may not answer the questions honestly or not reply at all. Then you should make three statements related to the three questions. For example, "Keith, you were swearing and name calling. That is against our classroom rules. You should not swear or call names of others." If the student continues to break the rule, then appropriate consequences should be delivered.

Give a Verbal Reprimand.   A straightforward way to have the students stop misbehaving is simply to ask or direct them to do so. This is sometimes called a ***desist order*** or a ***reprimand,*** and is given to decrease unwanted behavior. Verbal reprimands are effective with many mild and moderate behavior problems,

Teachers in Action

Some Alternative Responses

Barbara Lojka, fourth-grade teacher, Manhattan, Kansas:

If more than one child is involved in breaking a rule, I ask each of them to relate their side of the story and I make sure each story is told uninterrupted. Many times, by the time the stories are told, all the "fire" is gone from the problem. Just recently, one child said, "I'm sorry I got mad." The other child said, "That's okay." End of conversation!

Often, small problems—lack of attention, throwing erasers, talking to neighbors—can be solved in simple ways, such as by my standing close to a student; putting my hand on the student's shoulder; asking the whole class, "Are you super listeners?"; saying "Thank you" to those who are behaving; and saying "I'm looking for a super group." Fourth graders like being told that they or their group are doing well.

They seem to enjoy, at least they giggle, when I ask if their fingers, eyes, toes (or whatever part of their body is off-task) heard what was said ("Are your fingers listening?"). They also don't seem to mind being singled out if it is done with humor in a very silly voice: "Dixie, are your fingers listening?" She giggles, we proceed, and Dixie is now also listening.

I sometimes talk to a child privately about behavior. "Marie, I've noticed that you and Janice have been passing notes during reading." I ask if that behavior could please stop, and many times this is the end of the problem. If the problem appears again, a wink, nod, or quiet "no" finger gesture from me often stops the behavior. I also try to find an appropriate time for the behavior, such as, "Write the notes to your friend at recess."

Finding a quiet place for a child to regain control can stop unwanted behavior. The child can then return when in control. Sometimes, I can find the root of the problem by asking the child what's upsetting him. The child could feel better and be in better control after verbalizing his problem and behavior changes.

but by themselves are less successful with severe behavior disorders (Kerr & Nelson, 1989).

A ***direct appeal*** is a courteous request for the student to stop the misbehavior and to get back on-task. You might say, "Martha, please put away the comb and continue with the class assignment." A direct appeal often gives the student a sense of ownership for deciding to get back on-task and to do as you requested. The student feels a sense of responsibility.

As an alternative, you could use a ***direct command*** in which you take the responsibility and give a direction in a straightforward manner, such as, "Wayne, stop talking with your friends and get to work on the lab activity." With the direct appeal and direct command, the student is expected to comply with your directions. If the student defies your request or command, you must be prepared to deliver an appropriate consequence.

Most teachers think of reprimands as direct commands rather than simply requests to comply. Several studies provide guidance about effective ways to deliver reprimands. O'Leary and his associates examined the effects of soft, private reprimands versus loud, public reprimands (O'Leary, Kaufman, Kass, & Drabman, 1970). They reported that soft reprimands, audible only to the mis- behaving student, are more effective than loud reprimands in reducing disruptive behavior. When teachers spoke to offenders loudly enough for the entire class to hear, the disruptions increased or continued at a constant level. Soft, private reprimands do not call the attention of the entire class to the misbehaving student and may be less likely to trigger emotional reactions. Kerr and Nelson (1989) also recommend a private word instead of a loud remark.

Brief reprimands result in less off-task behavior than lengthy reprimands that encourage talking back (Albramowitz, O'Leary, & Futtersak, 1988). Reprimands are more effective when accompanied with eye contact and delivered in close proximity to the student (Van Houten et al., 1982). If reprimands are not used too often, and if the environment is generally positive and warm, students will usually respond quickly (Van Houten & Doley, 1983).

Reprimands given cautiously and properly delivered are effective in decreas- ing inappropriate behavior and helping restore order. The following guidelines should be considered when using reprimands (Malm, 1992; Rhode et al., 1992; Van Houten, 1980):

1. Be specific as to the behavior being reprimanded, a reason why the reprimanded behavior is not desired, and what behavior you want. Reprimand only one behavior at a time.

   An example of a well-stated reprimand is: "John, stop talking please or you won't hear the directions for your assignment." Examples of poorly stated reprimands are: "Billy, cut that out." "Jill, what in the world am I going to do with you?" "Steve, what's wrong with you?"

2. Use a polite command rather than a question. For example, do not use statements such as, "Isn't it time to do your work?" or "Wouldn't you like to start your work?" Instead make the request a polite command, such as, "Please start your work now."

3. Use a firm tone. Keep your voice deep and constant. Assume a quiet voice, do not yell. Emphasize key words.

4. Give nonverbal expressions of disapproval whenever possible. Facial expressions (e.g., a glare) and posture are effective.

5. Deliver reprimands when you are close to the student. Reprimands are more effective face-to-face. Maintain eye contact.

6. Be consistent and do not ignore misbehavior. Reprimands will be effective if they follow misbehavior consistently and immediately.

7. Accompany reprimands with praise and nonverbal signs of approval to teach new behaviors or replace the problem behaviors. Verbally reinforce compliance.
8. When reprimands do not produce the desired results, pair or replace them with other procedures that decrease behavior. Time-out, overcorrection, and response cost (e.g., loss of privileges) may replace reprimands.
9. Maintain control when delivering reprimands. It is counterproductive to be angry or to maintain a reprimand for longer than approximately one minute.

Use Differential Reinforcement. Differential reinforcement is a positive approach to misbehavior reduction in which the student can still obtain reinforcement, but at different rates depending on the nature of the behavior. Three types of interventions can be considered differential reinforcement (Evans et al., 1989).

- Differential reinforcement of infrequent misbehavior reinforces the student for keeping inappropriate behavior at or below a certain level. This applies to behaviors that may be tolerable or desirable but that occur too often or too rapidly. For example, a student may contribute many ideas to a class discussion, but 10 contributions may be too many because the student may dominate the discussion and deprive other students from contributing. You may identify three as an appropriate number of contributions. A schedule of reinforcement may be followed to gradually decrease or progressively eliminate a behavior.
- Differential reinforcement involves the delivery of a reinforcer for the *complete absence* of a designated misbehavior within a specified time. The student is reinforced for performing any, preferably appropriate, behaviors other than the inappropriate ones that are targeted. For example, a student may receive a star for not interrupting the class with inappropriate behavior.
- Differential reinforcement of incompatible behaviors decreases an inappropriate behavior and at the same time ensures that an appropriate behavior occurs. You reinforce a response that is incompatible with the inappropriate behavior targeted for reduction. The two behaviors should be mutually exclusive, opposing and competing, and impossible to be committed at the same time. For example, a student cannot be aggressive and cooperative at the same time, or be tardy and on time, or be talking and listening at the same time. Once you have identified the behavior to be reduced, you should strengthen its opposite. Of course, this approach requires the *presence* of the desired response.

MAJOR CONCEPTS

1. Situational assistance involves actions taken to help students cope with the instructional situation and to keep them on-task.
2. To provide situational assistance, you may remove distracting objects, provide support with routines, reinforce appropriate behaviors, boost student interest, provide cues, help students over hurdles, redirect the behavior, alter the lesson, provide nonpunitive time-out, and modify the environment.
3. If students are still off-task after situational assistance is provided, then mild responses can be used, including nonverbal and verbal, nonpunitive responses to the misbehavior designed to get the student back on-task.
4. Nonverbal responses may include deliberate ignoring, signal interference, proximity control, and touch control.
5. Various verbal responses can be used as nonpunitive, mild responses to the misbehavior. The purpose of the verbal responses is to get the student back on-task with limited disruption and intervention.

DISCUSSION QUESTIONS

1. What are the benefits of providing situational assistance?
2. What are the potential disadvantages of providing situational assistance?
3. What are the benefits and disadvantages of ignoring the behavior?
4. How does an I-message differ from an appeal or direct command?
5. Why not skip over mild responses and go directly to moderate responses when misbehavior occurs?
6. What are the benefits of asking "What are you doing?" along with the follow-up questions?

SUPPLEMENTAL ACTIVITIES

For Clinical Settings

1. Identify examples of student behaviors for which situational assistance would be appropriate.
2. Identify examples of student behaviors for which mild responses would be appropriate.
3. List several examples of student misbehavior and for each one write an appropriate I-message.

For Field Settings

1. Ask several teachers to identify ways they use situational assistance and mild responses to misbehavior.

2. Ask several students to describe ways their teacher nonverbally and verbally signals them to get back to work after they misbehave. Which techniques work best?

3. Ask several teachers what classroom routines they use. How do they affect behavior?

KEY TERMS

Cues	Positive phrasing
Desist order	Proximity control
Differential reinforcement	Punitive response
Direct appeal	Reprimand
Direct command	Signal interference
Extinction	Situational assistance
Hurdle helping	Surface behaviors
I-message	Time-Out
Mild response	Touch control
Nonverbal responses	Withitness
Peer reinforcement	

RECOMMENDED READINGS

Dreikurs, R., Grunwald, B. B., & Pepper, F. C. (1982). *Maintaining Sanity in the Classroom: Classroom Management Techniques,* 2nd ed. New York: Harper & Row. Includes sections on theoretical premises, effective democratic methods, coping with special academic and behavioral problems, and parental involvement.

Levin, J., & Nolan, J. F. (1991). *Principles of Classroom Management: A Hierarchical Approach.* Englewood Cliffs, NJ: Prentice Hall. Includes sections on the foundations of classroom management, prevention, managing common misbehavior problems, and managing chronic misbehavior problems.

Weinstein, C. S., & Mignano, A. J., Jr. (1993). *Elementary Classroom Management: Lessons from Research and Practice.* New York: McGraw-Hill. Includes 12 chapters covering such issues as rules and routines, gaining student cooperation, protecting and restoring order, managing seatwork, and other unique instructional settings.

REFERENCES

Abramowitz, A. J., O'Leary, S. G., & Futtersak, M. W. (1988). The relative impact of long and short reprimands on children's off-task behavior in the classroom. *Behavior Therapy, 18,* 243–247.

Bandura, A. (1986). *Social Foundations of Thought and Action: A Social-cognitive theory.* Englewood Cliffs, NJ: Prentice Hall.

Brophy, J. (1988). Educating teachers about managing classrooms and students. *Teaching and Teacher Education, 4*(1), 1-18.

Brophy, J., & McCaslin, M. (1992). Teachers' reports of how they perceive and cope with problem students. *The Elementary School Journal, 93*(1), 3-68.

Canter, L., & Canter, M. (1992). *Assertive Discipline: Positive Behavior Management for Today's Classroom,* 2nd ed. Santa Monica, CA: Lee Canter & Associates.

Evans, W. H., Evans, S. S., & Schmid, R. E. (1989). *Behavior and Instructional Management: An Ecological Approach.* Boston: Allyn & Bacon.

Glasser, W. (1969). *Schools without Failure.* New York: Harper & Row.

Good, T. L., & Brophy, J. E. (1994). *Looking in Classrooms,* 6th ed. New York: HarperCollins.

Gordon, T. (1974). *Teacher Effectiveness Training.* New York: Peter H. Wyden Publishing.

Gordon, T. (1991). *Discipline That Works: Promoting Self-discipline in Children.* New York: Plume (a division of Penguin).

Kerr, M. M., & Nelson, C. M. (1989). *Strategies for Managing Behavior Problems in the Classroom,* 2nd ed. Columbus, OH: Merrill.

Kindall, L. M., Workman, E. A., & Williams, R. L. (1980). The consultative merits of praise-ignore versus praise-reprimand instruction. *Journal of School Psychology, 18*(4), 373-380.

Kounin, J. S. (1970). *Discipline and Group Management in Classrooms.* New York: Holt, Rinehart & Winston.

Lasley, T. J. (1989). A teacher development model for classroom management. *Phi Delta Kappan, 71*(1), 36-38.

Levin, J., & Nolan, J. F. (1991). *Principles of Classroom Management: A Hierarchical Approach.* Englewood Cliffs, NJ: Prentice Hall.

Long, J. D., Frye, V. H., & Long, E. W. (1989). *Making it Till Friday: A Guide to Successful Classroom Management,* 4th ed. Princeton, NJ: Princeton Book Co.

Malm, K. (1992). *Behavior Management in K-6 Classrooms.* Washington, DC: National Education Association.

Morris, R. J. (1985). *Behavior Modification with Exceptional Children.* Glenview, IL: Scott, Foresman.

O'Leary, K. D., Kaufman, K. F., Kass, R. E., & Drabman, R. S. (1970). The effects of loud and soft reprimands on the behavior of disruptive students. *Exceptional Children, 37,* 145-155.

Redl, F., & Wattenberg, W. W. (1959). *Mental Hygiene in Teaching,* 2nd ed. New York: Harcourt, Brace and Company.

Redl, F., & Wineman, D. (1957). *The Aggressive Child.* New York: The Free Press.

Rhode, G., Jenson, W. R., & Reavis, H. K. (1992). *The Tough Kid Book: Practical Classroom Management Strategies.* Longmont, CO: Sopris West.

Shrigley, R. L. (1985). Curbing student disruption in the classroom—Teachers need intervention skills. *National Association of Secondary School Principals Bulletin, 69*(479), 26-32.

Van Houtin, R. (1980). *How to Motivate Others through Feedback.* Lawrence, KS: H & H Enterprises.

Van Houten, R., Nau, P. A., MacKenzie-Keating, S. E., Sameoto, D., & Colavecchia, B. (1982). An analysis of some variables influencing the effectiveness of reprimands. *Journal of Applied Behavior Analysis, 15,* 65-83.

Van Houten, R., & Doleys, D. M. (1983). Are social reprimands effective? In S. Axelrod & J. Apsche, Eds. *The Effects of Punishment on Human Behavior.* San Diego, CA: Academic Press.

Weinstein, C. S., & Mignano, A. J., Jr. (1993). *Elementary Classroom Management: Lessons from Research and Practice.* New York: McGraw-Hill.

chapter **15**

Using Moderate and Severe Responses

Objectives

This chapter provides information that will help you:

1. Determine the limitations of punishment and know how to use punishment effectively.
2. Describe the reasons for using moderate responses (removing desirable stimuli) when responding to misbehavior.
3. Identify ways that logical consequences and behavior modification techniques can be used as moderate responses to misbehavior.
4. Describe the reasons for using severe responses (adding aversive stimuli) to misbehavior.
5. Identify ways that overcorrection can be used as a severe response to misbehavior.
6. Describe the significant disadvantages of physical consequences as a punishment.

Situational assistance and mild responses should be used first as positive measures to address student misbehavior and restore order. If the student continues to misbehave, various types of punishment can be applied.

Punishment is the act of imposing a penalty with the intention of suppressing undesirable behavior. There are two procedures for achieving this purpose: (a) *withholding positive reinforcers or desirable stimuli*—through techniques such as logical consequences and behavior modification including time-out and loss of privileges; and (b) *adding aversive stimuli*—through overcorrection or physical consequences.

Withholding positive reinforcers is considered to be less harmful than adding aversive stimuli. Withholding positive reinforcers represents a ***moderate response*** to misbehavior, while adding aversive stimuli represents a ***severe response.*** Before you consider moderate and severe responses, examine some cautions and guidelines.

Especially for beginning teachers, dealing with misbehavior that requires moderate or severe responses can be very troubling. It is often helpful to talk with the principal, other teachers, or school counselors to obtain ideas and advice for dealing with students who exhibit more serious misbehavior. It is often useful also to contact the student's parents at any point to inform them of concerns you might have and to solicit their help in working with the student.

CAUTIONS AND GUIDELINES FOR PUNISHMENT

The effects of punishment are limited and specific. Much evidence (reviewed in Bandura, 1969) shows that punishment can control misbehavior, but in itself will not teach desirable behavior or reduce the desire to misbehave. Punishment is never a solution in itself; at best, it is only part of the solution. Punishment is sometimes necessary, however, and you should be prepared to use it when circumstances dictate. You should know when to punish, what punishment to use, and how to apply it.

Punishment is a last resort to curb misbehavior in students who know what to do but refuse to do it. It should not be applied when misbehavior is not disruptive or when problems arise because students do not know what to do or need further instruction. Punishment is called for in response to repeated misbehavior, but even with repeated misbehavior, it should be avoided if students are trying to improve.

You should express confidence in the student's ability to improve, and punish only when students repeatedly fail to respond to more positive treatment (Good & Brophy, 1994). Apply punishment as part of a planned response, not as a means to release your anger or frustration.

Disadvantages of Punishment

There are several potential problems related to punishment (Clarizio, 1980; Jones & Jones, 1990).

1. *Punishment has a transitory effect in suppressing inappropriate behavior and is not an effective method for changing student behavior.* Punishment merely slows down the rate of trouble behaviors. Emmer and Aussiker (1987) examined four approaches to discipline that were used in 120 school districts and found that the most punitive method (assertive discipline) was ineffective. When teachers were asked to increase their use of punitive control methods,

misbehavior actually increased from 9 to 31 percent of student behavior (Becker, Engelmann, & Thomas, 1975).

2. *Punishment does not teach the student appropriate behavior that can be used to prevent future behavior problems.* Punishment simply serves notice to stop inappropriate behaviors. It is important for students to have guidance in learning how to behave more productively.

3. *Punishment can produce avoidance behaviors.* Students sometimes avoid coming in contact with the teacher when they expect to receive a punishment for something they did. *Avoidance behaviors* include lying, cheating, skipping class, becoming sick, hiding, withdrawing, doodling, and the like. Such escape behaviors are rewarding to the student in that they remove temporarily, at least, the punishment. Yet the avoidance behaviors themselves can create problems.

4. *Punishment may lead to inhibition of socially desirable behaviors and the development of personal rigidity.* The effects of punishment are not always confined to the behaviors that are to be eliminated. Harsh punishments, especially those applied over a lengthy period of time, can inhibit socially desirable behaviors and result in a loss of spontaneity—students may become inactive for fear of doing something to receive a punishment. Punitive disciplinary practices may stifle assertiveness and competitiveness.

5. *The teacher becomes an undesirable model when using punishment.* Teachers who use aggressive techniques to control aggression tend to generate the same behavior in their students. Unwittingly, the student appears to learn that aggression should not be directed toward those more powerful but that it is permissible to be aggressive toward those of equal or lesser power. Furthermore, harsh punishment may be a source of additional frustration which, in turn, may facilitate further hostile feelings and acts.

6. *Punishment appears to inhibit learning* (Englander, 1986). Kounin (1970) substantiated an earlier study indicating that the students of more punitive teachers expressed less value in learning, were more aggressive, and were more confused about behavior problems. Studies also suggest that schools in which students learn more effectively are characterized by high rates of positive reinforcement and by somewhat lower rates of punishment (Mortimore & Sammons, 1987; Rutter et al., 1979).

7. *Punishment allows the student to project blame rather than to accept responsibility for the behavior.* Punishment tends to create a situation where the students become angry or blame those responsible for delivering the punishment rather than examining their own responsibility for the problem.

8. *Assigning additional homework or academic projects and lowering a student's grade as punishment may create a negative attitude*

toward these activities. It is not desirable to create this negative attitude as a result of punishment.

9. *The effects of punishment are usually specific to a particular context and behavior.* For example, assigning extra homework as a punishment for a student being out of his or her seat is not likely to keep the student in the seat on another day when there is a substitute teacher. That punishment is not likely to stop the student from misbehaving in other ways.

Guidelines for the Use of Punishment

Researchers and practitioners have identified factors that offer guidance for the appropriate use of punishment (e.g., Clarizio, 1981; Evans, Evans, & Schmid, 1989; Long, Frye, & Long, 1989; O'Leary & O'Leary, 1977; and Steere, 1988). Representing a synthesis of recommendations from these authors, the following factors are important to consider when effectively using punishment.

1. *Explain and discuss acceptable behaviors.* Acceptable behaviors should be emphasized when classroom rules are first discussed. Make it clear why the rules exist. Discuss the reasons for not engaging in behavior considered to be inappropriate. Most students will behave appropriately if they know what is expected.

Teachers in Action

Isolate the Motive behind the Misbehavior

Terri Jenkins, middle school language arts teacher, Hephzibah, Georgia:

It is all too common for discipline to reward misbehavior. When choosing punishment, always try to isolate the motive behind the misbehavior.

One year, I found myself holding perpetual detention for a student who persisted in misconduct. Over the course of time, the indiscretions became more frequent but they did not intensify. After spending innumerable detention hours with Karin, I confronted the possibility that I was rewarding her misbehavior instead of extinguishing it. She wanted my undivided attention, and she was getting it. I concluded that a student willing to suffer through daily detention with me was truly in need of adult companionship.

I began to create opportunities for us to spend "quality" time together other than detention. She assisted with class projects, graded papers after school, and accompanied me to school functions. Slowly, Karin's behavior was transformed. She became a model student, no longer finding it necessary to secure my attention through misbehavior. So it is important to identify the motive behind the misbehavior before determining the punishment.

2. *Clearly specify the behaviors that will lead to punishment.* Clarifying acceptable behaviors may not be enough. To help the students understand, examples of behaviors that break the rules and lead to punishment should be identified and discussed.

3. *Deliver a warning before punishment is applied to any behavior.* The warning itself could reduce the need for the punishment. If the student does not correct the behavior after the warning, punishment should be delivered at the next occurrence.

4. *Apply punishment fairly toward every student who exhibits the targeted behaviors.* You should treat both sexes the same way, and low-achieving and high-achieving students the same way.

5. *Apply punishment consistently after every occurrence of the targeted misbehavior.* Behaviors that reliably receive punishment are less likely to be repeated than behaviors that occasionally go uncorrected.

6. *Apply punishment immediately when the undesired behavior is expressed.* This can be done when the misbehavior is just beginning. Waiting to deliver punishment may cause the misbehavior to increase in intensity or spread to other students.

7. *Use punishment of sufficient intensity to suppress the unwanted behaviors.* Generally speaking, the greater the intensity, the longer lasting the effect. This does not mean that you need to resort to extreme measures. For example, the loss of positive reinforcement because of inappropriate behavior is better than shouting "Don't do that" with increasing intensity.

8. *Select a punishment that is effective and that is not associated with a positive or rewarding experience.* Not all aversive consequences may be seen as punishment. Some students, for instance, might think that being placed in a time-out area is a reward. In that case, a different consequence should be used which is not seen by the student as being positive or rewarding.

9. *Select the type of punishment to fit the situation. Different situations call for different actions.* Don't overreact to mild misbehavior or underreact to serious misbehavior. The seriousness of the misbehavior, the student, and the context of the situation need to be taken into account.

10. *Combine punishment with negative reinforcement whenever possible.* **Negative reinforcement** is the incremental withdrawal of a punishment that has been delivered, such as the loss of recess time. By combining punishment with negative reinforcement, students must do something positive to show good faith and escape punishment. For example, stating that students will lose a privilege for a specified time probably is less effective than stating that they will lose the privilege until behavior improves sufficiently to warrant removal of the punishment.

11. *Select a type of punishment that does not violate school and district policies, nor state statutes.* This guideline applies especially to corporal punishment, though schools may have policies about other punishments, such as detention.

12. *Prevent the opportunity for escape from the punishment.* The punishment will not have much effect if the student can ignore the verbal reprimand or if a trip to the office never culminates in a meeting with the principal.

13. *Avoid extended periods of punishment.* Lengthy, mild punishment such as missing recess for a week may have a "boomerang" effect. Punishment of short duration is more effective.

14. *Use punishment only when rewards or nonpunitive interventions have not worked, or if the behavior must be decreased quickly because it is dangerous.* Punishment should be used as a last resort when other techniques have failed.

15. *Administer punishment in a calm, unemotional manner.* If you deliver punishment while still emotionally upset, you may select an overly harsh punishment and may also provoke the student into further inappropriate reactions. Punishment should not be an involuntary emotional response, a way to get revenge, or a spontaneous response to provocation.

16 *Reward appropriate behavior.* Punishment is intended to weaken inappropriate behaviors. Reinforcement should be used to strengthen desired behaviors.

Decision Points

Let's assume that you have taken a teaching position in a school that has a history of discipline problems. You need to develop a set of rules, procedures, and consequences to establish an appropriate learning environment. Punishment can be used to suppress undesirable behavior. What guidelines will you establish for yourself for the appropriate and effective use of punishment? What might you do to reinforce or support desired behavior?

USING MODERATE RESPONSES

Following situational assistance and mild nonverbal and verbal responses, students might continue to misbehave. In that case, moderate responses should be used to correct the problem. The continuum of teacher responses to misbehavior (see Table 2-3) illustrates the movement to more directive responses if mild responses are not successful.

Moderate responses are intended to be *punitive ways* to deal with misbehaving *by removing desired stimuli* to decrease the occurrence of the inappropriate behavior. Moderate responses include logical consequences and behavior modification techniques. Since student behaviors that warrant moderate responses are more problematic than mild misbehaviors, it is often useful to discuss specific problems with the principal, other teachers, or the school counselor. Parents can be contacted at any point in an effort to inform them of their child's actions and to solicit their help.

Logical Consequences

Rudolf Dreikurs (Dreikurs, Grunwald, & Pepper, 1982) expanded on Adler's concepts of social acceptance. Based on Dreikurs' ideas, teachers can use natural and logical consequences to help misbehaving students behave appropriately and to restore order.

Dreikurs prefers to let students experience the consequences that follow their misbehavior. A *natural consequence* is the flow of events in which a person is faced with the unexpected effects of his or her behavior. For instance, if a student says mean things to other students, he or she will likely have few friends. Or, the student receives a low grade on incomplete homework. These are called natural consequences because they are directly related to the behaviors and happen without any outside influence or intervention. Natural consequences are not arranged or improved by the teacher or anyone else; they simply occur.

By allowing students to experience the natural consequences of their behavior, they are given an honest and actual learning experience. There are situations where, for the student's safety, you should not allow natural consequences to occur. For example, you should intervene when a student is behaving recklessly in an industrial arts, home economics, or art lab where injury may occur.

By contrast, a *logical consequence* is an event arranged by the teacher which is directly and logically related to the misbehavior. For instance, if a student leaves paper on the classroom floor, the student must pick the paper up. If a student breaks the rule of speaking out without raising his or her hand, you would ignore the response and call on a student whose hand is up. If a student marks the desk, the student is required to remove the marks. Students are more likely to respond favorably to logical consequences because they do not consider the consequences mean or unfair.

You may tell the student what the consequence is right after the behavior occurs. For example, "Milton, you left the study area a mess. You need to clean it up during recess." As an alternative, you may give the student a choice when inappropriate behavior is noticed. This tells the student that the inappropriate behavior must be changed or, if it isn't changed, that a particular consequence will occur. For example, you may say, "Joellen, you have a choice of not bothering students near you or you will have your seat changed."

When given a choice, students will often stop the inappropriate behavior. This approach can be very effective because the student feels a sense of ownership in solving the problem, and the issue is over quickly. If the problem behavior continues, you must deliver the consequence as you stated to the student.

At the start of the school year you should think of two or three logical consequences for each of your rules and inform students of these consequences. Logical, reasonable consequences are preplanned and you are not under the pressure of thinking up something appropriate at the time the misbehavior occurs.

Because of the variety of rules that you might develop, you might select a wide range of logical consequences; some may be considered behavior modification approaches, which are discussed in detail later in this chapter. Some examples of logical consequences include the following:

- *Loss of privileges.* As a regular part of the classroom activities, you may provide your students with a number of special privileges such as a trip to the library, use of a computer, use of special equipment or a game, service as a classroom helper, and other valued privileges. If the misbehavior relates to the type of privilege offered, a logical consequence would be to withdraw the privilege. For example, if a student mishandles some special equipment, the student would lose the privilege of using the equipment.

- *Change of seat assignment.* Students may talk, poke, or interact with other students in nearby seats. Sometimes a problem occurs because certain students are seated near each other. Other times, the placement of the seats enables easy interaction. If inappropriate interaction occurs, a logical consequence would be to relocate the student's seat.

- *Written reflections on the problem.* It is often useful to ask the student to reflect on the situation to help the student recognize the logical connection between the behavior and the consequences. You may ask the student to provide written responses to certain questions; this might be done during a time-out.

These questions may include: What is the problem? What did I do to create the problem? What should happen to me? What should I do next time to avoid a problem? Other questions may require the student to describe the rule that was broken, why the student chose to misbehave, who was bothered by the misbehavior, what more appropriate behavior could be chosen next time, and what should happen the next time the misbehavior occurs. See Figure 15-1 for a sample Incident Reaction Sheet.

Written responses to these or similar questions help students see their behavior more objectively and promote more self-control. You may choose to have the student sign and date the written responses for future reference. The written responses can be useful if the parents need to be contacted at a later time.

- *Time-out.* Sometimes a student is talking or disrupting the class in a way that interferes with the progress of the lesson. In such a case, the student could be excluded from the group; this is called a ***time-out.*** Removing the student from the group is a logical consequence of interfering with the group. An area should be established as the time-out area, such as a desk in a corner or partially behind a filing cabinet. As a general rule, time-out should last no longer than 10 minutes.

- *Detentions.* **Detention** means detaining or holding back students when they normally would be free to go and do other things. The student is deprived of free time and perhaps the opportunity to socialize with other students. Detention may include the loss of recess time or having to remain after class or after school.

Student's Name _____ Date _____

This is what I did:

This is the rule I broke:

I chose to break this rule because:

I could have done this instead:

Next time I will do this:

FIGURE 15-1   Incident reaction sheet

Detention can be a logical consequence for student behaviors that waste class time. A student might be asked to work on the social studies paper that wasn't completed during class due to inappropriate behavior. Students will soon see the logic that time wasted in class will have to be made up later, on their own time in detention.

Make sure the student understands the reasons for the detention. It should logically fit the offense, and the time should not be excessive. Five or ten minutes lost at recess, or 20 to 30 minutes after school would be reasonable. Confer with the student and work out a plan to help the student avoid detention in the future and to move toward self-control.

Detention after school can be viewed as unreasonable if the student misses the bus and is subjected to the hazards of the highway on the way home, or if the parents instructed the student to return home immediately after school. Consider these and related issues when preparing to use after-school detention.

Teachers in Action

Visiting the Parent at Work

Paul Couture, middle school English teacher, Claremont, New Hampshire:

By the time students advance to middle school, they may realize that there are limits to teacher control of student behavior. They may also know that teachers do not always contact the parents even when the situation warrants. The students may challenge teachers, knowing that the parents might not be contacted.

John had been a chronic disrupter in my English class, and I appealed to his sense of right and wrong in yet another after-school conference with him. He listened to me and then realized that none of my previous or current actions would change his behavior. I told him that I would have to contact his parents if his behavior did not change. Based on his previous experiences with teachers, John thought this was just an empty threat and he walked out.

John didn't know that I really would contact his parents. Immediately, I learned where his mother worked, drove there, waited at the time clock, and talked with her as she left. After we discussed several strategies for ensuring further communication, I asked her to tell her son once she got home that "I just met with your teacher at work about your behavior at school."

For John and the other students who heard about this incident, the meaning of accountability took on a new light. This direct, immediate, unexpected communication with the parent taught John that he was accountable. That made a big difference.

Decision Points

Over a series of days, two students in your ninth-grade class have heated words for each other. You have moved their seats and taken other steps to stop their behavior. Today, they almost get into a fight during small group work. You tell both students to come after school today for detention. What can you have the students do during detention to make this a learning experience and to help them see that detention is a logical consequence of their actions? What would be the value of written reflections? How might you handle this situation if one student had a dental appointment after school and could not stay for detention?

• *Contact the parents.* If a student repeatedly misbehaves, you may need to contact the parents or guardians. The logic here is that if all earlier attempts to extinguish the misbehavior are ineffective, it is appropriate to go to a higher authority. Parents may be notified by a note or a letter to inform them of the problem and to solicit their involvement or support.

You may choose to phone the parents instead. If the situation is fairly serious, a conference with the parents may be warranted. As illustrated by the accompanying Teacher In Action feature, unexpected, immediate contacts with parents show the student that they indeed are accountable for their actions.

• *Visit the principal.* In cases of repeated misbehavior or serious misbehavior such as fighting, students may be sent to the school office to see the principal. The principal may talk with the student in an effort to use his or her legitimate authority to influence the student to behave properly. Some schools have specific procedures to be followed when students are sent to the principal.

When the behavior problems reach this point, additional personnel, including the school counselor or psychologist and the parents, need to be consulted to help the student.

Behavior Modification Techniques

Behavior modification techniques can also be used as moderate responses to misbehavior to deliver punishment. Loss of privileges (response cost) and time-out are the two primary ways of removing desired stimuli in an effort to get the student back on-task and to restore order.

These techniques are intended to decrease undesirable behaviors. With these approaches, positive reinforcement should be used simultaneously as a means to reinforce students for appropriate behavior.

Loss of Privileges (Response Cost). *Loss of privileges,* or *response cost,* is the loss of positive reinforcement (e.g., privileges) because of inappropriate behaviors (Axelrod, 1983; Evans et al., 1989; Long et al., 1989). The consequence lost may be an activity, such as a privilege or a portion of recess time, or a token (Rutherford, 1983). Response cost provides feedback (via lost privileges) concerning what students should *not* do. The message is clear—inappropriate behavior will cost something.

To withdraw reinforcement, you need to be sure that reinforcement was there in the first place. Removal of a reinforcer then serves as a punishment. When combined with rewards, response cost can help students learn that appropriate behavior pays and inappropriate behavior does not.

Ideally, costs should be logically related to the offenses. For example, students who are persistently destructive with certain equipment will not be permitted to use the equipment for a time; students who do not get along with others will have to work alone. Response cost is popular in token economy systems in which points are earned for appropriate behavior, but may be withdrawn due to inappropriate behavior. To use this approach effectively, you should limit its use to highly disruptive behaviors.

The following guidelines should be considered (Evans et al., 1989). Behaviors that will result in reinforcement or withdrawal of reinforcement should be clearly explained. Balance must be maintained between reinforcers and penalties for misbehavior so that a student doesn't lose all available reinforcement. Fines should be reasonable, neither too high nor too low. You should not display anger or disapproval when intervening with response cost. Reinforce appropriate behaviors in conjunction with response cost. Reinforcers may be resumed if the student immediately returns to work.

Time-out.   With *time-out,* the student is physically removed from an attractive and reinforcing situation and from the opportunity to receive attention or rewards. It is intended to decrease unwanted behavior. When using time-out, you must be sure that positive aspects are associated with the classroom and that the time-out area has few positive aspects. The time-out area is understood to be undesirable while the classroom is desirable.

This moderate punishment is especially suited to reducing disruptive behavior of elementary students (Long et al., 1989). Powell and Powell (1982) suggest that time-out is not appropriate for managing all disruptive behaviors. They emphasize that time-out works best for behaviors that involve responses from other students (e.g., aggression, defiance). Conversely, these authors note that time-out is inappropriate for disruptive and interfering behaviors that are self-stimulating (e.g., rocking and daydreaming).

Time-out is effective in situations in which extinction (i.e., withholding reinforcement) and reprimands fail (Axelrod, 1983). Branter and Doherty (1983), Nelson and Rutherford (1983), and Harris (1985) offer further discussion of time-out.

Time-out may be confused with extinction. *Extinction* occurs when the teacher withholds positive reinforcement, while the student remains in the classroom. With time-out, the student is removed from the normal situation, and the opportunity to gain reinforcement is lost.

There are four time-out procedures, ranging from least to most aversive (Evans et al., 1989). At the start, the least aversive procedures should be tried. First, *nonseclusionary time-out* involves keeping the student in the reinforcing setting but denying access to reinforcers through manipulation of the environment (e.g., removing art materials the student is using, taking the student out of a game or activity).

Second, in *contingent observation,* or sit-and-watch time-out, the student is removed from the reinforcing setting. The student is asked to sit nearby and observe his or her classmates behave appropriately and participate in the usual activities.

Third, *exclusionary time-out* requires removing the student from the reinforcing situation and placing the student in an area with lower reinforcement value and in which he or she is not able to see classmates. One exclusionary time-out involves time-out in another classroom at the same or higher grade level for a specified period. The student thus is removed from peers whose attention he or she may be seeking. It is important that teachers agree upon the arrangements for sending and receiving students.

Finally, ***seclusionary time-out*** involves removing the student from the reinforcing setting and placing the student in a supervised isolation area or time-out room separate from all other potential reinforcers, including peers, teacher, classroom, and activities. Seclusionary time-out has been the subject of much negative publicity because it has been misused and mismanaged (Alberto & Troutman, 1986). Some schools contain a room for detention or in-school suspension. As mentioned previously, you may ask the student to provide written responses or reflections to certain questions during time-out (see Figure 15-1) to document the situation and to use in a conference with parents, if needed. It is helpful to tell the students why you are keeping their responses to the questions.

When using time-out: (a) choose an appropriate location that is safe, free of reinforcement, and can be easily assessed and monitored; (b) explain the procedure to the student during a period of good behavior; (c) limit time-out to about two to five minutes (Evans et al., 1989).

Decision Points

During a lesson in your fourth-grade classroom, a student has continually made noises, distracted other students, and interfered with the lesson. You decide to place the student in the time-out area for several minutes. What factors might you take into account when deciding what you will have the student do while in time-out? How will you help the student see that this action is a logical consequence of the disruptive behavior? How might your decisions be affected if this was a kindergarten classroom, or a ninth-grade classroom?

USING SEVERE RESPONSES

Sometimes withholding positive stimuli (i.e., using moderate responses) as a means of punishment does not work. One more intervention is then needed to deliver penalties as punishment; this represents the use of severe responses. The continuum of teacher responses to misbehavior (see Table 2-3) illustrates the movement to more directive responses.

Severe responses are intended to be *punitive methods* of dealing with misbehavior *by adding aversive stimuli* for the purpose of decreasing the occurrence of inappropriate behavior and restoring order. Common forms of ***aversive stimuli*** are overcorrection and physical consequences.

The strategies described on the continuum of teacher responses are appropriate for isolated cases of misbehavior; most discipline problems can be handled through situational assistance, and mild, moderate, and severe responses. If the earlier steps are successful, there may be few times when severe responses are needed. If you have students who are continually disruptive, however, even severe responses (adding aversive stimuli) may not be the solution. You may need to consider some alternative strategies discussed in chapter 16 about ways to deal with difficult students.

Overcorrection

Overcorrection involves having a student take responsibility for his or her own misbehaviors by practicing correct forms of the behavior and thereby learning appropriate behaviors (Evans et. al., 1989). Azrin and Besalel (1980) state that overcorrection should be used when the problem behavior is "deliberate, frequent, severe, or very annoying." If the problem does not meet those criteria, simple correction may be sufficient.

Simple correction requires the student only to correct the problem situation or eliminate the annoyance. For example, a class that runs to line up for lunch may be told to sit down and line up again. This incident does not meet the criteria for overcorrection.

There are two types of overcorrection: restitutional overcorrection and positive practice overcorrection (Ollendick & Matson, 1978). *Restitutional overcorrection* requires that disruptive students restore the environment to a better condition than existed before their disruptiveness. A student who continually litters in the classroom may be required to pick up every piece of paper, even though he or she may have been responsible for only some of the litter. Restitutional overcorrection might be used with a student who carves the desk top, tears down a bulletin board, or creates a mess in the classroom

---

Decision Points

One student in your seventh-grade social studies class has not helped her cooperative learning group clean up after each day's work. The student leaves papers on the desk and floor, and does not return books and supplies to their proper locations. How might you use restitutional overcorrection in this case? When would you have the student perform this overcorrection? How might you alter the guidelines for group work to minimize this type of behavior? How might you hold students accountable for cleanup?

Positive practice overcorrection requires that individuals exhibiting inappropriate behaviors practice positive behaviors that are incompatible with the inappropriate ones. For example, if a student frequently speaks without raising his or her hand, you may ask the student to practice hand raising five to ten times after speaking out (Evans et al., 1989). Positive practice overcorrection could be used with students who rock in their seats, argue, swear, or generally engage in undesirable acts that have obvious counterparts that could be practiced and serve as replacements for these acts.

While both types of overcorrection have promise for reducing misbehavior, they could pose problems (Long et al, 1989). Requiring a student to correct more than the actual damage may be misunderstood by students, parents, and administrators. You will need to withhold approval during overcorrection lest a student misbehaves in order to receive praise for correcting the misdeed.

Physical Consequences

Corporal punishment refers to punishment that inflicts physical pain or discomfort to modify behavior. Paddling, spanking, slapping, or pinching are examples. Physical consequences also include physical restraint and exercise, such as doing sit-ups, as consequences for a targeted behavior.

There are many disadvantages to physical consequences (Evans et al., 1989; Hyman, 1990). Inappropriate behavior may be suppressed only temporarily and appropriate behaviors may be suppressed as well. Other negative behaviors often emerge, such as escape (running away from the punisher), avoidance (lying, stealing, cheating), anxiety, fear, tension, stress, withdrawal, poor self-concept, resistance, and counteraggression. The student also may suffer physical harm. Furthermore, physical punishment may serve as a model of aggressive behavior for the student.

Because of these disadvantages, *physical consequences should not be used*. In fact, 20 states have banned corporal punishment in schools. Several other states are considering outlawing it. Many districts in states that allow corporal punishment have abolished it. Public statements opposing the use of physical punishment have been issued by the American Federation of Teachers, the National Education Association, the Council for Exceptional Children, the American Psychological Association, the National Parent Teachers Association, the National Mental Health Association, and many other organizations (Hyman, 1990; Wood, 1982).

In reviewing public opinion polls, Jones and Jones (1990) noted that during the past 20 years public opinion has gradually moved away from a favorable view of physical punishment. They indicate that it is likely there is considerably less public support for physical punishment with upper elementary and older children and that the public favors physical punishment only when other methods have not been effectively and systematically employed.

MAJOR CONCEPTS

1. Punishment is the act of imposing a penalty as a means of suppressing unwanted behavior. Two types of punitive responses are removing desired stimuli (moderate responses to misbehavior) and adding aversive stimuli (severe responses).
2. Because of inherent problems with punishment, certain guidelines should be followed when using punitive responses.
3. Moderate responses to misbehavior involve removing desired stimuli for the purpose of decreasing the occurrence of inappropriate behavior.
4. Moderate responses include logical consequences and behavior modification techniques.

5. Logical consequences are events arranged by the teacher that are directly and logically related to the misbehavior. Sample logical consequences include loss of privileges, change in seat assignment, time-out, written reflections on the problem, detentions, contacts with the parents, and visits to the principal.

6. Behavior modification techniques include loss of privileges and time-out. Loss of privileges involves the removal of positive reinforcers. Time-out is the contingent loss of an opportunity to obtain positive reinforcement for a period of time.

7. Severe responses to misbehavior include adding aversive stimuli. This can be achieved through overcorrection and physical consequences.

8. Overcorrection involves having the student practice correct forms of the behavior.

9. Corporal punishment is punishment that inflicts physical pain or discomfort to modify behavior. Corporal punishment should not be used.

DISCUSSION QUESTIONS

1. How can teachers justify the use of punishment?

2. What are the disadvantages of using punishment? How can the disadvantages be minimized or overcome?

3. Give some examples of logical consequences that are linked to the misbehavior.

4. Describe situations where time-out and loss of privileges would be appropriate.

5. What is the rationale for using aversive stimuli (severe responses) such as overcorrection and physical consequences?

6. Identify examples of student behaviors where simple correction and overcorrection would be appropriate.

7. What are the arguments for and against using corporal punishment?

SUPPLEMENTAL ACTIVITIES

For Clinical Settings

1. Consider what types of punishment you might use in your teaching, and identify guidelines that you will follow for their use.

2. List sample student behaviors that would warrant your removal of desirable stimuli (moderate responses) and for the addition of aversive stimuli (severe responses).

3. Establish guidelines for yourself concerning the effective use of reprimands.

For Field Settings

1. Ask several teachers to provide their recommendations for the effective use of punishment.

2. Talk to teachers to identify ways they use moderate and severe responses to misbehavior.

3. Find out the school policy about corporal punishment. Talk to teachers about it.

KEY TERMS

Aversive stimuli

Avoidance behaviors

Contingent observation

Corporal punishment

Detention

Exclusionary time-out

Extinction

Logical consequences

Moderate response

Natural consequences

Negative reinforcement

Nonseclusionary time-out

Overcorrection

Positive practice overcorrection

Punishment

Response cost

Restitutional correction

Seclusionary time-out

Severe response

Simple correction

Time-out

RECOMMENDED READINGS

Canter, L., & Canter, M. (1992). *Assertive Discipline: Positive Behavior Management for Today's Classroom,* 2nd ed. Santa Monica, CA: Lee Canter & Associates.
Includes sections on the assertive attitude, the classroom discipline plan, teaching responsible behavior, and dealing with difficult students. Elementary and secondary examples are provided.

Dreikurs, R., Grunwald, B. B., & Pepper, F. C. (1982). *Maintaining Sanity in the Classroom: Classroom Management Techniques,* 2nd ed. New York: Harper & Row.
Includes sections on theoretical premises, effective democratic methods, coping with special academic and behavioral problems, and parental involvement.

Evans, W. H., Evans, S. S., & Schmid, R. E. (1989). *Behavior and Instructional Management: An Ecological Approach.* Boston: Allyn & Bacon.
Includes chapters on assessing and targeting behaviors, intervening, increasing appropriate behavior, decreasing unwanted behavior, and related issues. Focuses primarily on behavior, its causes, and appropriate interventions to promote or inhibit certain behaviors.

Jones, V. F., & Jones, L. S. (1990). *Comprehensive Classroom Management: Motivating and Managing Students,* 3rd ed. Boston: Allyn & Bacon.
Includes sections on the foundation of classroom management, creating positive interpersonal relationships, increasing student motivation, minimizing disruptions, and responding to misbehavior.

REFERENCES

Alberto, P. A., & Troutman, A. C. (1986). *Applied Behavior Analysis for Teachers,* 2nd ed. Columbus, OH: Charles E. Merrill.

Axelrod, S. (1983). *Behavior Modification for the Classroom Teacher.* New York: McGraw-Hill.

Azrin, N. H., & Besalel, V. (1980). *How to Use Overcorrection.* Lawrence, KS: H & H Enterprises.

Bandura, A. (1969). *Principles of Behavior Modification.* New York: Holt, Rinehart and Winston.

Becker, W., Engelmann, S., & Thomas, D. (1975). *Teaching 1: Classroom Management.* Champaign, IL: Research Press.

Branter, J. P., & Doherty, M. A. (1983). A review of timeout: A conceptual and methodological analysis. In S. Axelrod & J. Apshe, Eds., *The Effects of Punishment on Human Behavior.* New York: Academic Press.

Clarizio, H. F. (1980). *Toward Positive Classroom Discipline,* 3rd ed. New York: Wiley.

Clarizio, H. F. (1981). Punishment: A new look. In H. F. Clarizio, R. C. Craig, & W. A. Mehrens, Eds., *Contemporary Issues in Educational Psychology,* 4th ed. Boston: Allyn & Bacon.

Dreikurs, R., Grunwald, B. B., & Pepper, F. C. (1982). *Maintaining Sanity in the Classroom: Classroom Management Techniques,* 2nd ed. New York: Harper & Row.

Emmer, E. T., & Aussiker, A. (1987, April). *School and Classroom Discipline Programs: How Well Do They Work?* Paper presented at the annual meeting of the American Educational Research Association, Washington, DC.

Englander, M. E. (1986). *Strategies for Classroom Discipline.* New York: Praeger.

Evans, W. H., Evans, S. S., & Schmid, R. E. (1989). *Behavior and Instructional Management: An Ecological Approach.* Boston: Allyn & Bacon.

Good, T. L., & Brophy, J. E. (1994). *Looking in Classrooms,* 6th ed. New York: HarperCollins.

Harris, K. R. (1985). Definitional, parametric, and procedural considerations in timeout interventions and research. *Exceptional Children, 51*(4), 279-288.

Hyman, I. A. (1990). *Reading, Writing, and the Hickory Stick: The Appalling Story of Physical and Psychological Abuse in American Schools.* Lexington, MA: Lexington Books.

Jones, V. F., & Jones, L. S. (1990). *Comprehensive Classroom Management: Motivating and Managing Students,* 3rd ed. Boston: Allyn & Bacon.

Kounin, J. S. (1970). *Discipline and Group Management in Classrooms.* New York: Holt, Rinehart & Winston.

Long, J. D., Frye, V. H., & Long, E. W. (1989). *Making It Till Friday: A Guide to Successful Classroom Management,* 4th ed. Princeton, NJ: Princeton Book Co.

Mortimore, P., & Sammons, P. (1987). New evidence on effective elementary schools. *Educational Leadership, 45*(1), 4-8.

Nelson, C. M., & Rutherford, R. B. (1983). Timeout revisited: Guidelines for its use in special education. *Exceptional Education Quarterly, 3*(4), 56-67.

O'Leary, K. D., & O'Leary, S. (1977). *Classroom Management: The Successful Use of Behavior Modification,* 2nd ed. New York: Pergamon.

Ollendick, T. H., & Matson, J. L. (1978). Overcorrection: An overview. *Behavior Therapy, 9,* 830-842.

Powell, T. H., & Powell, I. Q. (1982). The use and abuse of using the timeout procedure for disruptive children. *Pointer, 26*(2), 18-22.

Rutherford, R. B., Jr. (1983). Theory and research on the use of aversive procedures in the education of moderately behaviorally disordered and emotionally disturbed children and youth. In F. H. & K. C. Lakin, Eds., *Punishment and Aversive Stimuli in Special Education* (pp. 41-64). Reston, VA: Council for Exceptional Children.

Rutter, M., Maughan, B., Mortimore, P., Ouston, J., & Smith, A. (1979). *Fifteen Thousand Hours.* Cambridge, MA: Harvard University Press.

Steere, B. F. (1988). *Becoming an Effective Classroom Manager: A Resource for Teachers.* Albany, NY: State University of New York Press.

Wood, F. H. (1982). The influence of public opinion and social custom on the use of corporal punishment in the schools. In F. H. Wood & K. C. Lakin, Eds., *Punishment and Aversive Stimulation in Special Education: Legal, Theoretical and Practical Issues in Their Use with Emotionally Disturbed Children and Youth.* Reston, VA: Council for Exceptional Children.

chapter 16

Dealing with Difficult Students

Objectives

This chapter provides information that will help you:

1. Identify characteristics of difficult students.
2. Determine your responsibilities for working with difficult students.
3. Develop an action plan to deal with difficult students.
4. Determine when and how to seek outside help.

Most discipline problems can be prevented, or students can be redirected to positive behavior through situational assistance, and mild, moderate, and severe responses to misbehavior, as described more fully in chapters 14 and 15. Some students, however, continually misbehave even after preventive and coping techniques have been used. These difficult students can persistently upset the learning environment and disrupt order. It is important to know how to deal with difficult students so order is maintained.

What are the characteristics of difficult students? What responsibilities do you have in dealing with these students? What strategies can you use in the classroom to address these students? What sources of outside help exist when the problems are chronic and/or serious? What services can these outside sources provide? This chapter addresses these issues.

CHARACTERISTICS OF DIFFICULT STUDENTS

Difficult students are constantly disruptive, demand attention, openly confront your authority, or do not complete assigned work. They disrupt learning, interfere with the work of others, and may prompt other students to misbehave. Your regular management system may not work with difficult students. Before considering how to deal with these students, it is helpful to identify the behaviors difficult students exhibit, recognize influences that may have contributed to the development of the difficult behaviors, and understand that the behaviors may be symptoms of serious problems.

Behaviors

According to Curwin and Mendler (1988), 80 percent of students rarely break classroom rules, 15 percent break rules on a regular basis, and 5 percent break rules persistently. Rhode, Jenson, and Reavis (1992) estimate that some 2 to 5 percent of all students meet their definition of a *tough kid* who demonstrates excessive noncompliant and aggressive behavior or behavior deficits in self-management, social, and academic skills. In some school environments, these percentages may be higher. Tough kids who persistently break rules and sometimes become involved in serious misbehavior are an ongoing challenge in the classroom.

Difficult students often show *excessive noncompliant and aggressive behavior.* They argue with teachers, delay, make excuses, or do the opposite of what is asked. They also may destroy property, tease others, get into fights, and be verbally abusive and cruel. Difficult students may also have *behavioral deficits in self-management, social, and academic skills.* They may act before thinking, not follow rules, not cooperate, be off-task, and fail to finish work. Table 16-1 displays a summary of the behavior excesses and deficits of tough kids.

These disruptive behaviors can be categorized in different ways. In a study on how teachers perceive and cope with problem students, Brophy and McCaslin (1992) identified 12 problem-student types. At least five of the types relate to difficult students: hostile-aggressive, passive-aggressive, defiant, hyperactive, and distractable. The other types are less likely to be considered difficult students (failure syndrome, perfectionist, underachiever/alienated, low achiever, immature, peer rejected, and shy/withdrawn).

Many behaviors may be characteristic of tough kids. Let's look at one type of student who expresses these behaviors. A *bully* is a student who oppresses or harasses another student in a physical or psychological way (Germinario et al., 1992). Bullies are usually male, but some are female. They try to control their fellow students with aggressive behavior to relieve their own feelings of low self-esteem. Their observable behaviors include starting fights, teasing, verbal threats, answering back, and damage to or confiscation of possessions of their victims. It is estimated that 10 percent of all school children are habitual victims

TABLE 16-1 Characteristics of tough kids

1. *Behavior Excesses: Too Much of a Behavior*
   a. Noncompliance
      Does not do what is requested
      Breaks rules
      Argues
      Makes excuses
      Delays
      Does the opposite of what is asked
   b. Aggression
      Tantrums
      Fights
      Destroys property
      Vandalizes
      Sets fires
      Teases
      Verbally abuses
      Is revengeful
      Is cruel to others
2. *Behavior Deficits: Inability to Adequately Perform a Behavior*
   a. Self-Management Skills
      Cannot delay rewards
      Acts before thinking; impulsive
      Shows little remorse or guilt
      Will not follow rules
      Cannot foresee consequences
   b. Social Skills
      Has few friends
      Goes through friends fast
      Noncooperative; bossy
      Does not know how to reward others
      Lacks affection
      Has few problem-solving skills
      Constantly seeks attention
   c. Academic Skills
      Generally behind in academics, particularly reading
      Off-task
      Fails to finish work
      Truant or frequently tardy
      Forgets acquired information easily

SOURCE: Rhode, G., W. R. Jenson, and H. K. Reavis, *The Tough Kid Book: Practical Classroom Management Strategies.* Copyright © 1992 by Sopris West, Longmont, CO. Reprinted by permission.

of the 7 to 8 percent who are bullies (Olweus, 1984). Teachers in elementary and middle grades regularly identify about 12 percent of all boys as often harassing or oppressing others in physical or psychological ways (Hoover & Hazlet, 1991). Guidelines are available for ways to work with bullies (e.g., Germinario et al., 1992; Garrity et al., 1994).

Influences

In many of these students, there are underlying influences that may contribute to their persistent misbehavior. Many come from homes where they have been emotionally or physically abused or neglected. Some may have had traumatic childhoods due to organic conditions, such as attention deficit-hyperactivity disorder (estimated to affect 4 percent of school-age children), fetal alcohol syndrome, or addiction at birth. They may live in a home environment where one or more adults are addicted to alcohol, crack, or other drugs. Many students come from home environments where parents have little influence or control over their behavior.

Many students who chronically misbehave come from home environments in which the parents themselves have had a negative school experience. The student then carries this distrust to school with the expectation that school will not be a positive experience. The student also may have limited trust in adults and teachers. The student enters school with negative influences and expectations. Every failure diminishes his or her self-esteem and often leads to anger and distrust. These are the difficult students, the tough kids who must be reached.

The risk of violent behavior in schools is heightened with the increase in gangs and weapons. A **street gang** is a group of people who form an allegiance for a common purpose and engage in violent, unlawful, and criminal activity. Many gang members are of school age, and when they come to school confrontations arise.

Schools have struggled over how to address the influence of gangs. Strategies fall into three categories (Webb, 1993): (a) prevention—stopping the problem before it begins by teaching skills so they will never become violent; (b) intervention—singling out those who have shown violent behavior and working one-on-one to change their ways; and (c) suppression—keeping weapons out of schools through police style tactics. Prothrow-Stith (1993), a leading advocate of prevention programs, maintains that we must teach children how to avoid violence: how to keep conflicts from escalating, how to deal with anger, how to recognize dangerous situations, and how to avoid weapons. Fortunately, resources about reducing gang-related activities and preventing and defusing violence are available (e.g., Curcio & First, 1993; Lal et al., 1993).

The Justice Department estimates that 100,000 children carry guns to school every day. And guns are killing U.S. teenagers at the highest rate since the government has been keeping count 30 years ago ("Federal Tally," 1993). Each year, guns kill nearly 5,000 Americans under the age of 20, according to the National Center for Health Statistics. Among those aged 15 to 19, firearm deaths out-number those due to natural causes. Some experts estimate that seven times as many children are injured by guns as killed. Obtaining a handgun is no problem for millions of U.S. children, a recent Louis Harris survey indicates ("Survey Shows," 1993). Among sixth to twelfth graders, more than one in three say they could put their hands on a gun within an hour. Yet the study also shows that these students have anxiety and deep pessimism about their future in a culture of guns and violence. Some resources are available for understanding and dealing with behaviors that students express after trauma (e.g., Garbarino, 1992).

Symptoms of Serious Problems

Some of the behaviors exhibited by difficult students are troublesome while others are serious. Aggressive behaviors such as fighting, throwing tantrums, vandalizing, stealing, and exhibiting abusive behavior very seriously affect the student and the learning environment. Because of the immediacy of the events, you cannot ignore these actions, and immediate attention is needed.

Some difficult students, however, exhibit behaviors that may not demand immediate attention, yet they also may be a sign of serious problems. A student who does not comply with directions, has limited self-management skills, or has limited social or academic skills may be considered a difficult student. Whether overtly aggressive or passively noncompliant, difficult students exhibit behaviors that can disrupt their learning and that of others.

Some students may evince serious problems. Students who are viewed to be at-risk often are considered difficult students. *At-risk students* may have academic difficulties, a short attention span, low self-esteem, health problems, a narrow range of interests, a lack of social skills, the inability to face pressure, fear of failure, and a lack of motivation. They also may be disorganized, inattentive, distractable, unable to face pressure, and be excessively truant and absent (Lehr & Harris, 1988).

You should be alert to changes in students which may be indicators that serious problems are occurring. There may be changes in the type and degree of socialization with other students, or in their academic achievement. There may be changes in the student's activity level, as shown by absences, tardiness, or energy level. The student may change in physical appearance, health, or personality.

All of these changes may contribute to the student's being difficult to handle. Contributing factors may be very serious and beyond your influence to address or remedy. You should be prepared to contact other specialized professionals to help these students. Professionals may include counselors, psychologists, nurses, social workers, or even police officers. It is helpful to consult with the school principal before contacting those outside the school.

Decision Points

Let's assume that you have a student who exhibits some of the classic characteristics of noncompliance and aggression. The student breaks rules, argues, makes excuses, delays, teases, fights, and is cruel to others. In your judgment, which of these behaviors may be symptoms of serious problems? The problems may reach a point where they are considered serious enough to involve other professionals. What criteria will you establish when making the professional judgment about when to call on other professionals?

Teachers in Action

Guidelines for Working with Difficult Students

Michael Abbott, teacher in an alternative high school, Livonia, Michigan:

Our alternative high school has a high percentage of students who would be considered at-risk and challenging to work with. A sign in the school says "Soft on people, hard on issues." Probably nothing has helped me in my relationships with my students as much as this simply stated philosophy. To me, it says a great deal about human relationships and provides the following guidance as I work with challenging students:

- Self-esteem is easily damaged.
- People respond well to gentleness.
- It is not necessary to be cruel to be effective.
- People respond well if they know the issues.
- Expectations must be clear.
- Anticipate problems (be proactive rather than reactive).
- State consequences before anything has happened.
- Be consistent.
- Follow through.

TEACHER RESPONSIBILITY

To be successful with difficult students, you must assume responsibility for addressing the situation and take steps to get the student to behave within acceptable limits. There are several steps you can take to meet that challenge.

First, establish rules, procedures, consequences, and reinforcements. It is vital to develop a comprehensive management and discipline system for all students. This is the foundation for any additional actions that you need to take.

Second, make a commitment to help the difficult students succeed. Difficult students are sometimes accustomed to teachers trying to help them, then later giving up. Giving up on the student only reinforces and perpetuates the problem behavior; it will not end without intervention. This inappropriate behavior will continue unless you make the commitment to help the difficult student.

In doing so, you must clearly communicate your concern to these students. They must know that you will do everything possible to help them succeed. Since you may not be in a position to change any of the underlying, contributing factors for the misbehavior, you should focus on the inappropriate classroom behaviors. This commitment is essential in overcoming problem behaviors.

Develop a plan of actions needed to change the behavior. Handling each incident as a separate act is not sufficient. Planned, sequential actions are needed to systematically address the problem behaviors. Approaches to be followed in the classroom as part of this plan are addressed in the next section. Some guidelines and materials are available (e.g., Garrity et al., 1994; Jenson et al., 1993; Rhode et al., 1992; Walker, 1993; Young et al., 1992).

APPROACHES TO USE IN THE CLASSROOM

The goal is to help the difficult student be successful. To achieve that goal, you need to be committed to a planned, sequential set of actions to have the student stop misbehaving and get back on-task. A set of actions to achieve that goal is discussed below. Communication with parents is necessary. One of the following steps is to consult and inform parents; however, contact can occur at any point as the need warrants, even when you are assessing the situation.

Assess the Situation

Before taking any actions to remedy the situation, gather information and be reflective about the student, the behaviors, the environment, and yourself.

First, *find out about the characteristics of the difficult students and the influences in their lives.* You will then have a better understanding of them, and this information may help you decide on appropriate actions. You may obtain this information by talking with the student, through a questionnaire about interests, by asking other teachers who come in contact with the student, or other means.

Then, *examine your management system.* This is a necessary step to see whether there are factors in the classroom contributing to the misbehavior. This should include a review of rules and their consequences, procedures, space use, motivation, lesson delivery, reinforcement, and efforts to monitor students and promote cooperation.

Analyze the problem behavior and your response. It is important to precisely identify what the student is doing to create a problem. Some behaviors may be similar to those listed in Table 16-1. Checklists and observation systems are available to help record the behaviors (Rhode et al., 1992). One useful format is to list the type of student behavior and your response.

This step of looking at your own actions can be quite enlightening. To borrow from William Glasser (1969), ask, "What am I doing? Is it working?" If it is not working, stop doing it. When asking these questions, focus your attention on selecting an appropriate, workable response. By looking at the student's behaviors and your related responses, you can often determine the reason for the misbehavior. You then can act in ways to not reinforce the motive behind the student's misbehavior.

Teachers in Action

Calming an Emotional Student

Jane Holzapfel, middle school computer literacy teacher, Houston, Texas:

Emotionally disturbed students need a different approach for their misbehavior. By the time these students reach the middle school, every form of discipline has been tried. They are experts at undermining behavior modification or other attempts to get them to conform to class rules and decorum.

I had one such student, Shantana, in my sixth-grade computer power class. I had tried just about every form of discipline with her to no avail. When she was in eighth grade, she was enrolled in my computer literacy class. On the first day, she entered my classroom on the offensive by announcing that she didn't belong in a class with any seventh graders. She demanded that I change her schedule and then was verbally abusive toward the other students. She almost pulled one boy's pants down, trying to take his chair away. This was during the last class period of the day, and everything that had occurred earlier in the day contributed to the tense atmosphere.

I needed something to calm Shantana and give me the patience to deal with her. Whatever it was, I needed it as soon as she entered the room. She didn't respond to verbal contact; talking only escalated her unacceptable behavior. I discovered that by gently putting some hand cream on her hands and stroking her hands slowly in mine, her tenseness began to relax and so did her verbal mood. Stroking her hands let her know that I cared and that she was accepted by me even though I did not always approve of her behavior.

Most days, she calmed down enough to make it possible for me to begin the lesson without her abusive language toward me or the other students. Sometimes she would resist the hand cream gesture, but I persisted and soon it became the ritual that redirected her behavior. Occasionally several other students would ask to join us for hand cream. Together we shared a minute or two of hand rubbing, and the class seemed to work even harder on those days.

This step of self-examination can help you decide whether your expectations are reasonable. For example, many individual student differences may be apparent due to factors such as ethnicity, learning styles, academic ability, language, disabling conditions, socioeconomic status, and at-risk status. When considering students who are different from you, it is important for you to maintain reasonable expectations given their characteristics. Just because a student is different doesn't mean that he or she is a behavioral problem.

Keep Anecdotal Records

After you take the earlier steps, keep a written *anecdotal record* of incidents of misbehavior. An anecdote is a brief, narrative description of an incident. Anecdotal records can be simple, and may include a column format on a sheet. Information should include the student's name, the date and time of the incident, the location of the incident, a brief description of the student's behavior, and a brief description of your response. See Figure 16-1 for a sample Anecdotal Record Sheet.

Anecdotal records serve as a log for incidents of misbehavior and document the events. These records are very important if you need to contact the parents, principal, counselor, psychologist, or others. They provide documentation and help others who are consulted to better understand the nature and scope of the problems.

FIGURE 16-1 Anecdotal record sheet

Student's Name	Date	Time	Place	Behavior	Teacher's Response

Meet with the Student

Some consequences of misbehavior may have short-term effects. The students need help in making better decisions about their behavior. A one-to-one conference with the student is needed when the behavior is chronic or serious or there is a sudden change in behavior. The purpose of the conference is to provide caring and guidance to the student. You should listen to the student's concerns, firmly clarify your own expectations, and then work together to arrive at a practical course of action. There are several guidelines to consider when meeting with the student (Canter & Canter, 1993).

1. *Meet with the student privately.* The conference should be confidential, without other students around to overhear or disrupt the meeting. The conference should also be brief, with a maximum of 10 to 15 minutes.

2. *Show empathy and concern.* The conference is indended to help the student explore alternative, more appropriate behaviors. Therefore, you should help the student gain insight into his or her present behavior and choose more responsible behavior. The student should understand that this meeting is to help him or her, rather than to punish. The student should also know that you arc concerned and that you care.

3. *Question the student to find out why there is a problem.* Listen to the student's point of view rather than assume you know why the student is misbehaving. Question the student about the nature of the problem. It might be that the work is too hard or that something is happening at home or with other students that is contributing to the misbehavior.

Questions should be stated in a caring, nonaccusational manner. Avoid questions such as, "What is your problem?" Instead, ask "Did something happen today to get you so upset?" or "Can you tell me what's causing you to be so upset?" Listen carefully to the student and don't interrupt. Let the student talk. You will then have more information and fuller understanding of the student and the contributory circumstances.

4. *Determine what you can do to help.* Based on the answers to your earlier questions, you may discover there is a simple step to get the student back on track, such as moving his or her seat away from another student. In most cases, however, the solution is more difficult.

5. *Determine how the student can improve his or her behavior.* Part of the meeting should focus on what the student can choose to do differently to avoid problem behaviors. Talk about the situation and listen to the student.

At this time, it may be necessary to reteach appropriate behaviors for certain activities. Most students need only a single explanation of procedures for independent seatwork, discussion, cooperative groups, and entering and leaving the room. Other more difficult students need to be taught how to behave and be reminded often. While you will have previously taught appropriate procedures to the entire class, this one-to-one meeting with the difficult student provides an opportunity to reteach and clarify these procedures and expectations.

6. *State your expectations about how the student is to behave.* The student must understand that you are very serious about not allowing the misbehavior

to continue. You express a caring attitude to work with the student to solve the problem; the student must realize that predetermined consequences will follow if he or she chooses to continue to misbehave. Near the conclusion of the meeting, you might say something like: "I'm going to work with you to solve this problem. I know that you can behave responsibly. But you must remember that fighting is not acceptable. Anytime you choose to fight, you will be choosing to go to the principal."

7. *Disarm criticism.* Some difficult students may become argumentative and critical, and may blame you for all their problems. In that case, take steps to disarm the criticism by letting the student speak. Also, ask the student for more information concerning why he or she is upset with you. This can help calm the student, and he or she will see you as being concerned. This additional information will likely help address the problem.

8. *Document the meeting.* In addition to keeping anecdotal records, keep records of one-to-one meetings. Documentation should include the date of the meeting, a summary of the ideas generated in the meeting, and any conclusions that were drawn.

Decision Points

A student has been misbehaving in your tenth-grade math class, primarily due to limited self-management and social skills. It has reached the point where you decide that a special private meeting is warranted to express your concern, provide guidance, clarify your expectations, and to seek a practical course of action. How might you prepare for this meeting? How might you prepare for and conduct the meeting differently if the student instead showed behavior excesses such as noncompliance and aggression?

Consult and Inform Others

You may want to consult with others to obtain further information or advice. The principal, school counselor, psychologist, or other teachers who at any time dealt with the student may be consulted. They could share their experiences in dealing with the student and perhaps offer recommendations for strategies that you could take. The student's parents are also a source of information. Consultations are intended to help you deal with the student in the classroom; no referrals for outside services are made at this point.

Rather than wait until the behavior becomes very serious, inform the principal or parents about the problems. They will then know what you are doing and may be able to support you as the situation warrants. If indeed the problems become more serious, the principal and parents will appreciate this earlier contact rather than being surprised when a crisis develops. At a later time, the principal and parents may be involved in actions to address the problems if they persist or become more severe.

Provide Positive Support

Students need to receive reinforcement for their appropriate behavior through social reinforcers, activities and privileges, tangible reinforcers, and token reinforcers. Reinforcement encourages the student to continue the rewarded behavior.

Difficult students especially need to be reinforced for their appropriate behavior. Even though it may be easy to overlook delivering reinforcement to difficult students, they need to receive their fair share of rewards for their appropriate behavior. You may choose to make notes in your planbook as reminders to reinforce difficult students at regular intervals.

Difficult students need to receive additional positive support beyond that which is given to all students (Canter & Canter, 1993; Rhode et al., 1992). One way is to phone the student at home before the school year begins. (You will know which students to call based on information you hear from the student's teachers from the previous year.) You can ask the student for ideas about how the school year could be successful and express your confidence that you and the student will work together to have a good year.

You could contact the student's parents to express your caring about their child, get the parents' input about the student's experiences the previous year, learn what the student needs from you this year, emphasize that the student will be most successful if you and the parents work together, and express confidence that by working together the student will have a more successful experience at school. This early contact helps build a positive relationship with the parents before problems arise.

Another approach that can be used with all students but is especially useful with difficult students is to have them fill out a student interest inventory at the start of the year. Based on the questions you ask and the responses, you will have a fuller understanding of the difficult student's interests. You should be prepared to give personal attention and welcoming words to the difficult student when he or she enters the classroom. If problems occur during the day, you could call the student at home in the evening to express concern and to inquire about the problem.

Relating to the student as an individual is important. Take time to talk with the student or involve yourself with him or her in school activities. The individual attention of a caring adult can make a big difference. Visiting the student at home is another way of showing your concern.

Decrease Inappropriate Behavior

Your rules and consequences for the class apply to all students, including difficult ones. Since the consequences selected may not work for difficult students, you may need to select alternative consequences for these children only. Some discipline plans include delivery of a series of consequences based on the number of rule infractions the student has made.

Several consequences are discussed below. Determine the sequence of their use from the least to the most intrusive.

1. *Loss of privileges.* A number of special privileges may be provided. Withdrawing privileges can be an effective consequence, but you need to determine which privileges will have the most influence on correcting behavior if the privilege is withdrawn.

2. *Time-out.* Time-out involves removing the student from the instructional setting. The student is not given the opportunity to obtain reinforcement for the misbehavior. There are several types of time-out. One of the most effective is to remove the student from the instructional situation to be seated apart from the rest of the class; however, the student is expected to continue to do the work or listen to the lesson. The disruption stops, the rest of the class gets back to work, and the disrupting student is given an opportunity to calm down and get back to work.

You may ask the student to fill out an **Incident Reaction Sheet** while in time-out. This gives the student an opportunity to evaluate his or her behavioral choices while calming down. Questions may require the student to describe the rule that was broken, why the student chose to misbehave, who was bothered by the misbehavior, what more appropriate behavior could be chosen next time, and what should happen to the student the next time the misbehavior occurs. This reaction sheet should be kept on file as documentation of the incident, and it may be shown to others such as the parents, principal, or counselor as the need warrants.

3. *Time after class.* Keeping the student for about one minute after class can be an important consequence for students moving on to another classroom. This separates the student from peers, which can be perceived as a considerable penalty, and allows you to speak to the student about the behavior and the better choices that could have been made.

At this time, you could hand the student an index card on which to write a brief description of what was done in class to warrant staying after class. He or she could then sign and date the card for you to use as documentation in the event that the principal, parents, or others need to be contacted as the need arises.

4. *Detention.* Detention involves the loss of free time and the opportunity to socialize with other students. Loss of recess time or staying after school are two common detentions. Students should understand the reasons for the detention, and the time should not be excessive.

5. *Student calls a parent.* Having the student call his or her parent at home or at work in your presence can be a strong deterrent. The student is expected to explain the problem behavior and what will be done to improve. The call should be made as soon as possible after the incident when both you and the student can get to a phone in the building. This may take place at recess, at lunch, or at the end of the class period.

6. *Student writes a letter home.* Having the student write a letter to parents can also be an effective consequence. As with the phone call, the student describes the problem behavior and the better choices that could have been made.

7. *Time-out in another classroom.* If a student is highly disruptive, it may be useful to send him or her to another classroom at the same or higher grade

level for a specified amount of time. This approach is useful for students who seek attention, because they are removed from the peers whose attention they seek.

It is important that participating teachers discuss and agree to arrangements for sending and receiving disruptive students for a time-out. If students disrupt the classroom where they are sent for the time-out, they should know that the next consequence will be delivered, which may be a trip to the principal's office.

Decision Points

Students in your sixth-grade class are working in small groups when you notice that one student argues with others in the group, delays completing expected group work, and does the opposite of what is expected. To decrease the inappropriate behavior, what consequence would you select to deal with this student? What is the rationale for your choice? How might your selection be different if the behaviors occurred in a whole-class context? What effect did the grade level have on your decision?

Prepare a Behavioral Contract

A **behavioral contract** is a written agreement between you and the student that represents a commitment for the student to behave more appropriately. A contract includes: (a) a statement of the expected, appropriate behavior; (b) a specified time period during which the student is to exhibit such behavior; (c) rewards or positive support for exhibiting the appropriate behavior; and (d) penalties or corrective actions that will be taken if the student does not exhibit the appropriate behavior.

Behavioral contracts are not necessary for all difficult students. Some may respond favorably to the approaches already discussed. A behavioral contract should be prepared for students who do not respond, or if you are delivering further consequences to a particular student or are becoming frustrated or angry. A behavioral contract should then be drawn up.

Behavior contracting can be applied at any grade level, but is often more appropriate and effective with elementary and middle level students, as older students may resent obvious attempts to manipulate their behavior. The contract is effective also with special education students.

Know When to Involve Others

Consultations made earlier with the principal, school counselor, or psychologist were intended to provide information and advice in your dealings with the difficult student. Sometimes, however, students do not respond to any of your strategies, and the misbehavior continues to be chronic and serious. In such cases, it is necessary to involve others. Deviant and disruptive behavior warrants referrals to outside help.

Previously, informal contacts, telephone calls, and conferences with parents informed them of the student behaviors and your actions. Now, you need formal contact with the principal or counselors to solicit their assistance.

The principal can counsel or intervene with a difficult student. A referral to the school counselor or psychologist is warranted when you recognize that a developing problem is beyond your professional expertise. Remember that you have not been trained to be a psychologist, counselor, or social worker, and you should not view yourself as a failure when referring the student to someone with appropriate training. Some districts follow an intervention assistance team approach. Many district and community agencies work with schools and families, and these agencies also might be contacted.

SEEKING OUTSIDE HELP

After deciding to seek outside help, you need first to gather all the documentation you have prepared up to this time. You then need to decide upon the most appropriate person to contact.

Have Documentation Ready

By the time you are ready to seek outside help, you have exhausted all other efforts. You were keeping anecdotal records to document specific events of misbehavior indicating the date and time of the incident, the location of the incident, a brief description of the student's behavior, and a brief description of your response. You were keeping records of one-to-one meetings with the student and behavioral contracts that were developed. Incident Reaction Sheets that the student may have been asked to write during time-out are gathered.

All of these records document the incidents of misbehavior and the actions you have taken. This documentation should be made available to the consultants to help them better understand the nature and scope of the problems.

Decision Points

Two students in your first-grade classroom are involved in a heated argument about a lost set of crayons. One student had had no previous problems whereas the second student has had a series of difficulties in getting along with others. Will you make a written anecdotal record of this incident for both students' files? What factors will you take into account as you decide whether or not to have a written record? If an incident occurred with ninth-grade students, would you make the same decisions and select the same factors?

Referrals to Outside Help

It is common practice when outside help is needed to first contact the principal, who may take some actions or recommend that you talk to the counselor or psychologist. Parents may be involved at any point, depending on the recommendations of the principal, counselor, or psychologist.

Principal. When dealing with chronic or serious misbehavior, the principal has the authority to make certain decisions. The principal also may counsel or intervene when dealing with difficult students. Resources are available to help administrators work with aggressive and disruptive students (e.g., Black & Downs, 1993).

The principal might reward positive behavior. In consultation with you, the principal may be helpful in giving words of praise or other rewards when the student's behavior has improved. The principal might counsel the student by talking with the student. This additional guidance about the consequences of the student's choices can make a difference in turning the behavior around.

The principal might then contact the parents. This keeps parents informed of actions taken up to that time and they can be asked to support those actions at home. The principal might recommend that the parents come to school for a conference with the teacher or others.

The principal might approve new placements, services, or suspensions. Depending on the circumstances, the principal may take several actions such as changing the classroom placement, arranging for in-school suspension in a separate room, or referring the student to a counselor or psychologist. In more serious cases, the principal has the authority to seek placement in specialized educational settings outside the school, arrange for long-term suspension, or contact the police or other appropriate community agencies.

Counselors and Psychologists. Other than the principal, the school counselor is often one of the first people contacted when outside help is needed. The counselor may explore the student's behavior, the classroom environment, your teaching style, the management plan, or other related issues. The counselor then tries to provide objective feedback and suggestions for new approaches. By considering both your viewpoints and that of the student, the counselor can serve as an intermediary in any potential conflicts.

Sometimes a student's problems are rooted in deep and pervasive personality disturbances or family problems. The school psychologist can provide more intensive evaluation and diagnostic study. The psychologist will use the anecdotal and other records that you have accumulated and will supplement them with other tests, interviews, and observations. This analysis can lead to recommendations for actions to be taken by school personnel or may result in referrals to outside resources.

Problem-Solving Teams. In some schools a committee is available to assist teachers in dealing with classroom problems. *Problem-solving teams* consist of education personnel, parents, and other involved parties that meet

---

Teachers in Action

A Meeting with the Parents

Beth Schmar, sixth-grade teacher, Topeka, Kansas:

In the middle of March, my principal and I realized the Brad had taken control of the classroom. The other students hung on his every word and followed his every action. Brad was constantly seeking the other students' attention by rotating between being the class clown and the class bully. Either way, he had their admiration or awe.

From the start of the year, the principal and I tried many behavior management approaches, from a contract to suspension. In an act of desperation, we requested a meeting with Brad and his parents. We decided to include Brad for the entire meeting and to speak to him frankly. The principal and I shared our expectations for Brad's behavior and explained how his current behavior fell below these expectations. With the help of Brad and his parents, we developed a behavior plan that we all could live with.

We expressed to Brad genuine caring and concern about his future along with our own frustrations about his lack of success. Our honesty helped Brad react differently. He even commented to his parents later, "At least now I know the principal and teacher don't hate me." The meeting was the beginning of a new understanding that made our time together more positive.

---

systematically to discuss problems referred to them (Short et al., 1994). The teams provide collegial assistance with a minimum of bureaucracy. The teams also enhance commitment, communication, and morale by involving teachers and parents as expert resources and collaborators in problem solving.

The problem-solving team identifies needs, receives referrals, and plans and coordinates interventions with teachers, parents, other school personnel, and community agencies. Some teams become involved in preventive interventions, crisis intervention, and interagency coordination. Teams can provide (a) help for teachers in dealing with educational, behavioral, and discipline problems; (b) early identification and schoolwide prevention of the problems; (c) a means of in-school intervention; and (d) a mechanism for referral to appropriate educational resources.

Working with Parents

Many teachers, principals, counselors, and psychologists prefer that they be contacted before the parents are contacted. They can explore all appropriate interventions without prematurely involving the parents. If it becomes necessary to contact the parents, they are often more responsive when they learn that steps have already been taken. Parents may then visit you or others in the school. This is a more formal meeting than previous informational contacts, and the principal or others may participate.

The initial meeting with the parents gives all parties the opportunity to share information and formulate a common information base. Teachers and counselors, for example, may review the documentation about the series of incidents and actions that have taken place. The parents may share information about the child's attitudes and behaviors at home. Together, those present can develop a plan of action. Depending on the nature of the problem, they may conclude that an outside agency should be consulted.

The student may be asked to attend this meeting, or will be informed by the teacher, counselor, or principal about the results shortly after the meeting. The primary purposes of this meeting are to share information, develop a plan of action to help the child be successful, and gather the support of the parents.

Working with District or Community Agencies

Community agencies work with schools and families to help each child be successful. For example, Cities in Schools is a national nonprofit organization dedicated to decreasing the dropout rate. Its mission is to assist a targeted group of children to achieve academic and social success by coordinating existing community services to them and their families through the school. That agency might be contacted to assist.

Many districts or city governments include an office of substance abuse and violence prevention and intervention, and its resources may be useful. Social workers are available in community agencies. There may be other offices and organizations within the district or community that might be contacted for help.

MAJOR CONCEPTS

1. Difficult students often display *excessive noncompliant and aggressive behavior.* They argue with teachers, delay, make excuses, or do the opposite of what is asked. They also may destroy property, tease, get into fights, and may be verbally abusive and cruel. Difficult students may also have *behavioral deficits in self-management, social, and academic skills.* These may include acting before thinking, not following rules, not cooperating, being off-task, and failing to finish work.

2. For many difficult students, there are underlying influences that may contribute to their persistent misbehavior, such as emotional or physical abuse or neglect, organic conditions, drugs or alcohol, or gangs.

3. A comprehensive management and discipline system should be developed for all students in the classroom, and a commitment should be made to help the difficult students succeed.

4. To have difficult students succeed, you need to be committed to a planned, sequential set of actions to stop the student from misbehaving and get back on-task.

5. The plan of action involves assessing the situation, keeping anecdotal records, meeting with the student, consulting and informing others, providing positive support for the student, taking steps to decrease inappropriate behavior, preparing a behavioral contract, and knowing when to involve others.

6. Documentation should be available for review by the principal, school counselor, psychologist, or others who are consulted or to whom referrals are made. Each outside resource offers unique ways to assist in helping the difficult student succeed.

DISCUSSION QUESTIONS

1. Should teachers deal only with the student's problem classroom behavior or should they also try to address the underlying influences?

2. Why might teachers sometimes have difficulty in making a commitment to help tough kids?

3. What are the merits to the recommended sequence of approaches for dealing with difficult students in the classroom? How could that plan be improved?

4. What is the rationale for providing positive support for difficult students?

5. How might the principal help or hinder the handling of difficult students?

SUPPLEMENTAL ACTIVITIES

For Clerical Settings

1. Make a checklist of aspects of your management system that you will examine as you assess the situation in dealing with difficult students.

2. Prepare the format for an anecdotal record and a behavioral contract that you will use.

3. Establish criteria for the point at which you will refer to outside help in dealing with difficult students.

For Field Settings

1. Ask several teachers about particular strategies they use in dealing with difficult students in their classrooms.

2. Talk to the principal to see what role he or she plays in dealing with difficult students.

3. Talk with the school counselor and psychologist to find out about the referral process and their experiences in working with difficult students.

KEY TERMS

Anecdotal record	Incident Reaction Sheet
At-risk student	Problem-solving teams
Behavioral contract	Street gang
Bully	"Tough kids"
Difficult students	

RECOMMENDED READINGS

Canter, L., & Canter, M. (1993). *Succeeding with Difficult Students.* Santa Monica, CA: Lee Canter & Associates. [P.O. Box 2113, Dept. K, Santa Monica, CA 90407-2113; 1-800-262-4347]
Includes sections on reaching out to difficult students, meeting their special needs, communicating with difficult students, and additional strategies. Many examples are provided in each of the 12 chapters. Comprehensive coverage of the topics, and well written and organized. Examples are provided for K–12.

Karlin, M. S., & Berger, R. (1992). *Discipline and the Disruptive Child.* (revised ed.). Englewood Cliffs, NJ: Parker Publishing.
Opening chapters deal with the role of the teacher, identifying the problems underlying the problem behaviors, and basic methods. Separate chapters deal with particular difficulties (e.g., the fighter, the attention seeker, the unmotivated, abused children, children who abuse drugs). Focuses on the elementary grades, but many topics are applicable to the middle and secondary levels.

Rhode, G., Jenson, W. R., & Reavis, H. K. (1992). *The Tough Kid Book: Practical Classroom Management Strategies.* Longmont, CO: Sopris West. [1140 Boston Ave., Longmont, CO 80501; (303) 651-2829]
Includes chapters on characteristics of tough kids, unique positive procedures, practical reductive procedures for the classroom, and advanced systems. Includes useful tables and summaries. Has a K–12 focus.

REFERENCES

Black, D. D., & Downs, J. C. (1993). *Administrative Intervention: A School Administrator's Guide to Working with Aggressive and Disruptive Students.* Longmont, CO: Sopris West.

Brophy, J., & McCaslin, M. (1992). Teachers' reports of how they perceive and cope with problem students. *The Elementary School Journal, 93*(1), 3–68.

Canter, L., & Canter, M. (1993). *Succeeding with Difficult Students.* Santa Monica, CA: Lee Canter & Associates.

Curcio, J. L., & First, P. F. (1993). *Violence in the Schools: How to Proactively Prevent and Defuse It.* Newbury Park, CA: Corwin Press.

Curwin, R. L., & Mendler, A. N. (1988). *Discipline with Dignity.* Alexandria, VA: Association for Supervision and Curriculum Development.

Federal tally of gun deaths show U.S. teens are running record risk. (1993, March 24). *The Witchita Eagle,* p. 5A

Garbarino, J. (1992). *Children in Danger: Coping with the Consequences of Community Violence.* San Francisco: Jossey-Bass.

Garrity, C., Jens, K., Porter, W., Sager, N., & Short-Camilli, C. (1994). *Bully-proofing Your School: A Comprehensive Curriculum for Elementary Schools.* Longmont, CO: Sopris West.

Germinario, V., Cervalli, J., & Ogden, E. H. (1992). *All Children Successful: Real Answers for Helping At-risk Elementary Students.* Lancaster, PA: Technomic Publishing.

Glasser, W. (1969). *Schools without Failure.* New York: Harper & Row.

Hoover, J., & Hazlet, R. J. (1991). Bullies and victims. *Elementary School Guidance and Counseling, 25,* 212–218.

Jenson, W. R., Rhode, G., & Reavis, H. K. (1993). *The Tough Kid Tool Box.* Longmont, CO: Sopris West

Lal, S. R., Lal, D., & Achilles, C. M. (1993). *Handbook on Gangs in Schools: Strategies to Reduce Gang-related Activities.* Thousand Oaks, CA: Corwin Press.

Lehr, J. B., & Harris, H. W. (1988). *At-risk, Low-achieving Students in the Classroom.* Washington, DC: National Educational Association.

Olweus, D. (1984). Aggressors and their victims: Bullying at school. In N. Frude & H. Gault, Eds., *Disruptive Behavior in the Schools* (pp. 57–76). New York: John Wiley.

Prothrow-Stith, D. (1993). *Deadly Consequences: How Violence Is Destroying Our Teenage Population and a Plan to Begin Solving the Problem.* New York: HarperCollins.

Rhode, G., Jenson, W. R., & Reavis, H. K. (1992). *The Tough Kid Book: Practical Classroom Management Strategies.* Longmont, CO: Sopris West.

Short, P. M., Short, R. J., & Blanton, C. (1994). *Rethinking Student Discipline: Alternatives That Work.* Thousand Oaks, CA: Corwin Press.

Survey shows kids shadowed by fear of guns and violence. (1993, July 30). *The Wichita Eagle,* p. 3A.

Walker, H. M. (1993). *The Acting-out Child: Coping with Classroom Disruption.* Longmont, CO: Sopris West.

Web, T. (1993, March 22). Tough-talking programs strip violence of glamorous image. *The Wichita Eagle,* pp. 1, 4.

Young, K. R., West, R. P., Smith, D. J., & Morgan, D. P. (1992). *Teaching Self-management Strategies to Adolescents.* Longmont, CO: Sopris West.

appendix A

Beliefs on Discipline Inventory*

This inventory is designed for teachers to assess their own beliefs on classroom discipline. It enables teachers to assess to what extent they believe in the Human Relations-Listening; Confronting-Contracting; and/or Rules/Rewards-Punishment approach to discipline. Our hypothesis is that teachers believe and act according to all three approaches of discipline, yet usually one predominates in their beliefs and actions.

FORCED CHOICES

Instructions: Select either A or B. You may not completely agree with either choice, but choose the one that is closer to how you feel.

1. I believe that:
   A. Although children think, the decisions they make are not yet fully rational and moral.
   B. Students' inner emotions and decision-making processes must always be considered legitimate and valid.
2. Generally in my class:
   A. I assign students to specific areas or seats in the classroom.
   B. My seating (or work area) assignments are open to negotiation.
3. I believe that:
   A. No matter how limited the students' opportunities may be, students should still be given the responsibility to choose and make decisions.

---

* SOURCE: Wolfgang, C. H. and C. D. Glickman, *Solving Discipline Problems: Strategies for Classroom Teachers,* 3rd ed. Copyright © 1995 by Allyn & Bacon. Adapted by permission.

   B. Teachers need to realize that, in addition to their effect on students during school hours, students are greatly influenced by their own families, the neighborhoods where they live, their peers, and television.

4. When the high noise level in a classroom bothers me, I will more likely:
   A. Discuss my discomfort with the students and attempt to come to a compromise about noise levels during activity periods.
   B. Allow the activity to continue as long as the noise is not disturbing or upsetting any student.

5. If a student breaks a classmate's portable tape player that the classmate brought to school, I, the teacher, will more likely:
   A. Scold both students, one for disrespecting other people's property, and the other for breaking a rule that prohibits bringing radios and tape players to school.
   B. Avoid interfering in something that the students (and possibly their parents) need to resolve themselves.

6. If students unanimously agree that a classroom rule is unjust and should be removed, but I, the teacher, disagree with them, then:
   A. The rule should probably be removed and replaced by a rule made by the students.
   B. The students and I should jointly decide on a fair rule.

7. When a student does not join in a group activity:
   A. The teacher should explain the value of the activity to the student and encourage the student to participate.
   B. The teacher should attempt to identify the student's reasons for not joining and should create opportunities that respond to those reasons.

8. During the first week of class, I will more likely:
   A. Let the students interact freely and let them initiate any rule making.
   B. Announce the classroom rules and inform students how the rules will be fairly enforced.

9. I believe that:
   A. The students' creativity and self-expression should be encouraged and nurtured as much as possible.
   B. Limits on destructive behaviors need to be set without denying students their sense of choice and decision.

10. If a student interrupts my lesson by talking to a neighbor, I will more likely:
    A. Move the first student away from the others and continue the lesson because time should not be wasted on account of one individual.
    B. Tell students how angry I feel and conduct a dialogue about how the first student would feel about being interrupted.

11. I believe that:
    A. A good educator is firm but fair in taking disciplinary action on violators of school rules.
    B. A good educator discusses several alternative disciplinary actions with the student who violates a school rule.

12. When one of the more conscientious students does not complete an assignment on time:
    A. I will assume the student has a legitimate reason and will turn in the assignment when he or she completes it.

B. I will tell the student that she or he is expected to turn in the assignment when it is due, and then, with the student, we will decide on the next steps.

SCORING KEY INTERPRETATION

Circle your responses on the following table and tally the totals in each table:

Table I *(high control)*		*Table II* *(low control)*		*Table III* *(medium control)*	
2A	1A	4B	1B	2B	4A
3B	5A	6A	5B	3A	6B
7A	8B	9A	8A	7B	9B
11A	10A	12A	10B	11B	12B

Total number of responses in Table I _____ (Interventionist; high control)

Total number of responses in Table II _____ (Non-Interventionist; low control)

Total number of responses in Table III _____ (Interactionalist; medium control)

A high percentage of responses in Table I represents a leaning toward the Rules/ Rewards-Punishment approach (Interventionists) to discipline; in Table II, toward the Human Relations-Listening approach (Noninterventionists); and in Table III, toward the Confronting-Contracting approach (Interactionalists) to discipline.

By examining which table contains the largest number of responses, you can identify the approach to discipline that dominates your beliefs. The table with the second largest total of responses represents your second most prominent belief. The table with the fewest total responses represents the discipline approach that you least believe in.

If you have an equal number of responses in each table (or close to equal), this may indicate your approach to discipline is eclectic rather than clearly identified with any one of the discipline models.

This brief summary is not definitive. However, it ought to give you a general picture of how strongly you believe in each of these three discipline approaches.

appendix B

Audiovisual Resources

Items are listed here under topical categories. The title of the company or institution distributing the material is listed by the item, but the addresses for the companies and institutions are placed at the end of this appendix. Some companies offer a free preview of the materials prior to rental or purchase; contact the companies for specific information.

CLASSROOM MANAGEMENT

Classroom Management
Two 40-minute videotapes and a 16-page manual with each, $325; can be purchased separately each for $180. Illustrates effective management strategies for K–12 teachers; filmed in Oakland Public Schools. Tape 1, "Setting the Tone," shows eight teachers on the first day of school setting the tone for the school year and discussing expectations. Tape 2, "Taking Charge," shows six teachers dealing with disruptions and misbehavior in their classrooms, showing how teachers control their classrooms and communicate their authority. 1989.
Company: *Agency for Instructional Technology*

Classroom Management: Effective Techniques for Beginning and Experienced Teachers
Six 30 minute videotapes, $650 as a set or $125 for a single program. Produced by the Indiana University School of Education. Each tape includes live on-tape action sequences, discussions by behavior management experts, and commentary from teachers, parents, and principals. Originally designed as course material for undergraduate education students. Tape titles include: (1) Physical Intervention, (2 and 3) Working with Parents, (4) Social-Cultural Differences, (5) Alternative Curriculum, and (6) The Negotiation Process.
Company: *Kentucky Network*

Effective Management for Positive Achievement in the Classroom
Includes five videotapes (each about 28 minutes) and a workshop manual with participant activities and facilitator's notes, $795. Eight nationally recognized teachers offer specific approaches to classroom management in five segments: (1) How Teaching Styles Affect Classroom Management, (2) Creating a Positive Classroom, (3) Guidelines to Effective Classroom Management, (4) The Role of Student Contracts in Classroom Management, and (5) Discipline Approaches in the Classroom.
Company: *Universal Dimensions*

Managing Your Classroom
Six 26-minute videotapes, $795, may be rented. Each tape can be purchased or rented separately. Outstanding teachers at work in their own classrooms demonstrate specific strategies to elicit high levels of work involvement and low levels of misbehavior. These teachers then discuss their approaches. Program titles include: (1) Getting Ready, (2) Planning for Prevention, (3) Connecting with Kids, (4) Teaching Social Skills, (5) Responding to Misbehavior, and (6) Supporting Students At Risk. 1993.
Company: *Films for the Humanities and Sciences*

Strategies for Classroom Management
Includes four videotapes and a leader's guide, $390. Tapes can be purchased separately for $120. Pat Wolfe and Pam Robbins discuss ways to improve student attitudes and behavior in four videotapes: "Development and Teaching Classroom Rules," "Giving Clear Directions," "Using Transition Time Wisely," and "Creating a Positive Classroom Climate."
Company: *National Staff Development Council*

DISCIPLINE IN GENERAL

Bus Discipline: A Positive Approach
Four videotapes with leader's guide, $299. This program discusses the role of administrators, bus drivers, and teachers in promoting appropriate behavior on the bus. A step-by-step process is offered for solving recurring behavior problems. Developed by Randall Sprick and Geoff Colvin. 1993.
Company: *Teaching Strategies, Inc.*

Classroom Discipline
Includes one 30-minute videotape and a 24-page facilitator's guide, $125. Features Richard Curwin and Allen Mendler discussing how students can develop internal controls and self-responsibility when teachers abandon their traditional coercive, adversarial roles. 1992.
Company: *Agency for Instructional Technology*

Decision Points in Secondary, Junior High, Elementary, and Special Classrooms
Includes four 15-minute videotapes, $139 for each tape. Created by professors at Memphis State University, these programs included student-enacted open-ended vignettes; personalize solutions for different practices; catalyst for interaction and involvement; and facilitator's guide provided for decision making. Tapes include: (a) Room 309: Secondary Education (2 tapes); (b) Room 209: Special Education; and (c) Room 109: Elementary Education. 1987.
Company: *Insight Media*

Discipline and Motivation
Ten audiocassettes (order either the elementary or the secondary version), $59.95.
Each tape is 45 to 60 minutes long providing specific information on effective
management. Topics include problem prevention, effective consequences, motivating
the apathetic student, increasing on-task behavior, increasing student motivation,
implementing reinforcement systems, and others. Developed by Randall Sprick.
Company: *Teaching Strategies, Inc.*

Discipline: Appropriate Guidance of Young Children
One 28-minute videotape, $109. Differentiating between discipline and
punishment, the program demonstrates ways to handle difficult behavior in
preschool settings. Examines skills of cooperation. 1988.
Company: *Insight Media*

Discipline with Dignity.
Three 15–20 minute videotapes, $385. These videotapes are designed for
inservice training and staff development. These K–12, multicultural settings
demonstrate practical techniques for effectively dealing with diverse discipline
situations. The videos may be used as a primer to, in conjunction with, or as
reinforcement after training. They provide a quick, convenient way to motivate
your staff and to grasp the principles and techniques of Richard Curwin and
Allan Mendler's *Discipline with Dignity.*
Company: *National Educational Service*

Foundations: Establishing Positive Discipline Policies
Includes six hour-long videotapes and three texts, $850. This program will help
school administrators and staffs write or revise, implement, and maintain a positive
discipline policy. It enables preparation of a school-wide discipline policy. The
program authors are Randall Sprick, Marilyn Sprick, and Mickey Garrison.
Company: *Sopris West*

Managing Acting-Out Behavior
Two videotapes and a manual, $169. This is a staff development program to
prevent and manage acting-out behavior such as explosive behavior, physical
aggression, verbal abuse, severe tantrums, open defiance, and physical aggression.
Tape 1 describes various stages of acting-out behavior, and Tape 2 provides
nonconfrontational strategies to deal with these behaviors. The program author is
Geoffrey Colvin. 1993.
Company: *Sopris West*

Managing the Disruptive Classroom: Strategies for Educators
Includes one 60-minute videotape broken up into a four-part program, and a
32-page facilitator's guide, $295. The facilitator's guide features workshop
agendas, discussion questions, activity suggestions, blackline masters, and
directions for managing simulations. Designed for use in a staff development
program. Program content founded on William Glasser's reality therapy concepts.
The program authors are Robert Wubbolding and William Glasser.
Company: *Agency for Instructional Technology*

Managing Students without Coercion
One 74-minute videotape, $169. Presents methods designed to improve classroom
management using a collaborative approach with the teacher and students. 1993.
Company: *Insight Media*

Playground Discipline: Positive Techniques for Recess Supervision
Two 45-minute videotapes with instructions, blackline masters, and sample forms,
$249. Developed by Randall Sprick, this program helps staff teach students
responsible playground behavior and provides specific training for playground
supervisors in areas such as positive interactions, consistent supervision, crisis
situations, fighting, tattling, arguing, and helping children be more responsible. 1993.
Company: *Teaching Strategies, Inc.*

Preventing Misbehavior in Your Classroom
Two audiocassettes, $20. Betsy Geddes discusses techniques to work with the
student instead of against the student. The tapes outline 14 prevention
techniques to minimize student misbehavior.
Company: *Cline-Fay Institute*

Quality Schools
Includes one 30-minute videotape and a 24-page facilitator's guide, $125. Features
William Glasser arguing against traditional coercive management practices in
schools. He advocates teaching to students in ways that satisfy their needs and
convincing them of the importance and significance of what they are learning,
making discipline problems disappear and achievement rise. 1992.
Company: *Agency for Instructional Technology*

Quick and Easy Classroom Interventions
Three audio cassettes, $30. Jim Fay demonstrates ways to maintain classroom
control without taking time away from teaching. These practical techniques help
improve discipline, enhance student-teacher relationships, and return dignity to
both teacher and student.
Company: *Cline-Fay Institute*

Restitution
Includes four 20-minute videotapes, a facilitator's guide, and Diane Chelsom
Gossen's *Restitution: Restructuring School Discipline* text, $495. Based on
William Glasser's control theory, the restitution model stresses self-discipline. The
program gives teachers a process to redirect the student, yet does not diminish
the individual. Restitution manages students without sacrificing self-esteem, and
students begin to view problems as opportunities for learning. 1993.
Company: *New View Multimedia*

School-wide Discipline and Student Responsibility
Six videotapes and three texts, $850. Six videos take a school staff through a
step-by-step process of writing a positive and instructional discipline policy. Three
texts are included: (1) to describe the process of preparing a school-wide plan,
(2) to provide sample policies, and (3) to provide a workbook as a hands-on tool
to facilitate the writing. Developed by Randall Sprick.
Company: *Teaching Strategies, Inc.*

Solutions to Elementary Discipline Problems
Five one-hour videotapes, *The Solution Book* text, and instructor's manual with
reproducible handouts and practice assignments for participants, $850. Developed
by Randall Sprick, this program provides elementary teachers with practical
strategies for handling misbehavior and increasing student motivation. Tape titles
include: (1) Problem Prevention, (2) Motivating Students through Positive
Interactions, (3) Reducing Attention-Getting Behavior, (4) Effective Consequences
for Misbehavior, and (5) Systems for Increasing Student Motivation.
Company: *Teaching Strategies, Inc.*

Solutions to Secondary Discipline Problems

Five one-hour videotapes, two copies of *Discipline in the Secondary School* text, and instructor's manual with reproducible handouts and practice assignments for participants, $850. Developed by Randall Sprick, this program provides secondary teachers with practical strategies for handling misbehavior and increasing student motivation. Tape titles include: (1) Problem Prevention, (2) Effective Grading Systems, (3) Positive Interactions with Students, (4) Effective Consequences for Misbehavior, and (5) Motivating High Risk Students.
Company: *Teaching Strategies, Inc.*

Solving Behavior Problems: A 20-Minute Planning Process

One videotape with leader's guide, $145. This program provides an 8-step process that can be used by groups of individuals when designing a plan for systematically improving student behavior. The groups may be multidisciplinary teams, grade level or departmental teams, discipline committees, or others. The plan focuses on defining the problem, designing an intervention plan, and implementing the plan in the classroom. Developed by Randall Sprick.
Company: *Teaching Strategies, Inc.*

Success with Discipline: The Trials of Jenny Tippet

Includes three videotapes, $395. This is designed to help teachers and administrators manage middle-level student behavior through both individual classroom and interdisciplinary team approaches. The section titles are (1) Beliefs and Attitudes, (2) Prevention, and (3) Reacting to Discipline Problems. The program was a collaboration between Wavelength, a leading educational comedy ensemble of performers and writers, and Robert Shockley, an expert on middle-level classroom management. 1993.
Company: *National Middle School Association*

21st Century Discipline

One 75-minute videotape, $79.95. In a lively, humorous presentation, Jane Bluestein offers practical alternatives to using power or permissiveness to encourage student self-management; has an emphasis on prevention. Topics include ways to motivate student behavior, reinforce cooperation, encourage student self-esteem, help students solve problems, and intervene in negative behavior.
Company: *Instructional Support Services*

COOPERATIVE DISCIPLINE

Cooperative Discipline

Includes two videotapes, a *Teacher's Guide to Cooperative Discipline* text, a leader's guide with detailed instructions, and blackline masters, $474.95. This program is designed to provide a general overview in one session and then skill development in six subsequent staff development sessions; based on Linda Albert's cooperative discipline principles. This program offers dozens of intervention techniques along with encouragement strategies teachers can use to help students choose self-discipline and cooperative behavior. Teachers learn what motivates students to misbehave, how to reinforce desirable behavior, how to help students feel capable and connected, and more. A stimulating video provides realistic examples of ways teachers can deal with specific, immediate behavior problems.
Company: *American Guidance Service*

Responsible Kids at School and at Home: The Cooperative Discipline Way
Six videotapes with a leader's guide and supplementary materials, $289.95. This
program is designed for K–12 staff development and school improvement. The
program includes information about the causes of student misbehavior and
effective, cooperative approaches to address it. Program topics include the basics
of behavior, attention seeking behavior, power struggles, revenge behavior,
avoidance of failure, and building self-esteem through encouragement. 1993.
Company: *American Guidance Service*

ASSERTIVE DISCIPLINE

Assertive Discipline (Grades K–8)
Includes six programs on three videotapes (about 3 hours of viewing), a leader's
manual, the *Assertive Discipline* text, and two *Assertive Discipline Teacher Workbooks*, $495. Lee Canter discusses how elementary and middle-school teachers
can prevent classroom behavior problems by teaching students how to behave
and by positively recognizing them when they do. 1993.
Company: *Lee Canter and Associates*

Assertive Discipline for Bus Drivers
Includes two 30-minute videos, one leader's manual, and ten bus driver workbooks, $249. Lee Canter discusses how bus drivers can manage student behavior
to maintain safety and order on the bus. Techniques include ways to conquer the
most common problems occurring on the buses, establish rules on the bus, use
assertive communication skills, motivate students to follow their directions, and
use positive reinforcement.
Company: *Lee Canter and Associates*

Assertive Discipline for Paraprofessionals
Includes two 30-minute videos, one leader's manual, and ten paraprofessional
workbooks, $249. Lee Canter discusses how paraprofessionals can manage
student behavior in the areas they supervise. Techniques include ways to avoid
being hostile or nonaggressive, communicate in a positive and assertive tone,
manage large and small groups of students, prevent problems before they start,
and motivate students with praise and rewards.
Company: *Lee Canter and Associates*

Assertive Discipline for Secondary Educators
Includes four 30-minute videos, one leader's manual, and ten *Assertive
Discipline for Secondary School Educators Workbooks*, $495. Lee Canter
discusses how secondary teachers can set high expectations for student
behavior, maintain order, keep students on-task throughout the entire class
period, motivate all students to achieve success, and handle severe problems
like fighting and truancy.
Company: *Lee Canter and Associates*

Succeeding with Difficult Students
Includes four videotapes including 13 lessons (approximately 5 hours of viewing),
one leader's manual, one *Succeeding with Difficult Students* text, and ten video
booklet, $695. Lee Canter discusses the reasons behind the most severe student
misbehavior, how teachers can handle the anger and inappropriate behavior of

difficult students, and what steps the teacher can take to build positive relationships with these students. Includes some actual classroom videos where teachers model the techniques. 1993.
Company: *Lee Canter and Associates*

Success with Parents Inservice Video Program for Teachers
Includes three videotapes, three leader's manuals, and one *Parents on Your Side* text, $225. Videos are also sold separately. The tapes range from 35 to 50 minutes and are titled "Turning Parents into Partners," "Confident Parent Conferences," and "Positive Solutions to Difficult Situations with Parents."
Company: *Lee Canter and Associates*

BEHAVIOR MODIFICATION

Catch 'em Being Good
One 30-minute videotape, $495, or can be rented. This program has become "the classic" video presentation on the successful use of behavioral procedures in the elementary classroom. It is one of the most concise and understandable video programs available on behavior management techniques. The video contrasts the use of positive discipline, based on warm teacher-student interactions, with traditional but often less effective methods.
Company: *Research Press*

VIOLENCE

The Assaultive Student
One 30-minute videotape, $375. Examines the warning signs of physically assaultive behavior and staff responses to the out-of-control student. Illustrates effective restraint techniques and ways to de-escalate highly volatile emotional behavior. 1989.
Company: *Insight Media*

Freedom from Violence
Four 25-minute videotapes and two workshop manuals, $975. Designed for staff development programs, the videos integrate effective conflict resolution, anger management, and decision-making skills in the classroom. Tapes are titled: "Resolving Conflicts Peacefully," "Taking the Lid Off Anger," "The Gang Alternative," and "Safe School, Safe Environment." A demonstration tape is available.
Company: *Universal Dimensions*

Nonviolent Crisis Intervention
Five videotapes, $995; tapes can be purchased separately. Based on crisis intervention staff development programs used in many school districts. Designed to help safely defuse disruptive and potentially violent students. Tapes are titled: "The Disruptive Child," "The Disruptive Adolescent," "The Assaultive Student," "Fights at School," and "Reading, Writing, and Weapons."
Company: *National Crisis Prevention Institute*

Violence: Reversing the Trend
Includes three videotapes designed for viewing by teenagers, each tape is $275. Tapes are from 12-18 minutes long. These tapes deal with three factors related

to violence: guns, gangs, and conflict. The tape titles are "Weapons and You," "Crossing the Line: The Truth about Gangs," and "Getting Along."
Company: *Universal Dimensions*

HOSTILE AND RESISTANT STUDENTS

Broken Toy
One 30-minute videotape, $29.95. Designed for viewing by children in grades 4 and up. This tape addresses the problem of bully students. Through drama, it talks directly to children about put-downs, incessant teasing, and physical torment. It also teaches the importance of friendship and being a friend to all children, not just the popular ones. 1994.
Company: *Summerhills Group*

The Disruptive Adolescent
One 30-minute videotape, $375. Presents demonstrations and dramatizations of verbal intervention in secondary schools. Shows how confrontations can be transformed into orderly situations. Demonstrates safe, nonthreatening postures and reactions. 1989.
Company: *Insight Media*

The Disruptive Child
One 30-minute videotape, $375. Designed for elementary teachers, the program demonstrates techniques for responding to aggressive, disruptive children. Examines the four stages of crisis development. Presents specific ways to reduce tension. 1989.
Company: *Insight Media*

Working with Hostile and Resistant Teens
Two 45-minute videotapes and a teacher's guide, $159. Designed for teachers and counselors of grades 5–12, this program teaches effective anger management strategies in a school setting. Using role-plays with real at-risk students, the program examines the dynamics between the teacher/counselor and the hostile/resistant teen, and shows how to stay focused on the underlying problem. 1994.
Company: *Sunburst Communications*

AT-RISK STUDENTS

The Caring Connection
One 37-minute videocassette, $15. Produced by the NEA and the Iowa State Education Association, this videotape examines five successful programs designed to rescue at-risk students from academic failure. Appropriate for viewing by teachers and by community or parental groups.
Company: *National Education Association*

Interventions: Audio Presentations for Helping Teachers with At-risk Students
Twenty audiocassettes ranging from 15 to 55 minutes, $59. Developed by Randall Sprick, this program includes one tape for each of 16 specific interventions and four tapes on how to work collaboratively with classroom teachers. An accompanying book and resource manual with the same title is available for $49.
Company: *Teaching Strategies, Inc.*

Success with At-risk Students
One audiocassette, $10. Betsy Geddes and Jim Fay discuss love and logic's common sense, proven techniques with difficult students in many school settings.
Company: *Cline-Fay Institute*

ATTENTION DEFICIT HYPERACTIVITY DISORDER (ADHD)

ADHD in the Classroom—Strategies for Teachers
One 40-minute videotape with manual, $95. This program helps teachers better understand ADHD and equips them with techniques to address the needs of the ADHD student without neglecting the other students. Includes interviews with teachers, special education experts, parents, and ADHD students. 1993.
Company: *Menninger*

ADHD—What Can We Do?
One 37-minute videotape with manual, $85. Ideal for parent support groups, this program focuses on the most effective ways of managing ADHD in the home and the classroom. Parent-training strategies are detailed, and techniques such as home-token systems and others that can be used at home and school are demonstrated. 1992.
Company: *Menninger*

ADHD—What Do We Know?
One 36-minute videotape with manual, $85. The difficulties of living with ADHD are made poignantly real through interviews with parents, teachers, and three young people with the disorder. Provides a detailed look at how the disorder is manifested. 1992.
Company: *Menniger*

CONFLICT RESOLUTION AND PROBLEM SOLVING

Conflict Resolution
One 26-minute videotape and teacher's guide, $169. Designed for student viewing, grades 9-12. Teaches strategies for conflict resolution, helps students turn conflict into a positive experience. Shows them how to avoid conflict, resolve problems, and build better relationships. Winner of Media & Methods Awards Portfolio.
Company: *Sunburst Communications*

Conflict Resolution
One 30-minute videotape and a 24-page facilitator's guide, $125. Features Larry Dieringer discussing how effective conflict resolution both reduces the conflict and uses it as an opportunity for learning. An effective conflict resolution program can reduce classroom management problems and help students become skilled problem-solvers. 1993.
Company: *Agency for Instructional Technology*

Conflict Resolution for Grades 5–12
One 24-minute videotape, 17 staff handouts, nine student handouts, and a leader's guide, $149. Designed for teachers of grades 5-12, this tape shows peer mediation programs in action in a middle school and a high school. Includes conflict resolution specialists. Finalist in the Birmingham International Educational Film Festival.
Company: *Sunburst Communications*

Dealing with Anger: A Violence Prevention Program for African American Youth

Includes three videotapes, 30 skill cards, and a leader's guide, $495. Designed for student viewing. Each videotape begins with a vignette of a conflict situation that escalates into a potentially dangerous confrontation. The narrator freezes the action and describes a skill that can be used to defuse the violence. The same situation is replayed with use of the new skill.
Company: *Research Press*

Learning to Manage Anger

One 33-minute videotape and a leader's guide, $200, or can be rented. Designed for student viewing. The training program is designed to teach junior and senior high students a 7-step method for controlling anger and resolving conflict.
Company: *Research Press*

The Peer Mediation Video: Conflict Resolution in Schools

One 28-minute videotape and a 160-page program guide, $365, or can be rented. Shows how to establish a successful peer mediation program with students in grades 6-12. Peer mediation is a nonadversarial process in which trained student mediators help fellow students solve their own problems. Prepared by Fred Schrumpf, Donna Crawford, and Chu Usadel. 1993.
Company: *Research Press*

Student Workshop: Conflict Resolution Skills

One 30-minute videotape and teacher's guide, $189. Designed for student viewing, grades 5-9. Teaches the essential skills of conflict resolution by presenting a series of real-life conflicts, then demonstrates how the conflict resolution process, including mediation, works to find peaceful solutions.
Company: *Sunburst Communications*

Why Is It Always Me?

One 14-minute videotape and a leader's guide, $260, or can be rented. Designed for student viewing. The training program is designed to show young adolescents the difference between poor problem-solving skills and more effective techniques. Typical problems in the life of a 13-year old are highlighted.
Company: *Research Press*

Working It Out: Conflict Resolution

One 28-minute videotape and teacher's guide, $189. Designed for student viewing, grades 5-9. Teaches preteens and young teens an age-appropriate process for resolving conflict. Shows students how learning good communication skills, brainstorming for solutions, compromise, and mediation can turn conflict into a positive experience, build self-esteem, and improve relationships. Won the Silver Apple at the National Educational Film and Video Festival.
Company: *Sunburst Communications*

SELF-ESTEEM

Building Confident Kids

One 55-minute videotape in three parts with supplemental blackline masters, $129.95. This three-part series takes self-esteem theory and translates it into sound application. It promotes understanding of kids and their behavior

problems, and offers workable ideas for immediate classroom use. It is excellent for new and experienced teachers on the staff, classroom aides, and parents. Can be used in staff development program.
Company: *Sierra House Publishing*

Building Self-confidence

One 38-minute videotape and teacher's guide, $199. Also available in Spanish. Designed for student viewing, grades 6–12. Demonstrates that self-confidence is achieved in small steps: by taking a risk now and then, by learning to deal with put-downs, and through self-validation and encouragement from others. Finalist in the American Film and Video Association Film Festival.
Company: *Sunburst Communications*

Building Self-Esteem

One 26-minute videotape, 12 handouts, and a leader's guide, $149. Designed for teachers of grades 5–12, this tape focuses on two successful self-esteem programs, in a middle school and a high school. In-service Commendation at the CAVE Media Festival.
Company: *Sunburst Communications*

Go, Go, Goals! How to Get There

One 26-minutes videotape and teacher's guide, $169. Designed for student viewing, grades 5–9. Using scenarios typical of middle-schooler's experience, the program presents a step-by-step process that students can use to successfully set and achieve short- and long-term goals. Teens who are goal-oriented are less at risk for drug use or other self-destructive behavior. Won the Silver medal in the Questar Awards.
Company: *Sunburst Communications*

I Blew It! Learning from Failure

One 24-minute videotape and teacher's guide, $169. Also available in Spanish. Designed for student viewing, grades 5–9. Shows students how to turn failure around and use what they learn from it to achieve success. Provides a step-by-step process to help them re-evaluate goals and replace feelings of helplessness with a sense of control. Honorable Mention in the National Educational Film and Video Festival.
Company: *Sunburst Communications*

I Like Being Me: Self-Esteem

One 26-minute videotape and teacher's guide, $169. Also available in Spanish. Designed for student viewing, grades 5–9. Makes students aware of the effect of their self-esteem on their ability to behave in their own best interest. Shows how self-worth is fostered by positive feelings, and how it is forged in small steps that lead from one success to another. Finalist in the American Film and Video Film Festival.
Company: *Sunburst Communications*

No One Quite Like Me or You

One 16-minute videotape, eight student worksheets, and teacher's guide, $89. Designed for student viewing, grades 2–4. Encourages students to see differences as valuable, making each person unique; yet all of us are alike in important ways. Helps students accept and value differences in themselves and others. First place in the American Film and Video Association Film Festival.
Company: *Sunburst Communications*

Seeds of Self-Esteem
Two videotapes with video guide, $169. Exciting inservice training provides K–9 teachers with practical, easy-to-use strategies for building self-esteem. In the first videotape, "Self-Esteem Teacher Power," Dr. Robert Brooks presents a workable theory of self-esteem and highlights the positive impact teachers have in their students' lives. The second video, "Self-Esteem Teacher Strategies" offers effective strategies teachers can use to build self-esteem every day.
Company: *American Guidance Service*

Self-Esteem: Elementary Grades
One 29-minute videotape, 11 handouts and a leader's guide, $149. For teachers of grades K–6, this tape features two elementary schools with successful self-esteem programs. Silver Screen Award winner at the U.S. International Film and Video Festival.
Company: *Sunburst Communications*

Wonderful Me!
One 13-minute videotape, eight student worksheets, audiocassette, and teacher's guide, $89. Designed for student viewing, grades K–2. Using lively songs, scenarios close to student experience, and a storyteller to reinforce points, the program shows young children effective strategies they can use to feel good about themselves.
Company: *Sunburst Communications*

SOCIAL SKILLS

Asset: A Social Skills Program for Adolescents
Includes eight videotapes and a leader's guide, $1,400. Designed for student viewing. For a wide range of students, from those who are experiencing the typical problems of adolescence to those who are deficient in basic social skills. This is a research-based training program that uses behavior modeling videotapes, group discussion, role playing, and homework assignments to teach adolescents the skills they need for successful social interactions. It is designed for use with a wide range of students, from those who are experiencing the typical problems of adolescence to those who are deficient in basic social skills.
Company: *Research Press*

CARING CLASSROOMS

Creating Caring Classrooms
Includes one 30-minute videotape and a 24-page facilitator's guide, $125. Alfie Kohn and Eric Schaps argue for the creation of caring classroom communities that emphasize prosocial values. They detail how teachers are oftentimes just as responsible for helping their students achieve social, moral, and behavioral goals as they are for raising their test scores. 1993.
Company: *Agency for Instructional Technology*

The Ethical Classroom
One 90-minute audiocassette, $12.95. Ruth Charney, author of *Teaching Children to Care*, shares her thoughts on the teaching of moral and ethical behavior.

Includes strategies for creating caring classrooms, setting the stage in the first six weeks of school, collaborative and positive rule making, logical consequences, and time out.
Company: *Northeast Foundation for Children*

COMMUNICATION

Communication: The Person-to-Person Skill
One 37-minute videotape and teacher's guide, $199. Designed for student viewing, grades 7–12. Shows students that effective communication is the art of sending and receiving clear signals—both verbally and nonverbally. It pinpoints communication blockers. Winner of the Media & Methods Portfolio.
Company: *Sunburst Communications*

How to Talk So Kids Will Listen
Six 30-minute videotapes, $190 as a set or $39.95 for a single program. Based on the best-selling book *How to Talk So Kids Will Listen & Listen So Kids Will Talk* by Adele Faber and Elaine Mazlish, this program shares techniques to help listen to and understand children. Program titles include: (1) Helping Children Deal with Their Feelings, (2) Engaging Cooperation, (3) Alternative to Punishment, (4) Encouraging Autonomy, (5) Praise, and (6) Freeing Children from Playing Roles.
Company: *The Kentucky Network*

MOTIVATION

Boosting Student Motivation
One 25-minute videotape, $109. Explores incentives used to motivate students, focusing on the secondary school students. Offers tips on improving motivation. 1991.
Company: *Insight Media*

Goal Setting: A Tool for Motivating Students
One videotape and a leader's guide, $145. Developed by Randall Sprick, this program presents goal-setting procedures as a way to confer with students about increasing their motivation or improving their behavior. Actual classroom scenes demonstrate the procedures. Teachers learn how to confer with the problem student, how to correct the misbehavior, and how to reinforce the student for progress toward the goals.
Company: *Teaching Strategies, Inc.*

Motivation
Includes one 30-minute videotape, $139. Provides examples of what motivates people. Factors that influence motivation are explored. The program demonstrates behavioral extremes, and considers Maslow's hierarchy of needs. 1990.
Company: *Insight Media*

Motivational Opportunities for Successful Teaching (MOST)
Includes five videotapes (each about 28 minutes long) and a workshop manual with participant activities and facilitator's notes, $795. Raymond Wlodkowski offers a practical approach for planning to incorporate motivational aspects into instruction. The program titles are: (1) Attitudes: Positive Judgments to Influence Learning, (2) Needs: The Energy Behind Learning, (3) Stimulation: Continuing

Worthwhile Learning, (4) Disequilibrium: Unpredictability and Novel Changes in Learning, and (5) Competence and Reinforcement: Effective Endings for Effective Learning.
Company: *Universal Dimensions*

Motivational Thinking for Educators (MTE)

Includes six videotapes and a workshop manual with participant activities and facilitator's notes, $975. This is a follow-up to Raymond Wlodkowski's MOST program. In this program, he models many motivational strategies and learning strategies. The program titles are: (1) Motivation: Overview, (2 and 3) Motivation in the Elementary Classroom, (4) Motivation in the High School Classroom, (5) Motivation: Planning, Enthusiasm, Standards, and Measures, and (6) Motivation: The Coaching Process.
Company: *Universal Dimensions*

LEARNING STYLES

See 4MAT Run

This is lesson planning software for the Macintosh. 4MATION puts the power of 4MAT at your fingertips. It cuts planning time in half with a simple, easy-to-learn model for lesson development. It gives educators step-by-step guidance in creating lessons that capitalize on learner differences. As new lesson or unit plans are created, it provides a flexible system for cataloging and saving them to a dynamic database.
Company: *Excel, Inc.*

Teaching to Learning Styles

One 30-minute videotape, a 92-page leader's guide, and the accompanying book., *Marching to Different Drummers,* $398, may be rented. Introduces to teachers at all grade levels the practical ways of teaching to students' individual learning styles focusing on three guidelines. Winner of several film and video awards. 1992.
Company: *Association for Supervision and Curriculum Development*

COOPERATIVE LEARNING

Cooperative Learning Series

Five videotapes totaling over three hours of viewing, a 194-page facilitator's manual, the accompanying book, *Circles of Learning,* $1,180, may be rented. Explains what cooperative learning is, why it's such an important instructional tool, and how you can begin using it. Many practical ideas from several leading experts such as David Johnson, Roger Johnson, and Robert Slavin.
Company: *Association for Supervision and Curriculum Development*

Foundations of Cooperative Learning

One 58-minute videotape, $45. Spencer Kagan surveys the research and theoretical underpinnings of cooperative learning. He describes his own research and that of others in the areas of academic achievement, ethnic relations, and prosocial development.
Company: *Kagan Cooperative Learning*

I Can't, We Can: Songs about Cooperation
One 50-minute cassette tape, $10. Includes new recordings of ten songs about cooperation, including United We Stand, Lean on Me, Living Hand in Hand, He Ain't Heavy, and others. 1991.
Company: *Interaction Book Company*

Positive Interdependence: The Heart of Cooperative Learning
One 15-minute videotape, $50. Presents the nature of positive interdependence and how to structure it within cooperative learning lessons. Serves as a useful introduction to the topic. By David and Roger Johnson, 1992.
Company: *Interaction Book Company*

Teaching Students to Be Peacemakers
One 10-minute videotape, $25. Presents the steps in training students to negotiate wise solutions to interpersonal conflicts and mediate classmates' conflicts. Serves as a useful introduction to peer mediation programs. By David and Roger Johnson, 1991.
Company: *Interaction Book Company*

We Can Help: Songs about Cooperation II
One 52-minute cassette tape, $10. Includes new recording of 14 songs about cooperation, including Everything Is Beautiful, Getting to Know You, You've Got a Friend, What a Wonderful World, Wind Beneath My Wings, Stand by Me, and others. 1992.
Company: *Interaction Book Company*

EFFECTIVE TEACHING

Frameworks for Effective Teaching
Videotapes in five parts, includes one workshop manual with participant activities and facilitator's notes, $795. Demonstrating the 16 essential frameworks for effective teaching, this program provides guidelines to improve instruction and student performance. Includes some actual classroom demonstrations of techniques. The program is in five parts: (1 and 2) Time Effectiveness, (3 and 4) Motivation Teaching Framework, and (5) Productive Behavior Framework.
Company: *Universal Dimensions*

Maintaining Teacher Effectiveness
Seven videotapes with instructor's manual, $475. Tapes run from 38–60 minutes. The program provides principals and staff developers with a powerful tool for improving instruction throughout the school. It is also appropriate for use in preservice programs. Tape titles include: (1) Overview of Teaching, (2) Teacher Action, (3) Active Participation, (4) Motivation, (5) Anticipatory Set/Closure, (6) Reinforcement, and (7) Lesson Design. Presented by Don Maas.
Company: *Phi Delta Kappa*

Teaching in the Diverse Classroom
One 37-minute videotape, $150. University faculty and students explain why recognizing diversity is so important on today's college campus and demonstrate how instructors can be more effective teaching in an increasingly diverse classroom. They advocate four general strategies with specific examples: (a) include all students; (b) recognize different ways that individuals learn; (c) promote

respect in the classroom; and (d) acknowledge diversity through curriculum choices. 1991.
Company: *University of Washington, Center for Instructional Development and Research*

PARENT-TEACHER CONFERENCES

Building Parent Involvement: Elementary Grades
One 26-minute videotape, 20 handouts, and a leader's guide, $149. Designed for teachers of grades K–5, this program shows two schools with fully developed programs for involving parents in students' education. Includes Joyce Epstein, an authority on home-school collaboration, and Edward Joyner. 1994.
Company: *Sunburst Communications*

Motivation to Learn
Two videotapes, a leader's guide, and an accompanying text *Eager to Learn*, $290, may be rented. Shows how parents and teachers can team up to improve students' attitudes toward learning. Videotape titles are: (1) How Parents and Teachers Can Help, and (2) Guidelines for Parent-Teacher Conferences. Includes insights from motivation expert Raymond Wlodkowski.
Company: *Association for Supervision and Curriculum Development*

Parent-Teacher Conferences: Resolving Conflicts
One 37-minute videotape with a discussion guide, $135 purchase, $45 rental. The program shows how to involve parents in decisions and promote home-school collaboration when students have problems at school. Demonstrates a step-by-step process to help negotiate differences, find common ground, and arrive at creative solutions. Includes interviews with teachers and parents. 1992.
Company: *Menninger*

HOME-SCHOOL PARTNERSHIPS

Involving Parents in Education
One 30-minute videotape and a 54-page leader's guide, $340, may be rented. Helps educators and parents focus on common goals and possible solutions to common problems. Successful parent involvement programs are examined. Based on Joyce Epstein's work to get parents and the community to support school programs and to promote more parental involvement. 1992.
Company: *Association for Supervision and Curriculum Development*

Motivation to Learn
Two videotapes, a leader's guide, and an accompanying text *Eager to Learn*, $290, may be rented. Shows how parents and teachers can team up to improve students' attitudes toward learning. Videotape titles are: (1) How Parents and Teachers Can Help, and (2) Guidelines for Parent-Teacher Conferences. Includes insights from motivation expert Raymond Wlodkowski.
Company: *Association for Supervision and Curriculum Development*

Partners toward Achievement
Two 30-minute videotapes, $139. Designed for use in staff development programs or as part of a parent education program. This is a dropout prevention and

student enrichment program that promotes school, home, and community partnership as a basis for enhancing self-esteem and student achievement. Includes interviews and films of actual group sessions.
Company: *National Educational Service*

ADDRESSES

Agency for Instructional Technology (AIT)
Box A
Bloomington, IN 47402-0120
(800) 457-4509 or (812) 339-2203

American Guidance Service
P.O. Box 99
4201 Woodland Road
Circle Pines, MN 55014
(800) 328-2560

Association for Supervision and Curriculum Development
1250 N. Pitt St.
Alexandria, VA 22314-1453
(703) 549-9110

Cline-Fay Institute
2207 Jackson St.
Golden, CO 80401-2317
(800) 338-4065

Excel, Inc.
200 W. Station St.
Barrington, IL 60010
(708) 382-7272

Films for the Humanities and Sciences
P.O. Box 2053
Princeton, NJ 08543-2053
(800) 257-5126 or (609) 275-1400

Insight Media
2162 Broadway
New York, NY 10024
(212) 721-6316

Instructional Support Services, Inc.
160 Washington, S.E., Suite 64
Albuquerque, NM 87108
(800) 688-1960 or (505) 255-3007

Interaction Book Company
7208 Cornelia Drive
Edina, MN 55435
(612) 831-9500

Kagan Cooperative Learning
27134 Paseo Espada, Suite 302
San Juan Capistrano, CA 92765
(800) 933-2667

The Kentucky Network
2230 Richmond Road, Suite 213
Lexington, KY 40502
(800) 354-9067

Lee Canter & Associates
P.O. Box 2113
Santa Monica, CA 90407-2113
(800) 262-4347

Memphis State University
Denny Smith
College of Education
Media Productions & Sales
Memphis, TN 38152
(901) 678-3439

Menninger
Video Productions
P.O. Box 829
Topeka, KS 66601-0829
(800) 345-6036

National Crisis Prevention Institute
3315-K North 124th Street
Brookfield, WI 53005
(800) 558-8976

National Education Association
NEA Video Library
P.O. Box 509
West Haven, CT 06516
(203) 934-2669

National Educational Service
1610 W. 3rd St.
P.O. Box 8
Bloomington, IN 47402
(800) 733-6786

National Middle School Association
2600 Corporate Exchange Dr., Suite 370
Columbus, OH 43231
(614) 895-4730

National Staff Development Council
P.O. Box 240
Oxford, OH 45056
(614) 523-6029 or (800) 727-7288

New View Multimedia
P.O. Box 3021
Chapel Hill, NC 27515
(800) 441-3604

Northeast Foundation for Children
71 Montague City Road
Greenfield, MA 01301
(800) 360-6332

Phi Delta Kappa
P.O. Box 789
Bloomington, IN 47402-0789
(812) 339-1156

Research Press
Dept. J
P.O. Box 9177
Champaign, IL 61826
(217) 352-3273

Sierra House Publishing
2716 King Richard Drive
El Dorado Hills, CA 95630
(800) 255-3822

Sopris West
1140 Boston Avenue
Longmont, CO 80501
(303) 651-2829

Summerhills Group
P.O. Box 2219
Zanesville, OH 43702-2219
(614) 455-2035

Sunburst Communications
39 Washington Avenue
P.O. Box 40
Pleasantville, NY 10570
(800) 431-1934

Teaching Strategies, Inc.
P.O. Box 50550
Eugene, OR 97405
(800) 323-8819

Universal Dimensions
Altschul Group Corporation
1560 Sherman Avenue, Suite 100
Evanston, IL 60201
(800) 323-9084 or (708) 328-6700

University of Washington
Center for Instructional Development and Research
109 Parrington Hall, DC-07
Seattle, WA 98195
(206) 543-6588

Index